Ways *of* Being
ETHNIC
in Southwest China

STEVAN HARRELL

UNIVERSITY OF WASHINGTON PRESS

Seattle and London

Library of Congress Cataloging-in-Publication Data
Harrell, Stevan.
Ways of being ethnic in Southwest China / Stevan Harrell.
p.   cm. — (Studies on ethnic groups in China)
Includes bibliographical references and index.
ISBN 0-295-98122-9 (cloth : alk. paper) —
ISBN 0-295-98123-7 (pbk. : alk. paper)
1. Ethnicity—China—Sichuan Sheng.
2. Ethnic groups—Government policy—China—Sichuan Sheng.
3. Acculturation—China—Sichuan Sheng.
4. Sichuan Sheng (China)—Ethnic relations.
5. Sichuan Sheng (China)—Social policy.
6. Sichuan Sheng (China)—Social conditions.
I. Title.   II. Series.
GN635.C6 H37   2001   305.8'00951'38—DC21   00-068319

The paper used in this publication is acid-free and recycled from 10 percent
post-consumer and at least 50 percent pre-consumer waste. It meets the
minimum requirements of American National Standard for Information
Sciences—Permanence of Paper for Printed Library Materials,
ANSI Z39.48-1984. ♾ ⊕

To Deng Yaozong, who never let me give up

献给邓耀宗

一直不让我失望

CONTENTS

MAPS

the joys and tribulations of the field situation with Li Mingxi, Wang Chengxiao, Liu Xin, and Lan Mingchun in 1998; with Gaga Erri and Zhang Yong in 1993; and with Nuobu Huojy and Yan Dezong in 1994. Everyone was intelligent, kind, and helpful.

Several people have read and commented on earlier drafts of this book, and all of their advice has been helpful. They include Barbara Harrell, Miriam Kahn, Charles McKhann, Ren Hai, Yan Hairong, Colin Mackerras, Norma Diamond, Du Shanshan, and Bamo Ayi. At the University of Washington Press, Naomi Pascal has always been encouraging about the book and the Studies on Ethnic Groups in China series, and Lorri Hagman has been patient, persistent, and insistent enough to turn it into an actual book.

Other scholars have also provided intellectual help and advice; these include Lang Wei, Liu Huiqiang, and Yuan Xiaowen in Chengdu; Li Miao and Ma Yuanxi in Panzhihua; and Bamo Qubumo and Martin Schoenhals in Xichang. I gained much from the hospitality of Yang Liangsheng in Chengdu in 1988, of Bamo Erha and Liu Yulan in Xichang in 1994, and of my elder sister-in-law Zeng Qiansuo in Panzhihua always.

Finally, my greatest debt is to my scholarly elder brother, Deng Yaozong. He took me on in 1987 when I was an unknown quantity and made my project his own, as well as making me his project. He never allowed me to lower my standards, never failed to encourage me when I was down or even despairing, and never gave up his faith in my efforts. To him I dedicate this book.

Ways *of* Being
ETHNIC
in Southwest China

PART 1

THE
POLITICAL,
NATURAL,
AND
HISTORICAL
SETTING

1 / Some Ethnic Displays

INTERVIEWING IN A LIPUO VILLAGE, 1988

My research collaborators, mostly graduate students from Sichuan University in Chengdu, were a bit disappointed with our preliminary visit in 1988 to the Yi village of Yishala on the Yunnan border south of Panzhihua City. It was, they said, *tai Han hua*, "too Hanified." People there wore ordinary Chinese peasant clothes, lived in four-sided houses with central courtyards, and spoke fluent Chinese, even though they called themselves Lipuo and their daily conversation was usually in the Libie language, classified by linguists as belonging to the Central Dialect of the Yi Branch of the Tibeto-Burman family (Bradley 1998).

When we returned to the village for a two-week stay, there were weddings almost daily because it was the winter slack season immediately preceding the Chinese New Year. At one of these, we learned, a bride from the Mao lineage would be marrying into a Na family, and we asked about the origin of the two lineages.

"We Mao," they said, "come from Anfu County, Ji'an Prefecture, Jiangxi Province,[1] and our original ancestor was sent to the Southwest as part of a military detachment in the eleventh year of Kangxi [1672]. Our ancestors first came to nearby Dayao County and then moved to the current village site after a generation or two." The Maos have a genealogy, written entirely in the language of the majority Han Chinese, though they think that earlier on they might have had documents written in some sort of Yi script.

Surprised at the east-China origin of the Maos, I asked several men whether there were any Yizu (people of the Yi ethnic group) in Jiangxi today. Some said there must be some, but others thought that perhaps their ancestors were originally Han who had become Yi after moving here and marrying local

---

1. Anfu County existed until the Republican period. Ji'an Prefecture still exists, with its current seat at Ji'an County (Xie Shouchang 1931: 308; Ditu Ji 1983: 15).

women. One said he would very much like to go to Jiangxi and see if he could find any Yi.

The Qi lineage, by contrast, traces its origin to Nanjing, and the Na lineage to Huguang.

A VISIT FROM CENTRAL TV, 1994

It was an atypically cold evening in November 1994 in the valley-bottom city of Xichang (pop. 180,000), capital of Liangshan Prefecture, when former vice-prefect Bamo Erha (a Yi, or Nuosu) came to meet me and Martin Schoenhals, another American anthropologist resident in town, in the lobby of the shabbily luxurious Liangshan Hotel. A dinner was planned for a film-and-sound crew from Central Television Studios (Zhongyang Dianshi Tai) in Beijing, who had come to Liangshan to finish filming the documentary *Daughters of the Bamo Family* (Bamo jia de nüermen), to be broadcast as part of a national TV news-magazine a few weeks hence.

At the meal in the heated banquet room on the ground floor of the hotel, attended by various Nuosu dignitaries including a cardiac surgeon, the term "Yizu" was more in evidence than in any conversation I have ever engaged in. The meal was mostly ordinary Sichuanese cooking, but with the vital supplements of *mgemo* (bitter-buckwheat pancakes) and two kinds of boiled meat, known in the Han language as *tuotuo rou*, but in Nuosu simply as *yuoshe* (mutton) and *voshe* (pork). When eating was underway, the hotel help—young women in "hundred pleated" full skirts with horizontal stripes, elaborately appliquéd blouses, silver jewelry, and fancy embroidered headpieces (and also, since this was Xichang, makeup and medium heels)—burst in with red-yellow-black lacquered trays bearing matching shot glasses filled with expensive Sichuanese Wuliang Ye liquor and began singing, joined by the local guests:

> Su-mu di-vi wo
> Qo-bo go la su . . .
>
> [Guests from afar
> Come as friends . . .]

After a round of drinks, the waitresses sang the Chinese translation

> Yuan dao de gui bin
> Si fang de pengyou . . .

Another round. Then, not much later, another tray of glasses, and the assertion from the waitresses that

> Yizu you yiju hua shuo,
> "Zou lu yao yong shuang tui zou;
> He jiu yao he shuang bei jiu"

> [The Yi have a saying that goes,
> "When you walk, you should walk with a pair of legs;
> When you drink, you should drink a pair of cups"],

and so on through the evening. Even the two foreigners in attendance were trotted out to show how much they knew of Yi language and culture, for the rather overwhelmed but still good-natured Han guests from the capital.

The next two days the crew would spend filming Vice-Prefect Bamo's eldest daughter, Bamo Ayi, a fieldwork collaborator of mine and a professor at the Nationalities University in Beijing, out in the villages being an ethnologist and being Yi. The following December 13, the day before I left Chengdu to return home, I turned on the TV in my hotel room and was startled to find it broadcasting *Daughters of the Bamo Family*. I thought it rather superficial.

A WEDDING OF HAN AND ZANG, 1993

This wedding—most of it, at least—seemed very familiar to me, similar to those I had experienced in Han-Chinese communities in Taiwan and even closer to those I had seen a few years before in the Lipuo community of Yishala. In Yanyuan County, in the southwest corner of Liangshan Prefecture, I was attending a wedding between a groom who was Zang (a term only precariously translatable as "Tibetan") because of his mother, and a bride who was unequivocally Han.

I had spent the past few days beginning to try to unravel the complex web of ethnicity in Baiwu, a little town of about a thousand people divided among five different *minzu*, or state-determined ethnic categories. As far as I could tell, one of these groups, called Zang in local Han-language parlance, Ozzu when speaking Nuosu, or Yi, and Prmi in their own language (insofar as any of them spoke it anymore) was nothing like Tibetan, having been classified in the Qiang branch of Tibeto-Burman, related closely to such other languages as Qiang, Nameze, Gyalrong, Ersu, and Duoxu, but only distantly to Tibetan. I had been in their houses and seen a floor plan that seemed to link them to various other

7

local groups, but which was not much like those I had seen in pictures of Tibet, or even of the Khams area, usually thought to be "Tibetan," in western Sichuan. I had spoken with these people about their knowledge of Buddhism, and it was practically nonexistent. They claimed to have scriptures, written in Tibetan, but somehow nobody could ever find them. The rituals they performed in their homes honored a series of mountain and earth deities that seemed to be elements of a purely local tradition. Their clothes were not only unlike those of any Tibetans I had ever seen but were identical to those of two other groups in the same town: one clan that was classified in the Naxi *minzu*, and another single household, recently immigrant from elsewhere in the county, which called itself Naze in its own language but was also known as Ozzu in Nuosu and was called Meng (precariously translatable as "Mongolian") when speaking Chinese.

Out to deconstruct, nay to destroy, the simplistic errors of the Chinese state project of *minzu shibie*, or "ethnic classification," or more officially, "nationalities identification," I was stopped in my tracks in the courtyard where the wedding feast was being set out on low, square wooden tables, surrounded by benches, as one could see in Han or Yi communities anywhere in Yunnan or the nearby borderlands belonging to Sichuan. A drunken old man, dressed in ragged clothes with a large, dusty, faded turban around his head, was talking to me, the foreigner. Figuring, I suppose, that I did not speak any of the local languages very well, he pointed to his own painted nose and resorted to a sort of baby-talk: "Zangzu—Dalai Lama . . . Zangzu—Dalai Lama."

STOPPING IN A WOODYARD, 1993

The trip—nine Jeeps, thirty-some cadres of every local *minzu* but Han, six days of dusty roads and colorful maidens, several scenic wonders and one hot-springs bath—had landed us in the overflow yard of a logging camp, with no place to go and nothing to do but sit on rotted or otherwise unusable timber and talk ethnohistory.[2] While the cadres who made a difference were meeting somewhere, deciding how to divvy up the profits from one of China's last old-growth forests, I decided to talk to Mr. Fu, a vice-chair of the People's Consultative Conference for Ninglang County, Yunnan, right across the provincial border from Yanyuan, and a self-appointed spokesman for the Pumi people.

Mr. Fu was anxious to tell me about the history of the Pumi, who he thought probably came originally from what is now Qinghai but who had been in the

---

2. For an extended account of this trip as an idealized display of the New China as a multi-ethnic nation, see Harrell 1996b.

area of southwestern Liangshan for nearly two thousand years at minimum. His authority was "the *Hou Han shu* of Sima Qian" (*sic*),[3] which records a song sung by the king of Bailang, somewhere in the Southwest, at an imperial court banquet in Luoyang. Linguists, said Mr. Fu, had demonstrated that the language recorded was that of the Pumi, whose history therefore went back to that distant period.

Mr. Fu was, however, unconcerned that people in Sichuan who spoke the same language as he, practiced the same customs, and called themselves Prmi in their own language were classified as Zang rather than as Pumi. It stemmed, he said, from the local politics of the early 1950s, when the king of Muli—who was both abbot of a Gelug-pa monastery (and thus religiously subordinate to the Dalai Lama in Lhasa) and a *tusi* (local native ruler) enfeoffed by the Qing empire and allowed to continue in office under the Chinese Republic—had thrown in his lot with the Communists in return for making Muli into a Zang autonomous county that was part of Sichuan. In Ninglang, where there was no equivalent Prmi local official, the Prmi had remained "unclassified" until the late 1950s but through the good offices of Premier Zhou Enlai were eventually classified as a separate *minzu*. His Pumi and the Zang across the border in Sichuan cooperated just fine, he told me; in fact, even in my own area of scholarship, he was hoping to organize a local Center for the Study of Pumi History and Culture, and the Party secretary of Muli Zang Autonomous County in Sichuan had already agreed to contribute some timber revenues to the effort.

A WELCOMING PARTY, 1994

It had been a rather hard hike. I, the Westerner, was as usual carrying too much stuff, and it was a warm day and we had seven hundred meters to climb. Two teenage girls were scouting our arrival just around the corner from the mountain slope that is the seat of the headquarters of Dapo Mengguzu (in English, that usually comes out "Mongolian") Township, in the eastern part of Yanyuan County, and they ran ahead when they saw us, to tell everybody to get ready. As we marched into the little town, firecrackers started going off, and then we were between two long lines of schoolchildren and villagers, who chanted (in the Han language) as we went, "Huanying, huanying . . . relie

---

3. Sima Qian, of course, was author not of the *Hou Han shu* (History of the latter Han dynasty) but of the *Shi ji* (Records of the historian), written about three hundred years earlier. The primary author of the *Hou Han shu* was Fan Ye. This passage does in fact exist in the *Hou Han shu* (chap. 11).

9

huanying" (Welcome, welcome, heartily welcome). Up a slope, along a ledge, into a courtyard, and soon we were met by women in plain-colored skirts bearing large bowls of delicious, lukewarm beer. Since they were Mengguzu, they should have gotten *chiong* (as they call it in their own language), or *huang jiu* (in Chinese), they apologized, but it wasn't so common around those parts, so beer would have to do. After that hike, it did just fine.

Red papers with black writing on them adorned the walls and doorways of the school and the township government buildings; the slogans of welcome and celebration were in both Chinese and Mongolian, though only one local man, a schoolteacher, could sound out the letters of the latter. At the official ceremony the next day, the township Party secretary, resplendent in something resembling a Mongolian robe, or *deel*, presided in front of a framed message of congratulations on the establishment of the Mengguzu township in 1984. It had been given by the People's Government of Yikezhao League, in Western Inner Mongolia, and although it was written entirely in Chinese, it featured a silver leaping horse and a picture of crowds on a sunny day in front of Chinggis Khan's mausoleum in the Ordos (Khan 1995). I was told by the township head that although the language spoken here in Dapo (called Mengyu in Chinese or Naru in the local language) was superficially unlike that of Inner Mongolia, it really was 70 percent the same as the language of Western Inner Mongolia, at least. According to linguists, it too is a member of the Tibeto-Burman family (though its closer affiliations with one or another branch are disputed) and completely unrelated to Mongolian.

TWO CONVERSATIONS ABOUT ETHNICITY, 1988 AND 1994

It was already hot, even though it was only mid-morning when we completed our daily forty-minute trek through rice fields and banana trees from the Han Catholic village of Jingtang (Scripture Hall), where we were staying, to the minority village of Zhuangshang across an eroded streambed flowing into the Jinsha River. We were conducting interviews about household structure and economy. About 80 percent of the population of the village of Zhuangshang belongs to a group that called itself Laluo in its own language, back a few decades when anybody spoke it, and whose Han name was still in dispute in 1988. The household registration records, for example, had originally listed people's *minzu* affiliation as Shuitian, and in ordinary conversation in the Han language (the only language most of them knew) they continued to refer to themselves as Shuitianzu, or, perhaps more commonly, simply as *minzu*, a term that contrasted with Hanzu. The government, however, had recently determined that they were Yi, and the indication in the household registration records had been crossed out and written over to reflect this decision.

Ms. Hu Guanghui, a very helpful and intelligent middle-school graduate from the village, led me to my first household for the day, and I sat down on a wooden bench in the shade of the courtyard and got out my four-color ballpoint pen and my printed household questionnaire. I stood to greet the host, an uncle of Ms. Hu's, and he, seemingly already in his cups, although it was early in the day, greeted me perfunctorily, sat down on the other end of the bench, and pronounced, "When Old Man Mao [Mao Laoye] was alive, everybody recognized that we were *minzu*. Now that we have Old Man Deng, nobody recognizes that we are *minzu* anymore."

Mr. Hu's resentment was shared at the time by many other villagers with whom our research team spoke—they could not see why they, as a separate group of people, who were here first after all, had to be lumped in with the Yi (Nuosu), who were nothing but savages in the mountains with whom the local people had nothing in common. The village was poor, and the dispute about ethnicity was only one of the many beefs the local people had with the government.

In 1994 I paid a brief visit to Zhuangshang again and interviewed a local team leader. He regaled me for over an hour with success stories—tripling of household income, installation of electricity and running water in every household, a solution to their long-standing irrigation-water shortage, the possibility of developing commercial mango and pomegranate crops. But he simply would not be engaged in the question of the name of the local group. Yes, they were minorities; yes, they called themselves Shuitian; yes, it was alright to call them Yi—they were certainly a branch of the Yi.

THE CONTEXT OF THE DISPLAYS

All the preceding stories relate to the ways people present themselves as ethnic citizens in the southernmost parts of Sichuan Province and the immediately bordering areas of Yunnan, in southwest China. I conducted field research relating to the questions of ethnic relations in this area for three months each in 1988, 1993, and 1994, with brief visits in 1991, 1996, and 1998 also. This book is an attempt to make sense out of these presentations of self and the discourses of local, national, and global relations to which the presentations are directed.

When I first wrote, in a very formulaic and simplistic manner, about the specific local contexts of ethnic relations in this area (Harrell 1990), I ended up by paraphrasing the former U.S. house speaker Tip O'Neill, proclaiming that "all ethnicity is local." Like O'Neill discussing politics, I suspect, I was speaking a half-truth to emphasize a point. All ethnicity *is* local, in the sense that every person who considers him or herself a member of an ethnic collectivity does so in the context of interaction in a local community. But at the same time, all ethnicity, like all politics, is not *just* local. People in the modern world of nation-states are members of nationally—and often internationally— defined ethnic collectivities of which their local communities are a part, and the dialectical interaction between local, national, and cosmopolitan discourses is what shapes their lives as ethnic citizens of modern nations.

Southwest China is one of the places where such dialectical interaction and level-jumping between local and national is at its most involved and complex. Unlike Xinjiang, for example, or the Tibet Autonomous Region, boundaries here are contingent, shifting, negotiated; ethnicity in one context is not necessarily congruent with ethnicity in another; contexts shift over space and time and particularly from one language to another. Everybody here is Chinese in a citizenship sense; there is no question of an independent Yi or Pumi or Shuitian nation, but ethnic relations are vitally important in peoples' lives for many purposes. These include psychological self-understanding, the preservation or undermining of governmental and imagined national order, and the distribution of resources as varied as mining claims, admissions to teachers colleges, and birth-control quotas.

At the most basic level of understanding, then, it matters, in almost all contexts, what one's ethnic identity is. At one greater level of complexity, it may not matter in the same way in each context. But even this is too simple. To approach anything like realistic understanding of the phenomena, we must go to a still more complex level and understand that even though ethnicity matters differently in different contexts, the ways it matters in one context affect the ways it matters in others.

To approach this kind of realistic understanding of ethnicity and ethnic identity in context, one must combine field and documentary research. Documents reflect one context of understanding—official policy and the principles for its implementation on the local level. They do more than simply present an ideal or a sanitized version of reality; they also dictate categories that are used in scholarly discourse and in such real situations as meetings and the writing of reports. Anthropologists too often make the mistake of discounting the kinds of formulaic or categorical understanding found in official and scholarly documents, replacing it entirely with knowledge gathered in field research. Several parts of this book rely heavily on documentary sources, since these sources define certain kinds of understanding of ethnic relations, particularly what I call the official discourse of ethnic identification and the scholarly discourse of ethnohistory. The way that these two discourses interact with each other, the way ethnicity matters differently in each of them and in the interaction between them, is a key component of the analysis of ethnicity in Liangshan.

At the same time, however, this is primarily an anthropological account. Most of the data and most of the analytical positions taken in this book stem from the notes that I took during three long seasons of field research in Liangshan. The primary context in which this book approaches ethnicity is the context of the daily lives of local communities and their leaders, and the primary purpose of my argument is to show how ethnicity matters in this local context, along with the way this context interacts with those of the two official discourses carried out in meetings and documents. Without fieldwork, the most important leg of this triangle of discourses would be missing.

My own fieldwork in the People's Republic of China (PRC), however, has not conformed to the traditional anthropological paradigm of an extended stay in one place, or even to the more recent method of an extended investigation of a community defined by something other than kinship or locality. Nor has my work conformed to the usual anthropological practice of a single researcher dealing with data collection independent of local authorities or local scholars. Rather, this study, from the beginning, has been both regional and collaborative. I have traveled to many communities in Liangshan, visiting some of them for an hour or a day or two; some for a few days or weeks. I know no place intimately; I know a moderate amount about a large number of places. The disadvantage of this kind of nontraditional approach is that, even more than usual in the fieldwork experience, there is undoubtedly much important and relevant information that passed me by in every single place. The advantage is that I have not been tempted to take any particular place as typical, but have tried to cover as wide a range as possible, a strategy that has shaped the most central point of this book's argument: namely, that ethnicity in one locality is different from ethnicity in another, even if ethnicity in both places is shaped by the same triangle of discourses.

While the research for this book has been regional, it has also been collaborative. From January through March 1988, I was one of six members of a field research team officially affiliated with the Southern Silk Road Project, directed by Professor Tong Enzheng of Sichuan University. The primary object of investigation was family economy in three Yi villages and one Han village; I discovered the problem of ethnicity when I went to Yishala and found that the villagers were "*tai Han hua.*" During the whole time, I was monitored very closely by as many as five different agencies of the Panzhihua city government, and permission to conduct the research at all was contingent on cultivating good relations not only with local scholars but with cadres and bureaucrats as well. The whole project, in fact, was dependent upon the goodwill and tireless energy of Mr. Deng Yaozong of the municipal Artifact Bureau in Panzhihua; in order to go to the Nuosu village of Gaoping, for example, which was in an area closed to foreigners, we had to go together to the home of a vice-mayor of Panzhihua Municipality, unofficially to bring New Year greetings. Even after he approved the research, we had to promise not to do any research away from a road (fortunately, the Chinese word *lu* refers to trails as well as roads). After the research was finished, we had to report results to the municipal authorities.

For further research from January through March 1993, and from October to December 1994, I continued my collaboration with the Panzhihua Artifact Bureau but expanded to the Sichuan Provincial Nationalities Research Institute and the Liangshan Prefecture Nationalities Research Institute, both also government organs. My research with Ma Erzi in Yanyuan County in 1993 was possible because of his good relations with County Party Secretary Yang Zipuo, and because of Secretary Yang's open-minded attitude. Both the political climate toward foreigners and my own familiarity to local people had improved by this time, and there were fewer restrictions and requirements. Still, moving in on my own would have been impossible. In 1994 I continued these same collaborations and began to work closely with Professor Bamo Ayi of Central Nationalities University. This period of research was even easier. For our nine days in Manshuiwan, I did not even need official clearance, since Manshuiwan lies in Mianning County, long open to foreigners because of the satellite launching base there. Still, I will not forget when I asked Secretary Yang if I could go to Guabie, a remote area without roads that would have been totally off-limits to foreigners a few years earlier. His answer was, "Take care you don't get hurt."

This kind of close collaboration with officials and officially employed scholars brings with it an obligation to one's official and scholarly hosts, added on top of the obligations to the subjects of one's research. These may at times conflict with each other; the only defense is to think things through with professional ethics in mind. At the same time, there is also a danger of one's being co-opted to the scholarly views of one's collaborators, even if one has not acted unethically with regard to the research subjects (AAA 1976, Hsieh 1987). The views of ethnicity in the local context presented in this book are the views that emerged from conversations between me, my collaborators, local elites, and a less-than-representative sample of common people. All these people's views—particularly the views of my closest field collaborators, Ma Erzi and Bamo Ayi—have influenced mine. A different set of conversations might have revealed still different views; this would have happened with different collaborators as well as with different fieldsites. But I still think that the views expressed here are diverse enough to illustrate the contextual nature of ethnic identity; more views would reinforce that point but not substantially change it.

At the same time, collaboration has its advantages, and not only on the practical plane. The scholars and many of the officials and teachers I have worked with are thoughtful, dedicated, highly knowledgeable people, many of them possessed of an insider's knowledge that no foreign researcher could hope to match. I think that if it had been possible to conduct independent field research, I would have learned far less about Liangshan, its people, and their ethnic identity. And a very important result of this collaboration has been that many of the people I first met in field research have become my close friends and colleagues.

Finally, there is the language question. I speak standard Chinese (Mandarin, sometimes referred to in this book as the "Han language") very fluently; understand Sichuanese and Yunnanese accents to various degrees, but usually fairly well; and I can carry on simple conversations in Nuosu. I know no Prmi or Naze. This is not an ideal linguistic apparatus for a serious fieldworker, and it has meant a further reliance on my collaborators.

This short introduction to a long book does not have room for serious and detailed examination of the intellectual and ethical issues raised by regional, collaborative research. A forthcoming volume by Bamo Ayi, Ma Erzi, and myself will address these in great detail from three different perspectives. In the meantime, the data presented and the arguments made must be the standard by which the reader judges the work.

I begin with some general considerations about ethnicity and about Chinese history in chapters 2 and 3, give a brief historical overview of the Liangshan area in chapter 4, and present a series of case studies illustrating different ways of being ethnic in chapters 5 through 14. Chapter 15 assesses the significance of these observations.

2 / Foundations of Ethnic Identity

E thnic relations in Liangshan, complex as they are, are further complicated by the relationship between the local ethnic groups of the region
and the projects of the Chinese state and the putative Chinese nation.
Because the daily lives of the people—Nuosu, Prmi, Naze, Han, and others—
are so embroiled in China, we need to make a few initial observations about
what this China is that they are embroiled in. In order to do that, in turn, we
need to place modern China and its ethnic relations in comparative historical
and global perspective.

COLLECTIVITIES IN HUMAN SOCIETIES

Pre-State Societies and the Universality of Collectivities

Perceptions of difference—of culture, language, territory, kinship, and
physiognomy—have been a feature of relationships between human groups
as long as there have been societies. It seems clear, from ethnographic as well
as historical evidence, that humans, living in one place and associating with a
particular group of people, readily and universally classify humanity into selves
and others, attributing to the others different ways of doing things, different
ways of talking, different places where they ought to be, different relations of
kinship and descent, and different looks.[1]

As far as we can tell by modern ethnographic analogy, in the period of human
history before the origin of the state these culturally distinctive groups were
not subject to larger social and political entities, and thus were not in competition with each other for resources allocated by some central political power.
Neither were they part of any division of labor built on these cultural differences.

---

1. The salience of the racial component—imagined (whether real or not) differences in physiognomy between different collectivities—varies greatly from extreme in the United States to rather
minor in places like China or Egypt. Thus my ambivalence in including it as one aspect of collective self- and other-perception.

In that long stretch of past time between the emergence of *Homo sapiens sapiens* sometime in the Pleistocene and the emergence of the first states perhaps six thousand or eight thousand years before the present, there developed great diversity in customs, language, kinship systems, and those obvious physical characteristics we now associate with notions of race. Even into our own era of intensive investigation of other peoples and their cultures, there have persisted parts of the earth where local collectivities distinguish themselves according to language, territory, and customs but are not part of any larger political unit with power over the members of the local collectivities. We can take, for example, the interior of New Guinea, inhabited according to archaeologists for at least thirty thousand years and farmed for nine thousand (Lilley 1992), where people spoke a huge variety of mutually unintelligible idioms, where they called each other and themselves by a series of distinctive names for social groups (such as Etoro, Bosavi, and Onambasulu on the Great Papuan Plateau, or Fore, Jate, and Usurufa in the Eastern Highlands), and where the social groups had continuous or sporadic relationships of intermarriage, alliance, and military hostility. Similar examples can be found on the North American Plains in the eighteenth and nineteenth centuries, or in many parts of sub-Saharan Africa outside the influence of West-African states.

Here, clearly, are ethnic differences in their most embryonic form. Members of one collectivity, by virtue of speaking the same language, being demonstrably related by descent and marriage, practicing the same customs, living in the same place, and perhaps believing that they look somewhat alike, differentiate themselves from those folks in the next valley, who are not closely related to the people here, and who talk, act, and maybe look funny. They often have stories about how different "peoples" originated at the beginning of the world or some more recent time, and they more often than not think that their own way of speaking, acting, and looking is both inherited from their ancestors (and thus immutable) and superior to those of their neighbors (and thus desirable). They may intermarry or not, and relations with them may be peaceful or warlike, or may shift between the two.

Such relationships have both an internal and an external aspect. Internally, there are the characteristics that group members perceive that they hold in common with one another, and externally, there are the corresponding characteristics that group members conceive differentiate them from members of other groups. These characteristics, both internal and external, are primarily of two sorts: cultural and kin-based. Cultural characteristics are paradigmatic in the Saussurian sense: they include ideas of similarity within the group and of difference from people outside the group, in all the areas listed above. Kin characteristics, on the other hand, are syntagmatic: they include relatedness by descent and marriage among members of the group, and the lack of relatedness by descent or marriage between one group and another. The relative importance of inclusive or exclusive criteria of kinship or culture varies greatly from one set of intercommunity relations to another, but the presence of this kind of distinguishing criteria is pervasive in human societies.

In a nonstate society, this is about all there is to it. There is no ruling organization to confer or withhold people's rights according to their membership in one cultural-linguistic-local-racial-kin collectivity or another; there is no ruling class to appropriate surplus and aggrandize status; there is no written language that becomes a key to status and power, and if there is a lingua franca that enables people to communicate with one another, it carries no particular prestige. And, as Lévi-Strauss has pointed out (1966: 232), there is usually no sense of history as a series of changes that have led to the present. In other words, the goods that are in perennial short supply in any social system—power, wealth, and prestige—may be differentially distributed among collectivities, but this is not done by any central or overriding political organization.

Nevertheless, I think it is mistaken to draw too wide a line between cultural-local-linguistic-racial-kin collectivities in non-state systems, and such collectivities as they operate after the development and imposition of state power. The majority of the *bases* of differentiation—language, culture, territory, kinship, physiognomy—were there already in New Guinea or the Amazon or the North American plains in the absence of state systems. It is the *specific manner* in which these bases of differentiation are *used* that changes when the state appears, and changes again when the state takes the form of the modern nation-state.

Collectivities as Subordinate to the State

With the emergence of states in the last few millennia, these preexisting human proclivities to differentiate one's own from other people by means of similarities and differences in language, culture, physiognomy, common kinship, and territorial affiliation began to intersect with the increasing division of labor that is the development of social classes and the state, and thus the differences began to make a different kind of difference—they began to determine, or at least influence, the allocation of prestige, power, and wealth in a situation where prestige, power, and wealth were much less evenly distributed than in the prestate situation.

As far as we know, the first states to form (what Fried [1967] calls "pristine states") were rather local affairs, and most of them probably involved, at their core, members of only one local-linguistic-cultural collectivity, led by members of one or a series of allied kinship groups. The first states to form in north China, for example, the Shang in the mid-second millennium B.C.E. and perhaps the Xia a few hundred years earlier,[2] seem to have been based around alliances of a few powerful clans. These early, kin-based states were probably too small to contain many different cultural-linguistic collectivities, but within only a few centuries their territories expanded greatly—the Shang by the time of its conquest by the Zhou in 1049 B.C.E. probably directly controlled a territory on the order of magnitude of a modern Chinese province and a population in the hundreds of thousands (David N. Keightley, personal communication). When states such as this expand, neighboring peoples in the same region, who were not part of the collectivity that originally formed the state, come under the state's influence and must react to the threat that the state expansion poses. It seems to me that the neighboring collectivity can react in one of four ways:

1. It can imitate its threatening neighbors and form a state of its own, probably based on the same kind of clan alliance and rule. As a result, the territory will have two states rather than one. The Zhou, for example, may well have developed a state in imitation of, and to counter a threat from, the Shang; later the whole of what is now China proper[3] was occupied by states formed in this way. I call this process *imitation*.

2. It can organize itself in a more formal manner than before, giving explicit political power to certain leaders, rationalizing its political and military structure, and formalizing the rules of kinship, succession, and marriage, but stopping short of full state organization. The result is that the core of the region, perhaps the most populous and economically productive part, continues to be organized as a state, while the peripheral, less populous, and less productive parts become tribes, in the narrow sense of that word. This appears to have happened with many of the steppe peoples of Central Asia in reaction to the consolidation of Chinese state rule in the immediate pre-Imperial and

2. There has been considerable controversy over the existence and timing of the Xia dynasty, which according to traditional historiography preceded the Shang, but now looks as if it overlapped in time, if it existed at all. See Chang 1980: 335–55.

3. This is a term I hope will get revived in the current debates over national identity in China. The area I am thinking of includes all or part of each of the eighteen provinces of the Qing (though not some peripheral areas of some of those provinces, particularly in the Southwest), and probably also the three northeastern provinces, although those retain, in Western languages only, the ethnic designation Manchuria.

Imperial periods (Fried 1983), and the growth of the Iroquois confederacy from the sixteenth to the eighteenth centuries (Jennings 1984) was a similar process of *tribalization* in reaction to the incursion of state power in the form of European colonies.

3. It can be conquered or otherwise overcome and absorbed without much trace into the polity of the expanding state. Language, customs, and even physiognomy may retain traces of the former difference from the central norm, but descendants of members of the previously different cultural-linguistic-local unit come first to deny and then to forget them, voluntarily or involuntarily assuming totally the culture and language of the rulers, though perhaps as individuals initially retaining lower status in the society. Much of what is now south China has undergone this process of *assimilation*; people whose ancestors were unequivocally something else are now nothing but Chinese (Brown 1996).

4. It can be incorporated into the political structure of the state, but with a separate and distinct (and usually lower) status from that of the original subjects of the state rulers. Language, customs, religion, endogamy, separate territory, and sometimes race clearly distinguish the incorporated proto-ethnic group from the rulers and their cultural group at the center. The result of this process of *ethnicization* is an empire—a state and territory that include different peoples, as those are defined by the preexisting (but sometimes altered or even reemphasized) differences in language, customs, and so forth. Empires, of course, have existed in many parts of the world since the first millennium B.C.E.

These four processes are all characteristic of the expansion and strengthening of state power that has been the main trend in human history for the past few millennia. They may, of course, succeed one another temporally in a particular region: the inhabitants of the central Yangzi Valley, for example, may first have undergone tribalization (records are scanty) but certainly imitated the states to the north in the middle of the first millennium B.C.E., then were incorporated into the Chinese empire, almost certainly by ethnicization, in Qin (221–206 B.C.E.) and Han (206 B.C.E.-220 C.E.) times, and then were slowly assimilated until they became "nothing but Chinese" since at least the Tang dynasty (618–907). In a different sequence, steppe-dwellers of Central Asia tribalized over a thousand years ago were ethnicized into the Russian Empire and had their ethnic identity consolidated and strengthened under Soviet rule, only to experience a process of imitative nationalism with the breakup of the Soviet Union and the formation of the independent -stans in the 1990s.

With the exception of complete assimilation, these processes are potentially reversible. States may revert to tribal polities or even to collections of independent villages when external pressure goes away or when demography collapses. Ethnic groups incorporated into empires may aspire to or achieve political independence, either as states or as nonstate polities. And even assimilation can be reversed if it has not gone all the way to disappearance, as when long-lost ethnic identities, such as that of the Muslim Hui of coastal Fujian (Gladney 1991: chap. 6; Fan Ke n.d.), are revived for political and/or ethnic advantage.

In none of these four processes do the cultural differences themselves lead to the status of a people as an ethnic group, a nation, or simply a category inside or outside a state polity. The existence of these cultural differences is a necessary but not sufficient condition for the formation or persistence of ethnic groups. The cultural differences need not be great—they can be something as small as the memory of a language once spoken or the consciousness of a shared history, but there must be something there for ethnic identity to build on, to serve as what we call an ethnic marker (Keyes 1996). And in addition to cultural difference, there must be a sense of relatedness as a people, an ideology of descent from common ancestors (Keyes 1976), and marriage and affinity within the group. These, too, can be put in the foreground or laid aside, but as long as they are not completely forgotten, they can become the basis for ethnic identity.

With the emergence of the state—and particularly with the development of ideology as a buttress to state power, and the use of written languages to formulate, disseminate, and preserve state ideology—a third basis for in-group solidarity and out-group exclusiveness emerges: common and divergent history. Empires and nations both (see below) depend partly on history for their legitimacy, demonstrating that the in-group has a common past, and a past different from those of the other groups with which it comes into contact. With the advent of state power and ideology, then, history is added to culture and kinship as a possible basis for group identity. The different ways in which history-, kinship-, and culture-based ethnicity interact in local contexts are the main subject of this book.

The Empire and the Nation-State

Ways of Being Ethnic in Southwest China is concerned with a particular historical sequence during which the Chinese state has included under its rule peoples who distinguish themselves from one another by the aforementioned cultural, linguistic, territorial, and kin boundaries and share a sense of a common history and kinship, including descent from common ancestors (Keyes 1976). States that include such diversely perceived peoples are often divided into two types: empires and nation-states, with the former replaced by the latter in the last few centuries. Ernest Gellner, for example, asserts that

> there are two great types or species of the division of labour, of social structure, *both* of them being marked by very great complexity and size, but which differ radically in their implications for culture, in the manner in which they make use of culture. . . . One of these, which may be called advanced agrarian-based civilization, makes for great cultural diversity, and deploys that diversity to mark out the differential situations, economically and politically, of the various subpopulations within it. The other, which may be called growth-oriented industrial society, is strongly impelled towards cultural homogeneity within each cultural unit. (1987: 17–18)

Benedict Anderson's now-classic treatment (1983, 1991) similarly traces the process of development from the "dynastic realm," held together by divine kingship and a sacred "truth-language," to the modern nation-state, held together by ideas of citizenship and a common "national print language," the former consisting of diverse peoples bound by allegiance to the monarch and his associated clerisy, and the latter of a people with the perception that they share a common heritage and culture.

The attitudes toward cultural, linguistic, and kin-community difference are said to differ greatly in these two kinds of polities. In the empire or dynastic realm such difference is tolerated, even promoted, by state authorities, because it not only is accepted as inevitable but also facilitates both division of labor and political control in a society with a weak state and low revenue base. Examples abound in actual empires. The Ottomans, for example, minutely classified the population of their realm; Jews, Armenians, Greeks, Arabs, and Georgians each had their own religion, culture, language, territory, marital community, and, most importantly, their legally recognized position as part of the larger imperial community (Sonyel 1993, Batatu 1978).

The transition to modern Turkish nationalism under Atatürk eliminated all this qualified inclusiveness; Turkey was now the land of the Turks, who had their language (which was pointedly now written in the Roman alphabet, in contrast to the earlier Arabic one), and the minorities, though they were not entirely eliminated or assimilated, now had a problematical status: they were less than full citizens in the ideological sense that their cultural difference made them a kind of defective Turkish citizenry, rather than members of groups that combined to make an empire (Gunter 1994). Until very recently, Kurds were often not allowed to use their written languages in schools or other public contexts, and they were considered not only defective but rebellious if they did (Gunter 1994).

The same kind of process has occurred, in even more violent ways, in many of the new states that emerged from the decolonization of Asia and Africa after World War II. In many cases a national print language has had to be constructed, if not from whole cloth, at least from quite variable threads, as with Tanzanian Swahili and Bahasa Indonesia, and myths of origin in the remote past have been the basis of what I have elsewhere called "the hiding of a history of negotiation behind a narrative of unfolding" (Harrell 1996a). In the rare case where intellectuals attempt to create a nation (necessarily including a national historical narrative) in a relatively democratic environment, as in Taiwan or Belize in the mid-'90s, there develops a real puzzlement over what the national history ought to include (Zhuang Wanshou 1996a,b; Haug 1995). In most places, however, intellectual stooges in the service of a ruling class create a narrative that serves the fictitious but compelling idea that the nation—with a *common* culture, language, kinship, territory, physiognomy, and history—is an eternal thing, and citizens can and should point to a glorious past, a proud present, and a bright future.

In many polities, of course, the attempt to impose state nationalism on a multicultural population is not entirely successful; cultural and territorial minorities who are included in the new national whole may resent and/or resist. In doing so, they also incorporate the third basis of group identity—a common history—into their identity, along with culture and kinship. When this happens, ethnic conflict is born, with results obvious today from Tibet to Bosnia to Kurdistan. But direct resistance is not the only strategy available to leaders of local minority communities. Where the state attempts to co-opt the leadership and ordinary people of minority collectivities, it may be just as possible, and much more advantageous, for elites among the minorities to co-opt state policies for local purposes, especially where the policies are less than completely assimilationist and recognize some rights to cultural and other distinctiveness on the part of the minority collectivities. This can lead to a situation in which the central authorities and local leaders are using each other for rather divergent but not directly contradictory ends. (I see this as the prevailing mode of interaction in the area described in this book.) Resistance and accommodation are, of course, not mutually exclusive strategies, and members of minority groups may use both, either simultaneously or at different times. In either of these situations, however—resistance or accommodation—the ethnic identity of the minority people tends to be strengthened.

We must remind ourselves that the stable and rather unproblematic distinction between the ruling class and the protoethnic collectivities found in agrarian polities or empires, as well as the much more contentious distinction between the national culture and minority ethnic cultures characteristic of nation-states, are not fundamentally different from each other. Both are based on the aforementioned human universal of forming cultural, linguistic, local, and marital communities (along with, of course, other kinds of communities based on gender, age, occupation, or even artistic and musical interests). And nearly everywhere, whether in an empire, a nation-state, or even a prestate situation, members of such collectivities see themselves as being related by common descent and intermarriage (Keyes 1976; Horowitz 1985: 59), and in many cases they strengthen these feelings of commonality and difference by writing historical narratives demonstrating the inevitable unfolding of the group and its identity through time (Harrell 1996a). The difference is between the tolerance or even promotion of differences in empires and the suspicion and often attempts to eliminate them in nation-states. As Keyes points out, "Ethnicity has become a much more significant factor in social relations since the emergence of the nation-state" (1996: 153).

This distinction, however, like so many distinctions of ideal types, runs into problems when we look at actual cases. The Ottomans and Romans ran unequivocal empires, and the Turks and Italians have more recently run unequivocal nation-states in the same places, but certain cases are in-between, even at the end of the twentieth century. In other words, not all states in the contemporary world are unequivocally nation-states. The United States (whose very name connotes at least a nod toward pluralism) is riven by debate today over the extent of cultural commonality that ought to be required or expected of citizens; opponents of multiculturalism display the classical nationalist's fear that too much diversity will lead to separatism and disunity, while liberals see the United States as a political, rather than cultural, community. Muslims are now as much as 9 percent of the population of France (Tash 1997), and while the assimilationist project goes on in the schools, media, and town halls, there are voices arguing for a more pluralist society even in that locus classicus of modern nationalism. The issue of the nation-state is far from settled.

At the same time, not all state-minority relations are structured the same way, even in the same state. In the United States, for example, the relationship between the state (or the majority Euro-Americans) and Native American tribes—governed by treaty and administered territorially, and involving local government of the Native communities—is very different from the relationship between the state or the majority and African Americans, which involves no territorial base or governmental autonomy, and whose legal aspects are more ambiguous. At the same time African Americans pose a much greater threat to state legitimacy, because of their numbers and relative power in many social contexts, than do the few remaining Natives, living mostly in remote areas. In China the nations of the northern and western periphery have a very different relationship to the state and to the Han majority than do the nonnational ethnic groups of the South, Southwest, and Northeast. The case studies in this book deal with different ways of being ethnic even *among* the southwestern groups.

THE CHINESE CASE

Nowhere does the conflict between the two models of a political system—empire and nation-state—manifest itself more acutely or more ambiguously than in the People's Republic of China. China was once an empire, though more assimilationist and thus further from the ideal type than many, and in the world of nation-states today, it explicitly proclaims itself a unified, multinational state (*tongyi duominzu guojia*, lit., "unified country of diverse nationalities"), which in many ways looks somewhat like an empire. There are "autonomous regions, prefectures, and counties" for various minority peoples; there are special dispensations in language, religion, and even childbearing, made for members of minorities; there are officially promoted attempts to glorify the culture and the history of minority "nationalities" classified according to a meticulous, "scientific" process. At the same time, all the elements of the ideal type of a nation-state as outlined by Gellner and Anderson are there: the myths of a common origin and a glorious past; the idea of sacred territory, clearly distinguished from foreign soil, to be defended with the blood of its sons and daughters; a national print-language, also taught universally in the schools; and a visceral distrust (sometimes combined with envy or even admiration) of everybody and all things foreign.

This book is to a large extent concerned with the ways in which these two models of empire and nationhood conflict with each other in the context of their interaction with local cultural, linguistic, marital, and territorial collectivities. In other words, the people of Liangshan organize a great part of their lives in terms of strongly held, sometimes unquestioned beliefs that they are members of groups that share kinship, territory, and culture. As long as there have been people in the region, they have probably held these kinds of beliefs. But even before they faced the nation-building projects of the People's

Republic, the ways these groups were constituted, the characteristics they saw themselves as holding in common, and the nature of the boundaries between themselves and other groups were all quite variable. Since the project of ethnic (or "nationalities") identification (*minzu shibie*) began in the 1950s, the beliefs and practices of all these collectivities have been partially transformed in accordance with the categories in which they emerged from the project. The categories, in terms of their commonalities and boundaries, are more similar to each other than they were previously. The members of these groups have all been incorporated, unquestionably, as citizens of the Chinese state and as members of state-defined "nationalities," or *minzu*. But the differences in the nature and boundaries of these groups have not been eradicated by the state project; there are still different ways of being ethnic in the region, and this book is about them. Before we proceed to examine in detail the ways of being ethnic in Liangshan, however, we need to review briefly the process by which China came to the contradictory juncture of being both an empire and a nation-state.

The Rise of Chinese Nationalism

In the past century and a half, China has moved from being an empire that had many characteristics of nationhood (Townsend lists "a sense of a common history, with myths of origin and descent; a distinctive written language and literary forms associated with it; some common folklore, life rituals and religious practices; and a core political elite, with a common education and orientation toward government service" [1992: 125]) to being a modern state that still has one extremely important aspect of empire: rule over diverse ethnic groups whose cultures are, officially at least, promoted and celebrated rather than repressed or denigrated.

This does not mean, however, that China has, through the turmoil of the last 150 years, simply floated somewhere in a happy compromise between Gellner's ideal types. Rather, there has been a significant transformation in the ideas about and practice of relations between the core and the periphery of regions ruled from Beijing (or, very briefly, Nanjing) or, to put it another way, between those practicing the "core culture" that we usually refer to as Chinese and those coming under their influence, or in a third formulation, between Chinese living under Chinese jurisdiction and Chinese living elsewhere. In order to understand how Liangshan came to its present predicament, we need to explore how the center-periphery relations in which Liangshan is entangled got to be the way they are.

The Chinese empire, at least during its last few periods of dynastic rule, was characterized by a particular set of doctrines and practices that have come to be known as "Chinese culturalism" (Levenson 1968, Townsend 1992). A ruling elite defined itself and its criteria for membership not in terms of belonging to any particular kinship-and-culture collectivity, but strictly in cultural terms. Those who were able to master the principles of civilized political discourse embodied in certain texts known in the West as "Confucian classics" had the right and duty to rule. Most of those who achieved this mastery came in fact from the ethnic group of Chinese-speakers (known at least in the Qing dynasty as "Han people"),[4] but members of other ethnic collectivities, such as the Mongols of the Yuan and the Manchus of the Qing (1644–1911), could gain legitimacy in the eyes of the elite if they mastered the classical rhetoric and principles. This is why Mongols and Manchus could rule the empire and not be faced with constant, ethnic nationalist revolt.

At the same time, mastery of high culture and its consequent political and social status were hardly independent of Han ethnicity. The classical language in which not only the canonical texts but also the official documents of the Ming and Qing were written was a Han language; even though it differed greatly from any currently spoken form, it was much closer to those spoken forms than to any other language. Non-Han could and did master it—even the late Ming Jesuit Matteo Ricci seems to have come close—but it did not belong to them in the same sense that it belonged to Han officials and scholars. In addition, there were numerous and pervading resonances between the elite culture of Confucianism and the folk cultures of Han communities all over China and beyond. Operas and oral stories told tales that demonstrated the virtues analyzed and systematized in the classics; ancestor worship enacted Confucian notions of proper lineage and family organization; customary law of family and inheritance reflected Confucian notions of proper relationships and behavior. And most important, as there was no sharp dividing line between

---

4. The term "Han" has a varied history. It was the dynastic name adopted by the Liu family from 206 B.C.E. to 220 C.E. and came to be something of an ethnonym in later times. In the Yuan dynasty (1279–1368), however, it referred to the people of north China, including Khitan and Koreans (Endicott-West 1989: 13). The Qing dynasts, themselves Manchus, used the word when writing in the Chinese language to refer to what we now call Han or "ethnic Chinese," and it has come in modern times to refer unambiguously to this group. Hence I will use the word throughout this book for consistency, realizing that certain particular usages are anachronistic. Unlike certain authors, I do not want to use "Chinese" to refer to this group, since, in the Southwest in particular, there are millions of people who unequivocally consider themselves to be Chinese (Zhongguo *ren*, Zhoguoco, etc.) and just as clearly deny that they are Han.

ruling class and peasantry or merchants in Qing China, there was also no sharp line dividing elite from folk cultures. An unassimilated Yi or Yao who passed the examinations and became an imperial official had to be markedly bicultural, operating in the home sphere with one set of assumptions, practices, and vocabulary, and in the official sphere with quite another set. But a Han villager who made it in the official world simply had to shade over from a folk to an elite version of the same language, rituals, and manners. Elite Chinese culture claimed universality; this claim was justified in the sense that anyone could participate. But it was universality on the condition that one act in a literized (*wen*) manner, and the basis of that literization was Han culture.

In late Imperial China, the idea of a superior culture at the center went along with the imperial version of what I have elsewhere called a "civilizing project" (Harrell 1995a) but will refer to here with the neologistic but more accurate term "literizing project," since the basis of status was not urbanism but familiarity with texts. The universal validity of the high culture meant that anyone could adopt it; its moral superiority meant that the ruling class was duty-bound to acculturate others to it. If peoples were originally included in the Chinese empire by a process of ethnicization—political subjugation with minimal cultural change—the ideal of the literizers was still assimilation, making others literate and moral by persuading them to conform with norms dictated by the high culture, whose basis was Han. As Townsend points out (1992: 125), this amounted to "state nationalism"—pursuit of the idea that citizens of a state should have a common culture and thus constitute a nation—on the part of the imperial authorities. That this state nationalism was successful is of course demonstrated by the expansion of Han culture from the North China Plain in the third millennium B.C.E. to the eastern and southern oceans and the southwestern mountain walls by the twentieth century C.E.

What differentiates this imperial form from the present one, however, is very clear. In Imperial times, the high, literate culture was valid for everybody; no other culture was as good, for anyone. People around the peripheries were inferior because they had different and thus inferior cultures. Since the early twentieth century, the new versions of the high culture have been seen as the exclusive property of the Chinese (whether just the Han or all Chinese within the borders is still a matter of contention), and people around the peripheries have been thought to have different cultures because they are inferior. This transformation has come about as China has become a modern state, still struggling with whether it is really a nation-state.

Through a series of historical events beginning with the Opium War (1839–42) and proceeding to the semicolonial imposition of unequal treaties, the failed reforms of 1898, the Republican revolution of 1911, the May Fourth Movement of the late teens and twenties, the Japanese invasion, the Civil War, and the whole set of cataclysmic social changes brought about by the imposition of communism beginning in the late 1940s, Chinese intellectuals and politicians came to the realization that China would have to become a state like other states, and they set about creating such a state in much of the territory that had been ruled by the former empire. We need not rehearse modern Chinese history here, but we should outline briefly a set of processes that effected the change from imperial to national ethnic relations.

First, as intellectuals around the turn of the century increasingly despaired of China's ability to survive as an empire, Republicans began to identify China as a nation—an ethnic group with common descent, territory, and culture, but which was also politically sovereign. It was at this time that radical reformers, beginning with Liang Qichao in 1902, began to think and write of China as a *minzu*, a term probably first used in Meiji-era Japan (and pronounced *minzoku* in Japanese, but written with the same characters in Japan as in China) as part of the process of building a nation out of the fragmented feudal order that was Japan of the Edo period (1615–1868) (Morris-Suzuki 1996). When Liang picked up the term, he first defined it as a group with a common geographic origin, a common bloodline, common physical characteristics, common language, common writing, common religion, common customs, and a common mode of livelihood (Peng Yingming 1985: 9). For Liang and his associates, the unification of China as a nation could still be accomplished under the overlordship of the Manchu Qing dynasty, but radical revolutionaries who picked up the usage—the most prominent among them Sun Zhongshan (Sun Yat-sen)—began to identify the culture of the Chinese nation explicitly with a single ethnic group (the Han) and to exclude others (particularly the ruling Manchus) from this national-cultural community (ibid.: 9–10).[5]

But this explicit Han nationalism was unworkable unless the Chinese patriots who advocated it also wanted to give up half or more of the territory that had been under imperial rule. A strong China, for reasons of pride as well as natural resources and military defense, had to include parts of Central Asia, Mongolia, and Tibet, as well as the ethnically mixed areas of the South and Southwest. So the original idea of the nation-state, so effective in exciting anti-Manchu rebelliousness, evolved quickly into Sun Zhongshan's idea of a "Republic of Five Nationalities"—Han, Zang (Tibetan), Meng (Mongolian),

---

5. I am indebted to Zhang Haiyang for pointing me to Peng Yingming's invaluable essay discussing the earliest uses of the term *minzu* in China.

Hui (Muslim—but in this case referring to the Turkic speaking peoples of what is now Xinjiang), and Man (Manchu)—each represented by a stripe on the new Republican flag (Sun 1928: 12).

It is quite significant that the four minority groups represented in this formulation are all, in our modern sense, nations—large, territorially compact ethnic groups with reasonable, and in these cases historically founded, claims to political sovereignty. Though the Republicans opposed sovereignty for the Turkic or Mongolian peoples then within China's territory, they recognized its possibility. These groups' incorporation into the Republic would thus have to be in a process of ethnicization; previous imitation had precluded assimilation, at least in the short run.

There were no stripes on the flag, however, for any of the peoples centered in the Southwest, including the ones described in this book. In addition to cultural inferiority—something they at least implicitly shared with the Mongols, Manchus, Muslims, and Tibetans—they also had the added disadvantage of having no recent state sovereignty.[6] They were, in a sense, the peoples who remained on the far peripheries after those somewhat closer to the center had become assimilated; in the last centuries of the empire a few of them, such as the Nuosu, had responded by conscious tribalization, whereas others were in the process of being assimilated. Neither tribalization nor partial assimilation was perceived by Chinese nationalists as a barrier to eventual total assimilation, which became the explicit policy of the Republican government. When the Nationalist leader Chiang Kai-shek referred, then, to the *Zhonghua minzu*, or Chinese nation, he meant, ideally at least, a potentially culturally uniform national population living within China's borders (Chiang 1947: 39).

The Communist Variant

The Chinese Communist Party, upon taking power in 1949, inherited both the remnant cultural nationalism of the Republic and the very different Marxist-

6. One could argue that the Tai (or Dai) of Sipsong Panna (now called in Chinese Xishuang-banna Daizu Autonomous Prefecture) did have a functioning sovereign state into the twentieth century, but the combination of the fact that Chinese imperial regimes from the Yuan on had conferred titles on the ruler, implying his subordination, and the ignorance on the part of the Republicans about this area in general prevented the early Republicans from taking any Tai claim to nationhood very seriously. And of course the Tai state was small and weak, so no Chinese state was very afraid of its claims, though it is still not allowed in Chinese publications to refer to pre-1951 Sipsong Panna as a kingdom. See Hsieh 1995.

Leninist views on "the national question" (Connor 1984). This latter, of course, had to take priority in official policy at least, and it demanded that Han culture no longer be considered superior a priori and that no group be either legally disprivileged or subject to overt pressures of cultural assimilation. In short, Communist doctrine resisted both the empire model, in which ethnic groups were legally unequal, and the nation-state model, in which equality was based on the real or promised erasure of ethnic distinctions. The Communists could neither ignore ethnic distinctions nor make these distinctions invidiously, as either one would be cultural nationalism, or *da Han minzu zhuyi*—"great Han chauvinism." Instead, they had to create what they called a "unified country of diverse nationalities." What this meant was that all the ethnic groups in China, however many there turned out to be—and explicitly including not only the historical nations represented in the five-color flag but also the smaller and politically less organized groups in the Southwest and elsewhere—had to be recognized and accorded equal status as elements of the new state.

At the same time, the Communists were committed to economic and political development. As orthodox Marxist-Leninists, they espoused an idea of development that divided human history in general into five stages, originally systematized in Stalin's Soviet Union: the primitive, slave, feudal, capitalist, and socialist modes of production, in scientifically discovered historical order. It was empirically obvious in the China of the 1950s that members of different ethnic groups stood on different rungs of this ladder of human progress, and in general the Han (along with perhaps a few Hui Muslims, Manchus, and Koreans) stood at the top. The Communists thus formulated a policy of development that urged the "brother nationalities," or *xiongdi minzu*, to follow the example of the advanced Han and move quickly forward in history, even to skip some of the rungs on the ladder. One effect of this policy was to confirm the Han in their place of prominence as the most developed and the people whom the others should follow. The only difference between the Communist development project and the literizing project of the old Empire was thus the rationale: in Imperial times, peoples of the periphery had been urged to follow the Han example because it was morally superior in its own right; in Communist times they were urged to follow the Han example because it stood higher on an objective scale that was originally formulated without respect to who occupied its higher gradations, but conveniently placed the Han at the top.

Communist nationality policy was thus quite simple in its conception. First, the People's Republic's constituent "nationalities" (*minzu*) had to be identified, along with their position on the scale of progress. Second, they had to be given the opportunity (or coerced, depending on one's point of view) to develop in the direction of universal progress. Given the preexisting situation on the ground, particularly in such areas as the Southwest, identification was no easy task, and the development would be as hard or harder for the minorities as it turned out to be for the Han core. The ways in which these two prongs of Communist policy—ethnic identification and economic and cultural development—interacted with local categories and local society are the subjects of chapter 3.

3 / Ethnology, Linguistics, and Politics

I n any political system that involves relations among ethnic groups and/or nations, ideas of nationhood and identity maintain their salience only insofar as they are framed in categories relevant to the lives of the participants. Since ethnic groups and nations exist only insofar as people recognize their existence, their existence must be continually reinforced and restated by acts that communicate the continued salience of the categories. For example, as long as police in American cities differentially stop and question darker-skinned males simply for being in a particular part of town at a particular time of night, as long as census forms ask respondents to check one of several boxes labeled "race," as long as young men on certain street corners speak with a particular vocabulary and intonation pattern, the categories "black" and "white" will retain salience in American society. Similarly, as long as the personal identification cards of Chinese citizens carry a designation labeled *minzu*, as long as circle dances are performed in remote township squares on state occasions, as long as the language known to its own speakers as *Nuosu ddoma* continues to be spoken, and as long as members of certain categories are given preference in high school admissions, citizens of the Liangshan area will continue to be divided into the categories Yi, Han, Zang, and so forth.

Communicative acts such as those described above do not create ethnicity in the causal sense. The thing communicated about must have some importance for the communicative act to have meaning in the first place. But the communicative acts are necessary to sustain (and sometimes create) the facts of culture, kinship, and history that give their meanings such salience. Thus one way in which we can speak of ethnic identity is as a series of languages of communication about group membership and group relationships. In most systems of ethnic relationships, there are two general ways in which languages communicate about ethnicity, and each of these in turn is used in two or three specific types of languages.

The first way in which languages communicate about ethnicity is through the use of one set of symbols rather than another equivalent set, thereby communicating the ethnic aspect of the communicative relationship in which the symbols are used. Two kinds of languages can communicate about ethnicity in this way. The first of these is simply what we conventionally call languages, such as English, Black English, standard Chinese, and *Nuosu ddoma*. In many situations, merely using a particular idiom conveys a lot of information about the speaker and the listeners: whether I speak English or Chinese or *Nuosu ddoma*, when, and with whom, communicates things about ethnicity that are not necessarily explicit in the content of the conversation.

Signs other than speech and writing also communicate information about ethnic relations simply by being used. The whole series of cultural behaviors usually known as ethnic markers—which can include food, dress, housing styles, ritual, and many other things—are at this level nothing but signs, often conveying simple information about the ethnicity of the person employing them. People in the United States who wear yarmulkes or celebrate Passover are making a statement to each other and to outsiders about their Jewish ethnicity, for example, in the same way that people in Liangshan who preserve boneless pigs and worship the household deity Zambala are making a statement that they are either Naze or Prmi, but certainly not Nuosu or Han.

The second way that languages express ethnicity is by *talking about* it, by employing the categories that *refer to* ethnic groups and relations. In the Chinese case, and in Liangshan in particular, there are at least three different types of idioms that are used to talk *about* ethnicity. The first of these is the ordinary speech of people as they go about their business and have occasion to speak about themselves and their neighbors in terms of ethnic categories, which exist in all the languages spoken in the area, though the categories used in one language do not map exactly onto the categories used in another. This language often includes self-referential aspects, as people use their ethnic languages (in the above mode where the use of one language rather than another indicates something about ethnicity) to speak about ethnic relations, and even about the use of language, which in a polyglot area is an important aspect of their daily lives.

The second kind of language used to *talk about* ethnicity is the scholarly one of ethnohistory—the geographic and temporal story of the location and movement of peoples, presuming for the sake of argument that there are such things as peoples, civilizations, cultures. This language has been developed primarily by scholars, but the line between scholarship and local discourse is never clearly drawn. Thus the stories and legends of a local community are data for the scholars' systematic accounts, even as the systematic accounts, read and discussed in local communities, become incorporated into the local or folk narratives and classifications (Hanson 1989, Haley and Wilcoxon 1997).

The third language is that of the state discourse of ethnic identification, through which authorities in multiethnic states identify every citizen as belonging to one or another ethnic group or category. In the United States, this takes the forms of census categories and affirmative action goals, among others, and in China takes the form of the process of "ethnic identification," through which the Communist-led government, beginning in the 1950s, attempted to classify all of its citizens into one or another *minzu* (Lin 1987, Fei 1980). All official communications use this language of ethnic identification.

The manifestations of ethnicity described in this book can thus be seen as a series of communicative acts, performed in the kinds of languages described above. The remainder of this chapter describes how the formal languages of ethnic discourse have been formulated in the period of Communist rule, how the process of ethnic identification established the vocabulary of the official discourse and influenced that of the popular discourse, and how the work of ethnology and linguistics provided the language of ethnohistory to support and reinforce the categories formulated in the process of ethnic identification.

ETHNOLOGY, LINGUISTICS, AND THE LANGUAGES OF ETHNICITY

The Chinese Communists came to power in 1949–50 armed with two ideologies. The first of these was nationalism, through which they were determined to forge a "unified, multinational state" within their borders, including the minority regions around the peripheries. The second was Marxism-Leninism, through which they were determined to lead the inhabitants of that state in China proper forward from their "semifeudal, semicolonial" historical stage, and the inhabitants of the minority regions forward from whatever earlier stages of history they might then be at, into the future of socialism and eventual communism. To accomplish the twin goals dictated by these twin ideologies, the Communists needed the help of social scientists, particularly ethnologists and linguists, and these social scientists thus became closely implicated in the projects of state-building and national development, particularly as they applied in the peripheral areas. It was the ethnological projects that, in a sense, wrote the lexicons and grammars of the ethnohistorical and ethnic identification languages used in China today not only to talk about ethnicity but to attempt to regulate ethnic relations.

Chinese Ethnology before 1949

Precursors to Ethnology in Late Imperial Times. Description and classification of peripheral peoples have a long history in China. The earliest systematic general history, *Records of the Historian* (Shi ji), written by Sima Qian in the early first century B.C.E., contains chapters dealing with various peoples around the peripheries of the Chinese world, including "Record of the Southwestern Barbarians" (Xinan yi liezhuan). In only slightly later times, works such as *Records of Foreign Countries* (Huayang guo zhi) from the Jin period and *Book of Barbarians* (Man shu) from the Tang dynasty are entirely devoted to ethnology in the sense of describing the customs, habits, and ecology of foreign peoples.

By the Ming and Qing dynasties there had evolved two different, but connected, traditions of ethnological reporting about the Southwest. One was the writing of accounts of non-Han peoples in standard documents such as local gazetteers (*fang zhi* or *difang zhi*) and in the personal accounts of scholars and literati who administered or visited non-Han areas. The other was the pictorial ethnology of the *Miao man tu ce*, often called "Miao album" in English, a genre that is a sort of catalogue of minority "peoples" (including other groups in addition to those called Miao), each afforded a two-page spread consisting of a stylized picture and a brief description of physical characteristics, temperament, livelihood, and customs.[1]

Despite the very different levels of discourse embodied in these two genres, they share a common set of assumptions that still inform Chinese ethnology to a degree. First, they are driven by a classificatory impulse. Groups are named and categorized, and the categorization is anchored both in an assumption of a common history and in a set of characteristics of livelihood, temperament, customs, and so forth. Second, they are concerned with the distance of each group from the cultural ideal of the Han core. In many sources, groups are divided into two basic types. *Shu*, "cooked" or "ripe," peoples are those who, in spite of their obvious non-Chinese origin and their inferior customs and different languages, are still participants in the Chinese political order,

---

1. See Diamond (1995) and Hostetler (2001) for descriptions and analyses of Miao albums. The modern successor to this genre is perhaps the packets of postcards or trading cards of the fifty-six minzu of China printed in the 1980s; each has a picture on one side and a set of facts (population and area of habitation—analogous to batting average and RBIs?) on the other. I have two different sets of these cards, but the only Miao album I have seen, a rare manuscript, is kept under lock and key at the University of Washington's East Asia Library. It does not depict primarily Miao but rather peoples of Yunnan, mostly Tibeto-Burman, calling into question the name "Miao albums."

ruled either directly by the imperial field administration or indirectly by appointed local rulers, and often practice Chinese customs such as ancestor worship, are bilingual in their native languages and Chinese, and sometimes even participate in the classical educational system and the civil-service examinations.[2] *Sheng*, or "raw," peoples, by contrast, are those still beyond the influence of literization entirely, out of reach of any but the most sporadic and military government, ignorant of Han language and culture. Classification and scaling, the two basic principles of the 1950s ethnological project, are thus present already in literature from the late centuries of the Imperial era.

The Development of a Chinese-Western Hybrid Ethnology. After the fall of the empire in 1911, and especially after the beginning of the so-called May Fourth Era of iconoclasm and absorption of Western ideas beginning in about 1919, a flood of Western -ologies flowed into China, and among them were ethnology and anthropology. In the 1920s and early 1930s, such diverse systems of thought as evolutionism, German Kulturkreislehre, and British structural-functionalism caught the attention of Chinese scholars, first eager to look for scientific reasons why China had developed differently from the West, but soon thereafter thinking about the problems of the relations between China proper and the peripheral regions now included in the Republic's administrative borders (Chen Yongling 1998). Ethnology and anthropology were taught in universities in various parts of the country, including Peking University and Yenching University in Beiping, Zhongshan University in Guangzhou, and Xiamen University in the city of that name (Guldin 1994: 23–56).

Already in the period before World War II, foreign-educated Chinese ethnologists and their homegrown students had conducted considerable research among minority populations, but this research, paradoxically, grew in quantity and sophistication during the war years. Many intellectuals from the eastern and southern coastal cities moved inland to Sichuan, Yunnan, and Guangxi to escape the Japanese invaders, and a large number of them, along with scholars native to these areas, conducted field research among the minority peoples of the Southwest. Many of China's most eminent ethnologists, anthropologists, and anthropological linguists—such as Wu Wenzao, Fei Xiaotong, Liang Zhaotao, Lin Yaohua, Ma Xueliang, Yang Chengzhi, Feng Hanyi, Fu Maoji—and a host of others contributed to this effort as well as to the ethnological and ethnolinguistic projects carried out later under the Communists.

---

2. The participation of ethnically non-Han peoples in the civil-service examinations was a feature of local ethnic relations during the Qing period in many places in the Southwest, including the Nuosu village of Manshuiwan, described in detail in chapter 8.

The ethnology of these times is, as one might expect, a hybrid. While many of the scholars who wrote on the Southwest (such as Lin Yaohua, in his account of the Nuosu in Liangshan [1961]) were foreign-trained and incorporated the tenets of, for example, structural-functional analysis into their accounts, most of them still retained the classifying and ordering tendencies of their Imperial forebears. If the descriptions were more lifelike and less stereotypical, based on careful and often extended observation, the context was often still that of the descendants of certain peoples mentioned in the ancient texts, now known through science in greater detail but still retaining the character of their early ancestors.[3]

The kind of classification these scholars engaged in is indicated by the term for "ethnology" in standard Chinese: *minzuxue*, or "the study of *minzu*," a term that had acquired a second sense in addition to the nationalistic one described in chapter 2. That nationalistic sense has been perpetuated—in the term *Zhonghua minzu*, or "Chinese nation"—not only by cultural nationalists such as Chiang Kai-shek but also by the Communists, who used *minzu* to translate the Soviet Russian term *natsiya* (Connor 1984). *Zhonghua minzu* continues to be used in nationalistic appeals by China's Communist Party and government almost interchangeably with such terms as *long de chuan ren* (descendants of the dragon) and *Yan Huang zisun* (children and grandchildren of the emperors Yan [or Shen Nong] and Huang [or the Yellow Emperor]). In the ideology of China as a "unified country of diverse nationalities," all nationalities, or *minzu* in its second sense, are united in the greater Chinese nation, or *Zhonghua minzu*.

Ethnology, or *minzuxue*, however, is most concerned with the second sense of the term *minzu*, which refers to the groups that make up the nation. As mentioned in chapter 2, the term was originally used in this sense by such nationalist writers as Sun Zhongshan to refer to the major historical groups that made up the Chinese empire and were to be included as citizens of the new Chinese Republic and represented by the five stripes of the original Chinese Republican flag. The ethnologists working in the Southwest, however, quickly expanded the use of this term, using it in scholarly and administrative journals of the 1920s through 1940s to refer to the groups classified and described in their works. *Minzuxue* thus became the study of cultural and social difference, of the defining characteristics of the many and diverse peoples who inhabited China's border regions.

---

3. I have treated the nature of historiography and ethnology of the Yi peoples in the Republican and Communist periods in "The History of the History of the Yi" (1995b).

The Chinese Revolution and Chinese Ethnology

Emerging from this rather bourgeois, foreign-influenced background, Chinese ethnologists and linguists were asked, between 1949 and 1958, and again after 1978, to contribute to the Party-led projects of national unity and socialist development (Chen Yongling 1998: 25–33). From 1958 to 1966, the period of the Great Leap Forward and the subsequent famine and rebuilding, their role was restricted, as was the role of all intellectuals, many of whom were labeled as "rightists" after 1957. From 1966 to 1978, the period of the truly radical policies of the Great Proletarian Cultural Revolution, their role was practically nonexistent, except for a small amount of linguistic work (Guldin 1994: chap. 10). But after 1978 the project of ethnology literally continued where it had left off in the 1950s, to the extent that many articles researched and written in the 1950s, but judiciously tucked into drawers during the radical interlude, were taken out again and published in the 1980s. And despite the de facto turning away from socialism, and thus from much of Marxism-Leninism, as a formula for development after 1979, the project of nationalities unity was still a crucial one to the Communists, and development, though frequently changing its ideal form, had never lost its importance.

The contribution asked of the ethnologists and linguists was thus much the same in the 1980s and 1990s as it had been in the 1950s. In both periods, it began with new versions of the old projects of classification and scaling, structured since the revolution by the Soviet-derived notions of nationality and of the stages of history. From there it proceeded to various derivative tasks, such as recording the histories of the now-fixed entities, standardizing their languages and cultures, and, in the 1980s, reconstructing an economically developing, multiethnic polity out of the ruins of Cultural Revolution radicalism.

Identification: Determining Which Minzu Exist in China. With the advent of Communist Party rule in China, the term *minzu* in the second, more local sense became equated with the Soviet Russian term *natsionalnost'* (Connor 1984), which was defined by that eminent ethnologist Josef Vissarionovich Stalin as a group with four common characteristics: language, territory, economy, and psychological nature manifested in a common culture (Gladney 1991: 66–67). (Around the same time, *minzu,* so defined, acquired the standard English translation "nationality," which it retains, to the horror of Western ethnologists, in official and tourist literature on China today.)[4] These four cri-

---

4. I have noticed, however, that at least one of the regional *minzu xueyuan,* most of which translate their own name as "nationalities institute," has recently changed its name to the "Central

teria of *minzu* membership were the ostensible basis of the 1950s project of ethnic identification.

The identification project began when local groups were invited to submit applications for the status of *minzu*. According to later accounts (Fei 1981), over four hundred groups submitted such applications, which were then judged by teams of researchers, supposedly to determine whether they conformed to Stalin's four criteria. After researchers compiled data on the four hundred applications, the actual number of groups was determined to be somewhere in the fifties, stabilizing at fifty-four minorities[5] plus the majority Han in 1962, and having been augmented since then only by the addition of the Jinuo in 1979 (Du 1985).[6]

Recent retrospective scholarship, however, has shown that there was great variation in the extent to which the identification process actually used Stalin's criteria in determining group boundaries. In some cases they worked reasonably well. In such areas as Inner Mongolia, Tibet, and East Turkistan or Xinjiang, the conventional Chinese usage of the term *minzu* for Mongols, Tibetans, or Uygurs probably fits fairly well with an English speaker's intuitive feel for the idea of nationality, since these peoples lived in compact territories, were reasonably uniform culturally, and all had historical experience of independent statehood. Their inclusion in China (which many people in those areas continue to oppose) rather unambiguously makes the People's Republic of China a multinational state, as advertised.

In most of the Southwest, however, things are somewhat different, since different *minzu*, or different cultural and linguistic collectivities, live intermixed in that area, and there have been few historical instances of ethnically based states there, and none in recent centuries. In this kind of a situation, it becomes much more difficult to apply Stalin's criteria to nationality, and in fact Chinese ethnologists sometimes gave lip-service to his criteria while actually classifying *minzu* according to other standards. Lin Yaohua (1987) has shown, for example, that researchers in the Southwest discovered early on that the kind of

---

China University for Ethnic Groups." This does not really solve the problem of translation of *minzu* into English.

5. In this book, I reserve the term "minorities" for those ethnic groups that are officially designated or wish for official designation in the classification system of a modern state. In the People's Republic of China, "minorities" is a customary and reasonable translation of the official term *shaoshu minzu*.

6. For an officially sanctioned account of the process, see Fei 1981; for critiques by foreign scholars, see Heberer 1989 and Gladney 1991.

intermixture of ethnic groups found in that area did not conform to the model implied by Stalin's definition, and that researchers who still had to come up with policy recommendations thus fell back primarily on language as a criterion for identification.[7] Jiang Yongxing (1985), writing about Guizhou, has commented that the identification teams relied too heavily on "historical relatedness" of groups and not enough on local people's own wishes, with the result that many identities in Guizhou are still disputed and many groups are still "yet to be identified" (Cheung 1995a, 1996).

Despite the scientific premises and seeming finality of this project, there is still much dispute in certain areas over whether *minzu* were identified properly in the original project or the follow-up work that goes on in some places to this day. The uncertainties and disputes almost inevitably come from communities whose members feel their own *minzu* identity was wrongly determined in the classifying project. These are of two kinds. The most common are groups who feel they have been unjustly lumped with larger groups but ought to have a separate identity of their own. The Baima Zang of northwestern Sichuan are such a group; they have even printed and distributed a collection of historical essays that demonstrate their separateness from the Tibetans whose *minzu* they were included in, but it is reported that the opposition of the tenth Panchen Lama (who died in 1989) prevented the Zang from being broken up in this way.[8] Other examples are the Ge of southeastern Guizhou (Cheung 1995a, 1996) and, at one time at least, many of the Shuitian people described in chapter 13 of this book (see also Harrell 1990). The other type consists of people who claim minority status despite official classification as Han. Certain Hui of southern Fujian, described by Dru Gladney (1991: chap. 6) and Fan Ke (n.d.) are an example of this second type, in this case one that successfully won reclassification in the 1980s.

7. Lin explains the inability to classify southwestern groups according to Stalin's criteria by the fact that the criteria were designed for areas where the transition to capitalism was already initiated, while the peoples of southwest China were still at the feudal, slave, or occasionally even the late primitive stages. In fact, there was a debate in the 1950s as to whether to apply the term *minzu* to groups in the earlier stages of history according to the Morganian-Marxist paradigm, or whether to use distinctive terms such as *buluo* (tribe) or *buzu* (tribal ethnic group). For reasons of political equality, the debate was decided in favor of using *minzu* for all of the groups (Li Shaoming, lecture at the University of Washington, March 1999).

8. The Panchen's opposition is a widely circulated rumor that I have never seen in print. However, Zang scholars have begun to attack both the "separatist" ideas of certain Baima scholars and the whole idea of the Pumi as a *minzu*. See Sichuan Sheng Minzu Yanjiu Suo 1980 and Upton 1998.

The existence of continuing controversies over identification points out two important things about the identification project and about ethnic relations generally. First, the project is not a one-way thing, imposed top-down on passive local peoples. From the beginning, consultation with local leaders was an important part of the process, and from the beginning also, many if not most of the agents of the state who implemented ethnic identification and other aspects of the literizing project were themselves members of the minority communities. In other words, the language of ethnic identification is one that can be spoken by people of all ethnic identities and claimed identities. And the participation of people with local, changing interests ensures that even this attempt to determine classifications once and for all will always run up against shifting identities and interests of those being classified. In other words, the vocabulary of this language is not entirely closed or predetermined, though the ethnic identification project tried to make it as closed as possible. Second, classification is a vital issue in the minority regions of China. Not only people's pride and their understanding of their heritage and their place in the world, but also their access to resources are heavily dependent on it.

Description: Coming to Know the Minzu. Mere identification of minzu, however, is not enough of a contribution from linguists and ethnologists to enable the state to accomplish its goals in minority regions. Because the state project involves not only ruling the peoples within its territory but also economic and cultural development (defined as progress toward socialism and eventually communism, starting from wherever on the ladder of history a particular group might have been at the time of the Communist takeover), peoples must also be described in considerable detail, both in order to determine where they are on the ladder of development and also to provide specific knowledge about them that will be useful in various aspects of rule and promotion of economic and cultural development. To this end, the project of ethnic identification in the 1950s was combined with a massive project of ethnology, and many of the same scholars who contributed to the founding and early development of Chinese ethnology before 1949, along with younger scholars coming of age since the Communist takeover, were enlisted in this effort of data collection about the minorities' society, history, and language. Through this massive effort, continuing to this day, the scientific language of ethnology and ethnohistory was created and developed as a supplement to the political language of ethnic identification.

In the first heyday of this project, many investigations were conducted and reports written, and in preparation for the celebration of the tenth anniversary of the People's Republic in 1959, a large-scale effort began in 1957 to publish an encyclopedic series of reports on society and history. These first-generation reports, known colloquially as "white-covered books," or *baipi shu*, were compiled in great haste at the time of the Great Leap Forward, only to fall quickly under criticism for their insufficiently Marxist content, demonstrated by the fact that many of the senior scholars involved in their compilation were pre-revolutionary bourgeois ethnologists, some of them officially coming to be labeled rightists in the Anti-Rightist campaign beginning in summer 1957 (Chen Yongling 1998: 33–36). Many reports never saw the light of day, and went underground until the revival of ethnology and ethnology research institutes in the 1980s. During that decade they were then published, together with many results from research newly conducted in the 1980s, in the provincial collections of "reports of social and historical investigations" (*shehui lishi diaocha baogao*). These reports (over fifty volumes for Yunnan, for example, and ten or more each for Sichuan and Guizhou) consist both of individual reports on various topics and of ordered presentations of what is important to know about a particular *minzu* at a particular stage of development. For example, *Summary Volume of Historical and Social Investigations on the Yi of Liangshan in Sichuan Province* (Sichuan sheng Liangshan Yizu shehui lishi diaocha zonghe baogao) treats the following topics concerning the Nuosu of Liangshan, generally placed at the slave society level of development (Sichuan 1985: 5):

Part 1: Social Productive Forces
1. The principal sector of production—agriculture
2. Production activities that serve as subsidiary occupations: herding, fishing, forestry, and others
3. Handicrafts not yet separated from agriculture
4. Exchange of commodities that had not developed into a separate economic sector
5. Production and sale of opium and its effect on the productive forces in Yi Society

Part 2: Castes and Caste Relations
1. Caste structure
2. The means of production controlled by each caste, and its economic situation
3. Caste relations
4. Caste mobility
5. Class (caste) struggle and its form
6. Summary

Part 3: Land Relations
1. Land tenure relations
2. Land sales and pawning
3. The situation of land management
4. Other situations of rent and tenancy

Part 4: Clan system
1. Clans
2. Enemies
3. Household and marriage

The reports of social and historical investigations, along with various journals that have sprung up in *minzu* studies in provincial and prefectural institutes, as well as in departments of ethnology and anthropology at various universities and nationalities institutes constitute a rich corpus of ethnographic data spanning five decades (though concentrated very heavily in the 1950s and again in the 1980s and 1990s), but they do not simply present data in an empirical fashion. In accordance with the responsibilities of ethnologists and linguists to the state's minority projects, these works are concerned not only with identification, classification, and description but also with ordering. Each *minzu*, envisioned as a group with certain characteristics in common (Stalin's four criteria), must be regularized, systematized, normalized in Michel Foucault's sense (1977: 177–84), made to conform to a paradigm of what a *minzu* is. This standardization or normalization has taken many forms, including the ethnographic collections described above, but others have been particularly the province of scholars: the writing of histories and the preparation of linguistic materials.

Writing Standard Histories. Along with the reports of social and historical investigations, the State Nationalities Commission also published, in the mid- and late 1980s, a series of concise histories of *minzu* (*minzu jianshi*), one for each of the fifty-five officially recognized minority ethnic groups, or *shaoshu minzu*. Along with other historical works published by institutes and university presses, these standard histories set forth orthodox interpretations of the unitary history of each of the fifty-five minorities. Although these histories vary somewhat in content, they mostly conform to a standard format, one that places the history of each *minzu* into the framework of the history of China as a whole, and into the universal framework of the Marxist-Stalinist stages of evolution in human history. As Ralph Litzinger describes the volume on the Yao,

This history is a simplified, encapsulated version of how the Yao have progressed through history; it charts the obstacles they have encountered in their long and arduous path to realize full social and economic potential, to become a socialist, modern *minzu*.

[*Yaozu jianshi* (The concise history of the Yao)] takes the reader on a tour through the long historical stretch of Chinese history, as moments in the history of the Yao are situated in different dynastic regimes and related to social evolutionary stages. (Litzinger 1995: 130)

Works on other *minzu* are similar in their conception and construction (Harrell 1995b). There are three features to notice in these histories. First, there is no questioning of the idea that these *minzu* are real units, despite the fact that they were definitively identified for the first time in the 1950s and that some of their boundaries are still actively disputed. Second, the history of each *minzu* is calibrated to what I have elsewhere described as "history with a capital H, which stands for Han" (Harrell 1995b: 75). There is no doubt left that these *minzu* are part of the Chinese nation and have been for a very long time. Yet placing them in the context of the stages of human evolution makes it clear that they are a backward or inferior part of that Chinese nation. Third, much of the writing of these histories is done by scholars who are themselves members of the minority *minzu* in question. As representatives of their own *minzu* and at the same time participants in this hegemonic state project, they participate in the two-way process of co-optation mentioned above: their story gets told, and it is a glorious one, but it is told as a part of the larger story of the Chinese nation as a whole.

Standardizing Languages. One of the clearest indications of the Chinese state's ambivalence about its status as a present-day empire or a nation-state is its attitude toward minority languages. Although the Han language is clearly hegemonic, as the only one used in nationwide media and taught in all schools, the government, especially in the 1950s and again in the 1980s, has actively promoted the use of minority languages alongside Han Chinese. It has supported the development of print media in many of the minority languages (particularly those with large numbers of speakers), thus using one of the most prominent policies of nation-state building described by Benedict Anderson (1991), in the service of building a state that is not exactly sure of the sense in which it wants to be a nation.

In order to promote the use of non-Han languages, of course, linguistic scholars had to be enlisted in a linguistic project, much as ethnologists were enlisted in the project of ethnic classification, description, and history writing. If the languages of the minority *minzu* were to come up to the Han standard, they needed to be described, classified, standardized, written, and taught systematically in the schools. It has been the work of linguists, beginning with those attached to the ethnic identification teams in the 1950s, to accomplish these tasks with the minority languages.

Description, of course, involved a heavy investment in field linguistics, recording a large number of varieties. But merely recording and listing varieties was insufficient; these languages were those of the fifty-five minority *minzu*, after all, and each *minzu* needed to have its own language classified and related to those of other *minzu*. A standard *Stammbaum* classification was worked out by the 1980s (Guojia Minwei 1981: 585–86) that conveniently correlated, on a nearly one-to-one basis, *minzu* and their languages.[9] In addition, the varieties spoken by each *minzu* were further broken down into dialects (*fangyan*), and sometimes subdialects (*ci fangyan*) and local vernaculars (*tuyu*) (Bradley 1990, 2001). Only when the varieties spoken by members of a *minzu* cut across language families could a *minzu* have two languages; otherwise any variation was termed dialectal.

The linguistic project was not just descriptive and classificatory, however; it had and retains the practical purpose of using the languages in the modern context of nation-building and economic development. This means that standard varieties had to be chosen (for Yi, to take an example, this was a complex task, handled differently in the three provinces of Sichuan, Yunnan, and Guizhou [Bradley 2001]), and textbooks written for use in schools (Harrell and Bamo 1998). Those languages that had no written form prior to the Communist takeover had to have scripts invented for them (usually based on the Latin alphabet); those that were written previously often needed standardization if they were to be used in textbooks, newspapers, magazines, and other print media.[10]

The paradox of this linguistic project, of course, is that the minority languages are officially available only to promote the messages of national unity and development. Diversity is displayed by the use of the numerous vernaculars in a variety of media. But diversity can go only so far; the linguistic project grants voice to the members of minorities only insofar as they sign on to

9. The only exceptions to this one-to-one correlation were the Yughur, some of whom spoke a Mongolic and some a Turkic language; the Yao, some of whom spoke a Yao, some a Miao, and some a Zhuang-Dong (known in the West as Tai) language; and the Hui and Man, most of whom spoke Han (Guojia Minwei 1981: 586).

10. For fuller descriptions of the process of language recording, classification, and standardization in minority areas, see Harrell 1993 and Dwyer 1998.

the national project. Nevertheless, it is difficult to grant permission for people to speak, and give them the media to do so, while still keeping them from expressing any messages of conflict or separatism. Especially in the 1990s, divergent voices speaking for local ethnic groups have become more and more common, as related in the case studies in chapters 5 through 13 of this book.

INTEGRATION AND DEVELOPMENT IN MINORITIES WORK

Chinese ethnology is, then, in a sense a creature of and an important agent of the minority policies of the Chinese Communist Party. In order to carry out its programs of development and national integration, the Party needed the help of ethnologists, linguists, historians, and other scholars. They were the great normalizers, building the base of knowledge and vocabulary that allowed the substantive projects of national integration and development to proceed in the minority regions. But the work of the ethnologists was only a small part, though a vital one, of the overall program of development carried out by means of "minorities work," or *minzu gongzuo*.

When Mao Zedong launched the great systematic ethnological projects in the 1950s, he called upon the scholars and students participating in those projects to "rescue the backward," or *qiangjiu luohou* (Chen Yongling 1998: 31), for knowing who the minorities were, and placing them on the scale of history, were only preliminaries to the real objectives of minorities work. Though its content has shifted along with the Party line over the half-century of Communist rule, minorities work has still maintained its two primary objectives: including the minorities in the project of national integration, and developing the minority regions as part of the development of the country as a whole. The whole industry of creating knowledge of minorities, described above, from ethnological reports to standard histories to language textbooks and translation bureaus, was created *in the service of* these greater projects of including the minorities and the minority regions in the projects of national integration and development. The policy and practice of minorities work has been treated in great detail in works by June Teufel Dreyer (1976), Colin Mackerras (1994), and Thomas Heberer (1989, 2001) and, in its cultural aspect, by Louisa Schein (1999). The following summary places the present research in context.

Administration of Minority Regions

The earliest "nationalities policies" of the Chinese Communist Party emphasized the Party's willingness to grant a great deal of autonomy to local governments in minority regions that took its side in the civil war against the Guomindang (Kuomintang, KMT) forces (Gladney 1991: 87–91, Atwood 1995). As soon as the Party actually assumed power, however, its attentions were turned toward integration of all within its territory, and the nature of "autonomy" that actually emerged firmly subordinated governments of minority regions to the central government in Beijing. With the partial exception of Tibet before 1959 (Goldstein 1997), there was no opportunity whatsoever for local authorities to pursue policies at odds with those of the central government as formulated by the Party (Heberer 1989: 41). The designated autonomous areas—most of which were established in the 1950s but which had grown to comprise five provincial-level autonomous regions (*zizhi qu*) thirty-one autonomous prefectures (*zizhi zhou*), and 105 autonomous counties (*zizhi xian*) by 1989 (Heberer 1989: 40)—have in essence been under direct rule from Beijing since their establishment. The *degree* of relative autonomy that they have been able to exercise has varied greatly, however. During the 1950s and again in the 1980s and 1990s, many of the cadres in the Party and government have been members of minorities;[11] there has been wide latitude to use minority languages as primary or supplementary media of instruction in elementary and secondary schools, and since the Autonomy Law of 1984, there has been more local control of budgets than is the case in nonautonomous administrative districts. In the radical periods from 1957 to 1979, on the other hand, and especially during the Cultural Revolution, autonomy was nothing but a word in a title, and not only direct administration by mostly Han cadres, but deliberate attempts to suppress minority culture, religion, and customs were widespread (Gladney 1991: 91–92; Heberer 1989: 25–28; Guo 1996). The efflorescence of varied man-

11. I have, for example, been able to look at the records of all cadres appointed in Xide County in Liangshan (the site of Mishi, described in chap. 6), whose population is about 85 percent Nuosu and 15 percent Han. In this county, from 1976 until 1987 the position of county Party secretary was occupied by a Nuosu (Yi) for nine years and by a Han for three years. Of the seventeen vice-secretaries to serve during this time, eight were Nuosu, eight Han, and one Zang. Of Party department heads to serve during this time, only ten were Nuosu and twenty were Han; of party secretaries in the government, legislature, army, and other offices, thirteen were Nuosu and six Han. Although this is a higher percentage of Han among party secretaries than would be found in the county population, it does not appear to substantiate the charge that there are no minorities in responsible positions in the Party. It is interesting, however, that even within the Party, more cadres in technical positions (heads of departments) tend to be Han than do cadres in general leadership positions or those who serve as Party secretaries in administrative, legislative, and army units (CCP Xide 1991). Also, it is reported unofficially that since 1991 there has been a de facto policy of not appointing minorities to Party secretary positions at the prefectural level and above.

ifestations of ethnic identity described in the case studies in this book is partially explicable as a reaction to bad memories of oppression and persecution during the Cultural Revolution years.

The Democratic Reforms and the Displacement of Traditional Political and Economic Structures

Creation and staffing of administrative structures, however, are only a small part of development policy for minority regions. In the beginning, once it was determined where minority populations in various regions stood on the scale of human development, the authorities had to face the problem of social transformation. Nearly all the rural communities in China proper were rent sometime during the years between 1947 and 1952 by the Land Reform campaign, whose purpose was to depose former landholding elites and replace them with Communist Party cadres, and to transform the structure of landholding itself from its former "feudal landlord" basis first to individual peasant ownership and then within a few years to the collectives that were the basis of Chinese agriculture until the early 1980s.[12]

Land reform was also carried out in many minority regions, but only those where it was determined that the social system had already evolved to the stage of the "landlord economy," which is conceptualized as a later stage of feudalism (see Diamant 1999). In those areas where the society had developed only to the beginning stages of feudalism represented by the manorial economy—such as Tibet, the Sipsong Panna Tai kingdom, and much of the western part of Liangshan, or where social evolution was retarded at even earlier stages, such as "slave society" (most of the Nuosu areas of Liangshan) or even the late stages of "primitive society" (certain groups in southern Yunnan)—land reform was not carried out. Indeed, in many of these areas, native authorities, some of them long recognized by imperial governments as *tusi* or other native rulers, were allowed to remain in place alongside the new Party-led administration as long as the local land tenure systems were also in place. The separation of areas that underwent land reform, and those that did not, was often very local, with areas in the same township either reformed or temporarily left alone according to prevailing land systems in individual villages.

This delay in social reform lasted until 1956 in most areas of the Southwest;

---

12. For accounts of the land reform process in Han rural communities, see Hinton 1966; Potter and Potter 1989; Siu 1989; Friedman, Selden, and Pickowicz 1991.

when reform came, it was initially of a different sort from the violent class struggles of the Land Reform campaign. Instead, the previously untouched minority areas underwent a process called Democratic Reform (Minzhu Gaige, or Mingai for short). In this process, rather than inducing local peasants to struggle against and overthrow their indigenous leaders, Party nationalities workers made an attempt to co-opt as many local leaders as possible into the new administration (in some areas, many of them had been co-opted already). Those who cooperated with the Communists were made into vice-heads of three of the four arms of the state—the People's Government (Renmin Zhengfu), the People's Congress (Renmin Daibiao Dahui, or Renda for short), or the People's Consultative Conference (Renmin Zhengzhi Xietiao Weiyuanhui, or Zhengxie for short)—excepting in most cases the leading arm, the Communist Party. Though they were able to wield very little power in these vice- (*fu*) positions, they retained a measure of prestige as long as they cooperated.

Along with the co-optation of native leaders into local administration came a dismantling of traditional systems of land tenure, including manorial tenancy, serfdom, and slavery, and their replacement by individual freehold tenure, which was itself soon replaced by collectivization, sometimes within only a year or two of the original Democratic Reform. At the beginning of the reform process, it seems to have been a success in many areas, as it was carried out according to the so-called "five don't" principles: don't struggle, kill, settle old scores, raise old land claims, or jail people.[13] But the process did contain within itself the possibility of a much more polarized struggle, since people were classified, as in Han and other landlord economy areas, according to their relationship with the land in the old economy.

This possibility of conflict came to fruition in many parts of the country in the years 1957–59, as the Party's general line radicalized with the Anti-Rightist campaign, the establishment of People's Communes, and the Great Leap Forward. Many former local elites and landowners were dismissed from their largely honorary vice-posts at this time and often were branded as class enemies and struggled against. In many areas, such as the ethnically Tibetan districts of northwestern Sichuan, as well as the areas of Liangshan discussed in this book, some of these leaders, often taking a considerable number of loyal followers with them from among their former tenants or retainers, staged armed revolts and guerilla warfare against the Communist Party administration; these revolts in northwestern Sichuan probably contributed to the geopolitically more

13. Different people remember different lists. Peng Wenbin (personal communication) was told that the "five don'ts" were don't curse, beat, imprison, kill, or struggle.

significant 1959 uprising in Tibet; in Liangshan, the acute, large-scale phase of the insurrection lasted for one to two years in most areas, though there were holdouts in remote areas well into the 1960s. The final suppression of the insurrections was followed closely by the twenty tumultuous years of the Great Leap Forward and the Cultural Revolution; with the general loosening of nationalities policy in the 1980s, not only were many members of the old elites restored to their positions as vice-heads in the People's Congress and People's Consultative Conference, but there has been a cautious effort among many of these people, along with certain minority intellectuals employed in universities and research institutes, to rewrite the history of this period of ethnic conflict, though in doing so they continue to test the limits of tolerance of the propaganda departments that control publication; in general during the 1980s at least, *minzu* questions were considered much more sensitive than even such questions as the worth of socialism or the adaptability of the Marxist-Leninist model of development, and people had to tread very cautiously.

Economic Development

The tortuous course of economic development in China's minority regions proceeded in one sense parallel to that in the rest of China. When the Great Leap Forward mobilized huge numbers of people to build dams, roads, and other public works and to "manufacture" steel on former village threshing grounds, it mobilized in the minority districts also. When the Cultural Revolution took grain as the key link and expanded the area of its cultivation to what had been pasture or uncultivated areas, terraces appeared in newly cut forests on inhospitable mountains. And when agriculture decollectivized and there was a push for the development of what was first called a commodity economy and then a market economy in the 1980s and 1990s, minorities also decollectivized and were encouraged to produce for the market.[14]

The economic development of the minority regions has, however, been different from that in the Han areas, and in three important ways. First, in a situation reminiscent of colonialism or neocolonialism as described by world-systems theorists (Wallerstein 1984), China's peripheral regions have often been seen by central economic planners as sources of raw materials and markets for finished industrial goods. When I visited Xinjiang in 1994, for example, I watched trains of tankers full of oil proceed east toward China proper, while endless

14. For a dramatic example of the economics of decollectivization in a very remote pastoral region of Tibet, see Goldstein and Beall 1990.

lines of flatcars full of tractors passed them on the parallel tracks going west. This was pointed out to me as a common symbol used by Uygur and other minority peoples in Xinjiang to portray their dependent economic position (see Heberer 2001). Since minorities occupy over 50 percent of the People's Republic's surface area, they sit on top of a great proportion of its mineral and forest resources. Minority elites complain, albeit privately, that what is rightly theirs is being exported for the benefit of colonialists in the big cities and in China proper generally.

Second, since the minority regions of China are sparsely populated in comparison to China proper, central planners have at various times seen these areas as convenient outlets for surplus population. This availability of "nearly empty" territory, along with the desire to move more Han into the peripheries for security reasons and the lack of trained personnel among most of the minorities, has meant a great influx of Han settlers, merchants, cadres, teachers, and other government personnel into all minority regions at various times beginning in the 1950s. In Xinjiang, for example, approximately 5.7 million, or 38 percent of the 1990 population of 15 million, was Han; of those 5.7 million Han, 2.2 million were composed of the soldier corps, or *bingtuan*, the descendants of the armies sent to secure the area in the 1950s, who now dot the whole region with their massive agricultural colonies (Rudelson 1997: 22, 37). In Inner Mongolia, most Han in-migration has consisted of individual families moving at government instigation; they are more scattered, but Han now compose about 80 percent of the 22 million people of the Inner Mongolian Autonomous Region; Mongols, by contrast, are only about 15 percent (Borchigud n.d.). As a final example, Han migration into Tibet was not encouraged until the late 1980s, but since that time there has been considerable in-migration, which has been one important issue in the repeated civil unrest engaged in by local nationalists in Tibet (Schwartz 1994: 202–6). Almost nowhere are minorities entirely in charge of their own economic development. At the same time, members of minority groups in many areas nevertheless work hard, both as government cadres and as individual agriculturalists and entrepreneurs, to bring development to their own regions.

Third, even as the country has moved in the 1980s and 1990s away from the Marxist-Leninist strategies of development toward the strategy of building a market economy, a large number of minority regions have marketed a commodity available only to them: their ethnicity itself. Ethnic tourism, by both Chinese and foreigners, has come to China in a big way in the last fifteen years, and it is often promoted in minority regions as the way to create income in those areas for development (Oakes 1995, 1998; Cheung 1995a; Schein 1989, 1997,

1999; Swain 1989, 1990). In addition to bringing in revenue, ethnic tourism has been a factor in the revival of ethnicity during the reform era. Some areas, such as the Dali plain, home of the majority of the Bai people, who were quite acculturated to Han ways by the early part of this century, have seen a revival of ethnic things from clothing to religious ceremonies in order to provide an ethnic atmosphere for tourists. In this and other areas, along with the revival of ethnic cultural forms and customs has come private entrepreneurship on the part of minority individuals who manufacture and sell crafts to individual tourists while their communities are paid by tour operators (and indirectly, of course, by the tourists themselves) to display songs, dances, food, and other ethnic elements for the tourists to enjoy (Oakes 1995, 1998; Cheung 1995a; Schein 1999).

Variation in Minorities' Participation in and Reactions to Development

Economic development, in the form of both infrastructural construction and rising living standards, has been a real feature of life in minority areas of China since 1980. At the same time, minority regions have suffered almost uniformly from the twin plagues of resource extraction and Han migration, meaning that the benefits of development in most areas are less than what they might otherwise be. And as the state continues to promote nationwide development in a way that integrates the minority regions into dependency or interdependency with the geographic core of China proper, different regions react differently. In Tibet and Xinjiang, and to a large extent in Inner Mongolia also, many members of minority groups see development in quite critical terms, especially as it brings more and more Han people and Han culture into the regions. People are glad to have regained a measure of religious and cultural freedom but still wish, frankly, that the Chinese would go away. They tolerate and participate in tourism and even turn it to the advantage of the local separatist cause, since foreigners are likely to side with peoples campaigning for self-determination (Schwartz 1994: 201).

In other regions, such as the Southwest, there is enormous resentment toward Han people in general, over issues of resource extraction, immigration, and the superior, condescending attitudes of Han toward minorities. For example, I rode once in a car with a Yi driver, a Yi scholar and a Meng cadre to visit a Hui township. When we got going, the Meng cadre, a Communist Party member and rather fierce custodian of her unit's resources, burst out, in the local dialect of Liangshan, "Today's certainly gonna be fun. No Hans along" (Jintian yiding hui haoshua. Meidei Hanchu). The local leaders of ethnic minority communities, however, have bought in wholeheartedly to their membership in the

Chinese nation, and vigorously promote such integrative measures as ethnic tourism, showing the glories of their own culture to Han and foreign visitors; ethnic education to allow members of their own communities to participate in building up their own corners of China; and the ethnicization of the local administration, which allows them to set at least the details of the agenda of development, though they have little control over major extractive industries or immigration into their areas.

This book is about one of those areas where ethnically non-Han people, members of officially designated or self-promoted minority ethnic groups, are trying to make their way within the Chinese nation to a more respected position. Because they are parts of the Chinese nation, they communicate at least partly in the metalanguages of ethnic identification and of ethnology and ethnohistory. But because they also speak in their own languages, verbal and symbolic, and because their identity was differently constituted before and during the collective period, they have different approaches to being ethnic today.

The New Role of Ethnology: A More Open Conversation?

Since the late 1980s there also seems to have been a change in the attitude expressed by Chinese scholars of ethnology and ethnohistory toward the history and society of minority peoples. The old normalizing paradigm, based on the five stages of history supplemented by Lewis Henry Morgan's nineteenth-century account of cultural evolution, is no longer unquestionable orthodoxy, and class struggle is no longer a prescribed ingredient of ethnohistorical analysis. There is even a possibility of questioning both the premises of the language of ethnic identification: maybe Stalin's criteria are inapplicable, as suggested in general by Lin (1987) and Jiang (1985), and there may be situations, like that of the Naze described in chapters 11 and 12 of this book, where ethnic identity is so fluid that no conclusive identification can be made (Li Shaoming 1986, Li Xingxing 1994). In addition, the characterization of such modes of production as "slave society" among the Nuosu in Liangshan has also been severely questioned (Ma Erzi 1993).

If we compare a few article titles from the annual journal *Liangshan Nationalities Studies* (Liangshan minzu yanjiu), established in 1992, with the contents of the general report on Yi society cited above, we immediately see a difference:

"Nurturing the Market Economy Is the Key to Alleviating Poverty in the Poor Yi Districts of Liangshan"

"An Investigation into Commercial Activity by Village Yi Women in the City of Xichang"

"Miscellaneous Thoughts on the Clan Question among the Liangshan Yi"

"Mr. Leng Guangdian [a famous Nuosu leader during the Republican period], Who Encouraged Me to Attend School"

And, in a volume recently edited at the Nationalities University in Beijing, "A Trial Discussion of Remnant Caste Attitudes in Yi Areas of Liangshan" (Lin Yaohua 1993). It is clear that the disciplines of ethnology, ethnohistory, and linguistics, while still dedicated to the state projects of nation-building and development, no longer must do so within a rigid, normalizing paradigm.

In this new atmosphere, collaborative research with foreign scholars is not only tolerated but positively encouraged, even though the scientific paradigms of Chinese and foreign ethnologists are still widely divergent. Where they diverge most sharply, I contend, is in the presence of a self-critical discourse in Western anthropology since the 1970s and the virtual absence of such discourse in Chinese ethnology. There seem to cosmopolitan-trained anthropologists to be great similarities between the kind of colonial normalizing projects aided by European ethnologists during the first part of the twentieth century and the kind of applied anthropology in service of state- and nation-building described earlier in this chapter (Schein 1999, chaps. 4 and 5). But because of the unfree political atmosphere in Communist China, as well as the sincere belief of many ethnologists in the orthodox Marxist model of historical progression and its implications for projects of national development, the basic assumptions behind the state-directed and inspired projects are just now beginning to be questioned, and never publicly or in print. In addition, Chinese nationalism, as described in chapter 2, remains a powerful emotional force for almost everyone who has spent her or his life entirely in China, and even for some people who have traveled outside. To question the basic unity of the *Zhonghua minzu* is not only politically risky; for many people it is emotionally wrenching. Western scholars, by contrast, question everything, and as a result, collaboration between Western anthropologists and Chinese ethnologists remains uneasy, even with the relative opening of the Chinese field to new ideas.

It is in this kind of a situation that I conducted the three periods of field research and several short visits during which I collected the data for this book. In doing so, I did not simply observe and record the varied and changing bases of ethnic identity in Liangshan: I also participated in a minor way in their creation and formation. My essays on Yi culture and society will soon appear in a Chinese-language edition (Harrell 2000b), as, I suspect, will this book not long afterward. The fact that Nuosu and Han scholars will certainly be reading this book within a few years, and perhaps even Prmi and Naze scholars also, demonstrates perhaps better than anything else the interaction not only of the discourses of ethnohistory, ethnology, and ethnic identification within China, but also their increasing interaction with a global ethnological and critical cultural studies discourse. The process of discursive interaction is treated briefly in chapter 9; Louisa Schein (1999) treats it at far greater length. But here we must first sketch our own version of the discourses of ethnohistory, ethnology, and ethnic identification.

4 / The Land and Its History

The Liangshan-Panzhihua area (map 1) forms an inverted triangle jutting down below the fertile plains of historic Sichuan on the north and northeast, between the Yunnan-Guizhou Plateau on the southwest, south, and east, and the foothills of the Tibetan Massif on the northwest. It is a region of high, narrow ranges cut by the deep, steep-sided valleys of great rivers (fig. 1) and bisected by the wider, fertile rift valley in which flows the Anning River (map 2). The Anning Valley has an elevation of 1,550 meters at Xichang and only 900 meters at Panzhihua, and is characterized by mild, dry winters, scorching, dry early summers, and a rainy, warm season in late summer and early fall. Double-cropping is possible in the Anning River floodplain and in some of the lower-elevation small valleys and foothills. Where the land is reasonably flat, there are two agricultural seasons: the early, dry spring (*xiaochun*) season is used for wheat or barley (opium was formerly grown at this time), and the wetter, late or summer (*dachun*) season allows wet-rice cultivation (fig. 2). On slopes too steep for terracing, corn is grown instead of rice in the summer. The mid-level mountain areas, such as central Yanyuan, which lies at an altitude of 2,400–2,600 meters, have approximately the same yearly distribution of rainfall, most of it falling in late summer and early fall, but they are colder; they have no spring growing season, and only on the very warmest fringes can rice be grown during the summer. Otherwise, potatoes, corn, buckwheat, and oats are the main crops. In the winter, the weather in the mountains is usually dry, but it snows a few times every year, and the temperature drops well below freezing at night, though the high altitude brings brief warmth on sunny afternoons. In some of the great, deep river valleys such as those of the Jinsha (Upper Yangzi), Yalong, and Xiao Jin Rivers, the steep slopes next to the rivers are parched and covered with scrub vegetation; only when one rises a few hundred meters above the rivers is rainfall sufficient for cultivation. These rivers run cold and clear during the winter but turn into great brown torrents of mud during the rainy season. Valley-bottom alluvial soils

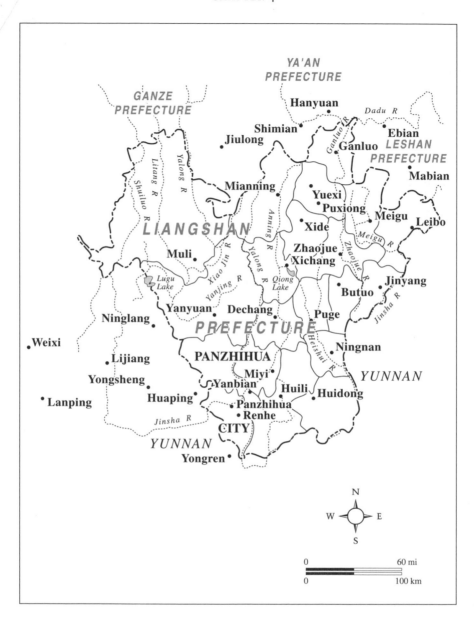

MAP 1. Liangshan and environs

FIG. 1. The valley of the Yalong River, between Xichang and Yanyuan

tend to be yellow or brown, but many of the hills are bright orange or dark red, strongly contrasting with the small, spindly pines that grow there after larger trees have all been cut at least once. At higher mountain elevations of 2,500–3,500 meters or so, there are still considerable forests remaining, especially in Muli and other counties on the western extreme of the area. Systematic logging, which has already denuded the middle elevations, worked on these higher regions at least until the logging ban imposed in late 1997; it is unclear whether this ban is enforceable enough to allow the forests to grow again. On the highest mountaintops, well above 3,000 meters, forest gives way to grasslands, and there is considerable pastoral economy, involving mostly yaks, goats, and sheep, though cattle and horses thrive in the lower regions of the grasslands.

Transport has always been difficult in the Liangshan-Panzhihua area. The only railroad is the Chengdu-Kunming Line, which was built at great expense of money and lives in the late 1960s, finally opening in 1972. There are places where the track, in order to gain or lose elevation, doubles back upon itself in a series of loops and curlicues, and along most of the route a passenger on the train gets the distinct sensation that he is inside tunnels more often than he is out. Since the late 1980s, a few paved highways have been built; there is a good

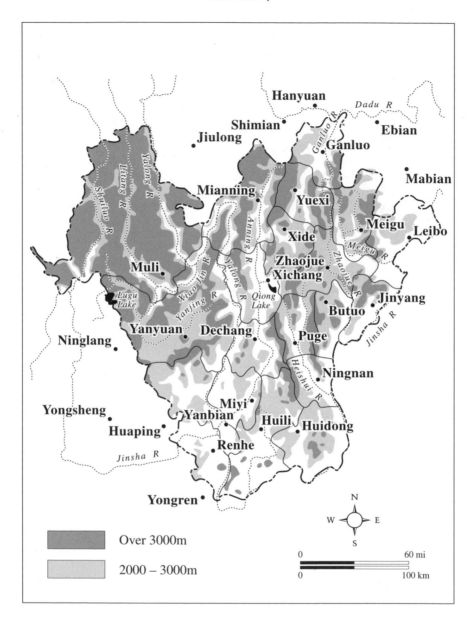

MAP 2. Liangshan in relief

FIG. 2. A fertile plain at Puwei in Miyi. The spring wheat crops
occupy the terrace as fruit trees are in flower in March.

highway grid within the urban sections of Panzhihua, which is strung out over
a fifty-kilometer length along the Jinsha River, and from Panzhihua north to
Xichang and Lugu the road is paved and very serviceable, though it turns into
dirt as it heads toward Yuexi and Ganluo. Side roads are more problematic;
all the county seats have motor roads, but some, such as the one from Xichang
to Yanyuan and on to Muli, are more like American logging roads than
American highways. Many but not all township government headquarters are
reached by dirt motor roads: the famous Zemulong, the most remote township in Panzhihua, had a road built in the late 1980s at great expense and effort;
the road was open for eight hours before a landslide closed it, and it was still
not reopened by 1998. Muli, the most remote county, has no paved highways,
and probably less than half its townships are motor-accessible. In most counties there are a few townships to which one still has to walk, meaning that the
old trade of muleteer is still not gone in Liangshan.

Outside the Anning Valley and the larger plains, or *bazi*, only a few villages—
mostly those that happen to be on a road going somewhere else—can be reached
by car. Bicycles, ubiquitous on country roads in China proper, are rare here

because of the steepness of even the motor roads, and only a few motorcycles have yet made their appearance, most of them in the towns and cities, since almost all villagers are too poor to buy them. People occasionally ride horses, but mostly they walk—to the fields, to market, to visit friends. The trails to most villages are steep, rocky, and often slippery with mud, and mud is the construction material for village houses in most places; in the areas to the west, bordering on the Tibetan foothills, where logging was possible at least until recently, many houses are made of wood, often in log-cabin style, and Prmi houses in Muli are built partly of stone, as are Nuosu houses in Ganluo near the Dadu River, where stone is abundant. Only in the commercializing areas near the big cities of Panzhihua and Xichang are any village houses built of brick or concrete.

Building materials differ by area, but house plans and styles differ mainly by ethnic group. On the whole, Han live mostly in the lowlands and foothills, though there are some Han families in very remote areas. Similarly, Nuosu are mostly in the mountains, but some live on the plains, including several places on the Anning plain near Xichang. Lipuo in the southern part of the area live in foothills and low mountains. Prmi and Naze are confined to the deep valleys and high plains of the western part of Liangshan and on over into Yunnan, while Lisu and Miao live in scattered enclaves, usually in high and relatively remote places. Most mountain townships in western Liangshan have ethnically mixed populations; some villages within these townships are ethnically pure and others are mixed. In the Anning Valley and some of the surrounding foothills, there are many areas whose population is entirely Han, while the core of eastern Liangshan is almost completely Nuosu. Often in a particular area, ethnic groups are arranged roughly by elevation, giving an interesting tilt to the idea of social stratification in what has been called a vertical society, or *liti shehui*.

The area where I conducted my field research thus contains a large number of different ethnic groups, whether we define these groups in the formal languages of ethnohistory and ethnic identification, or whether we explore them in more detail by examining their interactions through the everyday languages of ethnic identity. This chapter first takes the former, formal route of definition, examining from the standpoint of ethnohistory, and then from the standpoint of ethnic identification, the names, brief histories, and locations of most of the ethnic groups in the area. The following chapters examine in detail the ethnic interactions and ethnic identities of three kinds of people, each of which uses all the available languages in communicating about its ethnic identity, but uses them in very different ways.

AN ETHNOHISTORICAL VIEW

It is not clear who inhabited the Lesser Liangshan area in the pre-Imperial period (before the second century B.C.E.), but in the chapter "Barbarians of Zuodu" (Zuodu yi zhuan) in *The History of the Later Han Dynasty* (Hou Han shu), there is mention of a kingdom of Bailang in this area, whose king sent ambassadors to the Han court in Luoyang and some of whose songs were recorded by the court historians. Ethnolinguistic analysis by Chen Zongxiang (Chen and Deng 1979, 1991: 4) and others has suggested that the language recorded (in Chinese characters, of course) in that account is related to the modern Qiangic languages spoken by the Xifan, or Prmi, people in this area. If so, the Prmi can claim to be, if not the original inhabitants, at least the earliest ones who are still there.

Better established is the fact that the language spoken by today's Prmi people is one of perhaps twelve or so languages belonging to the Qiangic subfamily of Tibeto-Burman (Matisoff 1991) and that the other languages of this small subfamily are distributed along what is probably a historical migration corridor from the Qinghai or northeastern Tibet area south through the series of deep, north-south river valleys that parallel the eastern edge of the Tibetan plateau (see map 2). This seems to indicate that speakers of this group of languages migrated southward along this route, culminating in the Prmi, who are the southernmost Qiangic speakers.

The Naze, who are also early inhabitants of this area, likewise claim a northwestern origin, and may have come along the same route as the Prmi, or may have entered from the Southwest, where the Naze and their close linguistic relatives the Naxi initially established small chiefdoms during the mid-Tang dynasty (618–907), which continued during the period of the hegemony of the Nanzhao and Dali kingdoms, from the ninth to the thirteenth centuries (Shih 2000; Li Shaoming 1986). Naze and Prmi have lived intermingled in this area for hundreds of years and intermarry freely in many areas.

To the east, in the valley of the Anning River, there has long been Han settlement. This river valley and the surrounding foothills furnished the Shu Han general Zhuge Liang with the route of his "southern march" undertaken in the mid-third century C.E. as part of the three-way war between Han (or Shu), Wu, and Wei, immortalized in the great vernacular novel *Romance of the Three Kingdoms* (Sanguo yanyi). It is not clear exactly where he went, but he did establish administrative outposts in the area (Li Fanggui 1987). Nor is it clear when the earliest Han settlers entered Yanyuan and Yanbian, but they have certainly been a presence since the Yuan dynasty, if not before.

The Dali kingdom fell to the invading Mongols in 1253, and Prmi troops were reportedly instrumental in the Mongols' victory in the Lesser Liangshan area (Shih 2000). When the Ming expelled the Mongols from this area in the late fourteenth century, they founded about ten local administrations (*tusi*), essentially establishing local rulers as agents of the Chinese state (Fu 1982: 135–36), whose sway extended throughout Yanbian, Yanyuan, and part of what is now Muli, as well as enfeoffing the Naxi *tusi*, or local ruler, at Lijiang and the Naze ruler at Yongning near Lugu Lake. Han settlement in such towns as Lijiang, Yanyuan, Yanbian, and Mianning and in their surrounding river valleys, also increased during and after the Mongol and Ming conquests.

In the fourteenth through sixteenth centuries, Tibetan Buddhism began to spread into the Lesser Liangshan area. Monasteries of the Red, or Karma-pa sect, were established as early as the late sixteenth century (Rock 1948, 1: 204–10), and the Gelug-pa, or orthodox Yellow sect, which assumed the government of Tibet in 1642 (Goldstein 1989: 1), also began to build monasteries and to convert the population of Prmi and Naze peoples beginning soon afterward (Shih 2000). The monk-ruler of Muli, whose kingdom was established at the beginning of the Gelug-pa ascendancy over Tibet, spread his administration into what is now northern Yanyuan, and most of the Prmi-speaking people under his rule appear to have converted to the Gelug-pa sect during the seventeenth through nineteenth centuries. He was made a local official *tusi* of the Qing dynasty in 1729 (Fu 1983: 138), but it is unlikely that this changed his local political position or the ethnic composition of his domain.

Speakers of Yi languages, which belong to a different branch of Tibeto-Burman (Matisoff 1991), have been established in eastern Liangshan at least since the Tang dynasty (Ma Changshou 1985: 102) and appear to have entered western Liangshan in three waves. The first Ming emperor, Taizu, in order to consolidate his rule over the area after his defeat of the Mongols in the 1370s, also supported the establishment of local rulers near Xichang in the Anning Valley, as well as in Dechang and at Puwei in Miyi. All of them came from northwestern Guizhou or northeastern Yunnan and spoke languages of the Nasu group, a subgroup of the Northern Branch of Yi (Bradley 1990), or the eastern dialect, according to the official classification. Meanwhile, the Nuosu, or Liangshan Yi, maintained a basically tribal existence[1] in Greater Liangshan well into the twentieth century, with Han civilization encroaching only around the

---

1. I am using "tribal" here in the narrow sense suggested by Fried (1967: 170–74)—that is, a secondary, semicentralized polity that arises on the periphery of, and in response to pressure from, a state system. See chapter 2.

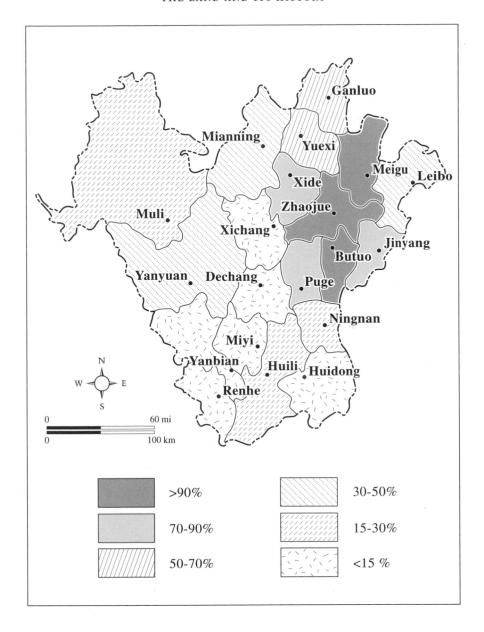

MAP 3. Percentage of Nuosu population by county
(Liangshan Prefecture and Panzhihua City)

frontiers of what came to be known in the West as "Independent Lololand." They continue to be the great majority of the population in the core counties of Greater Liangshan: in Xide County, site of one of the Nuosu villages covered in this study, Nuosu are over 80 percent of the population, and virtually 100 percent outside the river valley that contains the county seat, and they are over 90 percent in Zhaojue, Meigu, and Butuo, and 75 percent in Puge (see map 3).[2] But because of intertribal warfare in eastern Liangshan (Sichuan Sheng Bianji Zu 1987: 87–89; see chap. 6, this volume), perhaps brought on by population pressure, Nuosu began in the mid-Qing to cross the Anning River and settle in western Liangshan as well. This mass population migration continued into the mid-twentieth century, and Nuosu now constitute a majority of the population in Ninglang, over 40 percent in Yanyuan, and substantial minorities in Yanbian, Muli, Mianning, and Miyi. In the process of this migration, Nuosu have displaced Prmi and perhaps Naze people in the peripheral areas of all these counties; it is unclear whether they have also displaced Han populations. Other Yi, related to people in central Yunnan and speaking dialects of the Central Branch of Yi, who call themselves Lipuo, have lived in counties to the southwest, in Yunnan province, at least since the early Ming dynasty (1368–1644); the population of my first-ever fieldsite, Yishala, is 92 percent Lipuo. Today's Lipuo appear to be the descendants of Han troops, who entered the area during the early Ming, and local populations with whom they intermarried. Lipuo people have also come into the southern part of the Lesser Liangshan area in small numbers since the 1950s. In addition, there are pockets of Yi-speakers known as Yala, Shuitian, and Tazhi, whose origins and linguistic affiliations remain to be researched (see chap. 13).

Finally, there are enclaves of Lisu in Dechang, Miyi, Yanbian, and Yanyuan, as well as Miao populations in Yanbian and Muli. Most of them are recent immigrants; some were settled here by the Qing government in the late eighteenth and nineteenth centuries after being involved in disturbances in other parts of the country (Ye and Ma 1984: 111, 129).

The history of the migration of peoples in this area is thus exceedingly complex, and the resulting mix on the ground of local jurisdictions, languages, customs, and marriage alliances is as complicated spatially as it is temporally. Nevertheless, using the language of ethnohistory, it is possible to divide the current inhabitants into five sorts of people.

First, there are the early-resident groups of western Liangshan, who were the basis of the *tusi* political system of the area from the Mongol conquest until

2. Figures were collected from county and prefectural offices.

the twentieth century. A few of these are Yi (such as the Nasu *tusi* at Puwei), but most are either Qiangic- or Naxi/Naze-speakers. By the nineteenth century, many but not all of these people were adherents of one or another sect of Tibetan Buddhism, and many had picked up other Tibetan customs such as drinking yak-butter tea and barley beer. The influence of Tibetan civilization in this area, while rather late historically, is thus nevertheless profound.

Second, there are the Nuosu. They have long resided in eastern Liangshan but are among the latest of arrivals in the western area. Because of the massive numbers of their migrations, however, they now form a demographic plurality in most parts of western Liangshan as well. They have been remarkably resistant to acculturationist and especially to assimilationist pressures from Han or Tibetan civilization.

Third, there are little groups living in isolated enclaves. Three of these—the Miao, Lisu, and Tai—maintain relatively sharp ethnic boundaries, while others, mostly speakers of Yi languages other than Nuosu, are highly acculturated to Han customs and in some cases are becoming assimilated to Han identity.

Fourth are the Han themselves, people living on the most remote fringes of the world's largest civilization. They are a majority in the lowland areas of the Anning Valley and of course in the major cities of Xichang and Panzhihua, and a minority locally in many parts of the region, but everywhere attached by descent and culture to the billion-strong mass of Han Chinese. They include both peasants, who have been migrating here for many centuries, and educators and administrators who have come since the establishment of the People's Republic in 1949.

Finally there are the Hui, or Muslim Chinese (Gladney 1991), who live primarily in the towns and cities and are descendants of a network of traders that has been in Liangshan at least since Sayyid Ajall Shams ad-Dîn, governor of Yunnan from 1275 to 1281, recruited a large number of Muslim laborers to work on road building and irrigation projects (Peng Deyuan et al. 1992: 99). There are also a few rural Hui communities in lowland areas of Xichang and Miyi. In urban communities and concentrated rural settlements, they actively maintain an ethnic identity and their Islamic religious practices; in smaller towns they are rapidly becoming assimilated to the Han population.

TODAY'S *MINZU*

The project of ethnic identification (described in chap. 3) produced a map of the peoples of Lesser Liangshan that is drawn in a different language, based on the results of that particular project rather than on scholarly research in general. Because this map is drawn entirely in the categories of the fifty-six recognized *minzu*, which sometimes do and sometimes do not coincide with ethnohistorical and linguistic divisions, it is somewhat at odds with the map drawn in ethnohistorical terms above, and very much at variance with that described in chapters 5–14 in terms of the practical languages of ethnic identity. In Liangshan today the following *minzu* are recognized: Han, Yi, Zang (Tibetan), Meng (Mongolian), Pumi, Naxi, Hui, Lisu, Miao, Dai, and Bai.

Han

Han are one of the least problematic *minzu* to classify, though there are problems in other parts of the Southwest with people who claim minority status but are officially classified as Han. Basically, Han are those who are left over when all claims of minority status are either recognized or rejected. They are mostly city-dwelling teachers and administrators or valley-dwelling peasants.

Yi

Yi is a very broad, inclusive category. In this area it includes people whose autonyms are Nuosu, Lipuo, Nasu, Shuitian (or Laluo), Tazhi, Yala, and Bai. Nuosu are the least problematical: they are uniform in language, self-identification, membership in one of a series of linked clans, and strict ethnic and caste endogamy. For most Nuosu people, Yi is simply the Chinese word for Nuosu. Lipuo living in Renhe and in areas of Yunnan immediately to the south also accept their identity as Yi, though they recognize cultural and linguistic differences from Nuosu and do not intermarry with them. Nasu, also called Abu in some of the literature, are descendants of the families of the *tusi* of Puwei and the marriage partners of his clan; some of them accept their identity as Yi and some do not. Tazhi, living in Puwei also, appear to have once been linguistically the same as the Nasu but members of lower-ranking clans who did not intermarry with the elite. Yala, also living in parts of Miyi, are of undetermined origin but do not currently accept their identity as Yi. Shuitian or Laluo, living in Renhe district and in parts of Huaping in Yunnan, did not accept their identity as Yi in the late 1980s when I visited them; they were eager to distinguish themselves from the Nuosu, whom they considered barbarians (Harrell 1990). By 1994 they still referred to themselves casually as Shuitian, but did not object to being called Yi. Finally, some people classified as Yi insist that they are Bai, a problem I take up in chapter 13. The lack of identity among these Yi groups can be explained, according to the official categories, by noting that Nuosu prior to 1956 were at the slave stage of society, while other Yi had already entered feudalism, so there were differences within the Yi *minzu* in terms of historical stages, which made closely related societies seem quite different from each other.

Zang (Tibetan)

People who would be thought of as Tibetans by Western scholars (speaking one or another of the languages of the Tibetan branch of Tibeto-Burman, and with cultural affinities to the speakers of one of these languages) do not live in Liangshan, unless one includes the far northwestern corner of Muli, which is really part of another culture area, or a few cadres and teachers. But other people, mostly Qiangic speakers formerly known as Xifan, or "Western Barbarians," are classified as Zang. These include all Prmi speakers in Sichuan, many of whom were under the political jurisdiction of the monk-king of Muli, who was himself both an appointee of the Qing emperor and a vassal of the Dalai Lama in Lhasa. It was the wish of the last king of Muli that his realm be made a Tibetan autonomous region, and so the people living there and in adjacent areas of Sichuan were classified as Zang. Other Xifan groups in the corridor to the north are also classified as Zang.

Meng (Mongolian)

Descendants of the *tusi*—some of which were originally created by Qubilai, and some of which were established later, in areas that are now part of Sichuan—and of the retainers of these rulers, claim that their ancestors were members of Qubilai's Mongol army, which conquered this area, even though most of the earliest records of the recently deposed dynasties reach back only to the Kangxi period (1661–1722) (Fu 1983: 138–46). They thus claimed Mongolian identity in the ethnic identification project, and this was ratified by the authorities in the 1980s (Li Shaoming 1986). In practice, this means that all Naze or Naru speakers in Sichuan are officially classified as Meng.

Pumi

Prmi speakers in Yunnan remained unclassified in the early stages of the ethnic identification project, but in 1959 some leaders of local Prmi communities conferred with authorities in Beijing and confirmed that they did not want to be classified as Zang, because they thought they, as Xifan, were different from

Tibetans. They were thus made into a separate *minzu* called Pumi instead of the possibly insulting Xifan.

Naxi

In the 1950s Naze, or Naru-speaking, people in Yunnan, mostly around the Lugu Lake-Yongning region, were classified according to Stalin's criteria as Naxi because of similarities in language and origin stories with the larger Naxi group centered around Lijiang (McKhann 1995). To this day most of the Naze-speakers in Yunnan wish to be known in Chinese not as Naxi but as Mosuo, because of their divergent political organization and marriage customs. So far, they have failed in their attempt to be known as Mosuozu, but they have extracted the concession that they can call themselves Mosuo *ren*, or Mosuo people (He 1991), while remaining part of the Nazizu. There are also a number of unproblematical Naxi scattered in small pockets in Ninglang, Yanyuan, and southwestern Muli.

Hui

There are several Hui villages in the Anning Valley—I have visited settlements in Xichang and Miyi—and there are small Hui communities in the county towns of Yanyuan, Ninglang, and Miyi. These people tend to practice at least some Islamic customs, and there are rather ornate mosques at Guabang in Miyi and at Yangjiaoba in Xichang, recently restored with state aid. In smaller townships, people of Hui ancestry tend to lose both their religion and their endogamy, and to become assimilated to Han identity; I do not know if these people actually change their *minzu* identification when this happens.

Lisu

No problem here. There are Lisu townships in very remote mountain areas in Yanbian, Miyi, and Dechang, and they remain separate and isolated from their Han and Yi neighbors.

Miao

There is a compact Miao township in Yanbian (Li Haiying et al. 1983), separated by altitude from its Han and Yi neighbors. There are also about five thousand Miao in Muli, many of them living interspersed and intermarrying with

Han but not with Yi or Zang. These Miao belong to the southwestern branch of that ethnic category, call themselves Hmong in their own language, and are closely related to the Hmong who have migrated to America and Europe as refugees in the last twenty years.

Dai

Dai in this area are called Tai both in their own languages and in local Han dialects. They are descendants of detachments from Jingdong in Yunnan, sent by the first Ming emperor to help quell rebellions in the late fourteenth century (Sichuan Sheng Minzu Yanjiu Suo 1982: 94). They live in Renhe and Yanbian, commonly intermarry with neighboring groups, and are no longer Theravada Buddhists, if their ancestors ever were. Most of them still use Tai language at home.

Bai

Some people who are probably of Lipuo, Nasu, or other Yi ancestry have successfully, and some unsuccessfully, claimed identity as Bai. I discuss this further in chapter 13. There are also a few immigrants from the Dali region who are unambiguously Bai.

As can be seen already from these brief sketches, the *minzu* produced by the ethnic identification process are not the same as the ethnic groups defined in the practical languages of ethnic identity. These *minzu* categories, however, are far from irrelevant to people's daily lives. Censuses and social surveys, for example, often include data classified by *minzu* affiliation. More important, being classified as a minority of any sort, as opposed to a Han, brings with it certain affirmative action benefits. In Liangshan Yi Autonomous Prefecture, rural minority couples are uniformly allowed three children, whereas rural Han can have only two. In Panzhihua Municipality, quotas vary from township to township, but townships with heavy minority representation tend to have higher birth-quotas. There are special schools and classes for minorities throughout the area, and members of minority groups usually receive preference when applying for admission to regular schools.

Membership in particular *minzu* is also important. In the areas designated autonomous prefectures or autonomous counties, or in the smaller *minzu* townships, members of the locally predominant minority *minzu* tend to be appointed to positions of political power and authority in the four wings of the state bureaucracy: the Party, the government, the legislature, and the People's Consultative Conference. In addition, where there are programs of bilingual education, members of particular *minzu* are often offered the chance to become literate in their *minzu* language as well as in the national language, standard Chinese. For example, Prmi speakers in Muli, who are classified as Tibetans in a Tibetan autonomous county, learn standard written Tibetan starting in the third grade, using textbooks composed and printed in Lhasa. Prmi in Yunnan, classified as Pumi, are educated in Chinese only, since currently there is no written form of the Pumi language.

The Communist civilizing project has thus created a map of China, including the Liangshan area, that uses the metalanguage of ethnic identification and that channels administrative, educational, and developmental resources according to this map. In this sense, then, the map represents an important reality. It is not, however, quite the same as the reality of ethnic identity in the same region, which is the topic of the bulk of this book in chapters 5–14.

CONTEXTS OF INTERACTION BETWEEN DISCOURSES

These different languages of classification and representation are all relevant, in various ways and in various contexts, to the everyday lives of almost every person in Liangshan. For some, ethnicity is a fact of daily life, confronting them as soon as they step out the doorway in the morning, or maybe even before. People in places such as Baiwu Town or Shanhe Village in Gaizu live cheek-by-jowl with others who speak different languages, wear conspicuously different clothes, and occupy a different position in the local and regional political-ethnic order. For others, ethnicity is more remote but still relevant. Villagers in the mountains of Mishi see a non-Nuosu only when their child's teacher visits their home, if she does, or perhaps when they travel, once or twice a year, to distant markets at Lianghekou or Xide City. Similarly, for Han workers or bureaucrats on the streets of Panzhihua or Xichang, minorities are nothing but folks in colorful costumes whom they see but do not talk to. Even for these people, however, their ethnicity is important: Han urbanites know that Liangshan is a Yi autonomous prefecture and that Nuosu thus have certain affirmative-action advantages, such as schooling at the *minzu* middle school and less restrictive birth quotas. Mishi villagers may not see Han people very often, but their conversation seems obsessed with what they see as the Han state's encroachment in not completely comprehensible ways upon their land and lifestyle. Ethnicity thus flavors the life of everyone in Liangshan in a way that is simply not relevant for most people in China proper, where I have been told by several friends that they did not even know their own *minzu* (Han of course) until they were teenagers or young adults.

Ethnic difference and ethnic interaction are important for the people of Liangshan because they affect, and are expressed in, many concrete areas of people's lives. These include language, culture and lifestyle, marriage and kinship organization, education, and local and regional politics.

Language

Probably a majority of the population of the core counties of Greater Liangshan is monolingual in Nuosu, with only a rudimentary knowledge, if any, of the Liangshan dialect of Southwestern Mandarin. There is very little occasion for anyone to use any language other than Nuosu, especially with the increasing availability of books, newspapers, and government notices written in that language. Most Han in the Anning Valley and in other areas of concentrated Han settlement are also strictly monolingual: I once astonished an old Han lady, a lifelong resident of Yanyuan, when she overheard me speaking Nuosu on the street, since she did not understand a word and considered the Nuosu language to be impossibly difficult, even though it was all around her. For most members of minority groups in the Lesser Liangshan area, however, bilingualism is a fact of life. One has to know Chinese to deal in the market, to get an education, even to talk to some of one's neighbors. Of all the minority languages in the area, only Nuosu is readily available in written form (I have seen a few Lisu books, but never anything in Prmi or Naze, let alone any of the smaller Yi languages) or used formally in schools or for official documents, so literacy for many people means literacy in Chinese. At the same time, the daily environment for many people includes two or three vernaculars, so it is not uncommon to find people who speak three languages, especially if they are members of smaller groups who also have to deal with Nuosu as well as with Han or with the Hanophone state.

Small enclaves of speakers of languages other than Han or Nuosu have tended in recent years to lose fluency in their home languages. This gives rise to certain sad situations, such as visiting ethnologists yelling in the ears of poor deaf old ladies to elicit kinship terms or other ethnological gems, but most younger people I have talked to show little regret for the passing of their mother tongues. In some places, members of minority groups who do not speak each other's language converse in Han, or occasionally even Nuosu. I rode in a jeep with a Prmi and a Naze woman from Gaizu to Zuosuo: they were dressed identically and lived in identical houses, different from those of local Han or Nuosu, but they spoke Chinese to each other, since they had no knowledge of each other's language. Nuosu, by contrast, thrives even in small enclaves in the Anning Valley such as Manshuiwan (see chap. 8) and Yuehua.

In large cities, especially Xichang, by the second generation of residence most people of whatever ethnicity lose any language but Chinese.

Culture and Lifestyle

Certainly ethnic culture derives both from habit and from calculation: people retain the customs and costumes of their elders out of a feeling of comfort as well as out of a desire to communicate or display their identity in public contexts. There is no one-to-one correlation between customs and ethnic identity, especially over the broad geographic range of Liangshan. But in any particular local context, certain customs are singled out as markers differentiating between one ethnic group and another. In Liangshan, the most prominent cultural features used as ethnic markers are dress, food, housing, and ritual.

Ethnic dress is the most obvious indicator of group membership to an outside observer in Liangshan, and the most obvious item of ethnic dress is the skirt: all minority women have some sort of full skirt as part of their ethnic dress, while the only skirts worn by Han women are the straight, modern ones of younger women. Nuosu women in many areas, particularly in ethnically mixed areas of western Liangshan, wear the Nuosu skirt, blouse, and headdress all the time. In other areas, they may wear just the headdress, but there is no mistaking the ethnic statement made by full or partial wearing of ethnic dress. Members of other minority groups wear ethnic clothing more selectively; at present old women are more likely to wear skirts than are their daughters, but everyone wears them for special occasions. Nuosu men and women also wear the ethnically distinguishing *jieshy vala*, or felt cape and fringed cape, in cold weather.

Food and housing also bear ethnic messages. At least on feast occasions, Nuosu chunks of meat, along with Prmi and Naze fat pigback, attest to the ethnicity of the hosts, even in urban contexts. Houses tend to be built of materials that differ regionally, but the plans and furnishings are peculiar, in any one area, to a certain ethnic category.

Finally, religion and ritual are also salient ethnic markers. Members of all ethnic groups have some kind of ancestral altar in the main room of their houses, but it is in the corner for Nuosu, at the rear for Han, and in a variety of arrangements that differ regionally for Prmi and Naze. The nature of ancestral and spirit worship also differs, of course, from one group to another, as do wedding and funeral customs: Han bury their dead; Prmi cremate and leave prayer flags to mark the site of the ashes; Nuosu cremate and scatter the ashes on a mountain; eastern Naze cremate but hide the ashes in a mountain cache whose location is not revealed to any but their own clan. And there are minute differences even among the ways members of different ethnic groups celebrate the same holidays. Finally, some groups espouse Tibetan Buddhism, while others do not. All of these differences can be emphasized as aspects of ethnic interaction.

Marriage and Kinship Organization

In an area where members of diverse ethnic groups come into daily contact with each other, such as Liangshan, questions of ethnic endogamy and exogamy are bound to arise. Interviews in most villages elicit the idea that intermarriage is a modern thing, a consequence of social change and the Revolution. In some areas, this is no doubt true, but as with other aspects of ethnic interaction, each area displays its own particular pattern.

In general, Nuosu do not marry with other groups (even other groups classified as part of the Yi *minzu*) in the village context; they do not even intermarry among different castes of Nuosu. All other groups intermarry to a certain extent: Han will intermarry with anyone, anywhere, while other groups tend to be selective. In the cities and among educated people, all kinds of intermarriage are possible and frequent, with the possible exception of intercaste marriage among Nuosu. Any kind of intermarriage, of course, produces the problem of the *minzu* affiliation (and sometimes also the ethnic identity) of the offspring. In general, offspring of mixed marriages are classified as belonging to the non-Han *minzu*, because of the affirmative action benefits available. They may, however, acculturate to Han ways while retaining a minority identity; in chapter 13 I examine this situation in regard to the Lipuo case.

Marriage, however, is not simply a way of creating ties between groups; it is also used as a kind of ethnic marker to distinguish groups. For example, the ideal Nuosu marriage, reflected in the kinship terminology system (Harrell 1989, Lin 1961), is bilateral cross-cousin marriage, while other Yi-speaking groups such as Tazhi, along with Naxi (McKhann 1989) and patrilineal Naze, favor patrilateral cross-cousin marriage. This difference in systems not only serves as a marker, like any other custom, but renders marrying across the systems structurally problematical.

In addition to marriage, kinship organization also marks off one ethnic group from another in the local context. Naze and some Prmi in the Lugu Lake area are matrilineal and eschew marriage in favor of matrisegment households with visiting sexual partnerships. Han and Nuosu simply cannot participate in this kind of system; Naze who take up with Han marry them and live in patrilocal or neolocal families. It should be emphasized, however, that Naze in Guabie are patrilineal; since Guabie and Lugu Lake are several days' walk away from each other, difference in kin systems does not preclude identification in some contexts as members of the same ethnic group (see chap. 11).

Education

Schools in China, as in any multiethnic polity, attempt to teach not only literacy and other important skills but also to inculcate patriotic sentiment, at least in their overt lessons and curricular materials (Keyes 1991, Harrell and Bamo 1998, Hansen 1999, Upton 1999). The ways in which they have approached this task have varied, however, with the general variance in ethnic policy, and in the Reform Era since 1979 the strategy has been to use ethnic particulars to inculcate national sentiments. Nuosu language texts, for example, show little girls in skirts and headdresses (never mind that little girls rarely wear them), and little boys in turbans with horns on the front (something I have never seen on little boys) studying lessons that include Chairman Mao, Tiananmen Square, and the brave soldiers of the People's Liberation Army (PLA).

Beyond the politics of using the particular to inculcate the general, however, there are a number of other ethnic aspects to education in Liangshan. Which language to use, and in what proportion, is a continual subject of controversy, not only in mixed areas (Should Prmi and Han students be forced to learn to read Nuosu?) but also in the ethnically homogeneous Nuosu regions of eastern Liangshan (Which language should be taught first, and which should be used to teach subjects such as history and mathematics?). Should there be classes in such languages as Prmi or Naze, which do not have widely used written forms? Is teaching Prmi students in Muli to read and write Tibetan, because they are Zang, a worthwhile investment of resources? Whom does it benefit?

Special schools and affirmative action are also a feature of ethnic education policy. Most counties in Liangshan, as well as Yanbian in Panzhihua, have specific ethnic middle schools, or *minzu zhongxue*, which are usually the second-ranked middle-schools in their counties, below the central county school but above the local schools in the larger townships. (The smaller townships have only elementary schools.) Within regular schools, there are often special classes composed only of minority students (*minzu ban*) or classes taught primarily in the Nuosu language (*Yiwen ban*). Minority students are given bonus points in entrance examinations for upper-middle and normal schools, and sometimes for technical colleges and universities, and they also have available an alternative track of higher education in the Southwest Nationalities Institute (Xinan Minzu Xueyuan) in Chengdu, or, for the best of them, the Central Nationalities University (Zhongyang Minzu Daxue) in Beijing.

Local and Regional Politics

As Thomas Heberer points out (2001), the term "autonomous" (*zizhi*) in the titles of such administrative units as Liangshan Yi Nationality Autonomous Prefecture does not really denote any kind of federal system where local areas have much fiscal or policy-making autonomy that is guaranteed as a constitutional right. The granting or rescinding of autonomous decision-making powers (and, for that matter, the granting or rescinding of constitutional rights, which has happened several times in the history of the PRC) is in the hands of the Party. In addition, many of the natural resources—particularly timber and minerals—found in the prefecture are under the control of units belonging to either the central or the provincial government. And there is no local control over population movement into or out of the prefecture, meaning that national- and provincial-level units have been able to bring in large numbers of primarily Han people in the last forty years, significantly altering the population until Liangshan Prefecture is now only 40 percent Nuosu and 57 percent Han (Liangshan 1985: 2).

At the same time, the term "autonomous" is not totally empty of meaning, either. Autonomous prefectures (such as Liangshan) and counties (such as Ninglang, immediately across the border) are able to retain more of their tax revenues (Guo 1996: 56–86) and can apply for subsidies for construction projects from the Nationalities Commission bureaucracies as well as the ordinary ministerial bureaucracies. They are thus currently more autonomous in fiscal affairs than are ordinary prefectures (*diqu*) and counties.

Another aspect of the "ethnic" character of these units is the preferential appointment of minority cadres to positions of power and responsibility. This policy, of course, was widely followed in the early 1950s, but in the radical Maoist times, especially with the formation of the revolutionary committees in the Cultural Revolution to replace Party and government leadership organs, Han officials were in control. Since the Revised National Autonomy Law of 1982, however, minority officials have again had preference in these positions (see chap. 3, n. 11).

Along with the appointment of minority cadres to high positions (and the incumbent patronage networks that tend, of course, to have an ethnic flavor) comes a great elaboration of the ethnic flavor of political events. At official banquets in Liangshan, young women (in fashionized versions of traditional Nuosu clothing) and young men (in entirely fantasized versions) sing, play the pan-pipes, and offer liquor to guests of whatever nationality, who are eating (even at a round table with chopsticks) at least one plate of pork or mutton chunks and one of buckwheat cakes or potatoes, along with their stir-fried dishes and white rice. Government offices, celebratory banners, and even the doors of government logging trucks sport Nuosu writing alongside Chinese (or, in the case of Muli, a Zang autonomous county, Tibetan alongside Chinese, even though about one quarter of the population of the county is Nuosu [Muli 1985: 2]).

The implementation of ethnic preference policies also varies greatly with the jurisdiction. In the upland areas of Yanbian and Miyi, both of which are counties within Panzhihua City that have no ethnic autonomous designation, the population is nevertheless almost entirely Nuosu, and this is reflected in the designation of most of the high-mountain areas as Yi townships (*Yizu xiang*). But Nuosu writing is nowhere in evidence except on a couple of government signs—all documents are entirely in the Han language, as is all schooling. Those who can write Nuosu (and there are not many) have learned on their own. Similarly, Nuosu are not prominent in the county-level administration of these counties, except on the Nationalities Commission. There is, however, an ethnic middle school in Yanbian, as well as a highly regarded minority class in the No. 9 Middle School of Panzhihua City, showing that ethnic preference policies are only weaker, not absent, in those areas that do not have the "autonomous" administrative designation.

This chapter has summarized generally how ethnic identity (as experienced in the everyday life of local communities) and official *minzu* designations (which govern much policy implementation in government, language, and education) interact to affect the consciousness, political strategy, and opportunities of individual members of those groups. In a short summary such as this, however, the different textures of ethnic group solidarity and difference, and cooperation and conflict are not really palpable. The ethnic solidarity and ethnic relations of different groups are informed and upheld by different notions of ethnic identity. The following chapters explore these different modes of being ethnic for a series of different groups in Liangshan today. Within each group we explore a number of different local contexts to demonstrate more realistically the ways in which ethnic identity and nationalities policy intertwine in the lives of Liangshan's people.

PART 2

PRIMORDIAL ETHNICITY: THE NUOSU

5 / Nuosu History and Culture

N
uosu are the largest, most culturally distinct, and most ethnically separate ethnic group in Liangshan, and their ethnic identity is thus the
simplest to describe of all ethnic groups in the area. Nuosu are concentrated in most areas, scattered in a few; they speak four dialects that are fairly
mutually intelligible, and their customs and costumes vary slightly. But all
Nuosu are classified as Yi, and when they speak the Han language (as perhaps
half of them can do), they identify themselves as Yi. Nuosu life is influenced
by Han society and culture to varying degrees, to the point where members of
some communities in what Chinese ethnologists call the "nuclear area" (*fuxin
diqu*) rarely come into contact with Han people or culture, and then only in
official governmental or educational contexts, while Nuosu people in parts of
the Anning Valley retain only language and a few religious customs, along with
a sometimes-violated rule of endogamy, to distinguish themselves from the
surrounding, and numerically overwhelming, Han. But there are no communities where Nuosu cultural markers have disappeared altogether, and in fact
no communities where the language has disappeared, either. Acculturation,
that is, has never been anywhere near complete in Nuosu rural communities.
Even in the cities, ethnic identity is strong, and many educated Nuosu make
strong efforts to retain at least those elements of culture that will reinforce their
identity. In other words, no matter what degree of *acculturation* to Han ways,
there has been little or no *assimilation* to Han identity. For Nuosu, ethnicity
is a primordial thing, in the sense that they are all related, not only by descent
but also by marriage, and that non-Nuosu are not only descended from
different ancestors but also are not related by marriage.[1] For most Nuosu, ethnicity is also a cultural thing, but even where culture has been thinned by par-

---

1. In fact, the sense of kinship relations determining ethnic status is so strong that it was the
justification for the former practice of slavery and even for the caste system itself. Those of lower
status, while still related to their social superiors, are less pure in their ancestry (many of them
being descendants of captives from other ethnic groups). See Schoenhals 2001.

ticipation in Chinese urban society, the primordial, kin-based identity is never called into question. The case of the Nuosu is thus one in which all the languages of ethnohistory, ethnic group identification, and ethnic identity agree: they speak in different terms, but they come to the same conclusion: Nuosu are a primordially separate group.

In this and the following chapters, I first give overviews of Nuosu history and culture, and then provide a detailed account of Nuosu kin-based identity in a variety of contexts, from the most cultural (that is, the areas where the differences between Nuosu and Hxiemga [Han] culture are the least blurred and taken the most for granted) to the least cultural (where even language starts to fade, exogamy is possible, and only genealogy and consciously maintained cultural traits preserve the sense of identity). I do this by means of detailed accounts of four contexts (three local and one diffuse) where I have lived and worked, along with evidence from similar communities elsewhere in Liangshan (see map 4).

In this analysis, Mishi represents the cultural pole of Nuosu primordial identity. In fact, one could probably come up with a more ideal community, somewhere in Meigu or the outer reaches of Zhaojue or Butuo, but the overwhelmingly Nuosu population, the dominance of the language, and the absence of Han influence except in government and schools mean that in Mishi life is Nuosu; only the outside, the threatening, the somewhat incomprehensible other, is Han.

Baiwu is culturally less pure. The population of the areas around the town is only around 80 percent Nuosu, with significant minorities of Prmi and Han. Almost everyone except a few older women speaks Han in addition to Nuosu; in the villages closer to town, and in the town market, Han people and culture are a fact of everyday life. But the language, customs, religion, and ritual of Nuosu in this area are little influenced by Han culture; if anything, the effect of the Han presence in this area is to sharpen the sense of identity and ethnic boundaries, while blurring the cultural differences between Nuosu and others only a little.

In the lowland village of Manshuiwan, Nuosu culture is superficially unrecognizable. Houses look like Han houses, and there are graves in the hills where ancestors have been buried. Many people are highly educated, having attended schools teaching only the Han language, and not everyone even has a Nuosu name; some people use their Han names even when speaking the Nuosu language. Remarkably, however, *Nuosu ddoma* endures as the preferred medium of everyday speech, and the ideal of endogamy is still articulated (though some-

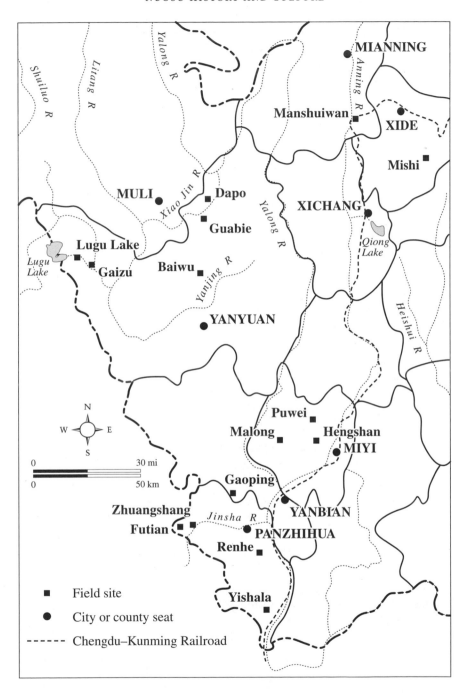

MAP 4. Field sites

times violated in practice). Here, where culture really is diluted and compromised, ethnic identity still seems a matter of course.

Finally, among educated officials, teachers, and scholars, in Xichang, Panzhihua, and distant cities such as Chengdu and Beijing, even the language is unevenly distributed, and marriage with other *minzu* is quite common. But in these cities, where cultural difference is no longer an unexamined aspect of ethnic relations, identity with and dedication to the cause of ethnic solidarity remains strong, and many people consciously preserve cultural elements in the service of preserving ethnic identity and pride. Whereas in a place like Mishi identity follows culture in an unself-conscious way, in Xichang culture is self-consciously mobilized in the service of identity.

NUOSU HISTORY

Both Nuosu genealogical and ritual texts and Han-language historical documents trace the origins of the Ni (Yi) peoples to northeastern Yunnan around the time of the Han dynasty. Where they came from before that is in dispute, though a lot of people think they were either in the area for a very long time or came in the first millennium B.C.E. from somewhere in the Northwest, perhaps Qinghai, along with the other Tibeto-Burman peoples (Ma Changshou 1987, Chen Tianjun 1987). The Wuman (Black Barbarians) and Baiman (White Barbarians) mentioned in the histories of the Period of Division (311–589), as well as the Cuan kingdoms of the Sui-Tang period (581–907), are thought to have been ruled by the ancestors of today's Yi, and at least one faction in an ongoing debate considers the Nanzhao kingdom, which ruled Yunnan and surrounding areas after 740, to have been a Yi-dominated polity (Qi Qingfu 1987). The descendants of the rulers and subjects of these and other kingdoms are said to constitute today's Yi peoples, who numbered 6.6 million in the 1990 census, with about 4.1 million of those in Yunnan, 700,000 in Guizhou, and about 1.8 million in Sichuan (Zimei 1992: 1).[2]

Those Yi living in Sichuan belong to the cultural and dialect group that calls itself Nuosu, and almost all of them live in Liangshan Prefecture or a few surrounding counties; in addition, a hundred thousand or more Nuosu live in Ninglang and other counties in the part of western Liangshan that is in Yunnan. How and when the Ni peoples came into Liangshan is a matter of

---

2. There are also about ten thousand Yi in Guangxi Zhuang Autonomous Region.

dispute; archaeological remains from the Han period in southern Liangshan seem to belong to some other ethnic group (Yi Mouyuan 1987: 303). Emperor Xuanzong (r. 713–56) of the Tang granted fiefs in the Anning Valley and at Yuexi to local lords who fought with the Tang against the Tufan, or proto-Tibetans, and later against the Nanzhao kingdom; these may have been ancestral to the Nuosu (Ma Changshou 1987: 101).

There is no doubt that by the Song dynasty (960–1279) Nuosu were firmly ensconced in the nuclear area of Liangshan, where they remain the overwhelming majority to this day. Their history since then has been one of keeping both the manifestations of Chinese power and the cultural influence of the Han at bay, while never forming an independent polity or even a society and culture completely free of Han influence. Nuosu people, while consciously preserving the distinct character of their culture and society, have always done so in a context that we can legitimately call ethnic; to be Nuosu is to be enmeshed in the outer webs of Chinese civilization, never truly independent but at the same time never succumbing, except selectively, to either the coercion or the blandishments of Chinese wealth and power, or of sinocentric cultural imperialism.

After the Mongols united China in the thirteenth century, including their conquest of Nanzhao in 1253, they established the *tusi* system of local rule that was to serve them and their successor dynasties and even the Republican government up to the Communist takeover of the area in the early 1950s. All over the Southwest, they enfeoffed local leaders as officers of the empire, giving them imperial seals and rights of local rule in return for the promise to be loyal and sometimes render various kinds of tribute. Liangshan was no exception to this policy. Members of the highest caste or stratum of Nuosu society, the *nzymo* (Wu Jingzhong 2001) were given various titles of *tusi* or the slightly lower offices of *tumu*, *tuqianhu*, and *tubaihu*. The most famous of these, enfeoffed during the early Ming dynasty, was the ruler known in Nuosu as the Lili Nzymo or, formally in Chinese, as Luoluosi Xuanweisi, or informally as the Lili Tusi. His headquarters were in what is now Meigu County, the heart of the nuclear area, and his nominal territory extended to the Dadu River on the west, the Jinsha River on the south, and into what is now Puge County on the southeast (Ma Changshou 1987: 106–7; Sichuan Sheng Bianji Zu 1987: 66–67). Other Nuosu *tusi* ruled in the more easterly and southerly parts of Liangshan.

According to tradition, sometime around the end of the Ming, the Lili Tusi's power was overthrown by the Hma and Alur clans of the *nuoho* or aristocratic caste because his exactions upon them were too severe. He moved to Xihewan in Zhaojue, but his family was again forced out of the area by a *nuoho* alliance, and he fled all the way to the outskirts of Xichang sometime in the early Qing dynasty (Ma Changshou 1987: 109). Similarly, other Tusi were forced out of the nuclear area at various times during the Qing by the increasing power of the *nuoho* clans; the most powerful remaining *tusi*, the Shama Tusi of Zhaojue, was gradually forced to Leibo by 1890, and Hedong Changguansi of the Leng family was forced from Yuexi to Tianba in Ganluo, where the early twentieth-century scion of that house, Leng Guangdian, became famous as a promoter of modern education and economic development during the 1930s and 1940s.

At one level, this ongoing struggle between the *nzymo* and *nuoho*, the two highest castes of Nuosu society, was fought over rights to land, retainers, and slaves as well as over the disputed rights of rule that the *nzymo* had over the *nuoho*. But at another level, one can see a larger struggle being played out, with the *nzymo*, ever drawn by official seals, offices, and power into the orbit of the surrounding Han civilization and culture, playing the cosmopolitan role that tied Nuosu society to China, and the *nuoho* playing the conservative, xenophobic role and becoming impatient with the *nzymo*, who began to look like agents of the Chinese.

The *tusi* system endured in the Southwest throughout most of the Ming and early Qing, with new *tusi* families being enfeoffed in the Kangxi period in many areas, including the Naze families described in chapter 11. But there was a countermovement toward absorbing formerly semiautonomous fiefdoms into the regular bureaucratic structure of the ruling dynasties. This movement, called *gaitu guiliu*, or "replacing the local and restoring the posted [officials]," began in the late Ming in some areas, but in Liangshan and adjacent parts of Yunnan did not really get going until the Yongzheng period (1722–36), when the emperor originally resolved to get rid of all *tusi* and replace them with regular bureaucrats appointed from the center. He tried this in Liangshan, where several county yamen were built, and those at Jianchang (modern Xichang), Yuexi, Yanjing (modern Yanyuan), Mianning, and Huili all gradually evolved into counties that remain to the present day. Attempts in the nuclear area, however, were unsuccessful, provoking revolts by local Nuosu, and in 1776 the Qianlong emperor (r. 1736–96), son of Yongzheng, gave up and created four new *tusi* who governed parts of the nuclear area, though some of them also lost out in battles with local *nuoho* clans (Yi Mouyuan 1987: 306; Sichuan Sheng Bianji Zu 1987: 1–3).

During the Qing period, however, *nuoho* clans did not fight only against local *nzymo*; they also fought each other for land, retainers, slaves, and honor. The battles were particularly noteworthy in Zhaojue and Puxiong, with the result that clans or clan branches defeated in these fights migrated first into Xide and Yuexi, where some remained while others continued across the Anning Valley into Mianning and the western parts of Xichang, and from there into Yanyuan, northern Yanbian, Ninglang, and Muli. They took with them many of their *quho* (commoner) retainers, with the result that the population of the latter areas is now 40–70 percent Nuosu, including a small number of *nuoho* and a much larger number of *quho* (Sichuan Sheng Bianji Zu 1987: 87–89).

At the end of the Qing and into the Republican period, then, most of the nuclear area was populated exclusively by Nuosu, and except for a few areas still under the control of *tusi*, there were no formal political organizations, only the informal leadership and customary law of the *nuoho*-dominated order. This order is reflected in a series of ethnographic reports compiled by Han scholars in the 1930s and 1940s, the best known of which, by Lin Yaohua, was translated by the Human Relations Area Files and published in English in 1962 as *Lolo of Liangshan*, despite the fact that Lin never used the demeaning term Lolo (Lin Yaohua 1961; see also Zeng Chaolun 1945 and Jiang Yingliang 1948). With increasing Han population pressure on the edges of the nuclear area, the nucleus itself became increasingly impenetrable by outsiders not under protection of local leaders, and large numbers of Han settlers, as well as a few Western missionaries and adventurers, were killed or captured into slavery during this era. At the same time, the peripheral areas were once again experiencing partial incorporation into the wider Chinese civilization, and such prominent figures as Yunnan governor Long Yun and educational reformer Leng Guangdian were among the Nuosu who participated actively in the politics of the early twentieth century.

The first meaningful contact with the Chinese Communists came when the Long March passed through Liangshan in April 1935, traveling from Huili to Dechang, Xichang, Mianning, Yuexi, and Ganluo, where the marchers made the famous crossing of the Dadu River described by Edgar Snow. Snow's picture of Nuosu people was on the romantic side:

> Moving rapidly northward from the Gold Sand River . . . into Sichuan, [the Red Army] soon entered the tribal country of warlike aborigines, the "White" and "Black" Lolos of Independent Lololand. Never conquered, never absorbed by the Chinese who dwelt all around them, the turbulent Lolos had for centuries occupied that densely forested and mountainous [land]. . . . The Lolos wanted to preserve their independence; Red policies favored autonomy for all the national minorities of China. The Lolos hated the Chinese because they had been oppressed by them; but there were "White" Chinese and "Red" Chinese, just as

there were "White" Lolos and "Black" Lolos, and it was the White Chinese who had always slain and oppressed the Lolos. (Snow 1938: 195–95)

The parts of Liangshan through which the Red Army passed were of course not the nuclear area, and by the 1930s leaders of local Nuosu clans were well aware of the ins and outs of Chinese politics. But there was very little "underground Party" activity after the Red Army left again, until they came back as national rulers in 1950 and 1951.

Liangshan was made a Yi autonomous prefecture; originally it had Zhaojue as its capital and included only the nuclear area and surrounding counties east and north of the Anning Valley; the remainder of the current prefecture was part of Xichang Prefecture. In 1978 Xichang Prefecture was abolished and the capital of the new Liangshan Yi Autonomous Prefecture, which included all of its present counties, was moved to the more accessible Xichang. Whether this change was made in order to dilute Nuosu demographic dominance can probably never be known conclusively, but it did mean the incorporation of many more Han, Zang, and other *minzu* into the prefectural population. Panzhihua City was founded in 1965 as part of the Third Front internal industrialization program (Naughton 1988); in 1978 Miyi and Yanbian Counties were brought under Panzhihua's administration (Dangdai Liangshan 1992: 10).

Specific policies of the Communists in the early period varied according to local conditions. In the Anning Valley and most other areas where Han settlement predominated, as well as in the Lipuo areas of Panzhihua and a few other areas where minority inhabitants were judged to have entered the historical stage of the landlord economy, or late feudalism, land reform was carried out in 1952–53, as it was in many Lipuo areas in Chuxiong (Diamant 1999). In the nuclear area and in high-mountain regions in Lesser Liangshan, the familiar pattern of putting cooperative traditional leaders into vice-posts was followed, and not until 1956 was there an attempt to transform the means of production. This went smoothly at first, as mentioned above, but after a radical turn of policy in 1957–58, many local leaders, some of them formerly officials in the Communist-led governments, organized a rebellion against the radical reforms that had deprived them not only of their wealth and power but, more important according to many Nuosu people, of their honor. As early as Leng Guangdian in the 1930s, they argue, Nuosu leaders knew the slavery system was doomed, but they refused to be treated with contempt, as in the struggle sessions so common to Chinese Communist political movements everywhere.

The rebels probably never posed a serious threat to centers of Communist rule or to the People's Liberation Army, but they did control many villages during the two big outbreaks in 1957 and again in 1959. More rebels probably died of sickness and starvation than from PLA bullets, and many more were captured and executed or imprisoned and died of disease in prison. But the latest holdouts surrendered by the early 1960s, and there has been no significant rebellious activity since then, though there was a brief "caste war" between *nuoho* and *quho* during the Cultural Revolution in the nuclear area.[3]

During the 1950s considerable attention was paid to development in Liangshan. Roads, clinics, and schools were all built, and local people participated in the initiatives and unintended disasters of the Great Leap Forward; even remote villages in Mishi had collective mess halls. The ensuing famine was not as serious there as in some other places, though locally many people did die of hunger, as they did in another local famine in 1974. Also in the 1950s and 1960s, there was a movement for script reform, replacing the old syllabary with New Yi Writing, a phonemic script using the Roman alphabet. By all reports, it was a total failure.[4]

The Cultural Revolution everywhere saw an attempt to eliminate many aspects of ethnic minority culture, and Liangshan was no exception. All education was in the Han language, and religious activities were banned, though they of course continued in secret in many places. Everyone tells me, however, that Nuosu women continued to wear Nuosu clothing during this time; that was something that "could not be controlled."

Since the end of the Cultural Revolution, and especially since the passage of the Autonomy Law of 1982, the emphasis has come back to the promotion of those aspects of Nuosu culture that are deemed harmless according to a now more liberally interpreted Communist morality. This has meant the replacement of Han officials in most administrations with minorities, primarily Nuosu; the official promotion of ethnic "culture" in the form of arts and crafts,

---

3. As far as I know, there are no published or publicly distributed sources that discuss this caste fight; I have heard of it from several Nuosu scholars. Apparently some young *quho*, imbued with the Red Guard spirit, attacked local *nuoho*, whom they considered unreformed backward elements, and *nuoho* fought back with militia of their own, after which the PLA intervened on the side of the *quho*, but quickly quelled the violence on both sides. My impression is that mortality was much lower than in the late-1950s rebellion.

4. This New Yi Writing, however, is the basis for the standard romanization system used in elementary school textbooks, and also to transcribe Nuosu words in this study. The Nuosu language has no syllable-final consonants, so the *t, x,* and *p* written at the end of syllables are used to indicate high, medium-high rising, and low falling tones respectively; syllables with no tone marker are in the mid-level tone. For ease of pronunciation for the average reader, we have eliminated the tone markers in this book.

song and dance, and often lavish, officially sponsored holiday celebrations; and the return of Nuosu language to education, this time in the form of a "regularized Yi writing" (*guifan Yiwen*), which is the old script used by religious practitioners, rationalized and cleaned of phonetic redundancy. Religious practitioners once again practice relatively freely, and in general it is difficult to tell what sorts of cultural practices—other than the old economic practices of slavery and other kinds of unfree tenure—are prohibited , and what others are judged innocuous and therefore allowed.

Liangshan is still one of the poorest prefectures in all of China (Heberer 2001), and grand schemes of development have left many, perhaps the majority, of Nuosu villages almost entirely untouched by such modern amenities as electricity, piped water, roads, clinics, organized recreation, and schools that go beyond the first or second grade. But the standard of living is rising in many areas, and more important for this study, the field is open for the assertion of ethnicity, short of political demands for actual autonomy. In this atmosphere, Nuosu culture and ethnic identity are once again important parts of people's lives.

NUOSU CULTURE AND SOCIETY

As is evident from the brief history recounted above, Nuosu society and culture have for a long time developed in conjunction with, or perhaps in opposition to, but never in ignorance of, the larger and more cosmopolitan culture of China. This means that certain characteristics are shared in common but are given a distinctive twist in each culture; the same elements are used one way by the Hxiemga and another by the Nuosu. This might be metonymically represented by the calendrical system of naming years, months, and days after twelve animals—Rat, Ox, Tiger, Rabbit, Dragon, Snake, Horse, Sheep, Monkey, Chicken, Dog, and Pig. The years represented by each of these animals are the same for the Han and the Nuosu, but the months are backward—for Nuosu the counting of months begins with Rat in the seventh month of the Chinese calendar, so that a melancholy Nuosu pop song intoning, "Go softly in the month of the Tiger" (Lahle tego iessa iessa bbo)—approximately October— is given the translated Han title "Bie zai jin qiu," meaning "Parting in the Golden Autumn." Many aspects of Nuosu culture and society are of this sort, looking similar to their Han counterparts on the outside, but carrying very different inner meanings, while others have no such resonance, standing instead in stark contrast to the corresponding aspects among the Han.

Clan, Marriage, and Kinship

The core of Nuosu society is the patrilineal clan, or *cyvi*.[5] When two Nuosu strangers meet, they immediately ascertain each other's clan and place of residence, asking, "Whose son are you?" (Ne xi sse nge?) of a man, or "Whose daughter are you?" (Ne xi mo nge?) of a woman, and also "Where do you live?" (Ne ka isu nge?). To be a member of Nuosu society, one must have a clan identity. Clans all have genealogies, which people learn to recite; some *nzymo* and *nuoho*, as well as *bimo* (priests), who always come from *quho* clans, can recite sixty or more generations of ancestors, while most *quho*, other than *bimo*, can spiel off ten to thirty generations. Nuosu customary law is based on the differential obligations of people of the same clan and different clans. For example, the penalties paid for murder or other lesser forms of homicide differentiate between killings within and outside the clan (Qubi and Ma 2001). Members of a clan are also expected to help each other out, in precedence to other people. When I was living in Mishi, there was a murder of a traveling merchant, who was not closely related or well acquainted with any local residents. Once it was determined, however, that he was a member of the Shama Qubi clan (one of the largest *quho* clans in Liangshan), local representatives of that clan (none of whom had known him personally before) took up a collection to enable the deceased's wife and children to purchase several animals to sacrifice and serve to guests at his funeral.

The local politics of prerevolutionary times were primarily those of intermarriage, feuding, and alliance among clans. The great *nuoho* wars of the late eighteenth through the early twentieth centuries, mentioned above, are examples of this, but so are local clan feuds between, for example, the Mgebbu and Qumo clans around Baiwu. After a Mgebbu woman married into the Qumo clan sometime in the 1930s and was mistreated, there was feuding and a prohibition on marriage between the two clans that has basically lasted to this day; no Mgebbu in our sample of over one hundred marriages was married to a Qumo, despite the fact that they live only an hour or two's walk away.

Clans are also strictly exogamous, meaning that marriage between clans

---

5. Hill and Diehl (2001) claim that the *cyvi* is best understood as a patrilineage. We have a friendly argument over this; my conception is that the local representatives of a *cyvi* are much like a patrilineage but that the conception of a *cyvi* as a kin group extending throughout Liangshan, with descent not necessarily readily traceable among branches, is a classic example of a clan. I use "clan" to refer to the *cyvi* as a whole, while sometimes employing "lineage" to talk about the local organization.

serves as a means of making alliances and creating ties of kinship among their members. This can be seen even at a casual level. I was sitting waiting for dinner in a little restaurant in Gaizu, near Lugu Lake, with my collaborator Vurryr and our driver Alur, both members of the Mgebbu clan. In walked a stranger, who spoke to the proprietor in Chinese, and a few minutes later Alur and the newcomer realized that both were Nuosu. When they did, they naturally asked each other's clans. The newcomer immediately told Alur that their two clans were affines (which, in a practical sense, probably simply meant that they both were *quho*), so he should call Alur *onyi*, or "mother's brother" (since the stranger was considerably younger), and he insisted on finding a chicken to sacrifice for the happy occasion. We already had noodles on the fire and finally talked him out of it, but this little incident is an indication of the depth of clan consciousness in everyday life. More generally, intermarriage among clans creates both strong local alliances, as repeated marriages to cross-cousins thicken the web of local kinship, so leaders of local lineages pay constant attention to marriage arrangements even today. Intermarriage also creates a more general net where most *nuoho* or *quho* clans are related to most others of the same caste (not to speak of the *nzymo*, who are very few anyway and thus limited in their choice of marriage partners), and thus call each other by affinal kin terms.

The practice of cross-cousin marriage is also reflected in the Nuosu system of kin terminology. In an ideal bilateral exchange, ego's mother's brother marries ego's father's sister, and mother's sister is often married to father's brother. Thus there are only six kinds of relatives in the senior generation: father (*ada*), mother (*amo*), father's brother or mother's sister's husband (*pavu*), mother's sister or father's brother's wife (*monyi*), mother's brother or father's sister's husband (*onyi*), and father's sister or mother's brother's wife (*abo*). For a man, the female cross-cousin (*assa*) is a potential spouse and thus a joking partner, as is the male cross-cousin (*onyisse*) for a woman. By no means all marriages are arranged with cross-cousins, so that the father's sister, for example, is not always the mother's brother's wife. But conceptually, the two categories are the same.[6]

The Nuosu emphasis on clan as a human matrix of social organization contrasts with the Han emphasis on attachment to place. There are immediate and absolute bonds of attachment between two clan-mates that override either local or affinal ties, and for many people these extend clear across Liangshan. In addition, whether it stems from a past of nomadic herding or swidden agriculture, or from a lack of territorially based government, there is a lack of attachment

---

6. For more detailed analyses of cross-cousin marriage and kin terminology, see Lin Yaohua 1994: 27–37; Harrell 1989; and Lu Hui 2001.

to place when compared to Han culture. The histories of *nzymo* dynasties and *nuoho* and *quho* clans alike are histories of migration; even rites for the soul of the deceased send it through a progression of places that reverses the migration, so that everyone ends up in the same place, unlike the Chinese underworld where one can be found by a bureaucratic address containing province, county, and village (Ahern 1972: 232). This is also reflected in a lack of attention to housing and environment in many places. Certainly Nuosu culture is famous for extolling the beauty of certain kinds of environments,[7] but the attachment to particular places is much weaker than the attachment to clans, and even the architecturally most interesting of houses are rarely built to endure or be passed down through the generations. Old people, who live separately from their sons in most cases, usually get some sort of little shack built for them; soon they will die and the house will be knocked down, and chances are their sons will move on anyway. In these conditions, the idea of a local community with continuity on the land does not arise; in its place there is the idea of the clan whose ties of solidarity transcend locality.

Caste and Class

Liangshan Yi society is famous in China because Chinese ethnologists have determined that it is one of the few remaining examples on earth of slave society, which according to Morgan, Engels, and Marx, came between the stages of primitive and feudal society. There are a great number of articles and books about this particular, concrete manifestation of a historical stage, and there is a Museum of Liangshan Yi Slave Society on a hill outside Xichang. As a consequence of this, Marxist writers in the 1950s and early 1980s tried to correlate the endogamous strata of *nzymo*, *nuoho*, *quho*, *mgajie*, and *gaxy* with places in a system of cruel and exploitative relations of slaveholding. More recent writers, however, have separated the two concepts, much as writers on India have long recognized that caste and class coexist and overlap, but do not coincide, in any particular village order (Mandelbaum 1970: 210–11).

---

7. Ma Erzi (2001) recites a song describing life in an ideal environment:
> We come to raise sheep on the mountains behind our house;
> The sheep are like massed clouds.
> We come to the plains in front of our door to grow grain;
> The piles of grain are like mountains.
> We come to the stream to the side of the house to catch fish;
> The fish are like piles of firewood.

The caste order of the Nuosu is best explained as the woof of the fabric whose warp is the clan system. Every clan is ambiguously *nzymo*, *nuoho*, or *quho*; members of the lowest strata have no clan affiliation and are thus liable to be held as slaves or serfs by members of clans of any stratum, including their own (Pan Wenchao 1987: 324).[8] One never asks the caste of a new acquaintance, but one does ask the clan, and unless it is a clan unrepresented in the local area, or occasionally one with a name similar to that of another clan of a different caste, one knows immediately the caste of the interlocutor. The most important factor that separates one caste from another is endogamy. *Nuoho* virtually never marry *quho*, on penalty of expulsion from the clan, and it is rare that *quho*, unless their own clan identity is suspect (in Nuosu, their "bones are not hard") marry members of the lower order. *Nzymo* ordinarily do not marry *nuoho* either, but in recent years there have been some marriages simply because of the difficulty of finding a spouse from the rarefied *nzymo* stratum, whose members are usually considered to have constituted only a fraction of 1 percent of the Nuosu population. Prohibitions on intermarriage are still taken very seriously today. Lin Yaohua (1993) recounts a series of cases from the nuclear area in the late 1980s and early 1990s in which *nuoho* clans either prevented marriages with *quho* or severely punished their members for going through with the marriage. I once asked a *nuoho* friend, a highly educated man completely at home in the Chinese scholarly world, what he would do if his daughter, then about fourteen, were to want to marry a *quho*. He said he would oppose it. I asked him if this were not an old-fashioned attitude. He admitted that it was, but gave two explanations. First, he said, he just wouldn't feel right inside. More important, other *nuoho* might boycott his family for marrying out, and they would thenceforth have trouble marrying within the *nuoho* caste. This had happened to some of his affinal relatives in another county.

It is important to point out at the same time, however, that caste stratification in Liangshan has never, as far as I can tell, included notions of pollution or automatic deference, which are so important in the Indian caste system. In areas where there are both *nuoho* and *quho*, they socialize freely with one another,

---

8. The relationship between caste and class in the lower orders of society is a matter of some contention. The strata known as *mgajie* and *gaxy* are defined primarily by their economic position—*mgajie* as serfs and *gaxy* as household slaves—but many people think of these as caste ranks as well, making the caste hierarchy *nzymo*, *nuoho*, *quho*, *mgajie*, *gaxy*. This view is strengthened by the fact that *quho* ordinarily will not marry *mgajie*. This kind of phenomenon, in which an occupational or economic status carries over into the exogamic hierarchy, is a feature that the Liangshan caste system holds in common with the *jati* manifestation of the Indian caste system.

eating at each other's houses and often becoming close friends. None of this, however, breaks down the marriage barrier; only among highly educated urbanites is intermarriage ever considered, and then it is usually decided against; most *nuoho* would rather have their daughters marry a Hxiemga than a *quho*.

The economics of the relationships between strata disappeared with the Democratic Reforms, but much retrospective research allows us to reconstruct a picture of what they were like. In the nuclear area, at least, class stratification was based primarily on personal labor and tribute obligations on the one hand, and slaveholding on the other. Not every stratum was represented in every area. For example, in Leibo around the headquarters of the Shama Tusi, there were no *nuoho*, and *quho* retainers were immediately subordinate to the *nzymo*, paying rent for land they held but having the right to buy and sell those land rights among themselves. Other *quho* were farmers on the *nzymo*'s own land, serfs who owed labor to the lord but also had their own allocated plots to raise their own subsistence crops. The independent *quho* farmers, as well as the *nzymo* families, could hold slaves belonging to the lower castes, who themselves were divided into several different orders, the higher of which could hold slaves from the lower orders. Slaves could be bought and sold among any strata who held them (Sichuan Bianji Zu 1987: 18–19).

The more common situation was probably one where there were *nuoho* but no *nzymo*, and often a large number of *quho* of one or more clans would be considered the retainers (called *baixing* in Han) of the *nuoho* lords. They owed small amounts of tribute and labor, as well as allegiance to the lords in fights, but they themselves often became quite wealthy, and the richest of them, like their *nuoho* lords, were also slave owners. A *quho* who was impoverished or unable to pay a debt might become a slave, but a *nuoho* could never become a slave of anyone, only a poor, ridiculous, fallen aristocrat.

The actual status of slaves has been a matter of some contention. Hu Qingjun (1981: 200) made the remark, infuriating to many Nuosu scholars, that the *gaxy*, or household slaves, were nothing but "tools that could talk," *hui shuohua de gongju*. Many Nuosu scholars dispute this analysis, and—while acknowledging that slaves were often captured in raids on other clans or, more often, on Han farmers in the peripheral areas, or when people ventured into Nuosu communities without adequate guarantees—also stress that customary law required that slaves be treated with some respect, and that although they could be ordered, they could not freely be insulted or maltreated without cause (Ma Erzi 1993). Certainly prerevolutionary analyses by Han scholars often opined that the life of a Nuosu slave was better than that of a poor Han peasant (Lin Yaohua 1961 [1947], Zeng Chaolun 1945); this opinion was no longer allowed once the Marxist idea of the place of slave society in human history became official dogma, since the assumption was that once humanity left its primitive condition, things were at their worst in slave society and became progressively better in manorial feudalism, landlord feudalism, capitalism, and socialism—a series of invidious comparisons that Marx probably would have laughed at, but that also indicates the involvement of the Nuosu with Chinese society, even in the understanding of their own institutions.

Specialist Social Statuses

Nuosu society, even leaving aside the obvious Chinese connections in the institutions of *nzymo* or *tusi*, was far from a homogeneous mass of farmers, landlords, and agricultural slaves. Several kinds of specialist social statuses were, and in some cases still are, important to the construction of society. Other than *nzymo*, the most important of these are *suga*, or wealthy person; *ndeggu*, or mediator; *ssakuo*, or military leader; *gemo*, or craft specialist; *bimo*, or priest; and *sunyi*, or shaman.

There is a Nuosu saying that "*suga* is the head of splendor, *ndeggu* is the waist of splendor, and *ssakuo* is the feet of splendor" (Ma Erzi 1992: 105). Ma explains this as meaning that in the prerevolutionary society of old Liangshan, with no officially recognized political statuses or offices (except for the occasional *tusi*), people stood out for their accomplishments and abilities in different fields. As in many societies, someone who could command wealth (in land, livestock, and/or slaves) was automatically prominent, and someone who was wealthy enough could move, for example, from a status of *mgajie* to that of *qunuo*, or the top stratum of the *quho* caste, whereas someone of a *quho* station who was poor could descend into slavery, and even a *nuoho* who was poor was a no-account.

The contrast between political position in Han and Nuosu society is revealed in another proverb: "In Han districts, officials are the greatest; in Yi districts, *ndeggu* are the greatest." "Judge" is an awkward translation of the title "*ndeggu*"; literally, it means a person who can cure evils, in this case the evils of crime and disputing (Ma Erzi 1992: 99). Ma Erzi describes the attributes of the *ndeggu* as follows: "wise in counsel, able to resolve disputes in Yi society, sharp at analyzing questions, decisive in using words to persuade people" (ibid.). There was no formal title, no initiation ceremony, no insignia of office for a *ndeggu*; there were only reputation and results. A *ndeggu* was simply someone (male or female, *nuoho* or *quho* or even *mgajie*) who could be called upon to settle questions and adjudicate disputes. But in a society with no formal political office, these people with the ability to interpret customary law and persuade others to make their decisions stick were granted the highest respect.

Little has been written about the status of the *ssakuo*, or brave warrior, but Nuosu traditional culture valued bravery as much as wealth or political and judicial wisdom. Liu Yu's characterization of Nuosu society as resembling the heroic age of Homeric Greece captures, I think, a bit of this flavor (2001). She quotes a series of proverbs that will have to serve here, in the absence of more detailed ethnography, to convey the flavor of the idea of bravery in Nuosu culture:

> One thinks not of thrift when entertaining a guest; one thinks not of one's life when fighting or killing enemies.
>
> No one makes way when wrestling; no one flees when caught in a hold.
>
> There is no boy who does not wish to be brave; there is no girl who does not wish to be beautiful.
>
> When one climbs high cliffs one does not fear vultures; on the battlefield one does not fear sacrifice.

Nuosu society also produced a variety of crafts and craft specialists. Known collectively as *ge* or *gemo*, "people of skill," they include blacksmiths, who make rounds from village to village producing agricultural and craft tools; silver- and goldsmiths, who produce jewelry and decorations for the wealthy; and the producers of the painted tableware (see chap. 7) that, in the revival of ethnic culture in the 1980s and 1990s, again is to be found in every house, from remote villages to the mansions of the elite in Xichang and other major cities.

Perhaps the most specialized occupation of all in Nuosu society, however, is that of the priest, or *bimo*. *Bimo* are always male (legend has it that a famous *bimo* tried to train his daughter as a successor, but she was found out by her two pierced ears, since men pierce only the left ear) and almost always are *quho*, usually from a few prominent clans, in which the knowledge is passed down from father to son; among the most famous of these are the Jjike, Shama Qubi, Ddisse, and Jili (Bamo 1994: 216). To become a *bimo* requires a long period of apprenticeship, and typically a father trains his sons, or if no sons are available or if they don't show the requisite abilities, perhaps other agnatic relatives or occasionally nonrelatives, who however must pay a stiff fee and cannot inherit all the ritual knowledge of the teacher (Bamo 1994: 215–26; 2001; Jjike 1990).

The life of a *bimo* centers around texts and rituals. Although Nuosu writing was used at various times in history for various political and administrative purposes, before the twentieth century the skills of literacy were almost exclusively in the hands of the *bimo*, whose books include rituals for a wide variety of purposes, from curing illness to success in war or politics to harming an enemy to the all-important funerary ritual of *cobi*, the so called "indicating the road" to the soul of the deceased back through all the places its ancestors had lived to the original home of the Ni (in Qinghai?) and thence to the heavenly regions.

Finally, in addition to the *bimo*, there is another kind of religious practitioner, the *sunyi*. *Sunyi* can be male or female, can come from any caste, and respond to inspiration rather than to heredity or apprenticeship. They become possessed by and drive out spirits, entering trance and displaying their spirit power by fire-eating and other feats, using drums and chants to cure and to exorcise. Little research has been done on the *sunyi*.

Family and Gender

Descent and inheritance in Nuosu society are of course patrilineal, and gender ideology values males as superior to females, but this is one more way in which superficial similarities between Nuosu and Han culture hide deeper contrasts. Perhaps most important, the relationship between generations in Nuosu society is more affectionate and not so hierarchical or authoritarian as that among the Han. As in most cultures, there is a cult of motherhood; a recent pop song about missing mother brings tears to the eyes of educated or village Nuosu who hear it on boom boxes or play it on car and bus tape decks, and folktales and folksongs emphasize the affection people have for their mothers.

In Han culture, this affection for the mother is balanced by a distant and authoritative relationship with the father, especially on the part of his sons, but Nuosu father-son relationships are not nearly so stern or one-sided. Even in peasant families, father and son often discuss issues of large and small import by the hour around the fire, contrasting with the almost total lack of communication between father and son in many Han peasant families (Yang 1945: 57–58). Sons do not live with their parents after their wives move in permanently several years after marriage, but set up separate housing, sometimes in the same compound but sometimes in distant parts of a village or cluster of houses. A man with adult sons can count on a minimum amount of support, but he has very little authority over them unless he is prominent locally within the lineage. For most practical purposes, then, a local lineage consists of agnatically related adult men, each of whom is the head of an independent nuclear household; there is no level of extended family household or property-based corporate segment between the household and the body politic of the lineage itself. People are closer to their own brothers and near cousins than to more distant relatives, but there are no corporate lineage segments.

Gender in traditional society is a difficult topic to get at. It is clear that gender differentiation and homosociality are a feature of Nuosu social interaction—all one has to do is to look at the people huddled on a hillside at a wedding or funeral, with knots of men here and knots of women there. The elaboration of gender in dress, adornment, and folklore is also extreme. At the same time, however, there are hints that gender roles in prerevolutionary society were sometimes fluid. There are stories (not folktales but recent reminiscences) of female *ndeggu* and even *ssakuo*, and prerevolutionary ethnologists, both Chinese and foreign, always compare favorably the position of Nuosu women to that of their foot- and housebound Han counterparts (von Eickstedt 1944: 168; Lin Yaohua 1994 [1947]: 47, 58).

It thus seems a bit paradoxical to me that, if anything, the status of Nuosu women in village society today shows greater differences from that of men in terms of their participation in contemporary public society and culture. We found, for example, in Baiwu that whereas Nuosu males were on the average better-educated than Han and Prmi males, Nuosu women had the least schooling. Village and township schools, in fact, typically have only a small minority of girl students. Very few Nuosu women become cadres or teachers, again in contrast to Han and, particularly, in my impression, to Prmi and Tibetans. In everyday interaction, around the fire in the home, women serve men, eat after them, and do most of the housework while men sit, talking and drinking. On the other hand, indulgence in psychoactive substances is not a male prerogative as it is among Han; almost all Nuosu women smoke and drink heavily. In conversation, the genders are mutually respectful, and women's opinions are listened to when offered but are not offered as often or as assertively as those of men.[9]

In the field of ethnology itself (to get really self-referential about this), however, the situation again seems somewhat egalitarian. There are a large number of Nuosu women professors, and so far all but one of the Ph.D. candidates of Nuosu extraction, whether from Chinese, American, or French universities, have been women. The disjunction between the retiring role of women in village life and their prominent participation in at least one aspect of wider culture awaits further research and analysis.

9. Hill and Diehl (2001) report the same impression.

Language, Writing, and Literacy

The Nuosu language belongs, according to Chinese linguists, to the Yi sub-branch of the Tibeto-Burman branch of the Sino-Tibetan family; other languages in this branch are Lisu, Lahu, Hani, Jinuo, and Bai (Guojia Minwei 1981: 585). Yi is in turn divided into six "dialects" (*fangyan*), with Nuosu constituting the Northern dialect. This classification, however, is politically determined by the results of the ethnic identification project; none of these "languages" is a single idiom or even has a single standard variety. A more linguistically based classification is that of David Bradley, who places four of the six "dialects" of Yi as delineated by the Chinese linguists into the Northern Branch of Yi (formerly Loloish); he places the Central and Western Yi dialects in the Central Branch, along with Lisu, Lahu, and some dialects of Hani (Bradley 1990, 2001). Like almost all Tibeto-Burman languages (Matisoff 1991), Nuosu is tonal, with tones serving a grammatical as well as a semantic function.

Unlike many Yi dialects from Yunnan, Nuosu has not in any manner given way to Chinese in the daily speech of Nuosu people. One hears the language not only on the streets and in the villages, but also in recordings, radio programs (though no television as yet), and official speeches at various levels of government. In addition, Nuosu has for at least seven hundred years been a written language. In the nineteenth and early twentieth centuries, the syllabic writing system, which seems to be completely independent of any other known script except for similar Yi scripts written in Yunnan and Guizhou, was almost exclusively the property of the *bimo*, who transmitted hand-copied ritual texts from generation to generation. In the mid-twentieth century, elite families in various parts of Liangshan began to use the script for secular purposes such as writing letters.

As mentioned above, a Romanized script failed to take hold during the 1950s, but in the late 1970s and 1980s a reformed version of the traditional script was promulgated and promoted and is now widely used for various purposes in Liangshan. School classes either teach in Chinese with Yi as a second language, usually starting in the third grade, or teach primarily in Yi with Chinese as a second language, usually starting from the first grade. There are standard textbooks for language and history all the way through senior high school, and texts for other subjects such as mathematics and sciences are being developed. I have watched elementary math classes taught in Nuosu, and it seems to excite the interest of the children much more than the equivalent material taught in Han, a language with which most of the children have to struggle. There is a provincial Yi-language school, or *yiwen xuexiao*,whose graduates often go on to Yi language and literature departments at Liangshan University in Xichang, Southwest Nationalities Institute in Chengdu, or Central Nationalities University in Beijing.

A commitment to using a language such as Nuosu as a second official language of public life means the development of a whole set of bureaucratic institutions of translation. Every county in Liangshan, as well as the prefectural government itself, has a language committee, or *yuwei*, whose task it is to translate government directives, forms, and reports from one language to another. Since most of the bureaucrats, even those of Nuosu ethnicity, find it more natural to write on administrative topics in Chinese, most of the translation is into Nuosu. It is not a meaningless exercise, however. For example, when I was working in Mishi, there was a cholera epidemic in nearby Zhaojue. Notices about cholera and what to do about it were posted in both languages on government bulletin boards. Similarly, the election ballots for the vote I observed in Baiwu were printed in both Han and Nuosu (fig. 3).

The problems of using Nuosu for bureaucratic communication go deeper than just habits, however. Until recently, the written (and spoken) Nuosu language did not deal with topics of modern technical or social innovations. In many places such as Baiwu, where nearly everyone has at least a rudimentary speaking knowledge of Han, this is customarily dealt with by inserting Han words into Nuosu conversation. Such terms as *xuexiao* (school), *yidian* (one o'clock), and *qiche* (motor vehicle) slip easily into Nuosu speech. The language authorities, however, feel it necessary to construct Nuosu equivalents for such words. This has produced calques for some terms, such as *ssodde* (studying place) for "school" and *teku cyma* (time one-count) for "one o'clock." For other terms, Han words are borrowed but with a Nuosu pronunciation, such as *guo-jie* for "country" and "government" (from the Chinese *guojia*), and *fizhy* for airplane (from the Chinese *feiji*). Once, out of curiosity, I looked in the massive *Han-Yi Dictionary* published by the Sichuan Nationalities Press and found not only "nuclear power plant" and of course "proletarian dictatorship," but, more surprisingly, "whale," translated as *jihxe*, a half-calque of Chinese *jing* (whale) and Nuosu *hxe* (fish) (Hopni Ddopssix 1989).

These examples demonstrate the most salient fact about Nuosu culture: it exists to a large extent by absorbing things from, adapting things out of, and inventing things in reaction to the larger, more socially complex, and more powerful Han culture with which it is surrounded. Ethnicity in Liangshan must thus be understood primarily in terms of kinship, rather than culture. This

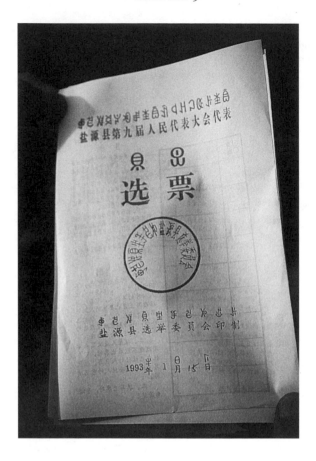

FIG. 3. A ballot for a local election in Baiwu, printed
in Nuosu and Chinese

does not mean that there are no circumstantial factors encouraging Nuosu ethnicity; obviously there are economic, political, and educational benefits to being
a minority in Reform Era China. What it does mean is that Nuosu people themselves understand ethnicity in primordial terms. They do not see it as contingent in any way. It is always, in every situation, abundantly clear who is Nuosu
and who is not; there is no blurring or contextual shifting of boundaries (see
also Schoenhals n.d.). In many places culture, as well as descent, is the thing
that makes some people Nuosu and others Hxiemga. In these places Han culture is either resisted entirely (as in Mishi) or selectively practiced while its
importance is denied (as in Baiwu). In Manshuiwan, Han culture has mostly

been taken over, but with no blurring effect on ethnic boundaries. Finally, in the cities, people whose basic, habitual practices are mostly Han consciously practice and display various aspects of Nuosu culture as a means of maintaining ethnicity. The following case studies will illustrate this continuum from cultural and ethnic separateness to cultural connection, and from ethnic separateness to ethnic identity as a reason for re-creating aspects of a separate culture.

6 / Mishi: A Demographically
and Culturally Nuosu Community

Mishi is written in Chinese with the characters meaning "rice market." It is reported by Nuosu cadres that PLA troops, coming into
the area to quell the rebellion in the late 1950s, looked at the map
and thought maybe it would not be such a hardship post after all; they would
at least be able to buy rice to eat. Alas for them, Mbi Shy in Nuosu means "yellow leech," and there was little rice to be had. Mishi Township (*zhen*) is a real
"Nuosu area" (*Nuosu muddi*). It lies in Xide County, about fourteen kilometers on a good dirt road built in the 1970s from the small railroad stop of
Lianghekou, where the Chengdu-Kunming railroad emerges from its descend-
ing curlicues in the high mountains and proceeds down the river valley to Xide
City. The township headquarters is a little cluster of whitewashed brick and
mud buildings along a U-shaped paved street, including an elementary and a
middle school, the official compound housing Party, government, and police
headquarters, a small hospital, and several apartment-style buildings housing
cadres, along with a few little commercial establishments. It lies at the south
end of a small alluvial plain where 680 *mu*, or about 45 hectares, of rice can be
grown in the wet summer season. Mishi Township is the headquarters for a
grouping called a "slice district" (*pian qu*) that also includes Luoha Township,
farther south on the same road, and two rural townships (*xiang*) that are not
accessible by motor road—Yilu and Rekeyida. The population of the slice district as a whole is about eighteen thousand; the population of Mishi Township
itself in fall 1984 was 5,782 people in 1,332 households, with a nonagricultural
population of 189, including cadres, teachers, and their families, along with a
few merchants who run barber shops, snack restaurants, and dry-goods stores.
About fifty of the nonagricultural residents are Han, all of them merchants or
teachers. All of the township cadres and police, and all of the agricultural population of all four townships are Nuosu, making Nuosu about 99.2 percent of
the population of the slice area.

Mishi's is still by and large a subsistence economy. The main crops are potatoes, corn, buckwheat, and oats; people also grow a bit of soybeans, broad beans,

and, on the scarce alluvial land, rice. Turnips, used to make pickles to put in soup, are the main vegetable; like most Nuosu, people in Mishi have little interest in green things to eat. After a long walk in the mountains, one can pull the mild, flat *voma* turnips from a trailside field and peel and eat them raw; they are cool and refreshing. Nonagricultural production is limited to two small township-owned workshops that produce indigo-dyed wool *jieshy* (pleated, unfringed wool-felt inner capes) and *vala* (woven wool-fringed outer capes), along with a spinning workshop and two small flour mills.

Electricity has lighted the homes and institutions of the township headquarters since 1992; it also reaches a few of the villages nearest to the town, all but one of them in Mishi Administrative Village (*cun*). The town had a generating station from 1979 to 1982, but they could not afford the maintenance, and it was closed down. Just up the road toward Lianghekou, a private entrepreneur, a native of the remote village of Vaha, was building a hydroelectric generating station when Bamo Ayi, Nuobu Huojy, and I lived in Mishi in October 1994, planned for completion in 1996. It has a planned capacity of 250 kilowatts, which would go a long way toward supplying the electricity needs of most of the villages in the township, but stringing the wires to those remote, roadless areas will take awhile. The entrepreneur, Qumo Vake, never went to school, but after marriage he joined the army in the 1980s and became a truck driver there. When he was discharged, he got a job driving a truck for the county government in Xide and then became the personal driver of the county magistrate. He accumulated enough money to finance a truck of his own and began to amass profits in the hauling business. He is now reported to have a large truck, plus a 4×4, of his own, and a house in Xide City worth about ¥100,000. The power station is costing about half a million *yuan*, of which Vake is reported to be putting up about ¥100,000; the rest comes from other private investors. After Vake became rich, he divorced his first wife, leaving her with their children in remote Vaha, about a three-hour walk from the road; in a brazen gesture of flamboyant upward mobility, he married a Hxiemgamo (Han woman) from Chengdu, who is reported by people in Mishi to be quite plain.

Aside from Vake, there is only one household in the township with an income of more than a few thousand *yuan* per year; they make around ¥20,000 from the commercial growing of apples and Sichuan peppercorns, or *huajiao*. Just about everyone else in the villages is an ordinary subsistence farmer. There are twelve administrative villages in the township, encompassing thirty-three cooperatives (called production teams during the period of collective agriculture) and about seventy or eighty natural hamlets (called *baga* in Nuosu and *puzi* in Chinese), though nobody has ever counted them. There are no settlements on the *bazi*, and none is reached by road; the closest two are a fifteen- or twenty-minute walk—including in one case fording a shallow but swift stream—from the town. The village of Matolo, where we spent two days drinking and interviewing, is considered typical—neither rich nor poor, high nor low, close nor remote.

Matolo consists of two cooperatives and five hamlets; the closest is little more than an hour's walk up a slippery trail from the township headquarters. Village cadres told us that there were about twenty households in Matolo Cooperative and about nineteen in Tuanjie, but they were not sure, since Nuosu people move around a lot. In the old society, people lived more scattered, except when they needed to group together for defense in wartime; they clustered into tight hamlets during the period of collective agriculture and now they are dispersing again. Houses are simple, built entirely of mud walls, with wooden doors and roof frames; in Matolo most of them now have tile roofs, a sign of prosperity, in contrast to the minority whose roofs are still of thatch. Houses all have dirt floors; as you come in the door you turn to the left, and the hearth, with its three stones or andirons, sports a split-log fire, often with something cooking on it. Often there are mats to the right of the fire where the guests sit; if you are an honored guest, such as a foreigner, they may offer you a little wooden stool, but the mats are more comfortable. There are beds in the main room and sometimes in side or back rooms; much of the main room is covered by a wooden loft used to store grain, potatoes, and agricultural implements. One reported cultural change is that women are now allowed in the loft, as they were not in the old society. The oldest houses in the main hamlets of the village were built in the early 1980s.

The major crops are corn, buckwheat, potatoes, oats, and soybeans; in the past few years agriculture has been good to people, and they have been able to make a few hundred *yuan* per household per year selling surpluses on the market. They save this money or use it to buy household goods; most families have an account at the local credit cooperative. Villagers also estimated that each household is able, on the average, to kill a large pig, a couple of small pigs, a sheep or goat, and five or six chickens for meat each year; occasionally they sell a pig or some eggs, but they eat most of the latter. Otherwise, they eat potatoes and buckwheat cakes, and mostly feed the corn to pigs (who in Nuosu villages are not penned but forage around and often live inside the houses, along with dogs, cats, and chickens). Village families altogether farm only twenty-two *mu* (1.5 hectares) of rice land down on the plain, so rice is a special treat.

Very few people from Matolo have left the village economy to work for wages, or *gongzuo*.[1] There is one boy who is now a college student, at the Southwestern Architectural College in Chongqing, and there have been three others who became cadres or workers of other kinds. The current cooperative head was in the army for awhile and speaks excellent standard Chinese, but he is now a plain farmer. Nevertheless, here as in so many villages, there is someone whose personal name is Gozuosse, a combination of the Chinese *gongzuo* with the Nuosu masculine ending. Ordinary farming people come and go as they feel like it; it is much easier to move now than it was during the period of collective agriculture.

HISTORY AND REVOLUTION

Mishi is a famous place in Nuosu history. When two branches of the *nuoho* Loho clan were forced out of Zhaojue eight or nine generations ago (probably in the late eighteenth or early nineteenth century), one of the first places to which they migrated was Mishi. Later some of them moved on to Mianning and Yanyuan on the other side of the Anning Valley, but others stayed, ruling over large numbers of *quho* and slaves.

According to local oral accounts, the most famous lord in the Mishi area in the 1930s and 1940s was Loho Anyu, who was overlord of most of the current area of Mishi and Luoha Townships, and had many retainers and slaves in all the villages. He lived at the small town of Lianghekou, where he also had land and slaves, and where he became the primary Nuosu ally of the local Han warlord, Deng Xiuting (Xide Xianzhi: 456). Under him were several lesser lords of the Loho and Lomu clans, who regularly intermarried. To the east of the town, where Matolo and Jiemo (see below) villages are located, the most important petty lords were Loho Sunyi, who lived on a hill above Matolo, and who had four wives and six daughters, but no sons, and, living just below him, Loho Kavuga, who was considered very oppressive of his slaves; he was captured and executed at the time of the Democratic Reforms. Under the rule of Loho lords, *quho* and *mgajie* moved in and out of the area. For example, the great-grandfather of the current adult males of the *quho* Alur clan came about eighty years ago; they lived over a little hill from the current hamlet of Matolo. Two of his sons, however, were driven out in 1944 for unspecified reasons by Loho Anyu and settled in a mountainous area above Xichang City. Three years later,

---

1. For discussions of the meaning of the term *gongzuo*, see Entwistle and Henderson 2000 and Harrell 2000a.

when they had amassed the sixteen goats the lord had required of them, they returned and built another house, where they lived until 1990, after which they came to Matolo.

One of the best-known leaders of the revolt in the late 1950s also came from Mishi; he was Loho Muga, son of Loho Anyu. Upon his father's death in 1943, Muga at the age of seventeen became leader of warlord Deng Xiuting's Yi militia and also inherited much of his father's land and about seven hundred slaves.[2] In the late 1940s Muga developed close relations with local Guomindang figures and often used his power to kill local Nuosu who cooperated with the Communists. Nevertheless, in early 1953 the Communist Party attempted to win Muga over to its side, and appointed him head of the culture and education office of the newly formed county government, soon afterward sending him to the Nationalities Institute in Chengdu to study. But he returned home when his mother became ill, and never went back to school. When the democratic reforms were begun in earnest at the end of 1955, he rebelled openly, allying with rebel leaders in many parts of the county in a guerilla effort that was not put down until 1958. But even then, Muga refused to surrender, and took to the hills, where he mounted sporadic attacks on various settlements for several more years. Nuosu cadres and intellectuals, themselves beneficiaries and active supporters of the revolution, still tell tales of Loho Muga's audacity and heroism, including such deeds as his personally killing seventeen PLA soldiers, and coming into villages in broad daylight to hold open planning meetings as late as May 1964 (Xide Xianzhi 1992: 155). One of the Nuosu intellectuals with whom I discussed this period said that I should not think of the bandits as being anti-Communist; basically, they were just anti-Han. Like all the rebels, however, Loho Muga was eventually defeated: after he held his open meetings, the prefectural government organized a special "small group to eliminate the Luo bandits" and alerted residents everywhere to be on the lookout for Muga and his nephew. In December the effort paid off when Muga was spotted in the forest by a woman cutting firewood, who contacted the local army unit, which called together army and people's militia members, who surrounded Muga and killed him and his nephews in a fierce firefight (Xide Xianzhi 1992: 456–57).

At the time of the Democratic Reforms, a large number of former *mgajie*

---

2. The Chinese term *nuli*, or "slave," is used in the Xide gazetteer (Xide Xianzhi 1992), from which this account is taken. It is unclear, however, whether this term refers to actual *gaxy*, which would seem quite unusual, or to retainers and dependents generally, which would include *mgajie* working on the land and quite possibly also *qunuo* retainers. The latter seems more probable to me.

and *gaxy* were liberated from their masters and formed the two villages that now lie close to the township headquarters. Some of these slaves are reputed to have been of Han origin, but none will now admit it. The two villages near the town were originally called Jiefang Cun, or Liberation Village, but that name sounds prejudicial, since to have been liberated one must have once been a slave, and slavery is something impolite to talk about in front of people who once experienced it. The villages are now called Jiemo and Vato, and are part of Mishi Administrative Village.

Some of the inhabitants of Jiemo and Vato had histories of oppression before the revolution. For example, one family of the Alur clan were slaves of Loho Kesse (*kesse* means "puppy"; I don't know if this was his formal name or a nickname) who was one of the aristocrats driven all the way across the Yalong River into Yanyuan and Muli by Deng Xiuting in the early 1940s. The man who told me the story was, along with his two brothers, orphaned in Muli, and when Deng died in 1944, Kesse returned, bringing his slaves with him, including the three boys. At the time of the Democratic Reforms, since they were orphaned slaves who previously had no home except that of the master, they settled down in what was then Liberation Village.

Two brothers of the Lama[3] family were slaves in Ningnan County, far to the east, before the Revolution. Sometime in the late 1940s, Lama Vusa and his brothers were moved to the Mishi area by the lord. Some of the family escaped back to Ningnan, but Vusa stayed here. Laqo, son of one of the escaped brothers, came to Mishi to join his uncle in the late 1980s and also settled in one of the hamlets of the former Liberation Village, now called Vato.

Vato and its twin settlement, Jiemo, close by the town, are much better off than Matolo. Village houses are noticeably larger, cleaner, and neater; they are lit by electricity and often sport Chinese-style collages of family photos on the walls, as well as cabinets and other store-bought furniture, and mosquito nets on the bed. People there drink boiled water and tea, unlike the highlanders, and their levels of education and literacy are much higher, and their incomes marginally so. These are the fruits of revolution; indeed Mishi is one of the few places I have been in China where, in the 1990s, revolution seemed still to be working; almost everywhere else, including other Nuosu communities, those who were rich before were rich again. Here the mostly *qunuo* families in Matolo still live the life of the hills, with almost no modern amenities or access to avenues of outward or upward mobility, while the former slaves down in the valley are

---

3. Lama is a common *quho* clan name and has nothing to do with Tibetan incarnations.

beginning, just beginning, to experience economic development. Just don't remind them that some of them may have been of Han origin.

LANGUAGE, LITERACY, AND SCHOOLING

A visit to Mishi Town on a school day would convey the impression of bustling educational life in the *Nuosu muddi*. At the primary school, the first-grade class has nearly fifty students crowded into desk space for about forty, so that some of the desks have three grubby, undersized, unwashed little tykes (the thirty-four boys sharing some desks and the sixteen girls sharing others), who thus fill up the desks intended for two. The first class of the day is language (*yuwen*), meaning Chinese. Since there are visitors today, the students first break into the Nuosu anthem, "Guests from Afar" (Sumu divi wo), and only after finishing the song do they stand for the middle-aged male teacher with the thick glasses and rumpled appearance, shouting at the top of their lungs, "Laoshi hao"(We wish you well, teacher) and then sitting down to business. After demonstrating some of the mistakes from the students' copybooks from the night before, the teacher proceeds to the day's lesson, which includes six new characters: *shang* (up, above, top, rise), *zhong* (middle, center), *xia* (down, below, bottom, sink), *da* (big), *xiao* (little), and *liao* (a perfective particle). The teacher leads the class in reciting each one in unison: "Shi-ang, shang, shi-ang, shang . . ." until he waves them off with his pointer, and they go on to "Xi-a-xia, xi-a-xia . . ." and so forth. Since the students at this time understand almost nothing of the Han language (Nuosu friends who grew up in villages typically tell me they couldn't really speak Chinese with any assurance until they were in the third or fourth grade), the teacher also explains what each character means: "*Da*, ayy nge" and so on. After he explains something or someone writes something, he asks, in Nuosu, if there are mistakes, and the class answers, in loud unison, "A jjo" (There aren't any), and they go on to the next topic.

The teacher then gives a writing assignment, telling them in Nuosu to write each character five times, and they get their dog-eared copybooks and stubby pencils out of their little shoulder bags, some of them using pocket knives to sharpen the pencils, and they set to work; the teacher strolls the room and corrects their handwriting and posture. The teacher tells us that the students have no trouble remembering how to write the characters, but they do have trouble with meaning and pronunciation, despite the repeated phonetic chants.

When the class period is over and the monitors have collected the copybooks, the class president stands, tells the students to say good-bye to the teacher, and they all yell, "Laoshi zaijian," and bolt for the door.

After recess, the same class has math. This is taught by the young school principal, who told me that first-year math was the hardest thing to teach, so he felt he ought to do it himself. He is outstanding at it. Teaching mostly but not entirely in Nuosu, he uses humor, challenge, and cajolery to get the urchins to understand addition and subtraction. Every time he asks for volunteers, hands shoot up in the air in some directions and elbows chunk down, fulcrumlike with the forearm vertical and the fingers waving, on the rickety desks in others. Most of the students work the problems on their fingers, and the teacher makes no effort to stop them. He calls on a little girl whose given name is Hxiemgamo (actually, a fairly common name) to do a problem at one side of the board, and thinks about it for a minute, then says, well, if we have a Hxiemgamo (Han woman) over here, we'd better have a Nuosumo (Nuosu woman) on the other side, and even the little urchins get the joke, since there are no actual Hxiemgamo, other than teachers, within miles of the place.

In both of these class sessions, there are four or five little punkins who are even tinier than the rest and who just sit there; they do not raise their hands, join in the chanting, or get out their copybooks to write characters or do math problems when the others do. The principal told me that most of these children are five-year-olds, whom the parents are sending to school early because they would like them to have a head start (there is no kindergarten or preschool here), or maybe because there is nobody to take care of them. He also said he thought that fourteen to sixteen of this year's students, including most of these little ones, would have to repeat the first grade next year.

There are a total of 208 students enrolled in the school; according to statistics they represent almost 70 percent of the elementary-aged children in the township, but this figure is clearly fudged, since we are also told that about 180 of the 208 students are from the two administrative villages of Mishi and Laiga, down near the *bazi*, and only about thirty come from the villages up in the mountains, of which Matolo is one of the closer ones. There are 38 girls and 170 boys.

Not everyone, however, who starts school does so in the township elementary school. Six villages have village schools, or *cunxiao*, and we visited the one in Matolo. It is a one-room mud-brick structure with no windows, only the open door and a couple of small skylights to let the daylight in, and of course no electricity (fig. 4). Until 1994 there were both first- and second-year students in the school, but now there are only first-graders, nine boys and a girl, ranging in age from six to nine. If they want to continue in the second grade next year, they will have to make the ninety-minute trip to the town. Last year, eight of the ten second-grade students continued.

There is a blackboard for the teacher to write on, but he has no desk, so he

FIG. 4. A class at the Matolo village school

puts his box of chalk on one of the students' desks in the front. He is a native of the village and a junior-high school graduate, and the villagers pay his salary as a *minban* (non-state salaried) teacher, which amounts to ¥400 per year. Under these conditions, he does a good job in language (Han) and math classes, despite great hardships. The lesson in the language class today, for example, is a text that reads, in translation:

> A big bird flies up into the sky.
> Wrong, wrong.
> It's an airplane.
>
> A big fish dives down under the sea.
> Wrong, wrong.
> It's a submarine.

For cosmopolitan, television-raised children in Shanghai or maybe even Xide City, this would be a fun lesson. But who knows what these little guys get out of it? They have probably seen airplanes flying over, but they have never seen so much as a rowboat, or a body of water larger than a mountain stream, let alone the ocean or a submarine. Still, they persist in a language they do not understand, and most of them will proceed down the hill the following year.

By the time these students get to the sixth grade at the Mishi school (which only about half of them do), they are fully accustomed to the culture of Chinese schools. There are two classes, or *ban*,[4] in the sixth grade, one of them an ordinary class, which is taught all in Han except for the Yi language classes, and another bilingual class (*shuangwen ban*), which uses Nuosu as the basic language for reading and writing, and as the medium of instruction for math, and uses both languages interchangeably in most of the other classes; Han language is not introduced until the third grade.

The first class of the day for the sixth-grade regular class is language, and the teacher is a twenty-year-old, pink-cheeked Han woman from nearby Mianning County, graduated only six months before from a normal school. She seems nervous, perhaps because of the presence of visitors, and teaches the text for this class, Hans Christian Andersen's story "The Little Match Girl" strictly by the book, as a realistic depiction of what life was like in the glory days of capitalism. When she calls on individual students, she walks over and knocks on their desks, seeming to have made no effort to learn any of their names. (My co-worker Bamo Ayi thought this was because Nuosu names were hard for her.) When the students are called upon to answer questions about the story, they read from the text, one syllable at a time, in exaggerated tones, as if the Han language is still a strain for them.

We then visit a Yi language class for the bilingual class. This class has nine girls out of seventeen students, and the teacher mostly explains the text without asking very many questions. He does, however, call the students by name. When they read the text individually, it sounds much more like natural speech, but when they read in unison, it sounds chanted, just like the Han texts, only with a different prosody reflecting different tonal patterns.

According to the principal and the teachers, this is the last time they will experiment with bilingual education in Mishi. It simply causes the students too much difficulty in testing into higher schools; they particularly get stuck on the differences between the *pinyin*, or romanized phonemic scripts, used to teach the two languages. Since schools tend to be evaluated according to their students' rates of testing into higher schools, having too many Yi-lan-

---

4. A *ban* is a group of students in a particular grade who take all of their classes together, often throughout the years they stay in a particular school. The bond between schoolmates of the same *ban (tongban tongxue)* is one of the closest non-kin bonds in Chinese society. For more on the *ban*, see Schoenhals 1993: 11-12.

TABLE 6.1
Enrollments in Mishi Middle School

Grade	Boys	Girls	TOTAL
Lower Middle 1	31	5	36
Lower Middle 2	21	7	28
Lower Middle 3	16	1	17
TOTAL	68	13	81

guage classes is an invitation to a low evaluation. Only in the four most remote townships of Xide County is bilingual education going to remain the standard policy. Left unsaid is the empirical observation, here and elsewhere, that bilingual or primarily Nuosu-language education tends to be a girl thing.

Of those who make it through to graduation, the best will test into the county middle school at Xide, and the next best to the *minzu* middle school in the town or perhaps to the vocational school at Lake in the northwestern part of the county. Some will drop out, of course, but those who want to continue but cannot test into one of the better schools will continue in Mishi Middle School, which has three grades, with the enrollments shown in table 6.1. It is more common to drop out than to graduate and not go on; a great many of those who graduate try to test into some higher school, usually a normal or vocational school.

The students learn language (sic), Yi language, mathematics, physics, chemistry, English, politics, physical education, health, history, geography, and music. We visited a second-year Yi language class, where the lesson was a poem of five-syllable lines concerning the knowledge and wisdom one could gain from one's elders, along with the reciprocal obligations of the elders in bringing up their children. The teacher conducted the class entirely in Nuosu, never using a single word of Han, and held the students' attention well (fig. 5). Bamo Ayi, who was observing with me, was impressed and proud that traditional Yi knowledge could be taught so well in a public school.

We also went to a third-year English class taught by a Han teacher from northern Sichuan who had just been sent to Mishi, having not found a job in a more desirable place. His English pronunciation and listening comprehension were not of the best; Ayi had to translate for him several times when I tried to speak to him in English. He was honest, neat, and hard-working, but I doubt the students learned much English from him. On this day, of course, whatever English they learned they learned from me.

FIG. 5. A teacher in a Yi-language class at the Mishi middle school giving
a lesson on respecting one's elders

The English teacher is not the only Han instructor at the middle school; in
fact five of the nine teachers, including the one woman, are Han. As in the town
elementary school, it is estimated that about 80 percent of the students are from
the villages down near the plain. In Jiemo, we found a large number of junior-
high graduates, considerable numbers who had gone on to vocational or normal schools, and two students at the Southwest Nationalities Institute.

It would appear from the foregoing that despite the pervasiveness of the
Nuosu language as the medium of everyday communication, literacy and mobility are dependent on learning Han. Mobility is, for sure, but literacy is a more
complicated issue and really cannot be understood except in relationship to
mobility. Bamo Ayi and I surveyed the populations of Matolo, up on the hill,
and Jiemo and Vato, down by the plain, and came up with the figures in tables
6.2 and 2.3. Official figures might well show 53 percent "illiteracy" for males,
and 86 percent for females, where we show 23 percent and 83 percent, respectively, because *wenmang* often means "unable to read and write the Han language," or sometimes even "did not attend school," though some official
statistics include the category "self-taught," which usually still means "self-
taught to read and write the Han language."

TABLE 6.2
Literacy and Language Competence by Age and Gender, Matolo

	Age 8–20	Age 21–40	Age 41+	TOTAL
1. Speaks Nuosu, no Han, no Writing				
Male	8	6	6	20
Female	21	16	24	61
TOTAL	29	22	30	81
2. Speaks Nuosu, writes Nuosu, no Han				
Male	0	0	1	1
Female	0	1	0	1
TOTAL	0	1	1	2
3. Speaks Nuosu, speaks Han, no writing				
Male	1	0	2	3
Female	0	2	0	2
TOTAL	1	2	2	5
4. Speaks Nuosu, writes Nuosu, speaks Han				
Male	0	3	8	11
Female	0	1	0	1
TOTAL	0	4	8	12
5. Speaks Nuosu, speaks Han, writes Han				
Male	6	2	1	9
Female	7	1	0	8
TOTAL	13	3	1	17
Literacy by Language				
Literate in both				
6. Speaks Nuosu, writes Nuosu, speaks Han, writes Han				
Male	6 (29%)	15 (58%)	6 (25%)	27 (38%)
Female	1 (3%)	1 (2%)	1 (3%)	3 (4%)
TOTAL	7 (14%)	16 (33%)	7 (14%)	30 (20%)

	Age 8–20	Age 21–40	Age 41+	TOTAL
Illiterate				
Groups 1, 3 (above)				
Male	9 (43%)	6 (23%)	8 (33%)	23 (32%)
Female	21 (72%)	18 (82%)	24 (96%)	63 (83%)
TOTAL	30 (60%)	24 (50%)	32 (65%)	86 (58%)
Literate in Nuosu				
Groups 2, 4, 6				
Male	6 (29%)	18 (69%)	15 (63%)	39 (55%)
Female	1 (3%)	3 (14%)	1 (4%)	5 (7%)
TOTAL	7 (14%)	21 (44%)	16 (32%)	44 (30%)
Literate in Han				
Groups 5, 6				
Male	12 (57%)	17 (65%)	7 (29%)	36 (47%)
Female	8 (28%)	2 (9%)	1 (4%)	11 (14%)
TOTAL	20 (40%)	19 (40%)	8 (16%)	47 (31%)
Han Spoken Language Ability				
No Han language				
Groups 1, 2				
Male	8 (38%)	6 (23%)	7 (29%)	21 (29%)
Female	21 (72%)	17 (77%)	24 (96%)	62 (87%)
TOTAL	29 (58%)	23 (48%)	31 (63%)	83 (56%)
Speaks Han				
Groups 3, 4, 5, 6				
Male	13 (62%)	20 (77%)	17 (71%)	50 (71%)
Female	8 (28%)	5 (23%)	1 (4%)	14 (13%)
TOTAL	21 (42%)	25 (52%)	18 (37%)	64 (44%)
Total population surveyed				
Male	21	26	24	71
Female	29	22	25	76
TOTAL	50	48	49	147

TABLE 6.3

Literacy and Language Competence by Age and Gender, Jiemo

	Age 8–20	Age 21–40	Age 41+	TOTAL
1. Speaks Nuosu, no Han, no writing				
Male	3	0	4	7
Female	12	5	13	30
TOTAL	15	5	17	37
2. Speaks Nuosu, writes Nuosu, no Han				
Male	0	0	2	2
Female	0	0	0	0
TOTAL	0	0	2	2
3. Speaks Nuosu, speaks Han, no writing				
Male	2	2	3	7
Female	2	7	4	13
TOTAL	4	9	7	20
4. Speaks Nuosu, writes Nuosu, speaks Han				
Male	3	1	3	7
Female	3	2	2	7
TOTAL	6	3	5	14
5. Speaks Nuosu, speaks Han, writes Han				
Male	6	10	8	24
Female	4	2	1	7
TOTAL	10	12	9	31

Literacy by Language

6. Literate in both
Speaks Nuosu, writes Nuosu, speaks Han, writes Han

	Age 8–20	Age 21–40	Age 41+	TOTAL
Male	18 (56%)	9 (41%)	7 (26%)	34 (42%)
Female	8 (28%)	2 (11%)	1 (5%)	11 (16%)
TOTAL	26 (43%)	11 (28%)	8 (17%)	45 (30%)

	Age 8–20	Age 21–40	Age 41+	TOTAL
Illiterate				
Groups 1, 3 (above)				
Male	5 (16%)	2 (9%)	7 (26%)	14 (17%)
Female	14 (48%)	12 (67%)	17 (81%)	43 (63%)
TOTAL	19 (31%)	14 (35%)	24 (50%)	57 (38%)
Literate in Nuosu				
Groups 2, 4, 6				
Male	21 (66%)	10 (45%)	12 (44%)	43 (53%)
Female	11 (37%)	4 (22%)	3 (14%)	18 (26%)
TOTAL	32 (49%)	14 (35%)	15 (31%)	61 (40%)
Literate in Han				
Groups 5, 6				
Male	24 (86%)	19 (86%)	15 (56%)	58 (72%)
Female	12 (41%)	4 (22%)	2 (10%)	18 (26%)
TOTAL	36 (59%)	23 (58%)	17 (35%)	76 (51%)
Han Spoken Language Ability				
No Han language				
Groups 1, 2				
Male	3 (9%)	0	6 (22%)	9 (11%)
Female	12 (49%)	5 (27%)	13 (86%)	30 (44%)
TOTAL	15 (17%)	5 (13%)	19 (40%)	39 (26%)
Speaks Han				
Groups 3, 4, 5, 6				
Male	29 (91%)	22 (100%)	21 (78%)	72 (89%)
Female	17 (51%)	13 (73%)	8 (38%)	38 (56%)
TOTAL	46 (83%)	35 (87%)	29 (60%)	110 (74%)
Total population surveyed				
Male	32	22	27	81
Female	29	18	21	68
TOTAL	61	40	48	149

In our own figures, we see some interesting patterns. Males are more likely at all ages to be literate in either language and to speak Han; literacy in Nuosu is either passing away or is acquired at later ages (or our figures may underestimate this slightly with the younger population, since we tended to concentrate on their school achievement). There has been, for sure, an improvement in male literacy in the Han language in the last forty years, and this undoubtedly reflects schooling. For women, the change has been less impressive, and fits with the observations that only a small minority of school children are girls. Somewhat more young women speak Han than do their mothers or grandmothers, but they are still overwhelmingly illiterate and monolingual.

The situation in Jiemo, down the hill and close to the town schools, is somewhat different, as shown in table 6.3. From careful examination of these tables, we see that the differences between Matolo and Jiemo are almost entirely in their competence in the Han language. Literacy in *Nuosu bburma* (Nuosu writing) is only slightly higher in Jiemo than in Matolo; in the younger age groups, a few more people in Jiemo are probably literate in Nuosu, because more of them go to school, and they learn Nuosu writing in school. But in the adult age groups, literacy in Nuosu is not very different—around 50 percent of the men, and only a small fraction of the women (15 percent or less) can read and write their language. This despite the fact that, as the villagers of Jiemo proudly told us, they had spontaneously been conducting their own adult literacy classes in the Nuosu language, and many women had attended them.

When we move to Han language ability, however, the differences between the two villages are striking. Male Han literacy is higher than female in every gender and age category, and Han literacy is lower in the over-forty age group than in the under-forties. But within every single gender and age category,[5] Han literacy is higher in the lowland villages. In other words, villagers of Jiemo have been able to go to school for the last thirty years, while villagers of Matolo have sent only a small number of their girls and only about two-thirds of their boys. Older women have rarely had the chance to learn to read and write in Han in either place, but in all the other categories, Jiemo villagers are more literate in the outsider language.

The same holds true for Han speaking ability, which is less closely correlated with schooling. Whereas a majority of males of all ages in both villages speak Han, the percentages are higher in Jiemo. Similarly, only a small fraction of Matolo women speak Han (13 percent), fully 56 percent of the Jiemo

---

5. Among women over forty, the difference is of course not significant, since there are only three such women in the two villages combined who can read and write Chinese.

women do, and much higher percentages do in the younger age groups. Much of this ability to speak Han is correlated with Han literacy, but not all of it; there are thirty-four people in Jiemo (23 percent of the total population) who speak Han but cannot read it, and 17 more in Matolo (12 percent of the total).

All of these differences in language ability are related to mobility. Men get about more than women, and lowland villagers more than mountain villagers. Mobility means going to the city (there is a road and a daily bus from Mishi Town, only a twenty-minute walk from the two Jiemo villages), it means going out to work (recall that only four villagers from Matolo have ever held salaried positions, while there are many cadres and others from Jiemo), and it means going to school (not only is attendance at the local school higher from the villages on the plain, but many more students have gone on to further education). And even here near the heart of Liangshan, where the government is making a huge effort to promote Nuosu as a language of schooling, bureaucracy, and mass media, the real route to success outside the tiny confines of Mishi lies in learning the Han language. This is why bilingual education is being relegated by Nuosu educational bureaucrats to the four most remote townships in all of Xide.

ETHNIC CULTURE AND CRAFTS

Ethnic markers such as dress, food, and housing have very little salience in the Mishi area, because everybody is Nuosu. After living in Yanyuan and visiting Nuosu communities in Yanbian and Miyi, where ethnic identity is a mosaic of chromatic textiles, with the Nuosu women the most colorful of all, I was astonished when I first arrived in Mishi that women did not wear Nuosu-style skirts or fancy jackets except for special occasions. They certainly had them; I purchased an exquisite embroidered jacket with rabbit-fur shoulder linings from a woman in the Mishi hospital who made such things for sale; and when the hospital workers wanted me to take their pictures, they all got decked out in their finest. But for the most part, in the town and in the villages, they went about in the usual trousers and tops of ordinary Chinese rural women, with only the embroidered head-cloth tied down by the long braids of the young women, and the black high-framed headdress on the mothers and grandmothers, distinguishing the village women from what Han peasant women would look like if there were any in the area, and not even that on many of the town women who worked in the government agencies. I asked all sorts of people why women did not wear Nuosu clothes for everyday wear here, as they did in Yanyuan and other areas, and the uniform answer was that such clothes were inconvenient for field and farm work. True enough, but presumably they are just as inconvenient, for example, for the road-building crews I saw in Malong and Guabie, which included women in pleated skirts. I think the real answer may be that there is no need for ethnic clothing to serve as an ethnic marker here, since everyone is Nuosu. Thus elaborate clothing can be saved for dress-up. Some people, both men and women, wear the *jieshy* and/or *vala* when the weather is cold, but this may be for the functional reason that these traditional garments are very warm, and at least as comfortable as the modern alternative, the green army overcoat.

Similarly, there is little fuss made about food. People eat potatoes most of the time, adding a little hot sauce and maybe drinking some sour-vegetable soup, and of course liquor when they can afford it. When guests come, they kill something, as is the custom everywhere. Housing, similarly, is a fact of life. These are certainly not Han-style houses; Nuosu people always have a hearth with three stones or andirons, an ancestral altar in an inner corner, and a half-loft above the main living area. But none of this serves as an ethnic marker; it is just how people live.

Paradoxically, however, there is one kind of ethnic marker that originates in the Mishi slice area that is less salient for the locals, because they do not need to mark their identity in any conscious way, than it is for the whole of Liangshan. This is the manufacture of red-yellow-black lacquered wooden din-nerware. It is practically impossible these days to go to an urban Nuosu house-hold in or out of Liangshan, and increasingly rare to go even to a farm family, where there are not at least a few pieces of this dinnerware, at the very least lit-tle shot glasses for downing grain liquor. Most of the dishes are now made in a pair of factories in Xide City and one in Zhaojue City, but the tradition is reported, by the local people at least, to have begun with the Jjivo clan in the village of Apu, which lies way up in the hills about halfway between Mishi and the township headquarters of Yilu, a quite poor, roadless township to which Apu belongs administratively.

Jjivo Munyu, a member of the dishes-making clan, is now vice-magistrate of Xide County and an amateur scholar of his own family's tradition. He writes that the Jjivo clan has a history of fifteen generations of manufacturing wooden dishes in Xide. According to the clan's own oral history, the first mem-ber to create wooden tools and dishes was Jjivo Jjieshy, a particularly skilled carpenter and woodworker. Jjieshy brought back advanced tools from Han areas at that time, and carved ritual implements in the shape of dragons and other animals for *bimo* to employ in exorcistic rituals. He also applied his skills to making various household implements such as buckets, and this was the begin-ning of the manufacture of dishes (Jiwu n.d.: 3).

Jjieshy's great-grandson moved to a place called Vaqiemu, where the craft was refined in two ways: lacquer pigments were extracted from local sources and applied to the wooden dishes, and the pit-lathe was invented for turning the dishes out of wooden blanks (ibid.: 4). Three generations later Jjivo Abi moved his branch of the clan to the present village of Apu, where further improvements have been made, generation by generation, in the selection of wood, improvement of pigments, and refinement of the designs. Finally, the high artistic standards of the present day have been achieved under the guidance and inspiration of Jjivo Vuqie, born in 1944, who now lives in Xide City.

We visited Apu in 1994 and recorded the process of manufacture in detail in writing and photographically. The following extract from my field notes, modified slightly, describes the process:

> The wood for any of the larger dishes is of a special kind. Wild cherry, called *huagao* in Han and *ngehni* in Yi, is cut and sold in the Mishi market by people from Bajjolomo, which is east of here, and is sold by the chunk, not by weight.
>
> They also make spoons (*ichy*), but the wood for them they can cut themselves in the neighboring hills—it is rhododendron (*shuohma*).
>
> When they first buy the wood, it has to dry out; they put it in an underground place where wind doesn't get to it, so that it will dry slowly. The piece we saw was coated with dirt when they first brought it out.
>
> The dishes are turned on a lathe, called *gedde*. It consists of two wooden seats, for one man each, which they sit on while they operate two long wooden foot pedals that are transverse to the seats, which lie one behind the other. The pedals are connected by a belt, formerly made of leather but now made from the inner part of a tire, which turns the rotor.
>
> The owner of the wood, who will make the dish, first hollows out a small hole (3 cm wide, 1 cm deep) in the middle of the blank, using an adze with a concave blade, about 3 cm wide and 1 cm deep, called a *zzo*. He then inserts the pointed end of the rotor in this hole. The rotor is called *zzowo* and consists of a 6– or 7–cm-thick, 60–cm-long wood cylinder, onto one end of which is hafted a conical iron blade, tapering to a point along a length of about 20 cm. This is pounded in with a wooden mallet made from a section of a pine trunk, with one side branch left as a handle.
>
> This assemblage (rotor, point, and blank) is then inserted between the two wooden rails that form the sides of the lathe. On the end where the blank is attached, there is a metal point called a *funzoddu*, and the mallet is used to pound the whole thing onto that point. In previous times, there used to be a similar point on the opposite rail; now they use a ball-bearing attached to the opposite

FIG. 6. Turning a bowl on the pit-lathe

rail—it turns more easily that way. The space between the rails, where the assemblage fits, can be adjusted for the depth of the blank.

Then the turning begins, with the carver giving instructions to the two pedalers when to start and stop (fig. 6). The carver turns the blank into the desired shape with a set of eight chisels, called *iku*, all hafted onto 60– or 70–cm-long rough, unturned pieces of wood. The chisels vary slightly in width and shape; all of them are hook-shaped on the end of a conical, iron base. . . . The carvers said that each slightly different one has a different use.

The carver alternates inner and outer surfaces of the dish. When the stump in the center where the rotor is pounded in is chiseled down to 1 cm or so thick, typically it breaks off, or the similar cone on the outside breaks off. The dish is then taken off the lathe and some more of the two cones are carved away using the adze.

We watched a bowl (ordinary rice-bowl size) being made, and I estimate that the whole process probably took twenty minutes from insertion to the final chopping with the adze. People told us that they can turn up to fifteen small or ten large dishes in a full day's work.

After it is turned, the dish still has to dry for a few days before it can be painted. The black is painted on first over the entire surface, usually excepting the bot-

FIG. 7. Lacquering a wooden bowl

tom (of any of the large, pedestal-bottomed dishes), as the base coat. Then it dries for a day, and the yellow is painted on, then it dries for another day, and they paint on the red.

They didn't have any blanks ready to paint when we were there, but one man demonstrated for us by painting over some of the red and yellow designs on a large bowl that was already painted (fig. 7).

The painter had a wooden box with a sliding top, which contained two small dishes for the pigments, and about twenty brushes. They make the brushes themselves using wooden sticks on the end of which various-shaped points of local goat wool are attached by wrapped thread. The brushes are called *ssema*, the little tiny one is called *qiema*, and the wooden paint-paddle, which has two flared ends about 4 cm long and 1.5 cm wide, is called a *ddivaddu*. The brushes have to be cleaned with tung oil, which is sold in the market.

Painting time varies greatly. One of the large rice dishes, with a fancy pattern, may require three to five days' work, or a full day's work for a simpler one. One large or two small soup tureens (*kuzzur*) can be painted in a day.

Only men work on the lathe, but both men and women paint designs on the dishes. Until recently, the tradition of painting belonged only to the Jjivo clan and their daughters-in-law, but in recent years affines marrying into the village have also taken up the craft, with the result that members of at least three other clans also know how to make and paint the dishes.

Since 1982 the craft of dish-making has spread beyond Apu, with the establishment of a factory in Xide City and another in Zhaojue. The dishes they produce are for the mass market and are turned on machine lathes, though they are painted by hand. They also include all sorts of nontraditional shapes and forms, including plates, rice bowls, tabletops, and even chopsticks. Jjivo Vuqie, the artist who inspired the latest refinements in design and technique, was originally hired as artistic director of the Xide factory, but in 1991 he became dissatisfied with two departures from what he considered the tradition—the high gloss coat that gives the factory dishes a modern sheen, and the change from a dull, slightly brownish-yellow color in the village dishes to a bright lemon-yellow in the factory ones. Vuqie thus became an entrepreneur, and now he has his own private factory, employing about twelve people, which uses machine techniques and continues the trend of innovative shapes but uses a lower-gloss paint and a duller yellow pigment.

A folk craft from one village in Mishi, passed down in a single clan for several hundred years and not well-known outside Nuosu society, has thus in recent years become an ethnic marker for Nuosu all over Liangshan and beyond. Museums covet the village-made utensils as a true folk art (I collected a set for the Burke Museum at the University of Washington, for example), but for most people, the factory dishes do just fine as an ethnic marker.[6]

HAUNTED BY THE HXIEMGA

The paradox of Mishi is that it is not one of those minority regions, such as the cities of Tibet (Schwartz 1993: 203) or even parts of Liangshan closer to main transport routes (Heberer 2001), where Han people are taking over. They are, in fact, almost completely absent in the daily life of most Nuosu people in Mishi. The cadres, the doctors, the extension agents, all are Nuosu; only a few teachers are actual Hxiemga. People are not ordinarily concerned with using ethnic markers to distinguish themselves from anyone else, and Nuosu cultural forms—house design, lack of attachment to place, clan solidarity, animal sacrifice, cape-wearing, and all sorts of rituals from weddings and funerals to exorcisms performed by *bimo* and *sunyi*—go on, especially in the post-

---

6. I treat the topic of Nuosu lacquerware, and its transformation from folk craft to ethnic commodity, more fully in Harrell 1999.

Cultural Revolution era, as taken-for-granted aspects of being human in such a place. But the physical absence of Hxiemga, and of corresponding Han cultural forms, hides a deeper-level, haunting presence. Even this ethnically homogeneous district has been incorporated into the People's Republic of China.

This is, for the people of Mishi, not necessarily all bad. They have some access to health care (though not much), some possibilities of outward and upward social mobility, some access to education, if they can afford it and get through the sometimes meaningless-seeming elementary grades. A few of them have joined the Communist Party or work in the government, or have become teachers. At the same time, there is a sense of loss, of something that seems to be gnawing the inside of the society, even though it comes from the outside. Consider:

> The villagers of Jiemo do not like to use the name Liberation Village, even though this would seem desirable in the communist order to which they belong. It would imply that they had been slaves, and having been slaves raises the suspicion that one's ancestors were Han. Still, at least one family there has named its daughter Hxiemgamo.
>
> A visit to a village by outsiders, themselves Nuosu (except for the curious American) prompts a serious discussion of what has gone wrong with society in the last few decades. A commonplace is repeated—before the Revolution, "there were no beggars in Nuosu areas" (Nuosu muddi zzahmo a jjo), because clans would take care of everyone, as was the case when the man was murdered while we were there. But now . . . there is a deterioration in social morals, and there are indeed beggars in Nuosu areas.
>
> Qumo Vake, the local boy who makes good, gives back to his own community by building a power station that may eventually light most of the homes. This is a right and proper thing to do. But then he overreaches; he adopts goals foreign to the community, just like the *tusi* who were driven out of the nuclear area in the Ming and Qing. He goes and gets a divorce and then marries a Hxiemgamo. People can say nothing about this, because he is rich and can do what he wants. And it is not terribly uncommon; I met a much richer entrepreneur in Ganluo who had the same ambition—he said he didn't think a Nuosu wife would respect him, if he cared so much about making money. But people feel uncomfortable with intermarriage, as if a haunting presence has taken one of their own. At least they say Qumo Vake's new wife is really ugly.

Recent writers on social memory (Abelman 1996) have talked about haunting—events of the past, though they are clearly in the past, are not safely in the past. In their absence, they continue to be present through memory. I would suggest that the presence of Hxiemga in places like Mishi is an analogous phenomenon, structured in space rather than time. Aspects of Chinese national culture, of Marxism-Leninism, of modernity (conceived of in Mishi as things of the Hxiemga, such as beggars and brash entrepreneurs) are more important in formulating the threat of Hxiemga than are actual Han people. These elements, which potentially represent the transformation of something familiar into something alien, are not present physically in Mishi, but they are an overwhelming presence in their absence.

Hxiemga is thus not so much another ethnic group to which to compare one's own, and certainly not any kind of people one sees very often unless one is a student or works in the schools. Hxiemga is a way of talking about selfishness, individual ambition, lack of solidarity, deterioration in social morals, the things that replace what is lost on the road to social change. It is also the bringer of education, material change, and opportunity. Individual Nuosu people adopt, sometimes enthusiastically, aspects of this outside presence—school, government service, Han language, entrepreneurship. But they do not trust it. Its presence is vague, distant, but no less threatening for that. *Nuosu muddi* can no longer be really autonomous, but then, of course, it never was. From enfeoffed *tusi* to slave raiding on the margins, Nuosu culture has always, from as early as we can discover, been shaped in reaction to the tempting, the corrupting, the haunting by those whose absence is such a huge presence in their lives—the Hxiemga.

7 / Baiwu: Nuosu in an Ethnic Mix

I f Hxiemga are a haunting presence for the people of Mishi, they are neighbors, rivals, and sometimes friends for many Nuosu people in Baiwu, a
township in Yanyuan, far on the other side of the Anning and Yalong Rivers.
There Nuosu, though now numerically dominant, were the last ethnic group
to arrive and have always lived with the everyday presence not only of Han, but
of Prmi, Naze, and sometimes other ethnic groups. In Baiwu, as contrasted to
Mishi, we come face-to-face with the operation of ethnicity and ethnic identity, where common history, descent, and culture all serve both to tie ethnic
groups together as collectivities and to mark the boundaries between them.

Baiwu Township is located thirty-five kilometers due north of the county
seat of Yanyuan, reached in less than an hour on a well-graded dirt road (maps
4 and 5). The little township headquarters seems much more like an actual town
than does the corresponding settlement at Mishi; in addition to the usual one-
and two-story courtyard buildings housing the township Party and government, the forestry bureau, the credit cooperative, the local hospital, and the
radio- and post administration, there are also a number of small shop-houses
that harbored, in 1993, three small restaurants, two video parlors, six lightly
stocked state stores (there were noticeably more a year and a half later), nine
privately owned stores, five one- or two-table pool halls, and two little hotels.
The smaller stores sell more or less the same things—liquor, beer, soft drinks
(which are too expensive for most people), cigarettes, matches, candles, toilet
paper, batteries. The larger ones offer clothing, and in the middle of the day
when the farmers come in to market, shopkeepers set out tables on the edge
of the single, paved street, offering clothing, cloth, and yarn, which Nuosu and
Prmi girls use to do their hair in fancy styles.

There is market activity in the middle of the day every day, and the street
in the winter sunshine is a riot of color, dominated by the bright skirts, blouses,
and embroidered headpieces of the Nuosu women and girls, along with the
more sedate, single-colored pleated skirts and embroidered aprons of the Prmi
women; bright blouses and blazers, in the city style, worn by young Han women;

129

FIG. 8. *Vala* as winter coat: Ma Erzi on a chilly morning

and the swaying fringes of the black, decoratively stitched *vala* of Nuosu men and women (figs. 8, 9). When farmers come in by horse or cart, one may glimpse a saddle painted in the same three-colored patterns found on the dishes from Mishi, and a few horses are often tied up near the unfinished fountain at the lower end of town. All of the stores are open at this time, and sheep or chickens may be for sale by people who have come in from the country; when someone comes with meat from a freshly killed yak, buyers cluster around arguing prices in several languages.

Contiguous with the town are two villages. Above the town is Hongxing (Red Star), whose population is entirely Nuosu, mostly *quho*, from the clans of Synzy, Lama, Ashy, Molie, and Jjike. Below the town is Lianhe (United) Village, which consists of Han, Prmi, Naze, and Naxi, with no Nuosu. Outside the immediate vicinity of the town, the population is almost entirely Nuosu; the only exceptions are a couple of villages that are part Nuosu and part Prmi. In sheer numerical terms, Baiwu Township is thus overwhelmingly Nuosu; the *minzu* distribution of the population in 1993 is shown in table 7.1. In Baiwu Administrative Village, however, the population is only 81 percent Nuosu, and this includes two more distant natural villages, Yangjuan and Pianshui, that are entirely Nuosu. In the villages attached to the town, then, the population

FIG. 9. *Vala* as ceremonial dress: a member of the groom's family
at a wedding, dancing to bring gifts to the bride's family

is slightly over half Nuosu and slightly less than half everything else, with 160
Han, 57 Prmi, and 60 Naxi. Nuosu who either live in Hongxing or come to
town thus have to deal with members of other ethnic groups on a regular basis.

Baiwu, like Mishi, was once the headquarters of a *qu*, a unit comprising four
townships, which was abolished in most of Liangshan in 1992. But Baiwu still
retains the government offices of the forestry bureau, grain administration,
postal administration, and hospital, and most important, it contains, like Mishi,
both a six-grade elementary school and a three-grade junior middle school.
Both schools are located on the upper side of town, contiguous to the Nuosu
village at Hongxing.

Despite its relatively good transport network and its proximity to town,
because Baiwu lies in Yanyuan, one of the poorer counties in Liangshan, economic development has proceeded slowly here, as in Mishi. Electricity was connected to the town only in January 1993 (I was there for the grand celebration),
and although it had reached most of the village homes in Hongxing and Lianhe
by late 1994, at that time it was still to be connected even to the nearby villages
of Pianshui and Yangjuan, and to the plateau area of scattered housing called
Lamata, let alone to any of the more remote villages around the edges of the

TABLE 7.1

Population of Baiwu Township by Ethnic Group, 1993

Minzu	Autonym	Name in Nuosu language	Population	Percent of total
Yi	Nuosu	Nuosu	9,734	92%
Han	Han	Hxiemga	307	3%
Zang	Prmi	Ozzu	359	4%
Meng	Naze	Ozzu	58	.6%
Naxi	Naxi	Naxi or Ozzu	46	.5%
Others			28	.3%
TOTAL			10,532	

Baiwu basin or in the foothills. There is no industrial or craft production whatsoever, and even agriculture on the broad Baiwu plain is restricted by the cold climate at this altitude, as well as the lack of rainfall outside the summer season. The township head told me that he thought the per capita income for 1992 had been about ¥340, but he managed to figure it in a manner that would reduce it to ¥240, which brought Baiwu in below the poverty line and thus retained eligibility for certain kinds of economic assistance. In fact, one of the cadres in the local finance office told me that the total tax and other monetary revenue for the local government was only about ¥80,000 per year (about ¥7 per person), compared to the state investment in development (mostly infrastructure) of around ¥300,000.

According to most local cadres and many other people, however, this "backwardness" was about to change; in 1993 and 1994 they saw Baiwu as on the road to development and prosperity, all because of apples. A wealthy entrepreneur who hails from Lamata in Baiwu Village explained it to me: Yanyuan apples are of the highest grade, along with those grown in only a few other places in China, some of them in Xinjiang. The market right now is unlimited, as urbanites strive to include more fruit in their diet, and even rural areas in the populous parts of Sichuan, not to speak of the expanding populations of Panzhihua and Xichang, will always buy more apples. All that is needed for the crop to really take off, he said, is to build a decent highway between Yanyuan and Xichang. This, he also said, would make up for the exploitative way that the Han-dominated government has treated the Nuosu homeland of Liangshan.

TABLE 7.2

Apple Orchard Ownership among Yangjuan and Hongxing Households

Number of trees	Mgebbu in Yangjuan	Former Slaves of Mgebbu, Yangjuan	Nuosu, Hongxing	TOTAL
None	28	9	25	62
1–50	7	4	5	16
50–100	0	1	4	5
100–200	9	2	9	20
200–500	7	0	1	8
500+	2	1	2	5
Mature trees	5	3	4	12

In fact, a large number of people all over central Yanyuan are planting apples, getting long-term leases (*chengbao*) on the land, and borrowing money from friends, relatives, and the agricultural bank to buy the seedlings. An incomplete but not systematically biased survey of 119 households in Hongxing and Yangjuan yielded the numbers in table 7.2. We can see from this table that nearly half of the Nuosu households surveyed (57 of 119) had planted apple orchards. In the mid-1990s, Han and other ethnic groups were also joining the rush. Many other families who had not yet planted in 1993 were preparing to plant. Everywhere on the Baiwu plain, one sees neat grids of trees, trunks whitened with a protective substance, all enclosed by mud walls that keep out marauding livestock.

Some of the orchards, as table 7.2 indicates, are quite large. Only a few of the orchards are mature, that is, planted six or more years ago and beginning to yield significant quantities of apples. The largest mature orchards in 1993 had 150 to 160 trees, which at a yield of 100 *jin* (one *jin* equals .5 kg) of apples per tree (some large trees yield several hundred), at a price of ¥.8 per *jin*, would bring in income of about ¥12,000, minus expenses. When the really big orchards, ranging up to 1,000 trees, come on line, if the price holds there will be a big infusion of income into this area, and many people are hoping that this will be the beginning of sustainable economic development. As of 1993, however, this was mostly a fond hope; the township head told me there were no more than four true ¥10,000 families in the township.

HISTORY

There is little doubt that the Prmi, Naze, and Naxi came to Baiwu before the Han or Nuosu. The area that is now Yanyuan and Muli was incorporated into the Chinese empire during the Han dynasty, lost again during the period of disunity, recovered again in the early Tang, but then lost to Nanzhao and Dali from the late eighth century until the Yuan reconquest in the 1250s (Fu 1983: 130–38); during the Ming period it was transferred from the jurisdiction of Yunnan to that of Sichuan. Around the old garrison town of Yanjing (Salt Well), imperial administration prevailed from the Ming on, but the specific political authorities that ruled the outlying regions date their imperial mandates as *tusi* back to only the early eighteenth century. The plains and valleys around Baiwu sat at the conjunction of the domains of three different *tusi*. The territory around the current site of Baiwu Town belonged to the Great Lama, or king of Muli (see Rock 1930), who was established officially as a *tusi* in 1710. He was ethnically Prmi but was also a monk-official of the Gelug-pa sect, which ruled Tibet, and was supported religiously by an incarnate lama whose seats were the same three monasteries, all within the boundaries of today's Muli County, from whence the Great Lama ruled.

In addition to the three great monasteries of the Great Lama's regime, there were also the "twenty-four little temples," one of which was only about a fifteen-minute walk from today's Baiwu Town. This temple, according to a descendant of the local official family, had from two to five monks in the early twentieth century. The civil administration was handled by an official of the Shu family (now classified as Naxi) called the *bazong*; other members of what are now the Naxi, Zang (Prmi), and Meng (Naze) *minzu* owed labor services to the *bazong*, and through him to the Muli administration, in return for farming the land. Some of the families also owned land privately in this area, and Han farmers came into the region at various times. They paid rent but did not owe labor services.

Toward the east of Baiwu Town, there were similar arrangements, but there the land belonged to the Guabie *tusi*, who was ethnically Naze, and also enfeoffed in the early eighteenth century. Finally, some of the land to the west of Baiwu Town was controlled by the Guboshu *tusi*, another Naze ruler enfeoffed at about the same time. Both of these *tusi* families professed Buddhism and supported small monastic establishments; unlike the Muli ruler, neither was a monk nor could boast an incarnate lama in his little monastery.

It seems probable that the population under the rule of these various *tusi* up until about 1800 was quite sparse; people report that even up to the 1950s, there were a lot more trees on the foothills and even on the plains than there are now. The small population consisted mostly of speakers of Prmi and Naze (and perhaps Naxi), who were nominally Buddhists but also practiced many rites of native priestly traditions called *hangue* (Prmi) and *ndaba* (Naze).[1] There may also have been Han tenants from time to time; although no Han families in the immediate Baiwu area now trace their ancestry back that far, there was a place called Yunnan Village, near the current settlement of Shanmen on the road from Baiwu to Yanyuan City, whose population was mostly Han at least six generations ago. There are still some Han living in Shanmen, according to township population statistics; I have not been there.

The ethnic composition of this area, however, was dramatically altered beginning with the migration of Nuosu clans out of Zhaojue and Puxiong eight or nine generations before the present (see chap. 5). Probably sometime in the late Qianlong period, in the late eighteenth century,[2] two branches of the *nuoho* Loho clan left Zhaojue, and eight generations before the present middle-aged men, they settled in various parts of Yanyuan and the remote northern regions of Yanbian. One of the regions where they settled was Baiwu, where most of them lived to the north and northeast of the town around the present site of Yangjuan.

Among the retainers who migrated with the Lohos or came a few decades afterward and became their retainers were the Mgebbu, Ali, Ddi, and Jjizi *quho* clans. These Nuosu clans, through both land purchase and warfare, gradually expanded at the expense of the representatives of the king of Muli, the *bazong* and his retainers. By the early twentieth century, about one thousand *mu* of land, mostly on the side of the river toward Baiwu Town, still belonged to the Ozzu (Prmi and Naxi); the rest was considered territory of the various Nuosu clans (both *nuoho* and *quho*), while individual plots were privately owned and patrilineally inheritable. In general, relations were peaceful most of the time, and there was considerable co-godparenthood between Nuosu and Prmi (and sometimes Han), to the point that my collaborator Ma Erzi calls a lot of people *shushu* (father's younger brother) who are Prmi or Han. But there were fights

---

1. I treat the relationship between Buddhism, older priestly practices, and ethnicity among Prmi and Naze, as well as many of their other customs that serve as ethnic markers, in detail in chapters 10 and 11. Here the point is simply to delineate the place of these people in the ethnohistory and ethnic relations of Baiwu.

2. It is always difficult to assign dates in Nuosu history, since the oral histories recited by members of different clans speak in terms of generations rather than years. This is the same problem encountered with the history of the Jjivo lacquerware makers (see chap. 6).

also, including a skirmish that reduced the territory of the *bazong* considerably in the 1940s, and other smaller feuds over real or imagined slights. For example, when one of the powerful Mgebbu elders was drinking with a local Ozzu shortly after one of the Nuosu elder's cattle got into the Ozzu's field and ate some of his grain, the Ozzu leader, a man with a very fierce reputation, became drunk and struck the Nuosu elder, at which point the Mgebbu went to an area called Gangou and rounded up about twenty clan relatives, who trashed the Ozzu's house and stole, slaughtered, and ate his best plow ox. According to the man who told me the story (the grandson of the Nuosu leader), the Ozzu realized he was wrong, and thus accepted compensation from the Nuosu rather than prolong the dispute.

It may be that such fights between Prmi and Nuosu were no fiercer or more common than fights among Nuosu clans themselves, such as that between the Mgebbus and Qumos in the 1940s and '50s, which resulted in a prohibition on intermarriage that has lasted until the present. In addition, of course, there were ruler-subject relations between the Lohos and their *quho* retainers. According to knowledgeable men of both clans, the obligations of the retainers to the lords included gifts of liquor and a pig's head at the New Year, weddings, and other occasions; fighting for the lord whenever he went to war against other *nuoho*; and three days' labor per month on the fields of the lords. Some *quho*, however, ignored the latter stipulation or, if they were rich, sent their slaves to fulfill it.

In the democratic reforms of the late 1950s, people were classified according to their ownership of land and slaves, rather than their caste position, with the result that many of the Mgebbus and other wealthy retainer clans were classified as slavelords or as wealthy producers, a term equivalent to "rich peasants" in the Han areas. Others, mostly *quho* and *mgajie*, were "half slaves," and of course slaves (*gaxy*) were classified as slaves. Some of the Lohos, as well as members of other *nuoho* clans with whom they intermarried, initially cooperated with the Communist authorities but turned rebel when the policy became harsh; certain Loho families lost large numbers of men to war and disease during this time. Other Nuosu, particularly poor peasants and slaves, joined the Communist Party, and some of them fought in the militias who put down the rebellions.

Nuosu seem to have been the only outright rebels against the reform policies of the late 1950s, but they were not alone in having their relations of production disturbed by the democratic reforms; the *bazong* family also lost its traditional base in land stewardship and became ordinary farmers.

Immediately after the democratic reforms came collectivization. At this time, there were large movements of population, which ended up producing the settlement pattern that persists to this day. The dispersed housing of Lohos, various *quho* clans, and slaves to the north of the town was disrupted when the Lohos all moved out, to areas near Yanyuan city among other places, leaving very few *nuoho* in the entire Baiwu area. The Mgebbus were called together by one of their leaders into the present village of Yangjuan, where they are now numerically predominant, while most of the *mgajie* and *gaxy* settled in Pianshui, a village that had a reputation during the time of collective agriculture as the poorest team in the brigade. Members of various clans who lived south of town were brought together in the new village (then a production team) of Hongxing, while members of every ethnic group other than Nuosu were clustered into the Lianhe production team, centered around the imposing old stone house of the *bazong*, which stands to this day. The longtime Nuosu Party secretary of Baiwu Village (then brigade) told me that the ethnic division was agreed upon by everyone. Not only would the Nuosu and other ethnic groups be able to conduct all their local affairs in their own language this way (all of the Prmi and Naxi spoke Han fluently), but also people just "felt better inside" being grouped with their own kind. North and northwest of town, however, the old pattern of dispersed housing remained and continues today, often with several hundred meters between each compound or little cluster of compounds.

From the time of the Great Leap Forward on into the Cultural Revolution, there was also an attempt to open up more land for farming, with the result that many great forests were cut down, and the plains and foothills around Baiwu have not regrown their former forest cover. Residents of the area lament this destruction almost constantly.

During the Cultural Revolution, Baiwu was not immune to the struggles and factional attacks so familiar to students of China proper. Red Guards from Yanyuan Town came as far as remote Yangjuan to attack former slavelords, and one man, who was twenty-two at the time of the democratic reforms, was strung up on the rafters of his own house for several hours while the Red Guards went to attend to other business. When they came back to administer a further beating, the former young slavelord's wife had enough, lashed out at the Red Guards with red-hot fire tongs, and cut her husband down. After this, the radicals did not return. Factional disputes also resulted in the temporary overthrow of the local cadres, but their positions were restored within a year.

In 1982 collective agriculture was dismantled, and land divided among individual households of all ethnic groups. There was, however, not much in the way of economic development until the late 1980s, with the beginning of the commercial fruit industry.[3]

LANGUAGE AND SCHOOLING

In Baiwu there is no single predominant language. Nuosu and Han vie for supremacy in different contexts, with Prmi relegated to a distant third, a locally moribund tongue used only by a few older people, and by them only at home. Both Nuosu and Han, on the other hand, are languages both of everyday conversation and of official discourse.

Just about everyone under fifty, and a considerable number of the older men and women in the town of Baiwu and its attached and nearby villages, are fluent in both Nuosu and Han. Sometimes this is not entirely obvious at first glance. For example, Ma Erzi is quite friendly with a family named Xu; he calls the father of the family Uncle Xu in the Han language. When we visited them several times in 1993, the father (a Han) and most of the children always spoke with us in Han, while the mother, a Prmi, spoke Nuosu. I assumed the father did not speak any Nuosu, but Ma just laughed at me. "He won't speak it with me or people around here who know Han, but he can speak it perfectly well when he has to deal with Nuosu from the mountains." In another instance, I heard a Mr. Chen, the team leader of Lianhe, joking with some Nuosu friends in the Nuosu language; he then used Nuosu to offer me a cigarette. When Nuosu and Prmi converse, they may speak either Han or Nuosu according to the context and the individual abilities of the speakers; nobody in and around the town who is not Prmi or Naxi knows more than a few isolated words of Prmi.

In the village of Changma, about an hour-and-a-half walk northwest from the town, the population is about half Nuosu and half Prmi, and the local schoolteacher there told us that by the time children are of school age, they all can speak both Prmi and Nuosu, and some have already picked up a fair smattering of Han, which makes teaching easier.

In Yangjuan Village, by contrast, where everybody is Nuosu, people of the older generations are less likely to know Han fluently. Many men sixty and

---

3. Some parts of this history of Baiwu are corroborated by more than one person; others are uncorroborated but fit. I am indebted to the following people for portions of the story: Mgebbu Lunzy (Ma Erzi) and his father Mgebbu Ashy (both originally from Yangjuan), Party Secretary Lama Muga (from Hongxing), Yanyuan local historian Loho Tuha (Hu Jin'ao) [the preceding all Nuosu], and Shu Maolin (Naxi), descendant of the *bazongs* of Baiwu.

over in Yangjuan know a little Han; when I speak with them we get by in a mixture if nobody truly bilingual is in attendance. Ma's father's elder sister (1919–98), did not speak more than a few words of Han, and this is probably typical for the elder generation of women there. In addition, children ordinarily do not learn much of the Han language until they are of school age; if they do not go to school, they still tend to pick it up in town, sometimes with explicit instruction from their families. Ma tells stories of not understanding much of what the teacher said in the first few years of school, and teachers in the Baiwu elementary school confirm that you have to be able to speak Nuosu if you are going to teach first or second grade, since you at least have to give instructions in Nuosu, even though the lessons themselves are in Han.

There are, in this kind of mixed linguistic situation, mutual influences between the two languages. Here as elsewhere, Nuosu has borrowed a lot of Han words, and Han speech has borrowed Tibeto-Burman syntactic and phonetic patterns: people often say, in Han, things such as "Fa[n] chile meiyou?" (lit., "Rice eaten not eaten?" or, "Have [you] eaten yet?"), which adopts the Tibeto-Burman subject-object-verb word order. Liangshan Han dialects in general, perhaps under the influence of Nuosu, which has no syllable-final consonants, have also converted their syllable-final n (and sometimes also ng) to a nasalized vowel, so that I was once told by a Nuosu entrepreneur, "Ngome yao fazha ngomedi jingji, yao duo mai pigu," which means "If we're going to develop our economy, we need to sell more apples," but sounds, in standard Chinese, like " . . . we need to sell more backsides." And Han of all ages, including those who speak no Nuosu, universally use the Nuosu exclamation of surprise, "Abbe!" instead of the "Aiya!" common in other dialects of Mandarin.

In official contexts, language appears in a great variety of mixtures. Most government documents are in Han (though some forms for filling out, and most government signs, are usually bilingual), and there is still very limited opportunity for the use of Nuosu writing in official contexts. But spoken language is another matter, as illustrated by the speeches given in a packed, fluorescently lighted room by government dignitaries at the grand ceremony celebrating the connection of the town to the electrical grid in 1993. The first speaker was Sha Decai, a Nuosu and head of the township government. He spoke entirely in Han, as did the next speaker, the former Party secretary of the now-defunct *qu*, or district. Then Township Head Sha introduced the highest ranking dignitary, Vice-Secretary Yang of the County Party Committee, a Nuosu, who spoke almost entirely in that language, inserting here and there a Han vocabulary item. He was followed by another vice-secretary, a Han named Chen, who apparently knew no Nuosu and spoke in Chongqing dialect, somewhat different from Liangshan Han speech, but still readily comprehensible to much of the audience. Once he had introduced these high-ranking officials, Township Head Sha seemed to relax a bit, for he used Nuosu to introduce the next speaker, a Mr. Li from the county electric company, a Nuosu from Yanyuan who has traveled all over China and even to Singapore. Mr. Li spoke a complete jumble of the two languages, but even when he was in the Nuosu sentence-mode, he used a lot of Han phrases, such as *guahao jianshe* (grasp construction), *dianshi ji* (television set), *lao baixing* (common people), the numbers for the prices of electric power, and the titles of government officials and organizations. A local Party cadre then spoke in Nuosu, Vice-Secretary Chen again in Han, and then finally the head of the county People's Consultative Conference (an office that, in Liangshan, would always be held by a member of an ethnic minority), gave another speech in which he switched, seemingly randomly, between the two languages.

It is difficult to understand this public use of Nuosu and Han languages in terms of the usual theories of code-switching, in which people in polyglossic situations switch from one language or variety to another according to the situation, the interlocutors, and the topic (Heller 1988: 6). Here the situation was the same for everyone, the audience also remained constant, and the topics all had to do with the benefits of electricity for economic development. What does seem clear is that many Nuosu cadres are, on the one hand, accustomed to the Han language governmental idiom used to speak of such phenomena as economic and infrastructural development. On the other hand, all of them unfailingly are saturated with ethnic pride and ethnic identity, and want to speak their own language when they can, especially to a Nuosu audience. These contradictory forces pull upon them whenever they are in their official role, and they thus code-switch without regard to context or content.

The names of the Nuosu cadres, however, tell us immediately that they come from a mixed area where the influence of the Han language is pervasive. All the Nuosu lineages in this area carry one-syllable, Han-type surnames, which are used in school, in official life, and any other time they are speaking the Han language. The local branches of the Loho clan, for example, carry a Han surname pronounced Hu in standard Chinese, but locally pronounced Fu. The Mgebbus are Mas (thus Mgebbu Lunzy is Ma Erzi, his father Mgebbu Axshy is Ma Ashi, and his nephew Mgebbu Vihly, head of the county animal husbandry bureau, is Ma Wei'er); the Hiesses are Lis, the Lamas are Mas (Mgebbu and Lama, both *quho* clans, can intermarry, even though their Han surnames are both Ma). Members of different local lineages of the same clan often carry different Han surnames as well (Shama Qubi is locally Sha, Ma, Qu, Qiu, Bai, or Bi), and of course several different surnames are shared by members of several ethnic groups; Prmi tend to be surnamed Yang, Dong, or Xiong, and Yang is also a common Han surname for Nuosu, and of course for the Han themselves.

This situation contrasts sharply to that in Mishi and other parts of the Liangshan nuclear area. There Nuosu clan names are simply transliterated into Chinese characters, so that for example Hielie becomes Hailai, Shama remains Shama, and Alur becomes A'er. In the nuclear areas, even the Han language preserves the original clan names; there the Han language must adapt itself to local reality, which is ethnically entirely Nuosu. In Yanyuan, by contrast, Han-language surnames are part of a common idiom shared by all ethnic groups in the area, but they do not necessarily conform to the kinship systems of the ethnic groups that use them.

Also in contrast to Mishi, the primarily Han-language educational system in Baiwu has produced a large number of graduates who have gone on to higher schooling and full participation in the larger Chinese society of Liangshan and beyond. Many of the Lohos, who left the area after the democratic reforms, are prominent in educational circles in Yanyuan and elsewhere, but the greatest achievement among the local clans has belonged to the Mgebbus. This is perhaps because the Lohos and Mgebbus had a head start on Han language education even before the Communist takeover. During the Republican era, it had become clear to political leaders in Liangshan, partly under the influence of the *tusi* and Whampoa Military Academy graduate Leng Guangdian, that the future lay in some sort of accommodation with Chinese society and political power, and the leaders of the Loho clan in Baiwu became part of this movement. In 1943 one of them went to Xichang and met a young man named Wu, a scholarly boy from central Sichuan, who was not able to go to middle school because of his family's poverty. The Lohos offered him long-term employment; he lived in the house of one of the Loho leaders, and in return for room and board taught a *sishu*, a traditional private school where local boys learned the Confucian classics. All of the students in the *sishu* were from the Loho and their retainer clans, including several from the Mgebbu.

Later on, Mr. Wu was succeeded by a Mr. Yuan, and after the democratic reforms, Teacher Yuan stayed in the village and settled down, but the *sishu* was abolished and replaced by an elementary school in 1956; many of the current county political leaders were students in the first few classes. Mgebbu students did well there also, and there have up until the present been ten college students from the Mgebbus of Yangjuan, studying at places such as Central Nationalities University, Southwest Nationalities Institute, Southwest Financial and Economic College, Liangshan University, and, most remarkably, the Central Music Conservatory in Beijing, where one young man in 1993 was completing a degree in vocal performance; he sang Verdi as part of the entertainment at a Nuosu village wedding.[4]

Baiwu and the neighboring township of Dalin now boast both a six-year complete elementary school and a three-year middle school in Baiwu Town, as well as twelve other elementary schools, ranging from one to six years. Enrollment in the Baiwu middle school (which, like its counterpart in Mishi, is never the first choice for graduates of the elementary school) was higher in 1994 than at any time since it became possible for elementary graduates to go elsewhere; there were 100 students in four classes. Similarly, the elementary school was bursting at the seams; 659 students in 14 classes were its largest enrollment ever. But even with the increased commitment to education in the past few years, there remains a large gender imbalance in both schools. In the middle school, just 18 of 95 Nuosu students were girls (as contrasted to 9 of 18 Han and Prmi students), and in the regular, Han language classes of the elementary school, only 143 out of 440 Nuosu students (and 10 of 28 Han and Prmi students) were female. It appeared that education, while increasingly common among boys, still failed to reach very many girls.

It is thus extremely interesting what happened when, in the spring of 1994, the principal of the Baiwu elementary school decided to organize a class to be taught primarily in the Nuosu (Yi) language. The regular classes, like those in Mishi, teach written Nuosu only as a single subject, and starting only in the third grade. But the "Yi-language class," the first to be recruited since 1984, would use the Nuosu language to teach all subjects except Han language and literature. Word went out to the villages, and the place was mobbed with registrants; 117 children signed up for the Yi language class and, reluctant to turn anyone away, the principal recruited another teacher (with no state salary available, the second teacher had to be *minban*, or paid for out of local tuition and fees). The most notable thing about the registrants, however, is that they were mostly girls—sixty, as opposed to fifty-one boys, in contrast to twenty girls and forty boys in that year's first-grade Han-language class—and that many of them were in their middle or even late teens.

The Baiwu elementary school first-grade classroom in fall 1994 thus presented the odd but inspiring spectacle of little first-grade age children in the

---

4. The story of education in Baiwu, in particular the ethnic dimensions of school success, is treated in the most detail in Harrell and Ma 1999. A briefer analysis of the ethnic dimension is also given in chapter 15.

front rows, backed up by fully-grown young adult women and a few adult men as well. The teenage students have exchanged their skirts and headcloths for ordinary trousers and bright-colored scarves, but they still stand out in a situation where no Han girl would wear a scarf, and they appear very intent and serious about the first-grade lessons. Ma Erzi and I tried to interview the students about their experience, but they were embarrassed and we were mobbed by younger students coming to look at the foreigner, so we could only ask a few basic questions of the students, and we talked to several of the teachers (all local Nuosu) about what had happened.

When the call went out for students to register for the Yi-language class, apparently teenage girls in several surrounding villages got together and talked about the possibility of starting school, even at their relatively advanced ages. They did not want to go through life illiterate, but had previously felt daunted by having to study in a language with which they felt insufficiently familiar. So they came in groups; in almost every case, there was more than one teenage student from a particular village. Many parents supported the girls' decision initially, but others opposed it, and some girls surreptitiously took Sichuan peppercorns from their families' harvest and sold them in the market to be able to pay for tuition and books. One twenty-four-year-old woman, already married but not yet living with her husband, who came was taken back home by her father, who did not want her to jeopardize the marriage.

In the school statistics, there are very few first-graders listed as being of advanced age. This is, according to the teachers, because the teenagers simply gave their ages as much younger than the actual figures, in order not to stand out among their classmates. When we interviewed them, several women who appeared fully grown and adult gave their ages as 12 or 13, plausible perhaps in the protein-rich American suburbs, but extremely unlikely for Nuosu in Liangshan.

It is difficult to predict how long this trend of Nuosu-language education for female students might last. Certainly the obstacles are formidable, not the least of them the fact that someone who starts at seventeen will not even finish elementary school until twenty-two, by which age almost all women are married. And there is no possibility of skipping grades, since there are no higher-level Yi-language classes as yet, though this of course may change. For this reason, one young teacher persuaded his nineteen-year-old first-grade sister to transfer to the Han-language class, where she could move faster, and of course offered her help, something that would not be available to most of the teenage girls. In 1996 she was in the sixth grade. But the eagerness of these teenagers to get a Nuosu-language education, even an elementary one, speaks against

the stereotype of conservatism and indifference to modern change often lev-
eled at the Nuosu. In Baiwu at least, what women seem to feel uncomfortable
with is not modern education, but Han-language education, and it is quite possible that if Nuosu-language primary education is expanded, the schooling and
literacy rates for women in places like Baiwu will increase dramatically in the
coming years.[5]

KINSHIP AND CULTURE AS DEFINERS
OF ETHNIC IDENTITY

Baiwu is like many other places I have visited, where Nuosu as an ethnic group
are defined not only by their history, as recounted briefly above, but also by
their common kinship and by cultural markers of ethnic distinctiveness.

Charles Keyes, in a now-classic article (1976) has pointed to belief in common descent as an important defining characteristic of ethnic groups, and certainly this is true both literally and metaphorically for Nuosu in Baiwu.
Everyone's primary identity is a clan identity, and that clan identity indicates
not only ethnicity but also caste membership; there are no more *nuoho* since
the Lohos moved out, but there are *quho* and *mgajie*, and the barriers are strict
between them. These barriers are maintained not only by genealogical recita-
tion, which enforces the stories of common descent, but also by strict caste
endogamy; not only descent but also affinity is an important aspect of kinship
that binds members of a caste together. In our survey of over two hundred
marriages, we found only two between *quho* and *mgajie*, and one more between
quho and *nuoho*.

Almost as strong as the marital barrier between castes is the prohibition on
intermarriage with other ethnic groups. Our survey recorded five marriages
between Nuosu and other ethnic groups in Baiwu; two of these have involved
high-school educated Nuosu and Prmi or Naze who have met in a partially
de-ethnicized urban context. There have, however, also been three interethnic
marriages between villagers, two of which took place before the Communist
takeover. One was a legitimate arranged marriage between a Mgebbu woman
and a member of a Naze family; another involved a Prmi from Changma Village
who was captured as a slave in a raid by the Lohos; he was sold to Zhaojue in

5. This may, in fact, happen in the next few years. Ma Erzi started, with overseas financial
help, a model elementary school in Yangjuan Village, which opened in fall 2000. This school is
taught bilingually and attempts to enroll equal numbers of girls and boys, as well as numbers of
qunuo and *mgajie* proportional to their population.

the nuclear area, where he married another slave of his owner, whom he brought back to the Baiwu area after the Democratic Reforms. The slave castes of the Nuosu were long replenished by marriage with captured Han, so this marriage does not fall outside of traditional Nuosu norms. Since the democratic reforms, there has been only one Nuosu-Han marriage among villagers; apparently a young Han woman who worked in a store in Baiwu town simply fell in love with a Nuosu from Lamata who often traded at her store; they now live in Lianhe (where mixed ethnicity is common), but their children are classified as Yi, in order to take advantage of affirmative action policies.

Nuosu practice of ethnic endogamy in Baiwu is typical of ethnically mixed areas I have visited in various parts of Liangshan. Places like Mishi, of course, are not at issue; there is nobody else to marry unless you are a shameless social climber. But in Gaoping, Yanbian, for example, the first Nuosu community where I lived, I first heard the sayings that "Yi and Han are two separate families" (Yizu Hanzu shi liang jia) and "Water buffaloes get it on with water buffaloes; oxen get it on with oxen" (Shuiniu shuiniu guo; huangniu huangniu guo), referring to the structuralist equation, universal in Liangshan, of Han with water buffaloes and Nuosu with oxen.[6] (In some places, such as Baiwu, where there are a lot of Prmi, associated with Tibetan culture and classified as Zang, they enter the equation as a third element—yaks, or *maoniu*.) And in Gaoping, there was only one recorded intermarriage, an urban-generated one between a Han schoolteacher and a Nuosu former county cadre. The situation was the same in Puwei and Malong in Miyi, as well as in Gaizu and its environs near Lugu Lake, and in Hema Township in Ganluo. Whatever other relations Nuosu have with different ethnic groups, friendly or hostile or a combination of the two, they do not intermarry.

At the same time, it is possible to use similar metaphors about animals to deliver a different message. More than once I have heard cadres, eager to promote the government line of harmony among *minzu* (*minzu tuanjie*), say that, well, water buffaloes are water buffaloes, oxen are oxen, but they are all cattle (*shuiniu shi shuiniu, huangniu shi huangniu, buguo dou shi niu*).

Common descent and endogamy are one group of the signs of ethnic solidarity and distinctiveness among the Nuosu; the other consists of those cultural features known as ethnic markers (Keyes 1996). The most salient of these are dress, architecture, and ritual.

Nuosu women's dress stands out in places like Baiwu as the single most vis-

---

6. In some places water buffaloes and oxen are replaced with goats for Han (because they sometimes grow beards) and sheep for Nuosu (because they traditionally did not grow beards).

ible sign of ethnic group membership and identity. Young women wear a "hundred pleated," ankle-length, full skirt, which in this area has a black border around the hem, two broad horizontal bands of bright colors in the middle, and a wine-red, unpleated band at the top. Jackets are usually sleeveless, with intricate embroidered and inlaid patterns of colored thread, and these days as often as not worn over store-bought blouses. An intricately embroidered head cloth is secured by means of long braids tied over it; in cold weather, plaid scarves may also be added. Colorful wooden beads are often complemented by fine silver rings and earrings. In the wintertime, women, like men, may also wear the felt *jieshy* and/or the woven woolen *vala* with the long fringe around the hem.

Nuosu women in other areas vary this outfit; indeed one can tell, with a little practice, not only the age and marital status of a woman (married women with children wear a black headcloth, and older ladies favor subdued colors) but her county and sometimes township of residence from her dress. Women from Gaoping in Yanbian, in the Suondi (southern) dialect area, for example, have a distinctive particolored band in the lower-middle part of the skirt, and when they are young wear a diamond-shaped, black cap secured with a red ribbon or yarn. When they grow older, they wear a floral-patterned towel as a headcloth. In Guabie in 1994, many young women wore artificial flowers in their headdresses. But there is never any overlap between the dress of Nuosu women and that of other groups; any woman dressed like this (or any man or woman wearing a *vala*) can immediately be identified as Nuosu.[7]

Still, as with the animal metaphors, there is room here for ethnic coalition-building. Twice I have paid visits in a Nuosu friend's company to wedding or holiday gatherings in Prmi or Naze houses and been greeted with the saying that "everyone who wears skirts [and metonymically, this includes their menfolk as well] is one family" (*fanshi chuan qunzide dou shi yi jia* or *nbo ggasu cyvi nge*) . This refers, of course, to the fact that minorities' ethnic clothing always includes skirts, while Han women wear pants.

Architectural differences are more subtle than sartorial ones, at least on the outside; in Baiwu it is difficult to tell a Nuosu from a Han house at a distance. When one approaches more closely, however, there is an important clue: Han houses have red paper couplets (*duilian*) pasted over their courtyard gates and the doors to their public rooms; Nuosu houses do not. On the inside, the houses are arranged differently. Han have an altar on the back wall of the main room, facing the doorway, at which they worship heaven, earth, country, the ances-

---

7. The details of Nuosu dress, and the ways in which they express social status variables, including gender, marital status, age, and home area, are treated in detail in Harrell, Bamo, and Ma 2000.

FIG. 10. A family seated around the hearth, waiting for dinner.
The family head at the right is a school principal.

tors, and the local spirit Tudi Ye. If they have a hearth, it is simply a fireplace
in the floor along the right-hand wall as one enters the house; they cook on
mud or brick stoves in the kitchen. The public area of the front room is walled
off from bedrooms, kitchens, and other rooms to either side.

Nuosu houses have much less distinction between public and private space.
In Baiwu (and Yanyuan generally) the hearth is right in the middle of the floor
as one enters the main doorway; it serves as fireplace as well as cookstove (fig.
10); water can be heated in a kettle hanging from the roof-beams, while food
can be cooked in pots or woks balanced on the three hearthstones or andirons,
or, if the fare as usual is nothing but potatoes, you can just put them in the
coals and take them out and eat them when they are done. Nuosu also have a
spirit-altar, but it is a high shelf in the right-hand corner as one comes in the
door. There are sometimes separate bedrooms in such a house, but it is rare
these days that there is not also a bed or two in the main room, sleeping on
beds having replaced the earlier practice of just spreading capes as bedrolls
around the fire.

Ritual is the final area in which culture serves as a marker of Nuosu identity. Nuosu celebrate a different series of holidays from the Han. Despite the

recent promotion, in the regional *minzu* discourse, of the Fire Festival on the twenty-fourth day of the sixth lunar month as the quintessential Yi holiday, this day is in fact celebrated by many ethnic groups, minority and Han, all over the Southwest. But the Nuosu do not celebrate the important Chinese holidays of Yuanxiao (fifteenth of the first lunar month), Qingming (April 5), Duanwu (fifth of the fifth lunar month), and Zhongqiu (fifteenth of the eighth) and they have only a rudimentary celebration of the Chinese New Year. Instead, Nuosu have their own New Year celebration, called Kurshy, which comes at various times in the late fall and early winter, differing from year to year and according to the area. Nuosu in Baiwu are, of course, glad for the festive atmosphere around the Chinese New Year, and Nuosu teenagers certainly set off enough firecrackers all over the town on New Year's Eve in 1993, but ritual is minimum; as was pointed out to me the next day, "Han celebrate the New Year, Nuosu play basketball" (Hanzu guo nian, Yizu da qiu).

More important than the yearly calendar are the rites of passage, marriages and funerals the most prominent among them. In a Nuosu wedding, like its Han counterpart, a bride is transferred to her husband's house and family, but the similarities end there. A Nuosu bride is visited by her husband's relatives before the wedding, and members of the two families splash each other with water during the evening's festivities. The next day, she comes to her husband's village with her male relatives (in Baiwu, some female relatives also come along, but this is not a universal practice), and they are greeted first by people from her husband's clan who serve them liquor, cigarettes, and candy outside the village, where they wait until the sun goes down, when the bride is carried into her husband's house on the back of a male cross-cousin of a clan other than her husband's. The husband takes no part in any of these ceremonies, but they may spend the night together before she returns with her relatives to her natal home. Before the bride and her relatives leave, the husband's relatives present them ritually with money and liquor to repay their effort in bringing the bride (fig. 9). She will visit increasingly frequently over the next few years, until, perhaps pregnant by this time, she finally moves in.

Funerals are also very different, for the simple reason that Nuosu cremate their dead (and thus, in this one single sphere of life, are uniformly judged by the government to be more progressive than their Han neighbors, who practice burial). A Nuosu funeral is a massive affair even for a poor village family; typically they slaughter several oxen and/or sheep, feeding several hundred people after the pyre is lit. At funerals as at weddings, young men from the clan of the deceased (and if the deceased is a woman, also from the clan into which she married) conduct song duels, chanting the glory of their clans and

FIG. 11. Nuosu women's clothing as ceremonial
dress: at a wedding

their exploits, while anyone who has hunting or militia rifles fires them off into
the air at random. When the body is reduced to ashes, no grave is prepared,
but the ashes are deposited on a nearby mountain, and the spirits worshipped
at the domestic altar.

This is not the place to go into the details of ritual symbolism at Nuosu weddings or funerals. The point is to demonstrate the extent to which these rituals are utterly unlike those of the neighboring Han (or, for that matter, of the
other *minzu* either). The language of ethnic markers comes into sharp play in
a place like Baiwu, where Nuosu are part of a local ethnic matrix. Unlike Mishi,

FIG. 12. Nuosu women's clothing as ethnic marker:
dancing to celebrate electricity

where dress is deemphasized because there is little need to mark ethnicity, where housing is simply the style in which people have always lived, and where weddings and funerals are primarily ways of cementing and altering social relations within and between kinship groups, all of whom are Nuosu, in Baiwu these communicative acts take on a second and perhaps more important meaning. Nuosu clothing, houses, weddings, and funerals all occur in full view of neighbors who belong to Han, Prmi, and sometimes other ethnic groups (figs. 11–13). They attend each other's ceremonies, visit each other's houses, and observe each other on the street and in the fields dressed in particular ways. Together with language, stories of common descent, and practices of marital exclusivity, these practices mark off what it means to be Nuosu in a community where there are other possibilities.

What seems most interesting about the use, even the efflorescence, of ethnic markers in a mixed community like Baiwu is that culture is more emphasized as it comes into contact with other, contrasting cultures, in a kind of Batesonian schismogenesis (Bateson 1958 [1935]: 171–97). Differences in these areas are emphasized at a time when Nuosu have more opportunity to participate in education, bureaucracy, economic development, and other facets of the wider Chinese society. Having realized, beginning as early as the

FIG. 13. Nuosu women's clothing as everyday gear:
building a road near Guabie

1930s and 1940s, that a completely isolated, independent *Nuosu muddi* was no longer possible or perhaps even desirable, people have not taken the path of assimilation. They were partially forced in that direction during the Great Proletarian Cultural Revolution, but as soon as the strictures were loosened in the early 1980s, they opted for conditional participation in the wider society—participation contingent on retaining a strict boundary in the spheres of family and certain aspects of culture while they participate in other, more cosmopolitan activities.

Nuosu in Yanyuan and other counties of Liangshan have not just reaffirmed their cultural distinctiveness as they have opted for participation in the wider society and economy. They have also attempted to turn the state programs of political integration and economic development toward local ends and purposes. When entrepreneurs who are heads of state-owned companies talk about Han invasion of their lands and exploitation of their resources, when intellectuals, some of them professors in Chinese universities, talk about the bandits of the 1950s as not being opposed to Communism, but only to the Han, we realize the complexity and contingency of participation in Chinese state- and nation-building practices. People will participate, and this already makes them very different from many outright ethnic nationalists in places such as

Xinjiang and Tibet.[8] After all, what country do Nuosu belong to, if not to China? But they will take full advantage of political "autonomy" and preferential policies in cadre appointment, school entrance, and planned birth, because they feel it is owed to them. There is risk in such participation, however, and one of the ways of buffering the risk is to strengthen the use of the Nuosu language in educational and political contexts, as well as reemphasizing the cultural markers of ethnic identity. Another way to buffer this risk is through psychological strengthening, which includes a reemphasis on the fact of ethnicity in many kinds of languages and conversation.

8. There are, of course, plenty of Uygur and Tibetans who also participate in Chinese state- and nation-building processes. But there is much more direct opposition in those places than in Liangshan.

8 / Manshuiwan: Nuosu Ethnicity in a Culturally Han Area

Nobody walking into Manshuiwan would suspect that he was in a Nuosu village unless he listened carefully. The village is a few kilometers northeast of the Xichang satellite-launching station, and stands astride both the main north-south highway of the Anning Valley and the Chengdu-Kunming railroad, which stops at a station, also called Manshuiwan, about four kilometers downstream. In the middle of the night, when the express from Chengdu comes through, the whole village shakes; after a few nights, however, one gets used to it and barely wakes up, if at all. All but three of the village's houses have been built in recent years, and they follow the southwestern Chinese rural variation on the classical Chinese four-sided courtyard, or *siheyuan*. Bright red couplets adorn the gate arches and doorways, and the front rooms of many houses are adorned with ancestral altars, prepared for the worship of heaven, earth, and country, and of the earth spirit. The little Nuosu-style altar in the corner of the front room is not at all obvious unless you look for it. The three oldest houses, built around the turn of the twentieth century, are even more classically Chinese, with wide concrete porches surrounding the central wells of the courtyards, which are paved with intricate pebble designs and open to the sky and to the full moon on clear nights (fig. 14). A few have elegant perennial and shrub gardens outside the walls, and numerous potted ornamental and medicinal plants in the courtyards. All this gives a sign of permanence that is utterly absent in the "slap it together and leave it when you're tired of it" style of construction in most highland Nuosu villages. People in ordinary Chinese clothing, many of them quite prosperous-looking, walk on dirt paths or lounge after harvest on piles of straw at the edge of the concrete basketball court, at harvest season temporarily given over to rice drying in the sun. If one did not know about Manshuiwan ahead of time, it would be a shock, when one came near, to hear those people conversing in *Nuosu ddoma*.

The initial appearance of prosperity in Manshuiwan is fairly accurate. The land is good, productive rice land, and all families received shares at the time

FIG. 14. The open courtyard inside an old Manshuiwan house

of decollectivization in the early 1980s. Two hundred forty *mu* (16 ha.) of rice land for 302 people means almost a *mu* per person, and there is plenty of water for irrigation, so people can grow a spring wheat crop and a summer rice crop on the same land. There is slightly more dry land than wet-rice land, and people grow corn (mostly for pig-feed) on the dry land during the summer season. They also have vegetable gardens around their houses, replete with fruit trees and pumpkin vines; there are fresh vegetables all year long. Unlike highland Nuosu, people here keep their pigs penned, usually in the same room as the toilet, so that all the manure can be collected easily to put on the fields. Members of the Wang, or Jienuo lineage, have also been very successful in educational and bureaucratic mobility, so that in many families of this lineage only older people and small children are left at home, while the young adults are work-ing in Xichang, Mianning, or other nearby cities. There is only one little store in the village; most people go to the town at Xihe, near the railway station, when they need to market. It is not far to walk or bicycle, but there are cars, trucks, and minibuses going up and down the highway at all hours, so that people walk-ing are likely to be able to get a ride, especially in the rain. There are still some quite poor families, particularly in the Li (Aju) lineage and in one branch of the Wang who are descended from slaves, as well as among the ethnically Han

Wu lineage and other Han families who live mostly above the railroad. But even these poorer people have electricity and running water, and some of them also black-and-white television sets and bicycles. It is fair to say that the poorest families in Manshuiwan, in terms of material standard of living, rank with the very wealthiest in the plains villages of Mishi, and with the upper-middle families in Baiwu.

Manshuiwan is one of several Nuosu village islands in the overwhelmingly Han sea of the upper Anning Valley, people who call themselves plains Yi, or *pingba Yizu*. In material and many other cultural terms, Manshuiwan is an ordinary Chinese village—probably of lower-middle standing on a nationwide scale, but certainly not poor—whose inhabitants just happen to be two-thirds or more minorities, namely Nuosu. This fact of ethnicity, however, is vitally important psychologically for almost all the villagers we spoke to. To understand how this situation came to be, we must take a careful look at Manshuiwan's village history.

HISTORY, ETHNICITY, DEMOGRAPHY: HOW MANSHUIWAN CAME TO BE

In the nicest old house in Manshuiwan, an eighty- or ninety-year-old classical-style structure of wooden posts and beams around a central courtyard open to the sky, with intricate carvings of birds and flowers in the windowpanes and live flowers in beds outside the gates and in planters inside, we met Wang Chenghan, a retired translator in the prefectural government at Xichang, whose most glorious moment came when he was called to interpret for Nuosu deputies to the National People's Congress in Beijing. Here, pieced together but altered very little from my English-language notes of three long conversations with Mr. Wang, is an account of the history of his clan, the Jienuos:

> The Wang or Jienuo clan is an offshoot of the Aho, which is one of the biggest *nuoho* clans in Greater Liangshan. Their original home was in Puxiong, where they did a lot of fishing along the rivers. Each family had a section of the river course where they could catch fish, but one day their earliest ancestor, who was eighteen years old, quarreled with a relative over the ownership of a particular stretch of river. He killed the other guy with a knife, and the penalty was for him to be exiled from the clan and be made into a *quho*. There is a Yi saying that if you kill someone at eighteen your mother will die when you're twenty, and sure enough, that happened. So he took his family and animals and slaves, crossed the Anning River, and went to live at the back (west) of Lushan (Lu Mountain)

above Xichang. But he noticed that everyone living there, especially the Han, had goiters, so he moved to someplace called Magong Jia, where the relations between Yi and Han were good, and his line prospered for two generations.

Meanwhile, around Manshuiwan there had been troubles between local Yi and the military colonies (of Han settlers) that had been sent here by various emperors. There was thus very little population, and a local *nuoho* lord gave the Jienuo clan title to a large area (about 20 km long) from the confluence of the Xiangshui and Mianning Rivers down to the Anning, which took up what is now the better part of two townships. The assignment of this ancestor, whose name was Jienuo Mosi, was to mediate relations between the Yi and the Han, and he did. This was ten generations ago.

Mosi had two sons, named Sada and Sala. Sala was first adopted by a local Han landlord, whose surname was Wang. The landlord had only a daughter— no sons—and so Sala ended up marrying the daughter and taking the name Wang, and his descendants became Han. Because of this relation, however, the descendants of Sada, who remained Yi, have also used the surname Wang. Sala, who took the name Wang Gang, was to be given a Han-style burial, with a Han-style coffin, but when the funeral procession was headed for the burial ground, his Yi relatives stopped it and took the coffin away. He was probably buried anyway (or maybe he was cremated), but there is a tomb about 3 or 4 km from Manshuiwan, and his descendants come every year at Qingming to sweep the grave.

In the Yongzheng period (1722–36) this whole area was subjected to *gaitu guiliu* (abolition of *tusi* rule) and this meant, among other things, that the Jienuo clan gave up both the slaveholding system and the distinction between *nuoho* and *quho*. This is a reason why they haven't intermarried in recent years with Yi from the mountains.

In the early and mid-Qing, the Yi were not allowed to take the imperial examinations, though many tried to sneak in. There is a story that in Ningyuan (Xichang), when you went into the examination sheds, there was a basin of water to wash your feet in, and they made it particularly hot. If you yelled "Acigi!" you were Yi, and found out, whereas if you yelled "Aiya!" then you were Han and could go ahead and take the examinations.

Local Yi objected to this and brought suit in a court at Chengdu, with the result that the governor ruled that Ningyuan Prefecture should henceforth have a first-examination quota of eighteen Han and five Yi. After this, at least two members of the Jienuo clan became examination graduates: Wang Wenhuan was a civil *xiucai* and later *juren*, and in the early Republic became head of education in Mianning County. This was Mr. Wang's grandfather. His father wrote (in classical Chinese): "Father was called Wenhuan, and had ambitions to study, so he received a *juren* degree from the Qing." Wang Wenming (younger brother of Wenhuan) became a military *xiucai*. Both Wenhuan and Wenming had previously studied at private schools in nearby towns, and later on at the Lufeng Academy in Xichang.

Twenty-two of the village's current sixty-eight households belong to the Jienuo clan. The other major Nuosu lineage is the Aju, or Li, which has twenty-eight households. It is fairly universally agreed that "in the old society"—that is, before the land reform of the early 1950s—the Jienuos were dominant, and thus their history is clearer. But the Ajus seem to have come through a similar route. Mr. Li Deming, an age-mate of Wang Chenghan, told us that the Ajus originally came from someplace called Dragonhead Mountain and may have already been affines of the Jienuos before they came here. There is a story that they received the surname Li when in their early migrations they ran into a Han official who asked them, in Chinese, what their surname was. They didn't understand, but wanted to act friendly, so one of them pulled some plums (*li* in Chinese) out of his shoulder bag, and Li thus became their surname.[1]

The third lineage represented in Manshuiwan are the Wus, who are ethnically Han. According to their tradition, they came from Wujiang County in Jiangsu to Dali in Yunnan in the Qing, and then dispersed to several different areas in the Southwest, eventually settling in Manshuiwan at the end of the dynasty. They were mostly owner-farmers, but one of their ancestors smoked away almost all of their resources right before the land reform.

In 1914, early in the Republican period, there was a slave rebellion in Yuexi

---

1. There are a lot of similar stories, usually told by Nuosu, about how Nuosu clans got their Han surnames. For example, the Loho in many parts of Liangshan bear the Han surname Luo, taken from the first syllable of their clan name. But those in Yanyuan and Mianning are called Hu. The story is that when they were crossing the Anning River from Puxiong on their way to Yanyuan, some Han officials stopped them and inquired about their surname. Scared and not understanding, they made *hu-hu* sounds, and these branches were thus assigned the surname Hu. This story is improbable, since the name is pronounced Fu in the local Han speech.

Another story concerns the Bamos, whose Han surname is An, pronounced Ngan locally. One of their ancestors was apparently better acquainted with Han language than the aforementioned Loho; when the Bamos were asked their surname, he understood but had no way to answer, because he didn't have a Han surname, so he just said "Nga . . . Nga" (I . . . I) in Nuosu, so the inquiring officials thought their surname must be Ngan.

These tales are typical of the stories Nuosu tell on themselves, about their being frozen with shame when confronted with their own lack of familiarity with Han language and culture.

and Mianning, which lasted two years (Zhou Xiyin 1987). Although the Anning Valley floor was not directly affected, the indirect effects were important, including a campaign from government authorities for the Nuosu in the valley to adopt "civilized" Han customs, under the slogan "Follow the Han example, practice Han customs, change your skirt for Han-style clothes" (Xue Han li, xi Han su, gaile qunzi chuan Han yifu).

During this time there were more private schools established in the northern Anning Valley. At least one member of the Li lineage studied at a school that was founded in nearby Xinghua by a series of nearby plains Yi—Nuosu lineages who, like the Wangs and Lis, had not only "followed Han customs and changed their skirts for Han clothes," but also had long adopted the Han economic institutions of landlordism and thus, according to local people, had given up the distinction between *nuoho* and *quho* for a distinction between rich and poor: "Zhi you pin fu zhi fen, mei you gui jian zhi bie." At least one of the Lis attended this school. The Wangs, on the other hand, were more prosperous at this time and had their own school in Manshuiwan, where several of their boys and a few of their girls learned the classics from Han teachers.

Slavery was not entirely gone in early twentieth-century Manshuiwan and nearby Nuosu communities, however. They may have given up the caste system, but there were at least four Jienuo families who still had household slaves. In 1918 a marriage was arranged between a bride from one of those Jienuo households and a young man from a Bamo family in Yuexi. As part of her dowry, she was given a domestic slave-girl, or *yatou*, a type of slave common in Han society in all parts of China (Watson 1980). In return, the Bamos sent a twelve-year-old male *gaxy*. As a *gaxy*, his clan affiliation, which was nominally Qumo, was quite weak, and at any rate he had no Han surname. So he took the surname of his new masters, Wang. People in Manshuiwan are unsure whether the little group of close agnatic relatives of the original slave-boy, which now numbers five households and twenty-three people, should be a branch of the Jienuo clan, or whether they are members of the Qumo clan who happen to carry the same Han surname as the Jienuos. At any rate, like almost none of the original Jienuos, all these households are now rather poor, and few of their members have been educated beyond elementary school.

Nearly everyone agrees that in the period immediately before the Communist takeover, the Wangs were dominant in this area. In the 1930s Wang Chenghan's family were wealthy landlords, with their tenants coming from the Lis, from local Han families, and even from some of the nearby mountain Yi who wanted to grow wet rice. But by the time of the Revolution, their family had already lost its land, and the most prominent families were those of Wang Wendou and Li Wanru, who was a minor local official under the Han warlord Deng Xiuting.

Since Manshuiwan lies in the Anning Valley, where the population is overwhelmingly Han, it did not wait until 1956 for full Communist institutional takeover, nor did it undergo the relatively mild form of social transformation known as democratic reform. Instead, like most of China, it underwent land reform, in which village residents were classified as landlords, rich peasants, middle peasants, poor peasants, or agricultural laborers, and the exploited classes were mobilized to struggle against the exploiters, eventually confiscating and redistributing their land. In Manshuiwan's land reform, there were originally no families classified as landlords or rich peasants, but then one of Chenghan's father's brothers, a former Guomindang official, went to Chenghan's family to seek refuge from his pursuers. When he was caught, this spurred an investigation, with the result that the family, having lost most of its property and been classified as "poor peasants," was reclassified as "bankrupt landlords" (*pochan dizhu*). By this time, however, it was the very end of the Land Reform campaign, and the family was not struggled against.

Two men from the Wang and one from the Li lineage became involved early in local government and Party politics. After the Communist takeover of the area in March 1950, the Communists organized an "ethnic cadres" class in Xichang, presided over by the Han PLA commander Liang Wenying, with the Nuosu reformer and military official Leng Guangdian as vice-head. Men who had joined this class, and several others from the village, have held various levels of political positions in the Communist bureaucracy ever since.

The village was a single production team during the period of collective agriculture, until the land was distributed to households in 1982. Since then, private agriculture has been the main means of livelihood, though there are twenty-two members of the Jienuo clan known to us to have worked outside the village, including one secondary and five elementary teachers, the head of the prefectural construction bank, several cadres in grain and commercial bureaus, and a physician. The Ajus have had only five members work outside, but they have included a county judge, the head of a *qu* (district), and several teachers. The Shi (Ashy) family, originally married-in affines of the Jienuos, have had a factory manager, a doctor, and a teacher, and even the Wus, the poorest lineage, have had a commercial bureau cadre, a teacher, and two factory workers. So while the Jienuos are clearly the most successful, the village in general has produced a considerable number of cadres, teachers, and workers—more, per capita, than even the Mgebbu of Baiwu, and certainly more than any single village in Mishi.

In 1994 there was only one industrial enterprise in Manshuiwan, a talc-grinding factory owned jointly by the village and team governments and a group of private investors, the largest of whom was the team head at that time, Wang Kaifu. The talc factory replaced a tannery on the same site in 1994; changes in the prices of hides had rendered tanning unprofitable. The factory employs fifteen workers, many of them local villagers who basically shovel rocks into a couple of crushing machines and bag up the powder that comes out at the other end. For this gritty work they will be paid piece rates, which were projected to run as high as ¥300 per month, but this level had not been reached yet in late 1994, since the larger of the two machines kept breaking down. It was not clear whether the talc operation would end up making any money.

ETHNIC INTERACTIONS

If the stories of its origins are true, Manshuiwan was born out of Nuosu-Han interactions, when Jienuo Mosi was called by local powers to "mediate Yi-Han relations." Since it is clear that the Nuosu lineages—Jienuo and Aju, but particularly Jienuo—have held a locally dominant position ever since, in a certain way local Nuosu-Han interactions have always been asymmetrical, with the Nuosu on top. But for the last hundred years at least, Manshuiwan and other plains Yi villages—such as Yuehua, Xinhua, Mianshan, and Hongmo in Mianning[2]—have been increasingly isolated islands in a Han sea. For example, in the current township of Manshuiwan, there are four administrative villages, of which Xihe is one, and the village of Manshuiwan is one team of Xihe Administrative Village. The total population of the township is six thousand, which makes the 230 Nuosu of Manshuiwan, who are the only Nuosu in the township, about 4 percent of the total township population. At Yuehua, about ten kilometers to the south, the plains Yi are scattered among four villages and number around 1,300 out of a total population of nearly 14,000, or 9 percent of the total.

In this kind of a situation, it seems logical that Nuosu would adopt many of the customs of the surrounding Han majority, and indeed this is the case. At the same time, they have unequivocally retained their sense of ethnic iden-

---

2. There is another nearby place called Hongmo, in Xide County, whose inhabitants are mostly Nuosu but are not plains Yi and maintain their caste identities. I am indebted to Nuobu Huojy for this information.

tity. But this identity is not exactly the same as that of the Nuosu living in the hills. People in Manshuiwan and Yuehua emphasize that they are plains Yi, who are to be distinguished both from mountain Yi (*gaoshan Yizu*) and from Han. Li Deming listed several cultural distinctions between the local Nuosu and their mountain relatives:

1. Our language has slightly different pronunciation, and we have borrowed vocabulary from Han. For example, we call our mother Ma, not Amo.
2. Our women don't wear skirts anymore, though some women still own them. This is because they're inconvenient for fieldwork.
3. Instead of painted wooden dishes, we eat from bowls with chopsticks.

He then went on to enumerate differences from Han:

1. They speak only Han, but Yi generally speak both languages. But in this village, the Han speak both languages also.
2. The Han celebrate only the Han New Year; we celebrate both [the Han and Nuosu New Years].
3. The Han celebrate the Fire Festival for only one day; we celebrate it for three days.

In the old society, Mr. Li said, intermarriage with Han was very rare. Now it is still fairly uncommon, but there is some; there has been one intermarriage in Manshuiwan. The reason why intermarriage is so rare is that the Yi are so few that intermarriage would cause them to die out. Relations with mountain Yi have always existed, but there has been little intermarriage. When they have intermarried, mountain women usually have come down to Manshuiwan; the sanitary conditions up in the mountains are not very good.

Wang Chenghan and Wang Kaifu confirmed that intermarriage with either mountain Yi or Han was formerly rare. The reasons that plains Yi did not marry with mountain Yi were:

1. Their lifestyle was different. Plains Yi "followed the Han example and practiced Han customs," while up in the mountains, Yi retained their original lifestyle.
2. From the time of *gaitu guiliu*, plains Yi have gotten rid of the slave system and with it the distinction between *nuoho* and *quho*.

The reasons why they did not intermarry with Han were also two:

1. The Han still have an arrogant, contemptuous attitude (*qiaobuqi*) toward the Yi in general.
2. In order to preserve the *minzu*, they might take in outside daughters-in-law, but would be reluctant to marry their own daughters out.

According to statistics that Bamo Ayi and I compiled, intermarriage with Han is in fact not particularly rare. Although we have more complete statistics on the provenance of Manshuiwan wives than on the marital destination of its daughters, the trend is clear in both directions from table 8.1.

Despite the rather wistful assertion by men of both the Wang and Li clans that it's better to take in Han daughters-in-law than to marry your daughters to Han, fully one-third of the Manshuiwan Nuosu brides in the last three generations of whom we have record married Han men, while fewer than one-fifth of the men took Han brides. By contrast, the sharp line between plains and mountain Yi seems to hold in fact as well as in ideology, and I think Li Deming probably hit it on the head when he said "the sanitary conditions are not too good up there." In today's society, where there is at least a modicum of redress for young people pushed into arranged marriages, no young woman from a place like Manshuiwan would agree to marry into a place like Mishi. Living with running water, rice and fresh vegetables, and a paved highway to market (and, by cheap minibus, eighty minutes to Xichang) is a different world from going to the stream, eating potatoes and buckwheat and pickled turnip greens, and a two-hour walk over a slippery trail to a once-a-week market that doesn't have much to offer anyway.

When members of the Wang and Li lineage do marry Han, however, they rarely marry with the Wus or the other Han families in Manshuiwan Village itself. This is clearly not a case of village exogamy, because there are a large number of marriages between the Wangs and the Lis. And it is not a case of hostile relations, either. There is just as much latent hostility between the Lis and Wangs, and between various families within each lineage, as there is against the local Han. In fact, there is an institution through which personal ties are regularly cemented between Nuosu and Han in this area: the practice of adopting each other's children as "dry relatives," what in the West would be called godchildren or godgrandchildren. Wang Chengliang explained how it works:

> You have a child who is doesn't play very happily [*buhao shua*], so you look for a person whose birth date is horoscopically compatible with that of the child, and decide to form a dry relationship. The natural parents have to bring the child [usually at the New Year] to the house of the dry parents, where they burn incense

TABLE 8.1

Endogamy and Exogamy among
Manshuiwan Nuosu

	Manshuiwan lowland Yi	Other lowland Yi	Han	Mountain Yi	Other	TOTAL
Sons' wives	8	41	12	2	1[b]	64
Daughters' husbands	8	14	11	0	0	33
TOTAL	8[a]	55	23	2	1	89

[a]The marriages in the top and bottom rows of this column are the same marriages. This is also reflected in the grand total at lower right.
[b]One man, the father of our landlady, took a wife from one of the Xifan or Zang peoples who live along the western rim of the valley.

to the dry parents' ancestors. The dry parents have to bring gifts at the New Year after that—including liquor, candy, and meat. They should also make an item of clothing for the child. These obligations ordinarily go on for only three years.

There is another way to do this, which is to leave a red piece of paper on the road, on which is written, "Tian qing di lü, xiao'er yi ku. Guo lu junzi nianguo, xiao'er bu ku," or "Green is the earth and blue are the skies; the little baby also cries. Kind Sir, passing by, if you read this off, the baby won't cry." Whoever comes by and picks it up assumes the obligations of dry kinship.

When this kind of recognition takes place, the adoptive parent chooses a [Han-style] name, including the adoptive parent's own surname, and gives it to the child. After this, the adoptive parent sometimes calls the child by this name. For example, Wang Chengliang's own son is called by his adoptive parents Wu Chang-shou. If you swear dry kinship with a mountain Yi, they may give the child a Nuosu-style name.

According to both Nuosu and Han villagers, dry kinship is primarily used to cement relationships between individual families across ethnic lines. Local Nuosu rarely do it with each other, they say, because there is already such a thick net of intermarriage as to make any further knitting of social bonds superfluous. We did not compile a complete list of dry relationships in Manshuiwan, but we recorded thirteen, of which two were actually between Nuosu, despite denials in the abstract that this practice exists.

Apparently the ethnic otherness of the dry parent or grandparent is of concern to natural parents, or I would not have been asked to be one by a family in the Wang clan—a household that had a twenty-day-old baby and a mother who was complaining that her breasts hurt and the baby was crying because he did not have enough milk. Like a mountain Nuosu, I chose a name in my own language—Henry—and left money to buy a suit of clothes at the coming New Year.

ACCULTURATION TO HAN WAYS

When I first visited the plains Yi village of Yuehua in 1993, I met a professor from the Southwest Nationalities Institute there; she was a native of the area and had come to visit on a family matter. Used to teaching language, and perhaps thus to speaking more clearly than the average person, she conversed with me mostly in Nuosu. I remember asking her a series of questions about cultural practices and remarking, "Here people don't wear Nuosu clothing, do they?" and her answering, "There are those who wear them and those who don't."

I think the professor was trying to impress me with her ethnicity, however, because I didn't see a single skirt in my brief visit there, nor did I see any even on the oldest women in my much longer stay in Manshuiwan. In fact, the early Republican injunction to "Follow Han ways, practice Han customs, and change your skirts for Han-style clothes" seems to have been successful, if indeed people in Manshuiwan in 1916 were still living like highland Nuosu, itself an unprovable proposition. Almost every material aspect of life in Manshuiwan is identical to those of surrounding Han villages, and contrasts with those of the highland Nuosu. Even ritual and spiritual life has acculturated significantly toward Han norms, though it is not so completely transformed as material existence.

Material life needs little emphasis here aside from the observations I have made earlier. The houses, old and new, are Chinese style, and the efforts of one village resident to demonstrate to me that the architecture was really characteristically Yi, because there were some *diaozhu* ("hanging" vertical posts that reach from the rafters to the beams but not to the ground), were drowned out by the overall plan, by the lack of hearths in the main sitting rooms, and by the ubiquitous presence of red couplets on the gates and doorways. Clothing is ordinary Chinese clothing—there is not much to say about it—and food is ordinary Chinese food, with the addition of an ethnic-marking pig or goat slaughtered and eaten in chunks at a holiday or in honor of a guest. With this latter exception, there is no material reminder of the Nuosu origins of the Wangs and Lis.

Spiritually, things are a bit more complex, but acculturation is still obvious, in the ancestral altars with incense burners; in the worship of heaven, earth, and country; in the observance of all the major Han holidays. But in other ways, characteristically Nuosu expressive forms reveal themselves, resulting in surprising mixtures. Some people are cremated, in the Nuosu style, but others are buried, and I went one morning with Bamo Ayi and her great aunt, in whose house we lived, to worship at the elaborate grave of the recently deceased great-uncle. They brought offerings of food and liquor, just as Han people would do when visiting a grave at Qingming. The grave was inscribed in the conventional way, with Han characters. And this is not a new practice; there is a grave in the village that was built in 1865 for a Jienuo ancestor, and it looks identical to a Han grave that might be found anywhere in China.

Other people, however, cremate their dead, in the Nuosu fashion, and some of them just build a little mound over the ashes, while others cremate and then build a grave, with or without an inscription. For the soul, however, a lot of people still insist on inviting a *bimo* (of which there are none in the area) to come and do the ritual of *cobi*, or conducting the soul back to the ancestral homeland. Others, however, never get around to having the ritual performed. And when people have a lingering illness or other problem, they may travel to a distant mountain village to invite a *bimo* to come perform a ritual.

It seems clear from these observations that culture is not a big part of ethnic identity in Manshuiwan. Nuosu people, in fact, are at pains to distinguish themselves from the Nuosu up in the mountains, where sanitary conditions are not so good, and nobody would ever think of marrying (one villager referred to mountain Nuosu as *manzi*, or barbarians). It is still absolutely clear in most cases who is Nuosu and who is not, and what that means, but it means common descent and history more than it means culture. The only cultural characteristic that is important to the ethnic identity of all Nuosu in the Manshuiwan area is language.

THE PERSISTENCE OF NUOSU LANGUAGE

Wang Chenghan tells a hilarious story about his experience as a young boy in the private Confucian school, or *sishu*, set up in the early twentieth century to educate the sons (and at least five daughters) of the Jienuos by the classical method.

The Jienuo boys and girls studied the classics in one of the old homes that is now standing in the village. There were several teachers over the years, all Han from nearby communities, and none of them spoke Nuosu. So when the little children started with *The Three Character Classic*, they had to have an interpreter to know what they were reading about. This led to classic little-boy deliberate misreadings. For example, for a text that read, in Chinese, "Can tu si; feng niang mi" (Silkworms extrude silk; bees ferment honey), the Nuosu boys read, "Cha du sy; vu nza hmi" (The string beans die; the sausages are done).

This story illustrates the linguistic tangle that is Manshuiwan even more graphically than appears at first glance. The Nuosu children heard nonsense syllables in a foreign tongue and gave them meaning, in much the same way as an American might hear a Chinese person saying *mai shu* and assume she was talking about her footwear rather than buying books. But the Nuosu words they heard in their mischievous bewilderment were, at least in part, borrowed from that very same language: *cha du* is a Nuosu pronunciation of the Chinese word for string beans, *can dou*.

Nowadays, children in Manshuiwan may learn either language or both, depending on where in the village they grow up. If they live below the highway, where all but one household is Nuosu, then they may well grow up knowing some Han but not speaking it fluently. In fact, some Nuosu families in this part of the village, if they have Han affines or friends, like to make sure their children get chances to play with their friends' or relatives' children so that they will not be at a disadvantage when they start school, which now, as in Republican days, is entirely in Han. If they grow up in the Wu lineage cluster way above the railroad, they might speak only Han. But even if they grow up in this upper section, depending on whom they play with, they may learn serviceable Nuosu, and children who grow up near the highway or between the highway and the railroad play with Nuosu and Han indiscriminately and will probably know both languages fluently before they start school.

It has probably been several decades since there were any monolingual adult Nuosu speakers in Manshuiwan; everyone, whether they have been to school or not (and almost everyone has had some schooling), speaks the local dialect of Han, at minimum as a fluent second language, and almost always equally well as they speak Nuosu. Manshuiwan Nuosu people are thus in a situation similar to those faced by people in small ethnic enclaves all over Liangshan and southwest China: they are no longer members of a speech community of any size and are thus uniformly fluent in the surrounding language, which here, as almost everywhere else, is Han.[3] In almost all of those other enclaves that I

---

3. As illustrated in the case of Baiwu, above, however, there are certain Prmi and Naze who are surrounded not by Han but by Nuosu, and whose second language is thus *Nuosu ddoma*.

have visited, once the number of speakers of the surrounded language goes below a few hundred, the language dies out in that community (see chap. 13). It is startling, therefore, to observe the resilience of Nuosu language in Manshuiwan, Yuehua, and other plains Yi villages in the Anning Valley. Very few people read and write it; everybody speaks fluent Han; most people also read and write Han—even farmers often read newspapers, notices, and technical books and magazines, and the large number of people working outside the village interact daily with an almost exclusively Hanophone world.

Yet there is no sign whatsoever that Nuosu language is declining in this village. Most overheard conversations in Nuosu families are in the Nuosu language, and it is still the first language of all children in the lower part of the village. Even some members of the Wu lineage speak it. The resiliency of the language requires some explanation, so I asked several people. The industrialist Wang Kaifu, who told me he had thought about this question a lot, had the most interesting answers:

1. The Yi came to Manshuiwan as clans and established their position early, and when the Han came later on, they came in small groups. So the Yi were always the majority in the immediate area.
2. The Yi and Han for the most part, even though they live in the same village and cooperate closely, generally live separated. The Han who live below the road or just above it generally speak Yi well, and all the children understand it, but those who live way up above the railroad don't necessarily. So the Yi have had a concentrated geographical environment in which to speak their own language.
3. The Yi feel strongly that their language is an important part of their identity and ought to be preserved, so they make a conscious effort to do so, even though obviously everybody is also fluent in Han.

Wang's third answer, I think, is the most interesting when viewed in comparison to similarly concentrated small communities elsewhere who have lost their former languages. It is, in fact, a conscious effort, which *stems from* a sense of ethnic identity. They do not identify as Nuosu because they speak the language; rather they speak the language because they identify as Nuosu. They have local traditions of common descent and common history (Keyes 1976) that shape their identity as a group, and part of those traditions is the idea that they are a group that has a language of its own. So they speak it.

Ideas of what is civilized and what is not, especially in light of the generally negative views expressed by Manshuiwan people about mountain Nuosu, may also help us understand the persistence of language. As mentioned above, there are very few "cultural traits" that Manshuiwan people have in common with Nuosu from outside the valley, and this is one perceived reason for not marrying them. Not only are such frequently used ethnic markers as dress, food, and housing in this village completely identical to what one would find one or two settlements away in exclusively Han communities, but also the kinds of ethnic stereotypes that are so common in highland villages of whatever ethnicity—of minorities as honest, lazy, straightforward, hospitable, generous, cruel—are notably absent in Manshuiwan people's discourse about themselves. But most villagers feel that this extreme acculturation cannot and should not lead to assimilation—because not only are Han people in general accurately perceived as looking down on all minorities, including the Yi, so that people might not be able to assimilate if they wanted to—but also they do not seem to want to assimilate. They are proud of their heritage, though they have no desire to readopt many of its habitual practices. So they need things to hang onto, and the language is an obvious one, especially since they have determined that it is no obstacle to mobility in the wider society, as some of the habitual behaviors or even stereotypical behavioral attributes might well be. So for the time being, at least, the Nuosu language, which in practical terms has very little use in the Anning Valley, continues to flourish, consciously employed as an ethnic marker and an important part of ethnic identity, in places like Yuehua and Manshuiwan.

KIN-BASED IDENTITY

Having completed a brief tour of three very different Nuosu communities, we can begin to look for things they all have in common. We can immediately rule out culture, in the conventional sense of common practices. Mishi and Baiwu may be culturally similar in this way, but they are not identical; in language and other areas, people in Baiwu have picked up a lot more Han "customs and habits," as the Chinese would say. And in Manshuiwan the habitual practices of daily life often thought to distinguish one ethnic group from another serve much better to distinguish the local plains Yi from highlanders in places like Mishi and Baiwu than they do to distinguish local Nuosu from local Han. Clearly the observation that Edmund Leach originally made in the 1950s still holds true at this level: whatever holds an ethnic group together, it is not common culture (Leach 1954).

This is not to imply, however, that culture is irrelevant to understanding

Nuosu identity in any of the three areas. In Mishi, people are immediately identifiable by their practices, which are unself-consciously different from what little they know of corresponding Han forms. In Baiwu, where Han are neighbors, friends, and rivals, cultural differences are acute, and consciously manipulated, even exaggerated, in order to display ethnic group unity and contrast. In Manshuiwan, where most aspects of distinctively Nuosu culture are gone, still people consciously hang on to one cultural form—Nuosu language—because they feel they ought to preserve things that belong to them as an ethnic group.

All this suggests that culture really does play the part of an ethnic marker, even where most of it has already acculturated to majority forms. But as a marker, culture's role in ethnic identity is secondary. The primary role, I think, must be given to ideas about kinship and about history. The Nuosu emphasis on genealogy (a feature of Nuosu thinking that probably stems originally more from the clan basis of social organization in the acephalous polity of Old Liangshan than from any concerns about preserving ethnic distinctions) is a prime example of an ideology of common descent as an important factor in ethnic consciousness. But kinship is more than descent; it is also affinity and intermarriage. And just as descent, the warp of the old political system, became a foundation of ethnic identity in situations of ethnic contact, patterns of exogamy and endogamy by clan and caste, the woof of the old system, have come to play an equally important part in ethnic identity. In places where the caste distinction still holds—much of the highland *Nuosu muddi*—caste endogamy and ethnic endogamy work in much the same way, to achieve in-group solidarity and out-group distinction. But even where caste no longer pertains—the Anning River plain—ethnic-group endogamy is an important aspect of ethnic solidarity. The fact that Manshuiwan people deny the prevalence of intermarriage with Han, even when it accounts for about a fourth of their unions, serves to illustrate the importance of endogamy, like descent, as an aspect of the kinship ideology that ultimately portrays all Nuosu as related, and as belonging to a "different family" from the Han.

As long as kinship—a primordial notion if there ever was one—remains the most important basis of ethnic identity for Nuosu people, Nuosu ethnic identity takes on two characteristics that distinguish it from the other forms of ethnic identity treated in parts 3 and 4 of this book. In an endogamous kin group, the boundaries are absolute; there is no room for absorption or leakage. Culture can acculturate to majority norms, or it can exaggerate the differences schismogenetically, and it makes little difference. None of the other groups described in this volume has in recent history been as endogamous as

169

the Nuosu; at the opposite extreme, of course, are the Han, who will inter-marry with anybody and thus absorb them into their ethnic community, mak-ing cultural practices (Chinese culturalism) the primary basis of Han identity throughout history (see chap. 14). Other groups lie in between on this dimen-sion, but in all cases their identity is somewhat contextual. For the Nuosu, descended from common ancestors and marrying only within the group, iden-tity is absolute no matter how culture does or does not change.

9 / Nuosu, Yi, China, and the World

T his chapter begins with a self-criticism. In the previous three chapters, describing Nuosu ethnicity in three very different rural communities, I have perpetrated a convenient fiction: the idea that one can describe ethnic identity and ethnic relations in a certain locality without considering the larger, national and international discourses of ethnicity and nationalism that pertain to the country in which the locality is situated. Certainly, chapters 6–8 did not treat Mishi, Baiwu, and Manshuiwan like the "primitive isolates" described in early twentieth-century ethnography. In this book imperial dynasties, warlord regimes, and modern revolutions sweep across Liangshan; people leave their communities to become educated, bringing back with them skills, knowledge, and even spouses from the outside; communities are collectivized in the 1950s and decollectivized in the 1980s, and are allowed to begin both capitalism and religion anew in the reform era. But throughout all this historical and geographical context, I have acted as if the important categories were the local ones: local Nuosu and outside Hxiemga in Mishi; Nuosu, Prmi, and Han in Baiwu; plains Nuosu, mountain Nuosu, and Han in Manshuiwan. I have neglected the fact that people who are Nuosu in local discourse, speaking their own language, and who are Yi (which in this context is nothing but a translation of Nuosu) when speaking Chinese, are also Yi or Yizu in a different sense: the sense that was created by the ethnic identification process, which made everybody a member of one or another of the fifty-six officially recognized *minzu*, or "nationalities." This category of Yi is not simply the local category of Nuosu or Yi writ large. It is founded on different principles, includes and excludes different people, and gives its members the potential to participate in a wholly different discourse of ethnicity, a discourse that seeks to lump rather than split, that takes Yi as an imagined community rather than as a face-to-face group (Anderson 1991), that invites, even requires, the creation of another whole series of myths of common history, descent, and, stubbornly enough, culture.

I committed this sin of omission knowingly, and for two reasons. First, I wanted, as an anthropologist, to focus in a serious way on the local, to attack the assumption that the official categories, the fifty-six mailboxes in a row, somehow reflect local reality. I wanted the local reality to be appreciated in its own right, to the point where I would not even assume that "Nuosu" meant the same thing in one community as it meant in another. Second, to do it all at once would be too complicated. So I postponed, as it were, the discussion of this larger-scale context of ethnic relations. But postponement is not cancellation, and now the rain check is due: it is time to focus not on the *minzu* discourse as something separate from the local relations in each community, but rather as something in which the same people participate and the same communities are involved, and ultimately as something that alters the vocabulary and syntax of the local language of ethnic identity. Local ethnic relations are a part of and influenced by larger-scale *minzu* relations, and there are several ways in which the fact that Nuosu are also Yi influences what it means to be Nuosu. But first we must talk about the participation of local community members in being Yi.

ETHNIC LEADERSHIP AND LOCAL PARTICIPATION

Nuosu people have not been entirely absent from the national stage of twentieth-century China. Probably the most prominent of all was Long Yun, a *nuoho* from Jinyang County in southeastern Liangshan, who went to study in military school in Kunming and later rose through the military ranks to become the ruler of Yunnan from 1927 until the Communist takeover extended to Yunnan in 1950 (Xie Benshu 1988, Lu Hui 1994). Also in the pre-Communist period, *nzymo* Leng Guangdian of Tianba in Ganluo was prominent in local political, military, and educational affairs, not only graduating from the Whampoa Military Academy in Nanjing but also returning to Liangshan in 1936 to mediate several local wars, as well as to establish the first modern school in a Nuosu area in Ganluo (Azha 1994, Wu Guoqing 1994). Both of these regional leaders lived on after the Communist takeover in Beijing, first honored as united-front personalities, then attacked as rightists in the 1950s, and finally rehabilitated (in Long Yun's case, posthumously) in the Reform Era. Two of Long Yun's sons emigrated to the United States, where they had successful careers in the restaurant business in Cambridge, Massachusetts, and Washington, D.C.

After 1950 certain Nuosu emerged not only as united-front personalities but at the mid-levels of the Communist Party structure itself. The most prominent of these has been Wu Jinghua, or Luovu Lapu (b. 1931), who came from a village just upstream from Mianning City, in an area where Nuosu and Han villagers lived interspersed, much as in Baiwu. Lapu and his male cousins went to a local elementary school in the city, from which several bright students were picked up and trained as cadres in the Revolution. Wu Jinghua rose to several prominent posts, most notably Party secretary of the Tibet Autonomous Region from 1985 until 1988 (Schwartz 1994: 18, 148) and also as Party secretary of the Central Nationalities Commission. A protégé of the late General Secretary Hu Yaobang, Wu fell from effective power after Hu's ouster in 1987; recently he has held a series of largely sinecurial posts. His three daughters have all studied for graduate degrees at the University of Michigan. Another Nuosu who has reached high posts is Feng Yuanwei, a plains Yi from Yuehua, who rose to the position of vice-secretary of the Sichuan Provincial Communist Party.

These are, of course, only four of the hundreds of Nuosu people who have had successful careers in Republican and Communist China. The point here is not to prove that Yi, too, can be stars, but to illustrate two things about the points of connection between the Nuosu world and the wider Chinese world. First, all four of these men came from mixed Nuosu-Han districts, and all had early contact with Han people, culture, and language. Both Long Yun and Leng Guangdian spent part of their childhood with Han families, Wu Jinghua went to school with Han children from age seven or eight, and Feng Yuanwei came from Yuehua, an acculturated environment much like Manshuiwan. Very few Nuosu from the nuclear area—Zhaojue, Meigu, Butuo—or from remote villages in the peripheral counties have made their mark in the wider world, even to the extent of becoming county or prefectural officials in Liangshan.

Second, whenever these men or people like them ascend the national stage, their ethnic identity as Nuosu, in the sense of being members of local and kinship communities like those described in the previous three chapters, is eclipsed by their *minzu* identity as Yi. In these wider contexts, the differences between Nuosu and other kinds of Yi, such as Nasu, Lipuo, Laluo, Sani, Samei, Ashi, or Nisu, to name a few, disappears, and Yi becomes a homogeneous category, rather like Han, with internal differences relegated to the rubric of "branches," or *zhixi*, and even these branches are rarely known to outside observers. To the adoring crowds who slaughter oxen when they visit villages, these Nuosu who have made it are just that, local boys who have made good in China and the world. But to the outsiders, they are Yi, and that is about all one needs to know. Nevertheless, Yi is a category that subsumes a lot of local and cultural difference, and in order to understand the place of Nuosu in the national scheme of things, we need to examine the category Yi in more detail.

YI AS A CATEGORY

The category Yi was not exactly invented by the Communists during the process of ethnic identification in the 1950s. For a long time, there had been both the category and the name, though they did not correspond. In the Qing period and the first half of the twentieth century, the Chinese term Luoluo was used for a wide variety of people, including most of the people now classified as Yi. There were several theories as to the origins of this term (there is even one group that calls itself Lolopo—see Lietard 1913, Mueggler 2001), but none is really conclusive. Westerners also picked up the term, beginning with missionaries and explorers in the late nineteenth century; most probably did not realize just how pejorative the term was. In general, it seemed to refer primarily to people who lived east or southeast of Tibet and spoke Tibeto-Burman languages, mainly those of what is now identified as the Yi branch. There were at the same time, however, a lot of local names for various peoples who might have been included in the broader Luoluo category. Several early Western explorers and missionaries commented on the problematic boundaries of the category: Alfred Lietard, for example, a meticulous and unbiased early observer of the Yi, included in his list of "Lolo tribes" the Lisu, now a separate *minzu* altogether (1913: 43–44). Herbert Mueller, in an authoritative summary published about the same time, included the Woni of Puer and Simao, a group now officially classified as part of the Hani *minzu* (Mueller 1913: 44). He also expressed a Westerner's exasperation with the problem: "But it is often difficult to decide which races should still be thought of as Lolo, and which as more independent relatives of this people" (ibid.: 40). And A.-F. Legendre, a doctor who spent years traveling here and there across Yi territory in Sichuan and Yunnan, was sure that the peoples in this category ought not to be classed together: "This time I became certain that one finds in Yunnan many tribes known as Loloish, and who call themselves that, who have almost nothing in common, physically or morally, with those of Liangshan" (Legendre 1913: 392).

It is easy to demonstrate that there is, in many cases, little in common among the various "branches" now assigned to the Yi *minzu*. For example, even though the six officially recognized dialects of the Yi language differ considerably in their vocabulary and pronunciation, and even though the Central and Western dialects are closer to Lisu and Lahu than to the Northern, Northeastern, Eastern, or Southeastern branches, Yi is considered a single language in official classifications. Similarly, there is extreme cultural variation among the groups. None but the Nuosu have the caste system (though others, specifically the Nasu, most closely related to the Nuosu, may have traces of something like it). Many Yi groups, especially in Yunnan, have had much closer contact than have the Nuosu with surrounding Han society and culture, particularly since the reabsorption of the Southwest into the empire in the Yuan, with its concomitant massive immigration of Han military and civil colonies to the area, and even more so since the *gaitu guiliu* of the Yongzheng era incorporated most of their communities into the regular civil administration. And in fact, many sources attribute the *divergence* of language, custom, and social practices specifically to the differential influences of the larger Han environment. For example, Chen Tianjun writes that the slave-feudal transition occurred at three different times in the three different areas of Yi settlement. In Yunnan, it came earliest, at the time Nanzhao was taken over by Dali, whereas it persisted in Guizhou and northeastern Yunnan until the Ming, and in Liangshan, in modified form at least, to the 1950s (Chen Tianjun 1987: 114–17).

It is still not entirely clear exactly why the limits of the category Yi were drawn during the ethnic identification project exactly where they were, to include the Laluo and Lolopo, for example, and exclude the Lisu and Woni. We do know, from retrospective accounts, that investigators put the burden of proof on those groups who wanted to be separate *minzu* (Lin Yaohua 1987). We also know that they paid heavy attention to language and to demonstrable common historic origins, even when those were not part of the local people's own versions of their history or origins (Jiang Yongxing 1985). But my best guess is that they included in the category Yi just about everyone who had previously been called Luoluo, either by Han neighbors or in written Han sources.

Whatever the principles of classification (and the search for principles may be futile, since the process was hurried and often ad hoc), the name for the category became a real question. Luoluo was clearly ruled out because it was pejorative, and there was no local term common to all groups or comprehensive of local groups and others included in the category. The solution came from the fact that in Liangshan and many other areas, Nuosu or other Yi, when speaking the Han language, often called themselves Yi 夷, an old term that originally referred to eastern barbarians but that had long been used in the ethnology and administration of the Southwest. Lin Yaohua, in his 1947 monograph, explains at the beginning that Nuosu people speaking Han call themselves Yijia, in contrast to Hanjia (from which derives, perhaps, Hxiemga), and that they almost never use the term Luoluo (Lin 1994 [1947]: 1). Yi 夷 itself seemed a bit derogatory, but the homophonic Yi 彝, seemed perfect, and aside from the fact that nobody who isn't one can remember how to write the character, the name has stuck, and become the Han translation of Nuosu, Lipuo, Nasu, Laluo, Sani, Nisu, and many other local self-appellations.[1]

In other words, ethnic identification lumped together a large number of local and regional communities whose origins seemed to be similar and whose languages were related, and who had some customs in common, such as texts for sending the soul back through a series of geographic place-names to the supposed point of origin. Before 1949, however, these "branches" had had very little to do with each other. This is demonstrated by the fact that, although the term Ni can be found in ritual texts from many areas, and it seems to refer to Yi as opposed to Han, Tibetan, or other peoples, there was never a term in common parlance in the local languages that referred to the whole group we now know as Yi.

There is lots of remaining evidence of the disunity of Yi as a category, in Liangshan and elsewhere. For example, in Puwei Township, Miyi County, there are officially three "branches" of the Yi: Nuosu, "Abu," and Tazhi. The "Abu" and Tazhi were relatives or retainers of the Ji *tusi* who ruled the area from the late Ming to the 1930s; the Nuosu came in the great migrations in the eighteenth and nineteenth centuries. Similarly, in neighboring Malong Township, there are Nuosu and Yala (Peng Deyuan et. al. 1992: 24). In neither of these communities do Nuosu intermarry with "Abu," Tazhi, or Yala, even though all of them are classified as Yi. The Nasu language probably formerly spoken by "Abu" and Tazhi is almost (but not quite) mutually intelligible with Nuosu, and the Yala language, though also classified as a dialect of Yi, is completely mutually unintelligible with Nasu and Nuosu.[2] There are even groups classified as Yi who want to be something else; most prominent among these are the Sani in Lunan (now Shilin) and Luliang Counties, east of Kunming, who even inscribe their tourist artifacts "Sani *zu*," elevating the Sani to the status of a *minzu* of their own; some of the Laluo (or Shuitian) people in Renhe and Huaping also objected, at least in the 1980s, to being classified as Yi. Despite this demonstrable diversity, the 1950s project generally has stood the test of

1. In the 1994 edition of Lin's book, titled *Liangshan yijia de jubian* (The great transformation of the Liangshan Yi), the modern character replaces the former in the title and also in the text, which otherwise seems to remain unchanged except for the addition of new material in some chapters. I will not analyze the politics of this graphic change here.

2. I treat the ethnic identity and ethnic relations of these and other "little groups" in some detail in chapter 13. Despite the fact of their classification as Yi (and only some of them dispute it), the nature of their ethnic relations is completely different from that of the Nuosu and is thus treated separately.

time; only the Jinuo of Sipsong Panna, once classified as Yi, have successfully obtained recognition as a separate *minzu*.

When I first tell Western friends about this situation, their sympathies immediately gravitate to the little guys, or in this case, the little groups of a few tens or hundreds of thousands who do not want to be indiscriminately lumped in with the huge category Yi. But ethnic identification did not create a situation that only opposed clunky, lumpy state categories against the reality of local discourse. The process in fact incorporated some of the local discourse (and more of the local people) into the larger discourse of the unified country with fifty-six *minzu*. And among ethnic elites, this has led to a counterdiscourse that suggests that the category of Yi is not too big, but rather too *small*.

A Nuosu scholar friend of mine, for example, expressed this view. He told me that he had traveled among many different ethnic groups in Sichuan and Yunnan, including not only various branches of the Yi, but also Lisu, Lahu, Hani, Naxi, and Mosuo. He found, everywhere he went, great linguistic and cultural similarities. And in fact, this is true enough. There is a basic Tibeto-Burman grammatical structure, with verb aspect markers, a subject-object-verb word order, a certain kind of pronominal structure, and so forth. The similarities are even closer if we take only the Yi branch (which includes Lisu, Lahu, Naxi, and Hani in addition to the Yi language). There were also cultural similarities—the aforementioned soul-sending rituals are common to most of these peoples (I myself have recorded some of the chants among the eastern Naze). From all this, he drew the conclusion that ethnic identification had probably been structured with the intention of breaking up the Yi into smaller units, so they would not be potentially so strong politically.

The unity of the category is a sensitive matter with ethnic elites generally. For example, I wrote an article (Harrell 1990) contrasting the nature of ethnic identity in three Yi communities: a Nuosu community in Yanbian; a Lipuo community in Pingdi, in southern Renhe; and a Shuitian community in Zhuangshang, in western Renhe. Though neither the Nuosu nor the Lipuo community had any problem with the category Yi, many Shuitian at that time did not like it. The article has been reprinted, in a Chinese translation, in the journal *Sichuan Minzu Research* (Sichuan minzu yanjiu), and although the description of the Shuitian community and its less-than-friendly relationships with the local Han was left in the article, any mention of their disagreement with being included in the category Yi was excised as too sensitive, particularly for Yi elites.[3]

---

3. In a similar vein, several small groups, including the Baima people of northwestern Sichuan, have tried to separate themselves off from the Zang, or Tibetan, *minzu*. The explanations that cir-

Outside of the elites, it is hard to know how much importance the unitary category of Yi has for local people. Clearly, in those areas where there are multiple Yi groups, many of whose animosities or lack of interaction reach back far beyond the period of ethnic identification, telling people they are all Yi has not materially changed their relationships with one another. And in areas where there is only one Yi group (such as most of Liangshan), the distinctions have little practical relevance. It is when members of local groups also participate in the wider national and international discourse that being Yi becomes important. And in these wider contexts, ethnic elites have gone to great efforts in many areas not so much to assert the unity of the Yi (which they assume without question), but to communicate the nature, the history, and, most of all, the glory of Yi culture to the Chinese world and to the world at large.

SCHOLARSHIP ON YI HISTORY AND CULTURE

There is now an enormous amount of scholarship on Yi ancient and modern history, on ritual and historic texts written in the Yi script, on the slave social system of Liangshan, on certain rituals and celebrations, and on prospects for economic development in Yi districts. In addition to the aforementioned collections of historical and ethnological materials, there are monographs (e.g., Zimei 1992, Bamo 1994, Wu Jingzhong 1993), all dealing with customs and religion (mostly in Liangshan) as well as essay collections on general topics (Xinan Minzu Yanjiu Xuehui 1987a and 1987b), and on specific areas such as literacy in *Nuosu bburma* (Sichuan Minzu Yuyan Xuehui 1990 and Sichuan Minzu Guangbo Diantai 1990) or household and family organization (Yuan Yayu 1992). There are now three journals—*Yi Research* (Yizu yanjiu), published in Chuxiong; *Liangshan Nationalities Research* (Liangshan minzu yanjiu), published in Xichang; and *Yi Studies of China* (Zhongguo Yixue), published in Beijing—devoted wholly or mostly to Yi studies. I have to confess right here that, despite the middling number of such articles and books cited in this volume, I have not yet begun to gain what historians have traditionally called "bib-

---

culate informally among the ethnology community for why their petitions have been rejected, time and time again, by the Nationalities Commission in Beijing, always center on the desire not to offend Tibetan elites, especially the late tenth Panchen Lama. There are, however, also scholarly arguments in Tibetan-language journals purporting to demonstrate on historical and philological grounds that these people (and the Prmi as well—see chap. 10) are unambiguously Tibetan (Upton 2000).

liographic control" of this literature, let alone to make a real dent in actually reading it. I do believe, however, that from even a cursory look at a very non-random sample of this literature, we can learn something about the enterprise that is Yi scholarship and how it fits into the general ethnic enterprise of promoting Yi culture both to the outside world and to the growing literate (mostly literate in Han, since that is the language of most of the scholarship), educated Yi public.

First, fitting both with the traditions of writing ethnohistory (*minzu shi*) and with the conclusions about the nature of *minzu* embodied in the project of ethnic identification, scholarship on Yi assumes the historical unity of the category, the objective reality of something called a *minzu* that endures through history. In order to establish the historicity of this reality, of course, historians must construct a *minzu* narrative similar in structure and function to the national narratives described by Bhabha (1990).[4] Whatever the shifting reality of ethnic relations, of local peoples and their alliances and conflicts, over the millennium and a half from the early Tang or even earlier to the present, it must be made to look like the unfolding of a single, unified historical narrative. To this end, historical writers such as Ma Changshou (1987) and Chen Tianjun (1987) speak of the existence of identifiably Yi people at least as early as the time of the Baiman and Wuman in Yunnan during the early Tang dynasty; the Wuman are said to be identifiable as the ancestors of the Yi. Qi Qingfu (1987), reviewing the establishment of the Nanzhao kingdom in the 740s, advances the now generally accepted hypothesis that the first ruling dynasty of that kingdom was Yi (and not Bai) and that all of the succeeding dynasties were Bai.

In order to make this assumption of a single historical *minzu* narrative convincing, scholars combine traditional Chinese historiography with Yi genealogical recitations (usually by *nzymo*, *nuoho*, or *bimo*), which lead back through several tens of generations to the time when "the six ancestors split up" (*liuzu fenzhi*). Two of these ancestors, called Qoni and Gguhxo in Nuosu, are traditionally considered to be the ancestors of the Yi of Liangshan; the other four are considered to be the ancestors of various groups of Yi in Yunnan, Guizhou, and Guangxi (Ma Changshou 1987: 10–31). *Nzymo*, *nuoho*, and *bimo* clans in Liangshan routinely trace their own genealogies to one or the other of these

---

4. I have elaborated on the structure of *minzu* narratives in Harrell 1996a. A similar (and similarly constructed) historical narrative for the Yao, another widely dispersed, culturally and linguistically diverse *minzu*, is described in Litzinger 1995.

two ancestors.[5] People who engage in the study of southwestern history generally, or Yi history in particular, now talk routinely of the breakup of the six ancestors as a historical event, even though many people now think that the six ancestors were six tribes of proto-Yi who were originally allied but then split up and migrated to various points in the Southwest.

Constructing a unified historical narrative in support of the idea of *minzu* unity runs into problems, however, when the great cultural and linguistic diversity of the present-day Yi peoples is taken into account. There are two ways to deal with this. One, of course, is the simple expedient of looking for commonalities in language, ritual, religious belief, and other areas of common culture. This is the tack taken, for example, in the Bamo sisters' *Record of the Customs of the Yi* (Yizu fengsu zhi), where the first chapter is devoted to a general account of the Yi, including a demonstration that the language is basically the same everywhere, though there are dialectal variations (Zimei 1992: 2–3). In this view, the differences are superficial and due to the lack of communication over long distances, as well as different historical conditions in different areas. The second possible strategy is to admit the great size of the differences between one group and another but use the simplified Marxist theory of historical stages, along with the progress of Han civilization and differential contact of various Yi groups with it, to explain why Yi society and culture are so different, for example, in Yunnan and in Liangshan. This is the tack taken in Chen Tianjun's aforementioned article (1987).

Much ethnological scholarship, covering such areas as religion, ritual, and customs generally (as well as folklore) can exist outside this unifying narrative, as particularistic accounts of local social and cultural phenomena. But in another sense, such literature on Nuosu society and culture assumes a particularly important place in the dialogue on Yi studies generally, precisely because of the purported isolation and slow development of Liangshan in comparison to other areas (Zimei 1992: 5; Chen Tianjun 1987; Ma Changshou 1987). Nuosu customs and culture become the typical, the original, the untouched and unspoiled versions, the pure phenomena that in other areas can only be glimpsed through multiple filters of Han influence and historic cultural and demographic change. This attitude is best exemplified by the idea of the slave system of production. Because of Marxist-Leninist historiographic stage models, the Nuosu slave system (which was real enough, but see Ma Erzi 1993), becomes the model for the slave system that *must have existed everywhere* before

---

5. E.g., see numerous examples recorded in Sichuan Sheng Bianji Zu 1987; each clan traces its ancestry to either Qoni or Gguhxo.

Han influence shoved history forward in other areas while it stood still in Liangshan.[6]

Second, scholarship on the Yi is designed to demonstrate to whoever is watching (and perhaps particularly to the Yi themselves) that Yi culture is something to be proud of, something that has many refined and highly developed features, something that can hold its head high in the face of the world. Part of the impetus for this kind of scholarly effort stems from the knowledge among Yi scholars that the Yi are usually considered one of the most backward (*luohou*) *minzu* in China and that the Nuosu of Liangshan, who exemplify Yi society because of their relative purity, are thought not only to be backward in the sense of dirty, poor, illiterate, and remote but also backward in the sense of having retained the slave system so much longer than all the other *minzu*. Because traditional scholarship, mostly by Han scholars, often used terms such as "cruel" to describe the oppression and exploitation of slaves, producing such gems as "tools who could talk" to describe the *gaxy*, Nuosu scholars have felt even more strongly the need to demonstrate the positive side of Yi life and culture.

One very commonly heard defense among Nuosu intellectuals goes something like "You can't take the conditions of Yi society in Liangshan on the eve of Liberation to represent the situation of the Yi throughout most of our history." According to this view, there were times when Yi culture was every bit as refined and developed as that of the surrounding peoples, including the Han. One piece of evidence often adduced for this opinion is the tradition of the *bimo* priests. Called "traditional Yi intellectuals" (*Yizu chuantong zhishifenzi*) in this discourse, *bimo* are praised for their knowledge of history, geography, medicine, physiology, agronomy, and a wealth of other humanistic and scientific fields, and for transmitting this knowledge down through the generations (Bamo 2001).

Another manifestation of this desire to demonstrate the value of Yi culture appears in scholarship and intellectual discourse on the origins of the various Yi writing systems. There is, in fact, little concrete, datable evidence of any Yi writing systems before the Yuan and Ming dynasties, at which time inscriptions ancestral to most of the scripts used by Yi peoples today are found on stone stelae, mostly in Guizhou, where Nasu *tusi* ruled during that period (Ma Xueliang 1982: 1–8). But the story circulates among educated Yi that in fact the Yi were the first in the world to invent writing and that Han and others learned to write from the Yi. The idea was first brought up in conjunction with the

---

6. Pan Jiao (n.d.) provides a particularly lucid analysis of the phenomenon of making Nuosu into prototypical Yi.

fifty-some single symbols found on pottery dated to the fifth millennium B.C.E. (K. C. Chang 1977: 113–14) at the early Neolithic site of Banpo, now in the city of Xi'an in the northwest of China proper. People thought these symbols might be ancestral to Yi writing of some sort, and made some speculations as to a possible course of evolution to present-day systems. The story, however, has gone beyond formal or even speculative scholarship. I have heard it several times in exaggerated form, perhaps best exemplified by a Nuosu militia captain I met in Baiwu, who told me that the symbols on the Banpo pots (which were probably twenty thousand years old) had remained a mystery to the greatest scholars in the land, including Mao Zedong's captive intellectual Guo Moruo, until they were shown to a Nuosu *bimo*, who could read fifty-four of the fifty-six symbols immediately. This demonstrated conclusively that Yi had invented writing, and Han had learned it from them.[7] A more general idea of the contribution of Yi peoples to civilization in general and Yi civilization in particular is contained in the Yunnanese Yi scholar Liu Yaohan's book *A New Approach to the Origin of Chinese Civilization* (Zhongguo wenming yuantou xintan), in which he argues that many of the innovations of ancient Chinese civilization, including the calendar, originated with the Yi and were later adopted by other peoples (Liu 1985).

This commitment of Nuosu and other Yi intellectuals to the enterprise they sometimes describe as propagandizing Yi culture to the world, or *xiang shijie xuanchuan Yizu wenhua* , carries over even to my own role and those of other foreigners who study one or another aspect of Yi culture and society. Senior and junior scholars alike have praised us for assuming whatever minor role we take in making the Yi and their culture known. The holding of two International Yi Studies Conferences (in Seattle in 1995 and in Trier, Germany, in 1998), along with the publication of the edited papers from the 1995 Seattle conference (Harrell 2001) are seen by many Yi scholars and intellectuals as an example of this broadcast function, which the Yi intellectuals themselves often take as their major mission in professional life.

7. In fact, Guo Moruo (1972), as well as Li Xiaoting (1969), did try to demonstrate the connection of these glyphs to the writing on shell and bone (*jiaguwen*) of north China about three thousand years later, and Ho Ping-ti, in his *The Cradle of the East* (1976) made similar claims. K. C. Chang's *The Archaeology of Ancient China* (1977: 114) shows a sample of these signs, and many of them do, in fact, duplicate or very closely resemble some of the syllabic signs in Nuosu writing. The same claim, however, could be made for the Roman alphabet: one can find the capital letters I, T, Y, X, Z, N, K, L, and E, along with an upside-down A.

CULTURAL DISPLAY

Another way to introduce Yi culture to the world (and to give Yi, particularly urban Yi, something to be proud of under the world's gaze) on a more popular level is the promotion of folk culture, or the modified forms thereof, for local and wider consumption. Since the adoption of the new Autonomy Laws and related policies in the early 1980s, this kind of activity has been one of the most politically innocuous ways of building or restoring ethnic pride without touching on sensitive topics that might get the perpetrators in trouble. In fact, as I have explored in more detail elsewhere (Harrell 1996b), one of the ways that the state *minzu* organs and local officials alike promote their project of nation-building in a "unified, multiethnic state" is to stress, for insiders and outsiders alike, the differences among *minzu* and local groups, while denying that those differences take the form of conflict. Many foreign writers (Schein 1989, 1997, 1999; Swain 1990; Oakes 1995) have stressed the interconnection of cultural display with the economics of the tourist industry: visitors want to see colorful ethnic costumes and customs, and locals want both to make money and to display their own cultures with pride, so ethnic color, in the form of clothes, dances, songs, and festivals, takes on a new life as a commodity.

There is a commodity aspect of ethnic color in Liangshan, as I will describe below, but I do not think commodification and tourism can be seen as the major reasons for this display, since there is very little tourism in Liangshan, by comparison to many places in Yunnan (such as Kunming, Dali, Lunan, Lijiang, and Sipsong Panna) or to tourist areas in southeastern Guizhou (Oakes 1995, Cheung 1996, Schein 1999). Foreign tourists are almost entirely absent, and even Chinese tourism usually passes the prefecture by on the way to more famous spots in Yunnan and Guizhou. I think the reason for the revival of cultural display in Liangshan is partly to increase the ethnic pride of the Nuosu themselves and partly to look impressive to the increasingly heterogeneous gaze of the Chinese reading and TV-watching public, as well as to visitors who come to the area primarily for reasons other than tourism but who like to experience a little ethnic color along the way. Ethnic color is thus less a commodity here than a form of symbolic capital whose value lies in insiders' ability both to enjoy it and to use it to impress outsiders.

An example of cultural promotion that is directed mainly at Nuosu themselves comes from the standardization, recording, and further innovation in Nuosu music and dance. Nuosu people in villages and small towns, like minority people all over southwest China (but pointedly unlike Han or Hui), do a lot of dancing in a circle or a line. At the head of the line a man plays simple, repetitive melodies on a high-pitched, bamboo transverse flute; the second dancer in line places his or her hand on the flutist's shoulder, and all trailing dancers hold hands, forming part or all of a circle. Each tune, according to its melody and tempo, has a particular step that goes with it; these steps, ranging from sixteen to thirty-two beats, are repeated until the flutist changes the tune. They are easy to learn, and a large number of people around a roaring fire on a cold night at a wedding or holiday celebration can have a roaring good time, especially when the dancers are also skilled enough singers to invent or remember mildly titillating or insulting verses to sing to the songs.

Nowadays, however, these dances have taken on a more standardized and explicitly ethnic flavor. First, since boom boxes are available in all but the poorest and most remote areas, when the flutist gets tired or wants a smoke or drink, the boom box can be set on a bench or table near the fire, and there is a standard tape that uses pop instruments to play some of the same tunes, eliciting some of the same steps. But there is only one tape of Nuosu melodies (there is another one for Naze/Prmi dances, which is only slightly different), and so once-through-the-tape becomes a kind of routine. Nevertheless, every Nuosu township I have ever been to has this tape, and it has become a kind of prescribed ethnic performance, especially for schoolchildren and young people, and, when one is available, for any kind of outside visitor, including foreigners. In addition, there is a series of melodies on the other side of the tape that are designed to accompany a complex square-dance type of performance by eight boys and eight girls; I don't know what the original source of this kind of dance may have been.

Not only circle-dance tunes, but drinking songs have also become standardized property of the Yi, though of course only Nuosu listen to Nuosu drinking songs. In particular, the drinking song "Guests from Afar" (Sumu divi wo) has become a kind of Nuosu anthem, which is sung for visitors when they enter a school or sometimes a village, and certainly at all manner of banquets, receptions, and dinners; there is even a Han language version now, as recounted in the story of the banquet for the television reporters told in chapter 1.

The appropriation of modern cultural forms in music goes beyond instrumentation, standardization, and recording, however. There is now a Nuosu pop/rock group, consisting of three young men, called (in Chinese) Shan Ying, or Mountain Eagle, which by 1994 had made two tapes, both widely available in Xichang record stores. The first, consisting mainly of pop-type tunes, is called in Han "Wo ai wode jiaxiang," or "I Love My Homeland," a translation of the Nuosu song title "Nga muddi nga cy mgu." Two of the songs on the tape express love for the singer's mother, especially when he is far away and misses her; these often bring tears to the eyes of listeners. Other titles include the aforementioned "Go Softly in the Month of the Tiger" and an original drinking song, simply entitled "Drink Up," or "Nry ndo." Their second tape, *Liangshan Rock-and-Roll*, includes more rocklike songs, and in a crossover effort, some of these are sung in the Han language. In 1994 these tapes were extraordinarily popular; I think every driver I rode with had them in his car and played them frequently, and there was much talk among urban Nuosu about the artists, the songs, and their content. The forms may be borrowed, but the content, with such themes as love for the homeland and longing for mother, is explicitly ethnic, both in its attachment to place and idiom and in its themes, which would have little resonance in most mass cultures today. I doubt that many non-Nuosu people other than ethnologists or folklorists have ever purchased copies of this tape.

Another revived (or perhaps more accurately, redesigned) cultural form that is now displayed primarily for internal consumption is the factory-manufactured red-yellow-black painted wooden dinnerware. As described in chapter 6, until the 1980s the dishes were primarily made by certain specialist clans in particular villages in various parts of Liangshan. In the early 1980s, factories were opened in Xide and Zhaojue, and by the early 1990s they could hardly keep up with demand. They print brochures, sometimes complete with price lists, for foreign and domestic customers, but most people buy them at the factory, in nearby stores, or in the department stores in the cities. A Nuosu home cannot be without them, but in a reversal of the pop-music case described above, here a local form has been adapted to a contemporary use. There are now hundreds of types of utensils, many of them designed for urban Chinese social life, such as beer glasses, covered teacups, chopsticks, and the plates and bowls that make up a rather fancy Chinese banquet-table setting. Nuosu people living in Xichang, who eat stir-fried vegetables or Sichuan spicy bean-curd more often than they eat chunks of mutton or pork, can still eat ethnic if they use these dishes and can display their ethnicity just by having them in the glass-fronted cupboard in the living room (fig. 15). Nuosu-style serving dishes are thus commodified, and unlike other cultural forms, they have become popular among members of other ethnic groups, including Han; one increasingly sees them used as fruit dishes and the like in middle-class homes in the region.

Many other forms of cultural promotion serve the purposes of both inside affirmation and outside display. For example, starting in 1993 some officials in the prefectural government decided to hold a modern celebration of the mid-summer Fire Festival, which has been designated the Yi holiday, though in my

FIG. 15. Nuosu-style lacquerware at an urban Xichang banquet

experience all ethnic groups in the Southwest, including the Han, celebrate it. So every August there is now the International Torch Festival, complete with sports events (wrestling and horse racing), song and dance shows, and even a beauty contest, in which young women dress in elaborate versions of Nuosu dress, and in addition to the talent competitions (which would be recognizable to an American or Chinese audience familiar with Miss Universe and the like), contestants parade around in a half-moon type posture in which they hold the hems of their pleated skirts out on each side and move with tiny, mincing steps. I once watched a tape of this contest while a four-year-old boy in the family I was visiting did a hilarious imitation in front of the VCR with a cloth tied around his waist and a towel piled on his head.

It is difficult to discern the target—external or internal—of another kind of cultural display, the coffee-table book. These have been produced for the Yi of Guizhou (Chen Changyou 1992) as well as for Liangshan. The Liangshan volume, under the general editorship of the art photographer Zhong Dakun, and published by the People's Fine Arts Publishing House in Beijing, contains technically outstanding, sometimes breathtaking photography, high quality printing, and a lot of features that situate it in nationalities politics and in Chinese official publishing. Inscriptions at the beginning were written by Wu

Jinghua, who is joined by Feng Yuanwei and other notables on the editorial advisory committee, and Liu Shaoxian, then party secretary of Liangshan, has written the preface. Depicted in photographs accompanied by Chinese and English texts (but no Nuosu text) are such conventional subjects as landscapes, houses, costumes, dinnerware, holidays, *bimo* and *sunyi*, and of course modernization and progress. It thus celebrates the Yi of Liangshan in the context of Chinese cultural politics. Nuosu intellectuals and entrepreneurs will definitely want the book, but it is too expensive for most people; I suspect the publishers are hoping for a market among urban Chinese in China proper, and perhaps among overseas Chinese (since it uses *fanti*, or unsimplified, Chinese characters). It stands somewhere between the poles of cultural capital creation and ethnic commodification (Zhong 1992).

Probably the most spectacular cultural display I have ever seen was the dinner for the visiting television crew described in chapter 1. The setting was the finest, by mid-1990s Chinese urban standards, that could be had in Xichang, and the food, most of it at least, was impeccably representative of modern Sichuanese haute cuisine. The people in attendance were of high (though not extremely high) status: a former vice-prefect, a cardiac surgeon, the head of the Foreign Affairs Office, several professors, some foreigners. It was probably the kind of crowd and the kind of service this television crew had seen in a hundred small- and medium-sized cities all over China. But the display of ethnicity overrode everything. All of the local attendees save one (not counting the foreigners) were Nuosu. The waitresses were dressed in Yi garb, singing Yi songs, telling the guests of Yi proverbs and customs. There were red-yellow-black shot glasses served from similarly painted trays, the factory sort, of course. The food had to include, at least for a taste, buckwheat pancakes and chunks of meat. The topics of conversation were, of course, Yi culture, Yi society, Yi customs, even Yi language. And the purpose, of course, was to facilitate a good treatment, in the forthcoming television newsmagazine segment, of three young women who had done the Yi proud by becoming a professor, an academy researcher, and a radio broadcaster.

It would be possible to bemoan the "inauthenticity" of a staged beauty contest (though there are things resembling beauty contests in traditional Nuosu culture), of drinking expensive Chinese liquor out of factory-produced lacquer cups, of coffee-table books with pictures posed just so that only girls dressed in the most Nuosu of costumes happen to enter the frame. Ethnic tourists, whose mission in their travels is to seek the ever-less-touristy and commercialized, ever-more-"authentic" place (Oakes 1998: 1–19) might be disappointed with any of these invented traditions. But the importance of this kind of display in

China's cultural politics—as Louisa Schein has shown for song-and-dance per-formances and official holiday celebrations among the Miao (1999), and as Almaz Han has shown for wrestling tournaments and summer fairs in Inner Mongolia (1999)—is that the impetus for these new versions of ethnic things comes primarily from the elites of the minority ethnic groups themselves. It is to instill pride in their own people and to gain respect and interest from out-siders (and of course to have fun and maybe make some tourist dollars) that these performances and displays are created and enacted. Nuosu cultural entre-preneurs, like Nuosu bureaucrats and economic entrepreneurs, are the insti-gators, leaders, and self-perceived beneficiaries of ethnically conscious activity, be it economic development, scholarly historical justification, or cultural dis-play. The creation, systematization, and display of ethnic things, old or new, is an important component in the revival of ethnic consciousness in 1980s and 1990s China.

FROM ETHNIC GROUP TO *MINZU* AND BACK AGAIN

Most of the groups and group relations described in the village case studies of chapters 6, 7, and 8 are of the sort that Western social scientists would call eth-nic groups and ethnic relations, or ethnicity. Groups of people, purportedly sharing common history and descent, and with some cultural traits in com-mon, display through a variety of languages, verbal and symbolic, their unity as groups and their differences from other groups with whose members (present or haunting by their absence) they interact more or less frequently. In the Nuosu case this ethnic identity is based most strongly in common kin-ship, including descent and affinity, and displays clear divisions between the we-group—Nuosu—and everyone else, whether or not there are large cultural differences that also divide them. If all ethnicity is at least partly local, the local manifestations of ethnic identity in Mishi, Baiwu, and Manshuiwan are clear, unambiguous, stable, and omnipresent in everyday life.

I think most urban Nuosu in Xichang feel their ethnicity at least as strongly as do their village relatives. But because they are educated, and because most of what most of them do all day is done in the context of contemporary China, their ethnicity is not just Nuosu, but consciously Yi. The *minzu* categorization may originally have been quite artificial. The ethnic identification project may have imposed an umbrella category on a large conglomeration of groups who were only distantly related and at that time had little consciousness of com-monality. But for urbanites in the 1980s and 1990s this commonality is impor-tant, for two reasons. First, they believe most of what they learn in school; they certainly believe that China has fifty-six *minzu*, and they believe this whether or not they also think that one of these, the Yi, or perhaps fifty-five of these, the minority *minzu*, have gotten a raw deal for the last forty years. So whether they think more in terms of opposition or of cooperation, it is in terms of their identity as members of the Yi *minzu*. Although the specific kinds of ethnic display found in Xichang are all derived from forms developed by Nuosu people in Liangshan, the content of scholarship suggests identification with a wider category, which is promoted by scholarly contacts at conferences and meetings with Yi from other parts of the Southwest, in the same way that cadres, who meet other Yi cadres, also have a face-to-face framework for this more-than-just-imagined *minzu* community. Consciousness is not uniform among the Yi, particularly not for little groups who are classified as Yi but feel little in common with their Nuosu neighbors, for example (see chap. 13). But for many people, what was originally an objective classification has become a subjective identity, and Yi is a true ethnic category.

For villagers, the process has not gone so far in most places, though it has certainly gone much further, for example, with college-educated officials and teachers in Manshuiwan than it has for illiterate farmers in Mishi. But with the gradual increases in education, media penetration, geographic mobility, and bilingualism that seem to be irresistible trends even in the heart of Liangshan, village Nuosu too will learn about the history and traditions of the Yi, about Yi in other places, even about the principles of *minzu* classification. For some of them, there might be a reaction, a formation of ethnic distinctions on the wider scene, such as that described by Hsieh Shih-chung (1995: 326) for Dai in Kunming, where people from Sipsong Panna and Dehong call each other, in the Han language, Xidai and Dedai, and have chosen to recognize little affinity. Or, perhaps, Yi—including all the multiple "branches" from Yunnan, Guizhou, and Guangxi—will become the relevant ethnic category for ordinary people, as it is now for governmental and scholarly elites. If this is true, if the local languages of ethnic identity and the metalanguage of ethnic identification begin to coincide in their vocabulary and syntax, then, paradoxically, China may begin to resemble the model set forth by Stalin, which was so unusable in practice for the workers of the ethnic identification project. It may also face in the Southwest, at that point, the kinds of ethnonational disputes and conflicts that have plagued the Inner Asian frontier areas of Tibet, Xinjiang, and Mongolia. For now, the Yi are not a nation, and the ethnic identity of the Nuosu—stable, discrete, and kin-based—works differently from that of other groups in Liangshan.

PART 3

HISTORICALLY CONTINGENT ETHNICITY: THE PRMI AND NAZE

10 / The Contingent Ethnicity of the Prmi

P rmi and Naze ethnicity works very differently from that of the Nuosu. Nuosu ethnic boundaries are definite. All Nuosu are Yi in *minzu* terms, and Nuosu are clearly distinguished locally from other ethnic groups (both Yi and non-Yi) both by recognition of difference and by endogamy, just as in larger contexts they are clearly distinguished as Yi from members of other *minzu*, and in many situations from other Yi as well. Prmi and Naze ethnicity, by contrast, is both less definitely bounded and more contingent. Boundaries between Prmi and Naze are blurred even in terms of recognition (some people are not even sure who is who), and still more so by frequent intermarriage between the two groups, as well as by intermarriage with Han in many contexts, and sometimes even with Naxi. In addition, both Prmi and Naze have had different *minzu* identities at different times and in different places—Prmi have been both Zang and Pumi; Naze have been Naxi, Mongolian (or anyway Mengguzu), and maybe Mosuo.

Prmi and Naze thus display what I call historical and contingent ethnicity. It is likely that, in the days before the ethnic identification project, they were not only known by a variety of names in a variety of languages but also identified themselves with a variety of different collectivities in different situations. The terms Prmi and Naze are autodesignations of the respective groups in their own languages. Prmi speak a language of the Qiang branch of Tibeto-Burman, whereas the Naze, whose language is closely related to that of the Naxi, speak a language variously thought to belong to the Yi and the Qiang branches. In other languages, however, these neat categories become blurred. In Nuosu, both Prmi and Naze are known as Ozzu, a category that also includes Tibetans. In classical and early twentieth-century Chinese sources, both groups were known as Xifan, or "Western Barbarians," and early Western explorers, ethnologists, and missionaries picked up this usage. The religious identification of both groups drew them partly toward Tibet through their Buddhism, but they also had their own priestly spirit-practitioners, called *ndaba* in Naze and *hangue* in Prmi, who are not affiliated with any wider religious community, though some of their rituals resemble those conducted by Naxi *ddobaq* or Nuosu *bimo*. At the same time, political allegiances drew some of the elite families of the Prmi toward Tibet (at least one Prmi ruler was a subordinate of the Dalai Lama) and of the Naze toward Mongolia (several local Naze rulers claimed descent from Qubilai's troops who conquered western Liangshan in the thirteenth century).

In short, we cannot reconstruct Prmi or Naze ethnic identity at any time in the past; we can only surmise that each local community presented a different picture. All we can do, in fact, is to look at the *current, local* picture in terms of the everyday languages of ethnic identity, and look at the past in terms of the metalanguages of ethnohistory and ethnic identification, and then examine how the metalanguages and the everyday languages interact to produce the present ethnic identities of the Prmi and Naze. We will find a picture so fluid that even the formally rigid categories of ethnic identification are subject to slippage in both the Prmi and the Naze cases. We begin in this chapter with the Prmi and their ambiguous relationships with the Naze and with the broader category of Zang; chapters 11 and 12 deal respectively with the ethnic identity of the Naze and with the Naze as a multivocal symbol in the discourses of others.

THE PRMI AND THEIR LOCAL ETHNIC RELATIONS

The three factors of culture, history, and kinship, which we have seen to be the bases of ethnic identity generally and among the Nuosu, also operate in the ethnic consciousness of the Prmi. But they operate differently: among the Nuosu, these three factors, to varying degrees, distinguish Nuosu from other ethnic groups; in the Prmi case, by contrast, they sometimes distinguish and sometimes fail to distinguish, making the ethnic boundaries themselves fuzzy and shifting in some (though not all) communities. In the cultural realm, Nuosu ethnic identity is distinct and constant regardless of culture. Prmi ethnic identity, by contrast, varies as culture varies, but not uniformly. Many aspects of Prmi culture serve as ethnic markers in local communities, in two ways. First and unsurprisingly, ethnic markers serve to distinguish local Prmi from other local ethnic groups. But in other situations, culture and ethnicity do not coincide. Sometimes common cultural patterns unite Prmi and Naze (and sometimes even Naxi) in contrast to other groups such as Nuosu and Han; at other times cultural similarities between Prmi and Naze fail to unite the two, because they are overridden by factors of history and kinship that serve to preserve a Prmi/Naze distinction; and finally, sometimes cultural differences between Prmi and Tibetans are ignored, and Prmi and Tibetans are placed in the same category of Zang for religious or political reasons.

Ethnicity and Cultural Markers

In 1990 there was a total of about 57,000 Prmi, distributed as follows: In Yunnan, where Prmi are classified as Pumi, there were 14,000 in Lanping Bai and Pumi Autonomous County, 8,000 in Ninglang Yi Autonomous County, and another 4,000 in Weixi and Yongsheng Counties and in Lijiang Naxi Autonomous County. In Sichuan, where Prmi are classified as Zang, there are about 26,000 in Muli Zang Autonomous County and 5,000 in Yanyuan County (Yan and Chen 1986: 1–2; maps 1 and 5). A number of cultural traits sometimes, but not always, serve as ethnic markers to distinguish them from surrounding Nuosu, Han, Bai, Naxi, Miao, and perhaps other groups. These include language, religion, dress, and housing.[1]

Language. Most authorities agree that the Prmi language belongs to the Qiangic branch, or *Qiang yuzhi*, of the Tibeto-Burman subfamily of Sino-Tibetan (Matisoff 1991: 482; Guojia Minwei 1984: 585; Yan and Chen 1986: 2). Chinese official classifications recognize only one other language—Qiang—in that branch, but this classification has a political motivation (Harrell 1993); both Chinese and Western linguists (Matisoff 1991: 482; Liu Huiqiang, personal communication) also include eight or nine other languages, most of them spoken by people who, like the Prmi, were originally known to local Chinese as Xifan (Wellens 1998) and to Nuosu as Ozzu.

In Muli, the Prmi language is spoken by the largest single ethnolinguistic group, and is the everyday vernacular of peasants and officials alike; the language is also flourishing in parts of Ninglang. In Yanyuan, people still speak Prmi in Mianya Township, where the population is about 10 percent Prmi, and also in Gaizu Township, where Prmi are about 5 percent, but concentrated in a few villages. In Baiwu Township, by contrast, knowledge of the language is very scattered. For example, in Changma Village, about an hour-and-a-half walk from Baiwu Town, the population is about half Nuosu and half Prmi. Children of both *minzu* were reported by the local team leader to be fluent in both languages by middle childhood. In the Lianhe (United) team of Baiwu Town, on the other hand, where there are only 57 Prmi along with 160 Han

---

1. This account of ethnic markers in Prmi culture is based on Yanyuan, Muli, and Ninglang Counties, which I have visited, but does not necessarily hold in its details for the Lanping-Weixi-Lijiang area or for Yongsheng, where I have not been.

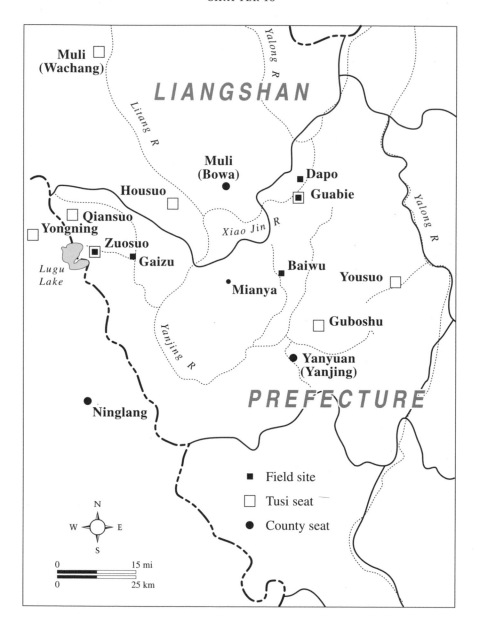

MAP 5. Yanyuan and surrounding areas

and 60 Naxi, knowledge of the language is fading. Some older people still speak it fairly fluently, but middle-aged people have limited vocabularies and do not use the language for conversation. Few young people can speak the language at all. Most Prmi there use a mixture of Han and Nuosu languages in their everyday conversation, with Han predominant (see chap. 7).

In both Muli and Yanyuan, people speaking the Han language uniformly and unambiguously refer to the Prmi language as Zangyu. More than once, after learning that I spoke Nuosu, Prmi have asked me in their own language whether I spoke Prmi (they use the term Prmi when asking, though I don't understand the rest of the sentence). They then ask me, in Han, "Ni hui shuo Zangyu ma?" (Do you speak Zang?). And this identification is followed through in the schools in Muli. Like their counterparts in Xide and Yanyuan (chaps. 6 and 7), the county authorities in Muli have recently made a commitment to bilingual education (*shuangyu jiaoyu*), with schoolchildren beginning the study of Han in the first grade and of their own ethnic language in the third. But of course there are no textbooks in the Prmi language, since it has no written form at present. And since the Prmi are a branch of the Zang *minzu*, the bilingual education is in the Zang language, that is to say Tibetan, using the "Uniform Teaching Materials for the Five Provinces and Regions," textbooks written and composed in Lhasa for members of the Zang *minzu* in Tibet, Qinghai, Gansu, Sichuan, and Yunnan (Upton 1999: 119).

I questioned several cadres and intellectuals (as well as a few members of rural households) in Muli about the relationship of their own language to the Tibetan spoken in Lhasa or the Khams dialects spoken by Tibetans in Western Sichuan, including the six thousand or so in the northern part of Muli County. They uniformly answered that the spoken languages were mutually unintelligible but that this was perfectly understandable in terms of dialect variation within the language spoken by a particular *minzu*. Han people from Beijing, Shanghai, and Guangzhou cannot understand each other either, one Prmi cadre said to me, but does this mean that they are not all Han just the same? The logging trucks that haul the old-growth forests of Muli up the treacherous highway to Yanyuan and then on to Xichang have the name of Muli Zang Autonomous County written on their doors in Chinese and Tibetan.

In Yunnan, of course Prmi are Pumi and do not study Tibetan in school; all their instruction is in Han unless they live in heavily Nuosu areas, where they may get some classes in *Nuosu bburma*. Though Prmi is not now written, there are indications that it may have been in the nineteenth century, using Tibetan script, and in 1993 local leaders in Ninglang told me that they were

FIG. 16. The monks at the Yongning monastery

making efforts to translate old texts and perhaps to revive the use of the written language.[2]

Religion. Prmi have two religious traditions. The first is Tibetan Buddhism; the second is the Dingba or Hangue religion, which has been defined by Chinese ethnologists and Pumi leaders as an indigenous religious tradition separate from Buddhism (Yan and Chen 1986: 71–74; Hu Jingming, personal communication 1993), a complex of folk beliefs and rituals that includes offerings to ancestors and nature spirits and may or may not include a written, textual tradition (Wellens 1998). The degree of adherence to both of these religious traditions varies greatly among the Prmi communities that I have visited.

With regard to Buddhism, a few examples will illustrate the range of variation. In the areas around the south shore of Lugu Lake in Ninglang County, as well as in most of Muli Zang Autonomous County, most Prmi are practicing Buddhists. Many families have formal shrines in their houses, complete with oil lamps burning constantly, pictures of the Dalai and Panchen Lamas, and

2. Charles McKhann and Koen Wellens (personal communications) also report the existence of texts written in the Prmi language, presumably using the Tibetan alphabet, in various remote areas in Muli.

the custom of inviting monks to perform calendrical rituals and rites of passage. Many families have had members enter the monkhood, and since the
revival of religious practice after the liberalization of the early 1980s, thirteen
of Muli County's monasteries have been partially or wholly refurbished, and
they are now training a new generation of monks, most of them Prmi. The
large monastery at Yongning, a township in the northern part of Ninglang,
is also newly flourishing, with a mixed population of Prmi and Naze monks
(fig. 16).[3]

In the township of Gaizu, about ten kilometers to the east of Lugu Lake,
Buddhist observance is still common, but the culture of Buddhism seems to
lie thinner on the landscape. The four ethnic groups that are resident in the
township roughly follow a pattern of vertical geographical stratification, with
Han and Meng (Naze) in the valleys, Zang (Prmi, locally called Xizu in the
Han language) on the middle slopes, and Yi (Nuosu) in the highlands. In the
central village of Gaizu, there are more Naze and Han than Prmi (and no Nuosu
at all), while the population of Shanhe and Sanjia, two villages across the river,
is mixed Naze, Prmi, and Nuosu, with no Han. More remote villages, according to local records, are exclusively Prmi and Nuosu.

The nearest temple for these villagers is at Zuosuo, near the southern shore
of the lake. There are two Buddhist priests[4] in Gaizu, and two in the Shanhe-
Sanjia area, but all four of them are Naze; people remark that it is ironic that
even though Buddhism comes from Tibet (Xizang), the Naze (or Meng) are
more religious than the Prmi (or Zang). None of the three priests we interviewed was very knowledgeable about Buddhism. The eldest, who was over
eighty in 1994, read to us from a Tibetan-language ritual text from his small

3. Naze in Ninglang, as elsewhere in Yunnan, are known in the Han language as Mosuo. A
fuller discussion of the various terms for Naze is to be found in chapter 11.

4. It is a real problem knowing what term to use for these men. They are called lamas in Chinese,
according to the usual usage in that language, but this is confusing to Western readers, who usually think of "lama" in its original, Tibetan sense of an incarnation or "emanation-body" (spelled
bla-ma in Tibetan), who is the reincarnation of a particularly important spirit such as a bod-
hisattva. In Tibet, ordinary celibate males in monastic establishments who wear red robes are called
grwa-pa, and in the Naze and Prmi languages the borrowed term djaba is commonly used for these
religious. In English, we call them monks. But the Prmi and Naze religious are not celibate and
do not live in monasteries. Chinese scholars writing in English have followed the Chinese usage
and called them lamas (Shih 2001, Weng 1995), but this is misleading to Westerners who know
anything about Tibetan Buddhism (in Chinese, an incarnate lama is called a huofo, which sometimes gets translated into English as "living Buddha"). Since the primary function of djaba in these
villages is to conduct rituals for lay clients, I have adopted the term "Buddhist priest," to distinguish them from the native priests (Prmi hangue and Naze ndaba).

FIG. 17. An old Naze priest reading a Tibetan-language text

collection, but he freely admitted that he could understand only part of the content (fig. 17). Nevertheless, all Prmi and Naze in this area profess themselves Buddhists, and they all call upon Buddhist priests for funerals, ancestral rites, curing, and other rituals.

In Baiwu, Buddhism is little more than a name. All Prmi there claim to be Buddhists, but no one knows much about Buddhism. Families I talked to claimed to have Buddhist texts, written in Tibetan, but could not produce them for me to look at, and nobody could read the Tibetan-language inscriptions posted over some families' doors at the Chinese New Year—they were written by a relative from a more devoutly Buddhist area, who had since returned home.

I know little of the Hangue religion and have never managed to meet a priest, or *hangue*. Mr. Hu Jingming, a Prmi leader from Ninglang and the vice-chair of the Ninglang County People's Consultative Conference, told me that the Hangue tradition is comparable to other non-Buddhist priestly traditions in the general area—the *ddobaq* of the Naxi and the *ndaba* of the Mosuo. People in Gaizu told me that there are some *hangue* in more remote mountain areas and that they perform rituals similar to those of the *ndaba* and *bimo*, including sending the soul back to the original homeland. The *hangue* may have had written religious texts in the past—the texts mentioned above, which Mr. Hu has collected, are probably ritual texts, and Mr. Yan Huaqian of Gaizu told me that *hangue* from the nearby mountains had Tibetan-script texts. Mr. Hu said that the Hangue religion was predominant among Prmi in the southern part of Ninglang, near Yongsheng, in contrast to the overtly Buddhist areas around Lugu Lake.[5]

Prmi religion of both kinds—Hangue and Tibetan Buddhist—serves as an ethnic marker, distinguishing Prmi from both Nuosu and Han, neither of whom practice either of these traditions.[6] Even though the practices of Naze *ndaba* are very similar to those of the *hangue*, and even those of the Nuosu *bimo* show some resemblance, the existence of *hangue* texts in Tibetan script (whatever language this script may turn out to represent) and the language used in the oral rituals distinguish *hangue* practices from those of the *bimo*, whose texts are in Nuosu, and from those of the *ndaba*, who have no written texts at all. Other groups with whom Prmi come in contact, however, also practice Tibetan Buddhism, including Naze in particular, as well as some Naxi. Buddhism thus creates a kind of unity among Naze and Prmi, particularly in the areas around Lugu Lake, where it is so visible in the lives of the people, but also in those areas where people do not actually know much about the faith or practice many of its rituals. In fact, Buddhism is only one of several aspects of life in which Prmi and Naze together form a kind of ethnic collectivity; others in the cultural realm are dress and housing, and still more can be found in the areas of common history and kinship relations.

Dress. In most areas I have visited, Prmi women's dress differs from that of neighboring groups such as Han, Nuosu, and Hmong. In Yanyuan, Ninglang, and Muli, there is a Prmi women's outfit, which consists of a long, pleated skirt of a single color (usually blue, black, or gray), over which they tie a rectangular apron with an embroidered edge. They top this with a wide belt, usually red, of homespun hemp; wear a wool or felt vest closed with frog-buttons in the front; and wrap their head in a turban of black cloth, or in the case of young women on festive occasions, sometimes multicolored yarn (fig. 18). This outfit is embellished with silver or other jewelry.

This style of dress serves to distinguish Prmi from Han, who never wear skirts, and from Nuosu and Hmong, who also wear skirts, but of very different

---

5. Charles McKhann (personal communication) observed *hangue* conducting a funeral in southwestern Muli in 1996. Koen Wellens began a research project on the Hangue religion in 1998.

6. There are certainly isolated Han Buddhists in this area, but they ordinarily do not follow Tibetan conventions or rituals, observing instead Chinese Mahayana (primarily Pure Land) forms.

FIG. 18. A Prmi bride and groom clowning for the camera.
She wears ceremonial dress.

design. On the other hand, when Prmi want to emphasize friendship with
Nuosu, they can haul out the proverb "Everybody who wears skirts is one big
family," thus including Prmi and Nuosu in one category that excludes the Han.
And even though many Prmi in Muli consider themselves to belong to the same
Zang group as the Khams-pa or Ba, whom the Prmi call Gami, their dress is
completely different.

Distinguishing ethnic groups by women's dress is of course pervasive in
southwest China. I was once riding in a jeep with a local Nationalities Office
cadre, who asked me if there were *minzu* in America. I said yes, and then he
asked me, "How do you tell them apart? Do they wear different clothes?" But

dress in fact tells a more complex tale about ethnic relations than the naïve correlation with *minzu* would indicate. For example, when I first visited Baiwu for a single afternoon, in September 1991, the Nuosu cadre who acted as my host wanted me to be able to visit one household of each of the five *minzu* represented in the two villages contiguous to the town. In each place, I asked about language and various other customs, and also about women's dress. The latter question inevitably produced a volunteer to pose for a photograph, and I came home with a roll of slides including Yi, Meng, Zang, and Naxi couture. But when I had the slides developed and projected them, I could not remember which was which; only the Nuosu and Han stood out, the Nuosu because their clothes are really different, and the Han because they were not included, since they don't have "costume" (*fuzhuang*), only "clothes" (*yifu*). The Naze, Prmi, and Naxi outfits were indistinguishable because they were identical. In fact, in every Prmi community I have visited, the ethnic dress of Prmi women is identical to that of the local Naze, and the Naxi families in Baiwu in Yanyuan, who were retainers and officers of the Prmi king of Muli, also maintain this style of dress.

Dress thus joins Buddhism as an ethnic marker that not only marks off Prmi clearly from Han and Nuosu, but also fails to draw a line between Prmi and Naze. And as with Buddhism, the importance of ethnic dress as a marker persists even in the absence of the marker itself. In all these places, most Prmi women usually wear pants and blouses, the ordinary Chinese rural dress, when they are working in the fields or around the house, so that it is not always possible to distinguish a Prmi from a Han woman by dress alone. But, like Buddhism, the clothes can be taken out of the closet when necessary, particularly on ritual occasions when it is important to display one's ethnicity.

Housing. Housing is another clear ethnic marker that differentiates Prmi from Han and Nuosu but not from local Naze. All over western Liangshan, housing styles of all ethnic groups are adapted to local building materials. This means that in any particular area, houses occupied by members of disparate ethnic groups will have a superficial similarity: all houses in Baiwu, which has no remaining great forests, are built of mud, while all houses in the Lugu Lake region in both provinces, as well as around Gaizu, are built in the "log cabin" (*muluo*) style. But floor plans, furniture, and household ritual paraphernalia distinguish the dwellings of various ethnic groups.

I have visited three styles of Prmi houses. In Shuzhu, a village almost directly above the county town of Muli, they have walls of stone, of stone and mud, or of wood in log-cabin style, and are centered around an interior room approached by a corridor from the front door. In the center of the room is a

FIG. 19. The interior of a Prmi house near Baiwu, looking from the
women's to the men's side of the room

hearth, surrounded by mats, and sometimes by chairs and tables, for sitting
and eating. Altars to spirits and ancestors are on the left-hand wall as one enters
the room, while Buddhist altars are directly above the hearth. There are no Naze
in this immediate area, but there are both Nuosu and Han in the same village,
and their houses have different, much less elaborate floor plans.

In Baiwu and its environs, the outer appearance of Prmi houses is identical to that of local Nuosu and Han houses; they are built of mud walls. But the
interior is easily distinguished. There is usually a walled courtyard, with one
or two of its sides given over to storage sheds and animal pens. On another
side of the courtyard is the main room, with a dirt floor in most cases (replaced
by concrete if people have become wealthy). This room is entered by a door
at one corner; along the wall on the door side are beds on which women can
sleep; on the other side, the beds are reserved for men. These beds are part of
the conceptual division of the room into male and female halves; at the end of
the room opposite the door, there is a hearth around which people sit; usually
men sit on the male side of the room and women on the female side (fig. 19).
Above the hearth is a whitewashed mud altar for the household deity Zambala;
here the head of the household makes offerings of liquor before meals (fig. 20).

FIG. 20. The Prmi household head offering liquor to Zambala
before a meal

There are other altars in the two corners of the house on the male side; the
ones at the front are for ancestors and those at the back are for various earth
and sky spirits. Han and Nuosu houses in these communities are fundamentally different from those of the Prmi and Naze in their layout—neither type
has a conceptual division into male and female halves; Nuosu living space is
divided into host and guest halves, and Han space, though marked by a single
altar opposite the main door, is not divided by gender or social role. But both
Naze and Naxi in this area build their homes with layout and ritual spaces identical to those used by the Prmi.[7]

Moving to the Lugu Lake region, including Gaizu and its environs, a similar pattern of resemblance and differentiation obtains. The log-cabin style
houses of the Han and Nuosu look like those of the Prmi and Naze from the
outside, but once one walks in, one notices the difference immediately. The
predominant Prmi and Naze house style in this area is that described in recent
ethnological works on the Naze by Shih (1994) and Weng (1995); the court-

7. This dualistic, gender-based division of space is quite different from the spatial-cosmological
arrangement of the Naxi of Lijiang, as described by McKhann (1989).

yard has downstairs animal pens and upstairs bedrooms on one side, a Buddhist shrine at the end opposite the entrance, and the large, elaborate main room (described more fully in chap. 11) on the side opposite the bedrooms.

Prmi culture is thus not a uniform thing. In many places Han influence has been extreme, to the point where the Prmi language itself is no longer spoken or no longer being taught to the young. But in every community I have visited, there are still some ethnic markers that set Prmi off from Han, Hui, Nuosu, Hmong, or other neighboring peoples. These include language, whether actively spoken or not, dress, housing, and a large number of ritual and calendrical practices that are too boring and redundant to be described in detail here. In those communities where there are no Naze, these markers operate as they do for other ethnic groups—as a kind of label for what makes "us" different from "them."

The problem with cultural markers and ethnicity, however, comes in those communities (which are numerous) where both Prmi and Naze live. The languages are completely separate and mutually unintelligible, though fairly closely related. But the other things that serve to mark off Prmi from Han and Nuosu do not mark them off from Naze, since Prmi and Naze seem to converge toward a common form, whether it be in dress, housing, or ritual, in each local community, and to covary perfectly with each other. So I have been in the presence of two middle-aged women, each wearing basically identical "ethnic dress," speaking Chinese to each other, since one was a Prmi and the other a Naze. Prmi and Naze often learn each other's languages, but they do not always do so. Culture, and the use of culture as ethnic markers, seems to be unable to tell us whether Prmi and Naze are one ethnic group or two. Can kinship and history help us understand this matter?

Ethnicity as a Set of Kin Relations

Prmi, at least in Yanyuan and Muli, belong to named patrilineal clans, and an individual's name in the Prmi language consists of the clan name plus a personal name, with the personal name used alone in most circumstances. Most Prmi also have a Han-language name consisting of an ordinary Chinese surname and given name. Marriage is not allowed within the clan, but it is often the case that two or more clans have the same Han surname, so that it appears to Han people that Prmi can marry close relatives. As with most non-Han groups in this area, Prmi often practice patrilateral cross-cousin marriage, which itself becomes an ethnic marker in that many educated Han consider it not only barbaric but genetically dangerous. Patterns of avoiding or encouraging marriage with other groups can also be ethnic markers, and Prmi patterns of intermar-

FIG. 21. Members of the groom's family blowing the conch shell
at a Prmi wedding to celebrate the new union

riage with various groups in different places vary from free intermarriage to none
at all. Prmi in Muli laughed at the suggestion that anyone would even consider
marrying Hmong, and I know of very few marriages with Nuosu, even though
Prmi seem to have no explicit prohibition. This may be due to the fact that the
Nuosu prohibit such intermarriage in most situations. Intermarriage with Han
is more ambiguous. As far as I know, Han people never prohibit marriage with
any other group, and whereas Prmi in Shuzhu, a Prmi/Nuosu community in
Muli that I visited, insisted that they had never had any intermarriage with Han
or Nuosu, in Baiwu, Prmi-Han intermarriage is quite common.

Between Prmi and Naze, on the other hand, intermarriage is free and frequent in every area I know about where the two groups live in close proximity. In this situation, where dress, religion, and other customs are nearly or
completely identical between the two groups, *minzu* membership becomes more
like simple descent-group membership than like an ethnic difference, except
for the fact that Naze and Prmi do not share the same language.[8] This is par-

8. I am reminded of the situation described by Jean Jackson in the Vaupés area of Colombia,
where language exogamy is a requirement (which it is not among the Prmi), but there are few if

ticularly true in the Lugu Lake/Yongning area, where some Prmi have adopted what most people assume was originally a Naze custom of duolocal "walking" marriage, in which husband and wife continue to live in their respective maternal houses, the husband visiting his wife at night (He Xuewen 1991; Yan and Chen 1986: 40–44; Hu Jingming, personal communication, 1993).

Ideas and practices of kinship thus seem to support the thesis that Prmi and Naze are culturally very similar peoples, making up a kind of ethnic category above the level of *minzu*. They are tied together not only by the paradigmatic resemblances in housing, dress, religion, and other areas but also by two kinds of kinship bonds. First, their kinship systems, like their housing, clothing, and religious practices, tend to converge in each locality toward a common form of practice—both are patrilineal and practice virilocal marriage in many areas (e.g., in Baiwu), and both husbands and wives live with their mothers throughout their lifetimes, practicing "visiting marriage" in parts of the Lugu Lake area. Second, they are united syntagmatically by frequent intermarriage and, in the case of the matrilineal areas, intervisiting. In a certain sense, the local logic of everyday practice seems to have overridden the larger-scale, classificatory logic of ethnic identification. But in fact things are not so simple. In no community are Prmi and Naze actually classified as belonging to the same *minzu*, and the fact of this classification pulls Sichuan Prmi in the direction of unity with other Zang. To understand this counterforce, we have to discuss the Prmi in the metalanguages of ethnohistory and ethnic identification, and show how the classification in these languages also affects their ideas of ethnic identity in their daily lives.

ETHNOHISTORY AND ETHNIC CLASSIFICATION

It seems clear that the peoples known as Xifan, roughly the speakers of the Qiangic languages (Matisoff 1991), were the earliest people to inhabit the western Liangshan area whose cultural and linguistic descendants still live in the area today. The Qiangic-speakers today include local groups who call themselves by a variety of names, including Qiang (the only one that is an unambiguous *minzu* in its own right), Gyalrong, Ergong, Minyak, Qiuyu, Zaba, Ersu, Duoxu, Xumi, Nameze, and perhaps others,[9] as well as Prmi. When they first

---

any cultural differences between speakers of different languages other than the languages themselves (Jackson 1983).

9. Some of these names are approximations of autonyms in the groups' own languages; others are taken from approximations written in Chinese characters (see Peng n.d.).

came to western Liangshan is unclear, but most ethnologists think their place of origin should be spotted somewhere to the northwest, perhaps in today's Qinghai Province. That the ancestors of today's Qiangic groups were in the area by the later Han dynasty seems to be a matter of little doubt. The earliest reliable mention comes from the story of the king of Bailang, which is recounted in *The History of the Later Han Dynasty*. The king is said to have visited the court of Emperor Ming Di at Luoyang in 100 C.E. and to have sung the famous "Song of Bailang," which is recorded in *The History* in a phonetic representation in Chinese characters. Chen Zongxiang, a respected (Han) ethnohistorian from Chengdu, published an article with linguist Deng Wenfeng in 1979, and a collection of essays in 1991, suggesting that the language of the song is none other than Pumi; this identification has been used by scholars who have written on the Prmi to connect them historically to the Bailang kingdom (Yan and Chen 1986: 7–8).[10]

For the last few hundred years, most of the Prmi in what is now Sichuan, perhaps all of them, were subjects of the kingdom of Muli (Mili in the Prmi language), which was headed from 1661 until 1951 by a theocratic ruler usually known in Chinese either as the *tusi* of Muli or, more romantically, as the Great Lama. This local ruler was a Tibetan Buddhist monk of the Gelug-pa (Yellow) sect but, unlike some more famous Gelug-pa rulers such as the Dalai and Panchen Lamas, he was not an incarnate lama but rather an ordinary monk who passed the office of ruler to a younger brother or nephew in each generation. There was an incarnate lama in the Muli monastery, but his office was separate from that of the ruler. The tenth generation incarnation died in the early 1970s; because of the strict repression of religious activity at that time, his successor was not sought again until the mid-1980s, and the eleventh generation incarnation was officially confirmed in November 1992. When I visited the Muli monastery in early 1993, the lama was finishing high school in Muli County Town. Quite naturally, he was reported to be a star student. The Muli ruler's domains were centered on three monasteries within the borders of what is now Muli Zang Autonomous County, as well as the eighteen "small temples" (including the one at Baiwu mentioned in chap. 7) that were scattered about his domains and housed from three or four to several tens of monks. The great monasteries and small temples administered lands,

10. Any such identification is of course an anachronism, as Norma Diamond has pointed out to me. Not only must there have been considerable linguistic change in almost two thousand years, but there was probably no group called Prmi for the king of Bailang to have identified with at that time.

collected taxes, and raised armies; their tenants were mostly Prmi, Naze, and Han peasants.[11]

In the ethnic identification project, most of the "Xifan" groups were incorporated into the broad category of Zang, which is usually translated into English in both Chinese official and Western ethnological sources as "Tibetans." The only exceptions are the Qiang proper, resident primarily in Maowen Qiang Autonomous County, northwest of Chengdu in Sichuan, who are recognized as the Qiang *minzu*, and the Prmi of Yunnan, who are recognized as the Pumi *minzu*. Members of some of the groups classified as Zang, such as the Ersu in Ganluo County[12] and the "Baima" in northwestern Sichuan, object to the designation as Zang and are trying to get it changed, so far unsuccessfully. It is reported "on the wire" of Chinese ethnologists that a separate status for the Baima was originally blocked by the late Panchen Lama, who did not want to split up the Zang people, but now no new *minzu* are being recognized anywhere, so it is not surprising that the Baima, Ersu, and others have failed in their quest for separate status.

How the Prmi in Sichuan got classified as Zang, and the Prmi in Yunnan as Pumi, seems a prime case of historical contingency. In the early 1950s the Chinese Communist Party, while not yet ready to attempt transformation of social and political systems in such areas as Muli, was still actively soliciting the support of local rulers such as the Great Lama. Accordingly, Party leaders invited the last Great Lama to visit Beijing in 1951 to negotiate an agreement. His conditions for alliance with the Communists were rather simple—he wished Muli to be part of the system of local *minzu* autonomous administrative districts that was being set up at that time. Since he was a Gelug-pa monk, educated in Tibet and fluent in the Tibetan language, his primary political identification was with Tibet rather than with any kind of Prmi unit, so he requested that Muli be made a Zang autonomous county, or *Zangzu zizhi xian*, and so it has remained, even since the incorporation of Muli into Liangshan Yi Autonomous Prefecture in the 1970s. Quite naturally, the Prmi residing within the king's former domains, now Muli Zang Autonomous County and

---

11. In the southern parts of his domain, the Muli Great Lama was apparently losing power and influence to Nuosu, who began moving into the area from the east at the end of the eighteenth century; Nuosu interested in local history uniformly claim that they, unlike Han and others, never paid any rent or taxes to the Great Lama's government, although some local Prmi dispute this claim.

12. Peng Wenbin (personal communication and n.d.) reports that there are three schools of thought among Ersu cadres and intellectuals in Ganluo. One views Ersu as members of the wider Zang category; the other two would prefer a separate *minzu* identity, some of them choosing the name Ersu and others partial to Fan (drawing on the old name Xifan).

a few more southerly townships given to Yanyuan in 1960, were classified in the later ethnic identification process as Zang, along with the six thousand or so Khams-pa Tibetans who live in the northernmost parts of Muli. (This story was related to me jointly by Hu Jingming, a Pumi from Ninglang, and Dong Yunfa, a Prmi Zang from Yanyuan who was then magistrate of Muli County and was promoted to Party secretary in 1994.)

In Yunnan the process was analogous, though the outcome was quite different. Mr. Hu Wanqing, a Pumi from Ninglang and the father of Hu Jingming (who told me the story), was called to Beijing by Premier Zhou Enlai himself in 1957 or 1958, at a time when the Communists were actively engaged in the projects of ethnic identification and Democratic Reform, to transform the social and political systems of areas inhabited primarily by non-Han *minzu*. At that time they discussed the problem of *minzu* identity, and the prime minister asked Mr. Hu whether the Ninglang people were Xifan or Zang. Hu said that they were Xifan but preferred to use their own self-designation of Prmi, so Zhou ordered the investigation teams to confirm their identity, after which they were formally recognized as the Pumi *minzu* (but only in Yunnan) in 1960.

The Prmi in Yunnan are thus a separate *minzu*, and however much they may be culturally similar to and maritally connected with their Naze neighbors (this varies from very similar and very connected in Ninglang to almost totally unaffected in Weixi and Lanping, where there are no Naze),[13] there is no thought that they might be Tibetans. Prmi in Sichuan, on the other hand, are unambiguously Zang, even to the point where the old man in my story at the beginning of chapter 1 tried to place himself in my consciousness by invoking the Dalai Lama. What exactly does this mean?

In many of the very local contexts of ethnic interaction discussed above, it does not matter much whether Prmi are Zang or some other *minzu*. For example, in Baiwu they are the only Zang anybody ever sees, and they fit neatly into a long-established pattern of ethnic relations. They are the third term, the Ozzu, the yaks added on to the Hxiemga water buffaloes and the Nuosu oxen, and this would not change if they were suddenly to become Pumi. In other local contexts, however, there is a difference. In Muli County there are about twenty-six thousand Zang, of whom six thousand, living in the far north of the county, are what most Western ethnologists would call Tibetans, or, more specifically, Khams-pa. They speak a dialect of Tibetan, not Qiangic, and they are unambiguously Buddhist. The Prmi refer to them as Gami, but their own

---

13. In those counties, however, Prmi are closely interspersed with, and culturally and linguistically interact with, both Lisu and Bai (Koen Wellens, personal communication).

name for themselves is Ba, and they call the Prmi Rang-nyi, which means "lower-elevation farmers" in their own dialect of Tibetan.

The assumption of linguistic unity between Prmi and Ba, mentioned above, is not confined to the realm of language, but also affects scholarship on other aspects of culture. The description of Zang culture in *General Description of Muli Zang Autonomous County* (Muli Zangzu Zizhixian gaikuang), for example, proceeds through descriptions of such cultural practices as housing styles, dress, weddings, funerals, and holidays, describing in every case the practices of that small section of the Zang *minzu* who are Ba (also called Khams-pa or Gami) and only mentioning in passing that there are some variations in dialect and customs between people living in different parts of the county—in other words, that there is a linguistically only distantly related and culturally quite distinct group of Prmi who are also included in, and in fact form the majority of, the Zang of Muli. The local (Ba) version of *Tibetan* culture thus becomes the standard for all Zang in the county, including the great majority who are not Tibetan but Prmi (Muli 1985: 17–28).

It is thus clear that the majority of Prmi within the borders of Sichuan (who are slightly more than half the total number of Prmi) have varying degrees of reason to identify with Tibet and Tibetans. For those who are Buddhist, and especially for those who were once subjects of the Muli kingdom, this was always true to an extent. But as I speculated in the early part of this chapter, before the Communists assumed control and divided everyone into *minzu*, the identification with Tibet, based mostly on religion and perhaps also on political loyalties, was situational and contingent. What the ethnic identification project has done, along with the whole apparatus of scholarship and curriculum creation that has followed in its wake, is to attempt what I have elsewhere called a "crystallization" of a formerly fluid identity (Harrell 1996a). It would seem that it is no longer possible to be just Buddhist or just a Prmi-speaker or just a subject of a particular *tusi*; one must be a member of a *minzu* and roll all one's identities into a single packet.

What is striking about the Prmi case, however, is how unimportant this packaging has turned out to be. On the one hand, there are still several contexts in which Prmi people in Sichuan identify with groups other than Zang. For example, in the area to the east of Lugu Lake, in Gaizu and its environs, the local Han dialect word for Prmi outside of the official discourse is not Zangzu, not Pumi, but rather Xichu, which presumably derives from the earlier term Xifan. This area was not subject to the Muli king but rather to the local Naze *tusi* at Zuosuo, and we should recall that the stereotype of the Prmi is that they are less devoutly Buddhist than the Naze, so it should not be surprising that their identification with Tibet or with the Zang is not strong. At the same time, however, nobody seems to object to the term Zangzu; it just sounds a little remote and official.

In another example of the continued fluidity of identity, every (Zang) Prmi I asked in any of the communities I visited in Sichuan—whether cadre, schoolteacher, or ordinary peasant—freely acknowledged that the Prmi in Sichuan were just like the Prmi in Yunnan and that the classification of the former as Zang and of the latter as Pumi was an affair of the government, a historical contingency. One peasant, for example, told me that they were culturally and linguistically the same people but that government investigators in his area had told him that there was no such thing as a Prmi *minzu*, so that they would have to be Zang.

On the other hand, the identification of Prmi as two different *minzu* in two different provinces does not seem to bother anybody local. Mr. Hu Jingming of the Ninglang People's Consultative Conference told me that he had plans to found and fund an Institute for the Study of Pumi Culture and History in Ninglang and that the plans for funding were to use iron-ore revenue from state-owned mines in Ninglang, as well as timber revenue from the vast old-growth forests of Muli, where the Prmi are not Pumi at all, but rather Zang. Dong Yunfa, also a Prmi and then the magistrate of Muli (since promoted to Party secretary) was sitting right beside us at the time and indicated to me that he enthusiastically supported the proposal. Yet neither he nor any of the other Prmi I spoke to in Sichuan was disturbed by the fact that they all are classified as Zang. Discussions with Prmi cadres and intellectuals on both sides of the border yielded none of the resentment that is common among so many small ethnic groups who feel they have been misclassified (Harrell 1990; Cheung 1996; see also chap. 13).

Thus, through a historical process of political negotiation mixed up with the project of "ethnic identification," the local ethnic identity of Prmi, manifested in all the linguistic, religious, and other cultural markers discussed above, became overlain by two different *minzu* identities, Zang in Sichuan and Pumi in Yunnan. But instead of lamenting or forming some sort of resistance to state policy on this matter, the leaders at least of the Pumi and Prmi Zang in the two provinces have accepted and begun to assert and manipulate their respective *minzu* identities, and I have indication that ordinary people as well are incorporating these identities into their consciousness. But they do not use these identities as a basis for conflict. In a paradoxical way, the ethnic identity of the

Prmi in the 1990s is as fluid, contingent, and multivalent as it has ever been, with the added dimension that now Prmi leaders can use the official classifications as yet one more aspect of their identity that they can manipulate, whether for identification with the larger entity of the Zang *minzu*, for fostering local pride in the history and traditions of the Prmi themselves (who were here well before the Tibetans, if we believe the story of the King of Bailang), or for both at the same time.

On the other hand, the identity of the Prmi does bother some Tibetans. The desire of the late Panchen Lama to preserve the unity of the Zang was already mentioned, and a young Tibetan educational cadre of my acquaintance in Chengdu was quite indignant when I brought up the split identity of the Prmi with him. He said that the *pr* or *pu* in "Prmi" or "Pumi" was clearly the same syllable as "Böd," which is the Tibetan name for Tibet, and that *mi* means "people" in a lot of Tibetan dialects, so that "Pumi" itself means "Tibetan people" and should never have been a designation for a separate *minzu*. Similarly, a Tibetan ethnologist translates "Pumi" in a Tibetan-language publication as "Böd-mi" (people of Tibet) in order to ridicule the notion that these "people of Tibet" could be a *minzu* separate from the Tibetans (Upton 2000).

The contrast between the ethnic identity of the Prmi and that of the Nuosu is thus extremely clear. In any particular local community in which they both reside, such as Baiwu or Changma or Sanjia and Shanhe, they are simply two groups who may or may not speak each other's languages but at any rate are culturally quite different and do not intermarry, and they may have had conflicts over resources in the past or in the present. But when we move to the larger context of *minzu* politics at the county level and above, their situations are quite different. Nuosu are internally solidary, externally clearly distinguished from all other *minzu*, and, in the case of their cadres and intellectuals, chauvinist to a fault about the glories of the greater Yi or Ni civilization, of which they consider themselves the purest representatives. They are not a nation, but they are a clearly demarcated ethnic group and someday might have national aspirations (though one hopes not). Prmi, on the other hand, may not even be much of an ethnic group, if we use our definition that requires internal solidarity and external distinction, both maintained by reference to culture, history, and kinship. They could never conceivably be a nation (there are far too few of them, only a fraction of the population of a typical Chinese county), and even as a category they are subject to continuing negotiation.

The biggest paradox of all in the Prmi situation is the contrast with the Naze. Prmi and Naze are culturally almost identical to each other, with several traits covarying between the ethnic groups from one place to another; they intermarry freely; and their ethnic identity in political contexts beyond the local community is contingent and shifting. But the ways in which this contingency works out in actual political practice in the arenas of *minzu* relations and *minzu* politics are completely different for the two groups. There is fierce fighting within and without the Naze ethnic group about their identity, their affinity, their language, and their name in a variety of languages. In the following chapters, I turn from the fluid, manipulable identity of the Prmi to the turbulent, conflict-ridden identity of their cousins and occasional spouses, the Naze.

11 / The Contested Identity of the Naze

U
nlike their Prmi cousins, at peace with their identity and almost unknown to the outside world, the Naze are caught up in intersecting swirls of controversy about who they are and whom or what they represent. To what *minzu* do they belong—Mongolian, Meng, Naxi, or perhaps Mosuo? How are they related to the Mongolians? How are they related to the Naxi of Lijiang? Are they a matrilineal people? Were they originally? If they are, does this indicate a shameful primitivity, a valuable remnant of a distant past, a hope for women's liberation, or a sign vehicle for the psychosexuality of the Han Chinese male? These controversies rage not only among the Naze themselves, where they are hotly enough debated to have resulted in fistfights among cadres, but also in the arenas of Chinese and international ethnic politics and ethnological and feminist scholarship. In this way, the ethnic identity of the Naze is even more historically contingent than that of the Prmi— it is not only local history that is involved, but the history of the nation and, from several perspectives, that of the human species in general. Many people have a stake in these controversies: ambitious Naze cadres and intellectuals, who promote their versions of the Naze cause in forums ranging from local nationalities commission (*minwei*) meetings to international conferences; their rivals among the Naxi of Lijiang, who see the Naze as just one branch of their own, heavily tourism-oriented *minzu*; Chinese ethnologists looking to validate the model of human history put forth by Morgan and canonized by Marx and Engels; cosmopolitan anthropologists continuing to argue the nature of matriliny and its relationship to power and prestige relations between the sexes; Chinese male writers, intellectuals, and curiosity-seekers, eager to find an alternative with which to criticize or maybe just circumvent the sexual repression of Han and Communist values; domestic and international promoters of tourism, looking to promote the newest Shangri-la for profit; and feminist historians looking for that shred of empirical evidence that equality and partnership, their proposed alternative to what they see as the current bat-

tle of the sexes, did exist in what they imagine is the past and was left over by neglect on the shores of Lugu Lake.

Caught up in these controversies, whether they know it or not (and many of them are probably only dimly aware of it) are about fifty thousand Naze people, living mostly in Ninglang, Muli, Yanyuan, and Yanbian. Since the large-scale Nuosu incursions of the last two hundred years, Naze settlements have been concentrated in a few enclaves in these counties, most of them in high basins or the bottoms of deep valleys, surrounding the small towns that were, until the twentieth century, the seats of Naze *tusi* enfeoffed by the successive Yuan, Ming, and Qing dynasties. In the more westerly of these locations—most prominently around Lugu Lake and the former *tusi* seats of Yongning in Ninglang, and Zuosuo and Qiansuo in Yanyuan, as well as Wujiao, Xiangjiao, and Shuiluo Townships in Muli (Weng 1995: 6)—Naze have matrilineal clans, duolocal (Murdock 1949, Gough 1961) residence (in which everyone lives with his or her mother) and are closely associated with one or another branch of the Tibetan Buddhist church. In the more easterly of the Naze enclaves—around Yousuo, Guabie, and Guboshu in Yanyuan—Naze have patrilineal clans, patrilocal marital residence, and loose ties, if any, with Tibetan Buddhism. Most Naze have been and continue to be subsistence farmers, growing some rice but mostly corn and other highland crops, and raising cattle, pigs, and sheep for consumption and income (see map 5).[1]

Nowadays the overwhelming majority of the population of the middle and upper slopes surrounding the Naze enclaves is Nuosu, and in the enclaves themselves Naze mix with Prmi, Han, or both. The boundaries between Prmi and Naze are quite permeable locally, and in fact, despite the idealization and romanticization of Naze by Han writers as the exotic and incomprehensible other, there is also considerable interaction and often intermarriage in some areas between Naze and Han. There have even been a few marriages in Yanyuan between Naze and Nuosu. But Naze identity is not, unlike that of some of the small Yi groups described in chapter 13, subject to erosion by the inexorable forces of Han civilization. Historically contingent as it is, it remains strong, and this is one reason why Naze themselves have been active participants in the controversies surrounding their identity. I consider ethnic identity in this chapter, and representation in the next.

---

1. On Naze household economy, see three recent Ph.D. dissertations from North American universities, by Shih Chuan-kang (1994), Weng Naiqun (1995), and Guo Xiaolin (1996).

THE QUESTION OF IDENTITY

> We are Mosuo. We are a separate people with an ancient history
> and are completely different from the Naxi. . . . But because of mis-
> takes made in the ethnic identification process in the 1950s, we mis-
> takenly got lumped in with them.
>
> —He Jiaze, 1993

> Whatever you do, tell the truth. Tell them we are Mongols. Don't go
> writing that we are some other *zu.*
>
> —Wang Wenzhi, 1994

The questions of Naze identity have historical roots going back to the immi-gration of the forebears of the Naze into the Liangshan area, perhaps in the early centuries of the common era, and to the consolidation of rule from the center by the Mongol Yuan dynasty in the late thirteenth century. But they became questions of identity per se with the ethnic identification project in the 1950s, which determined that the Naze were closely related to the Naxi, a larger group living mostly in Lijiang County, to the west of Yongning. So closely related, in fact, that they were branches of the same *minzu*, speaking dialects of the same language. The Naze were Buddhist and the Naxi rather less so, the Naze were matrilineal and the Naxi patrilineal, and the languages were not mutually intelligible, but these differences could be explained by the flow of time separating the peoples and especially by outside influences—Buddhism from Tibet and patriliny both from the surrounding dominant Chinese cul-ture and from the natural evolutionary process through which patriliny replaces matriliny with the advent of private property, something that had hap-pened sooner among the Naxi than among the Naze, because the Naxi home-land of Lijiang was more exposed to the feudal influences of the greater Chinese social system (McKhann 1995).

It is unknown to outside scholars (and perhaps by now unknowable) what the Naze of Yongning in the 1950s or 1960s thought about being classified as Naxi. But we do know that there were other kinds of opinions among Naze on the other side of the provincial border, in Yanyuan and Muli Counties in Sichuan. As early as 1936 those people were identified as Mongols, or *Menggu ren*, in the Yanyuan County gazetteer, and members of the ruling families of several local political units set up under the Ming and Qing dynasties referred to themselves as Mongols, one family even filling in *dazi* (which is now thought of as an ethnic slur upon Mongols, in Inner Mongolia as well as the

Southwest) when asked to indicate their *minzu* on a form in 1954 (Li Xingxing 1994: 8). Others referred to themselves as Mengzu, a shorthand way of saying Mengguzu, which may or may not have a slightly different connotation (Li Xingxing 1994). Despite this early self-identification, the Naze in Yanyuan, Yanbian, and Muli were determined to be Naxi until the 1980s (ibid.: 9). By 1982, however, the Naze in Yanyuan had successfully petitioned for the right to call themselves Mongols on that year's census returns (there is a "Menggu" [Mongol] among the fifty-six recognized *minzu*, but no "Meng"). In 1984, Dapo, in northeastern Yanyuan a long way from Lugu Lake, and Yanhai, along the eastern shores of the lake, along with Xiangjiao and Wujiao in Muli to the north, were established as Mongol townships. In the 1990 census, however, the Yanbian people had still not won the right to be Mongols (ibid.: 10).

Back on the Yunnan side of the border, however, sentiment in the 1980s was not in favor of being identified as Mongols. People there were agitating instead for the Naze to be recognized as a separate *minzu* altogether. But they could not call themselves Naze; that was a term in their own language not used in the hegemonic discourse of *minzu* identification. They opted, instead, for the designation Mosuo, which in fact had occurred in many Chinese-language historical sources dating back to the Tang dynasty (Li Shaoming 1986: 285; Li Xingxing 1994: 10) but usually was used for both Naze and Naxi.[2] By 1990 they had successfully petitioned the Yunnan Provincial People's Congress to be allowed to call themselves Mosuo *ren*, or Mosuo people, but were still unsuccessful in petitioning the national government to allow them to use the designation Mosuo *zu*, which would have made them the fifty-seventh *minzu* in the "great family of nationalities" (ibid.). It was in this context that He Jiaze, quoted above, approached me after a banquet in Ninglang City in 1993—he wanted to see if I could do anything to bring foreign pressure on the Chinese government to recognize the Mosuo as a *minzu*. He was no dissident, either, being chief of staff (*mishuzhang*) of the Ninglang County Communist Party Committee.

Even more recently, some Naze living in Yanhai,[3] on the Sichuan side of Lugu Lake, and therefore classified as Mongols, have begun to reconsider their

2. I understand that in Taiwan, until the opening up of relations with the Mainland at the end of the 1980s, the term "Mosuo" was still used in ethnological circles to refer to the Naxi and Naze (Hsieh Shih-chung, personal communication). There are many variant characters used to write this name; the ones used now (see the glossary) have only recently become standard.

3. In 1994 the official name of this township was changed from Yanhai *xiang* to Lugu Hu *zhen*, perhaps to reflect hopes for more urban development, with a new road scheduled to be completed from Yanyuan City the following year. But people still referred to the place, in the local vernacular, as Yuan Hai.

position. Recognizing that they and the Mosuo on the Yunnan side all are Naze, that they regularly intermarry (or whatever you call it when they live in matrilineal clan households) and speak the same language, and that the provincial border itself isn't even marked except where a rare road happens to cross it, some of them have advocated getting together, under one name or the other— Mongols or Mosuo—and trying to make common cause in persuading the state to create a common administrative entity that would encompass Naze areas on both sides of the border, perhaps in a Mosuo autonomous county. Others, however, while liking the idea of an autonomous county, would rather not have the name Mosuo in the title, since they consider that not only a Han name that they would not apply to themselves, but an appellation that does not distinguish them sufficiently from the Naxi. Meanwhile, Naze in other parts of Yanyuan County identify strongly as Mongols and take issue with the idea that they might be anything else. Wang Wenzhi, an official on the Liangshan Prefecture Nationalities Commission and a native of Guboshu in central Yanyuan, a person who helped me materially with a lot of bureaucratic aspects of my own fieldwork, really seemed like she meant it when her parting words to me in December 1994 reminded me that the Naze were Mongols. The issue is still hotly debated.

CULTURE AND ETHNIC IDENTITY

Use of culture as one criterion for identifying *minzu* has created a situation in which intellectuals among the Naxi in Lijiang have tried to use cultural commonalities to justify the inclusion of the Naze (almost always called Mosuo in Chinese writing) in the broader category of the Naxi *minzu*. At the same time others, including Naze intellectuals and cadres themselves, as well as western anthropologists such as Charles McKhann, have used the same cultural criteria to cast doubt on this identification.

The issue here seems to come down to the relationship between culture and history, which in turn depends on a particular scholar's vision of history. Nobody doubts that there are cultural differences between the Naxi of Lijiang (sometimes called Western Naxi) and the Mosuo of the Lugu Lake region (sometimes called Eastern or Yongning Naxi). These include patrilineal vs. matrilineal clan organization; patrilocal vs. duolocal residence; much larger household size among the Naze; reliance of non-Buddhist priests among the Western Naxi on a corpus of texts written in an indigenous script (called in Chinese *dongba wen*, after the Naxi word for priest, *dobbaq*), whereas the Naze priests, or *ndaba*, rely entirely on oral transmission and memorization of texts;

the loose association of the Naxi with the Karma-pa sect of Tibetan Buddhism, and the rather closer association of the Yongning Naze with the Gelug-pa sect; different styles of domestic architecture, reflecting different roles for and conceptions of the two genders in the household; quite different styles of that most pervasive of ethnic markers, female dress; and, most notably of all, the mutual unintelligibility of the languages of Lijiang and Yongning (McKhann 1995).

At issue here is not the reality of these many cultural differences, which are easily observable, but their significance. For Chinese ethnologists, especially from the 1950s to the 1980s, these differences were merely the result of historical processes of cultural evolution. Everyone knew that matriliny preceded patriliny and that oral traditions gave rise in the course of history to written ones. So if the Naze were matrilineal and the Naxi patrilineal, this merely reflected the geographic isolation of the Naze, who had retained their primitive customs in their remote mountain habitat, while the Naxi, influenced earlier by the surrounding "Han culture," had followed the natural sequence from matrilineal to patrilineal and from an oral to a literate priestly tradition (Yan 1984, Yan and Liu 1986, Yan and Song 1983). With the similarity in their languages and the possibility of documenting historical connections between the two (see below), there was little doubt that the two groups belonged to the same *minzu*, and in fact they were classified as such in the ethnic identification project.

For Western anthropologists, the issue was more complex. They recognized the same cultural differences and might even have considered that under certain circumstances the Naze displayed an earlier form of the same culture. In fact, Western anthropology could argue either for cultural difference, as McKhann did in his 1995 article, or for a common origin and blending at the margins, as his more recent researches suggested (personal communication). But for Western students of ethnicity, this is ultimately beside the point when we are considering issues of identity. In the tradition of Western ethnicity theory, what is important in determining ethnic identity is not the visible criterion of cultural similarity or difference, but the subjective consciousness of belonging or not belonging to the same group. Most of the Naze with whom Westerners have come in contact in the Lugu Lake area have been adamant about their separate ethnic identity as Mosuo, so, according to the ideas of Western ethnicity theory, they are a separate ethnic group. And their efforts to gain recognition on the basis of cultural separateness seem to have borne fruit in China as well, whatever the evolutionary sequence from matrilineal to patrilineal. They have, in fact, been so successful as to gain recognition as Mosuo *ren*. Yan Ruxian, who wrote one of the original books on these people as the

Yongning Naxi, calls them Mosuo in her second edition of that work, written in the 1990s, explaining in the preface that she was not allowed to publish the work with the name Mosuo in the early 1980s. And Bai Hua, whose romantic fantasy of Mosuo life is discussed in chapter 12, never mentions anything in his book about the Naxi.

It would seem, then, that the controversy over whether the Naze are Naxi or not is settled, at least in any forum less exalted than the State Council, which is simply not recognizing any more *minzu* in the current political atmosphere. But in fact, other aspects of the identity question are not settled. For one thing, Naze living in the western part of their territory, the area around Lugu Lake and extending into southwestern Muli, are divided by the border between two provinces. If those on the Yunnan side have gained practical recognition as Mosuo, those on the Sichuan side are still classified as Mongolians, or at least as Mengzu. How to get together in the face of these divisions of province and *minzu* is still a problem, in spite of cultural commonalities and intermarriage.

The Naze themselves are culturally split between the western section, where people are matrilineal and Buddhist, and the eastern section, where they are patrilineal and their affiliation with Buddhism is much looser. Spokespeople for the Eastern Naze are less than thrilled about being associated with matriliny and its primitive connotations, they do not like the term "Mosuo," and they are to varying degrees proud of their Mongol heritage. Whether to get together in the face of these divisions of culture is a real problem for these people, in spite of common *minzu* affiliation. This is the problem Ma Erzi and I investigated in both Eastern and Western Naze communities in 1994.

CULTURE AND ETHNICITY IN EASTERN AND WESTERN NAZE COMMUNITIES

Guabie district in 1994 was one of the last two *qu* (abolished administratively in 1992, but still referred to popularly) in all of Liangshan Prefecture to lack road access.[4] Wodi Township, the former *qu* seat, lies in a dry, hot valley a hundred or more vertical meters above the Xiao Jin River; it was the seat of the Guabie *tusi* from the nineteenth century until the 1950s, located first in a yamen on the mountainside a few hours' walk away, but moved to the present site of Wodi Town in the 1920s. The population of Wodi Township is 6,095, of whom 1,211 are Naze, most of them concentrated in the river valleys, particularly around

4. A road was under construction in late 1994, and I understand it was completed by 1997, but I have not been back to the area.

the sites of the two yamen. In Ngodzi Village, which is contiguous with the administrative center of Wodi Township, there are about twenty-seven households of Naze people, plus ten or so Han households and one Nuosu family. The other thousand or so Naze in the township are dispersed among four villages, with about half of them living in Jiala Village, which is the seat of the former yamen of the local *tusi*.

Naze culture, or the northeastern version of it, still thrives in Wodi and serves as a clear cultural marker between the Naze and members of other ethnic groups residing in the town and its surrounding villages. Dress, for example, is a strong marker of Naze ethnicity in Wodi. Naze women of forty or older wear plain-colored pleated skirts, immediately distinguishing them from Nuosu, who also wear pleated skirts, but with horizontal stripes of different bright colors, and from Han, who do not wear skirts at all. Most younger Naze women, however, dress in trousers just like the Han.

Another aspect of Naze culture that serves as an ethnic marker is housing. Naze houses (see diagram 11.1) are immediately distinguishable from those of the Han and Nuosu—although built of the same materials (mostly mud walls), they have a distinctive floor plan, somewhat similar to the Prmi plans used in Baiwu and described in chapter 10. It includes a floor-hearth next to the wall to the left of the entrance; a plastered mud altar at the base of the wall next to the hearth; and altars for the nature and ancestral spirits in the corner above the hearth on the side opposite the door, and for a hunting or warrior spirit in the corner away from the hearth on the back wall. A half-story loft, built of wood in an L-shape, extends along the door- and hearth-sides of the room. Two thick, round pillars stand in the middle of the room; the one nearest the door represents the female and the other the male. Places around the hearth also reflect this division, with the spots nearest the wall on the male (inner) and female (outer) sides of the hearth, respectively, reserved for the most senior male and female members of the household, and lower-ranking people of each gender seated farther from the wall on each side (fig. 19). Beds line the door-side of the room and the side opposite; predictably, women sleep on the door-side and men along the inner wall. There may or may not be extra bedrooms in addition to the beds in the main room.

The plan of the Naze house reflects the religious practice of spirit worship carried on by the *ndaba*.[5] In Ngodzi hamlet there are two of these native priests;

---

5. The native priests among the Lugu Lake Naze are usually referred to in the English literature as *daba*, which is a romanization of the Chinese-language version of the term, used in Chinese ethnological reports. I asked several times in Guabie, and always heard the prenasalized *nd* sound;

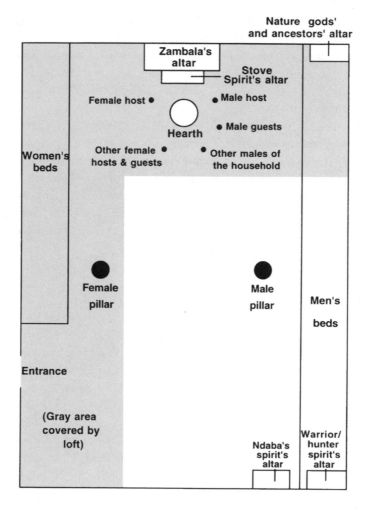

Nature gods'
and ancestors' altar

Zambala's
altar

Stove
Spirit's altar

Female host •

• Male host

• Male guests

Hearth

Women's
beds

Other female •
hosts & guests

• Other males of
the household

Female

pillar

Male

pillar

Men's

beds

Entrance

(Gray area
covered by
loft)

Ndaba's
spirit's
altar

Warrior/
hunter
spirit's
altar

DIAGRAM 11.1. Eastern Naze house

the elder is training two men in their twenties to be disciples. People call on these priests for curing and life-cycle ceremonies. There were some Buddhist monks in the *tusi*'s yamen in the old days, but there are none there now, and most people I interviewed knew little about Buddhism. The Eastern Naze house

I thus reproduce the word this way, without passing judgment on whether the conventional form *daba* reflects a dialect difference with the Lugu Lake area, or just the absence of a way of representing the sound *nd* in Chinese characters.

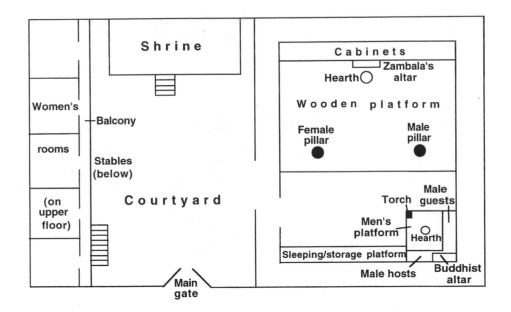

DIAGRAM 11.2. Western Naze (Mosuo) house

plan and the cosmology it represents are utterly different from the symbolic structures expressed in Han and Nuosu houses in the same and neighboring communities. When one walks into a house in this community, one immediately knows the ethnicity of the owners.

At the same time, this house plan, which is also shared by Naze at Guboshu on the high plain of central Yanyuan, is quite different from that used by the matrilineal Naze (and Prmi) in the Western area around Lugu Lake (see diagram 11.2). Naze in Luguhu Township live in log houses built around an entirely enclosed courtyard. The main room, like that in the Eastern Naze houses, is also divided into male and female areas, but in a more complex pattern. The end of the room away from the door is occupied by a plank platform about 20 cm above the level of the dirt floor; the altar of Zambala, next to the cooking hearth, is thus in the middle of the platform (fig. 22). This platform is in a general sense female space, although men can and do sometimes join women around the main hearth. On the opposite end of the room, the corner away from the door is occupied by a square platform, about 60 cm above the dirt floor. The corner of the platform toward the interior of the room has a carved wooden pillar that is used, in the majority of houses that are still without electric

FIG. 22. Meal preparation at the hearth
in the middle of the low women's platform

FIG. 23. Guests *(left)* and hosts *(right)* sitting around the small hearth
on the men's platform. The carved pillar is used
to burn pine-resin to light the room.

FIG. 24. Meat hanging from the rafters; on the wall
are pictures of the Ten Marshals.

lighting, for pine-resin torches to light the room; in the middle of the platform
there is another hearth, where people can get warm or roast snacks such as
peanuts or sunflower seeds. The side of the platform along the long dimen-
sion of the room (facing the door) is for male guests; the side facing toward
the Zambala end is for male hosts. Above this platform on the door end is a
Buddhist altar (fig. 23). Two pillars hold up the roof beams; the one on the
inner side is the male pillar, and the one on the outer side is the female. Older
members of the household, along with children, can sleep on their gender-
appropriate sides of this room; younger women usually sleep in the upstairs
bedrooms across the courtyard, and younger men visit their partners.

These houses are built with extreme care and considerable elaboration, and
are large, roomy, and seemingly permanent, complete with enormous cobwebs
and occasional birds' nests in the high ceiling space under the rafters. Two or
three sides of the main room, particularly the Zambala end, are usually occupied by rows of wooden, sometimes carved and painted, cabinets, and walls
are festooned these days with a startlingly eclectic mix of posters and paint-
ings, usually including some Buddhist icons, portraits of pretty girls from previous years' calendars, photos of famous landscapes or tourist sites in China

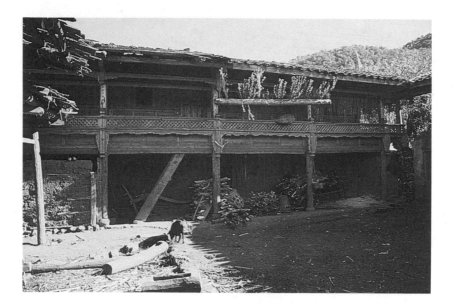

FIG. 25. The women's rooms are upstairs on the side of the courtyard
opposite the main room.

proper, and almost always a shiny new portrait of Chairman Mao (and sometimes also the Ten Marshals[6] of the PLA) (fig. 24).

Across the open courtyard from the main room there is a two-story structure; the bottom floor houses cattle and pigs, while the upper story (fig. 25) is
where the women of the household ordinarily sleep, often entertaining their
husbands or lovers during the nighttime.[7] And at the end between the two wings
there is an elaborate Buddhist shrine (fig. 26); if the household includes a
Buddhist priest, he may sleep there if he is not visiting his wife or lover. In the
poorer and less commitedly Buddhist community at Gaizu, twelve kilometers
inland from the lake, the houses are similar but most lack the shrine.

Each house plan, in fact, reflects the particular kinship structure of the people

6. The original Ten PLA Marshals were Zhu De, Peng Dehuai, Lin Biao, Liu Bocheng, Chen
Yi, He Long, Xu Xiangqian, Nie Rongzhen, Luo Ronghuan, and Ye Jianying. Since Lin Biao was
disgraced after 1972, current portrait sets actually depict only nine marshals.

7. For detailed and accurate descriptions of Naze household and kinship structure, see Shih
2001 and Weng 1995, both of which are based on extensive fieldwork in primarily matrilineal
communities, Shih at Yongning in Yunnan and Weng in Muli.

FIG. 26. A shrine (Bön in this case) occupies the end of the
courtyard facing the entrance.

who employ it. The plan used in Guabie and the other Eastern Naze areas fits
a structure of patrilineal kinship, in which people are organized into exogamous, named clans, and women from one clan marry into the household of
another. Brothers and their wives often stay together with the brothers' parents for many years after marriage; when the joint family divides, if the parents are alive they ordinarily stay with the youngest son. In our survey of the
community, there were fourteen solitary or nuclear families, eight stem families, and five full-fledged patrilocal joint families. Household size ranged from
two to nineteen, with a mean size of 6.6 and a median of five.

At Lugu Lake, on the other hand, house structure and household structure
fit the classical matrilineal pattern described in so many ethnographies of the
Naze (Yan and Song 1983, Yan and Liu 1986, Shih 2000, Weng 1995, Guo 1996).
We did not have time to make a detailed survey of household structure ourselves, but the following two households are illustrative of the typical pattern.
The household of a local Luguhu schoolteacher described in diagram 11.3
follows the classical matrilineal and duolocal principles exactly. Each of the
first three generations consists of brothers and sisters, with the next generation down containing the sisters' children, of both sexes. The schoolteacher,

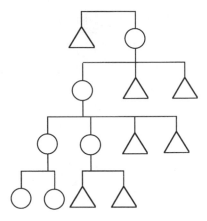

DIAGRAM 11.3. A strictly matrilineal household at Lugu Lake

the youngest brother in the second generation, is in a permanent "walking marriage" with a woman who lives with the couple's children in her own household across town. His father, a prominent Buddhist priest, lives a few households over but visits regularly to conduct rituals and to visit with the menfolk of the household.

The Naze household featured in diagram 11.4 is in Gaizu, an outlying township where Naze cultural institutions, including Buddhism, are not as self-consciously pursued, and where people in recent years have not held as strictly to the matrilineal principle, but where the core of household organization is still based partly on matrilineal principles. As we can see, this very large household is really a hybrid. The grandmother was married, and her husband, who is a very old man, still survives as part of the household, but no longer takes any part in the management of household affairs, which are in the hands of the four sisters in the second generation, though the eldest sister is the formal head and takes the lead role in household management. Two daughters of the household head have married out and live with their husbands, and the eldest son is in a relationship with a woman who used to live in this household but no longer resides here. The household head's next five children, A-E in the diagram, are all in walking relationships, though the two daughters as yet have no children. F, our source of information about this household, is twenty-seven years old and in a walking relationship, but as we can see, his younger cousin has brought a wife into the household, and they have a child who is living there.

Along with these contrasting systems of household organization, we also

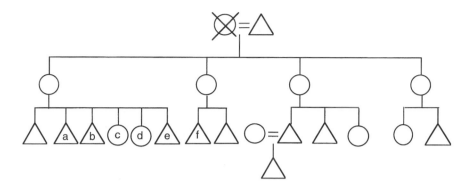

DIAGRAM 11.4. A mostly matrilineal household in Gaizu

find correspondingly contrasting systems of kinship terminology. This is not the place for a detailed analysis of the whole system of kinship terms, but the terms used for close relatives in the ascending generation are diagnostic of the differences between the two systems. Diagram 11.5 shows the kinship termi-nology as employed in the Eastern Naze area. As one can see, it fits with a patri-lineal system, in which cross-cousin marriage is the norm and married couples live together. In the first ascending generation, the parents are distinguished from all aunts and uncles, and there are two terms for aunts and uncles of each sex: *abu* is the term for FB, FZH, and MZH, whereas *avu* applies only to MB; similarly, *mala* is the term for MZ, MBW, and FBW, while *ane* applies only to FZ. In addition, a woman calls her husband's father *avu*, since in the preferred system of cross-cousin marriage, she marries her MBS, and MB=HF.

The emphasis in this system is thus on the marriage relationships between patrilineal clans; there are three terms for each sex in the ascending genera-tion. One (*mamo* or *ada*) singles out one's own parents; another (*ane* or *abu*) singles out cross-aunt or -uncle (MB or FZ), whose son or daughter one ought to marry in the ideal system, and the other (*mala* or *abu*) takes care of the resid-ual relatives.

The system as it exists in the Lugu Lake area, in Yanhai and Gaizu, is com-pletely different and reflects the matrilineal system found there (diagram 11.6). This system of terminology also reflects the household system in the area. The equal signs for marriage have been replaced by the sign for "roughly equal," since marriage is optional between couples and does not occur in the same household. Here, rather than three terms for each sex in the first ascending

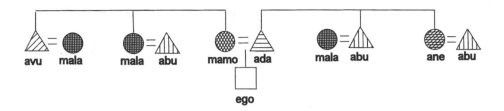

DIAGRAM 11.5. Kin terms used by patrilineal Naze at Guabie

generation, there are three for males and two for females: *ada* refers to the father only; *evu* to the mother's brother; *abu* to FB, FZH, and MZH. *Abuo* indicates mother or MZ; *emi* is used for FZ, FBW, or MBW.

In other words, while *ada* singles out the father, *abuo* does not, like the roughly corresponding term *mamo* in Guabie, single out the mother. Rather, the term *abuo* refers to the elder-generation women of one's household, including one's mother and her sisters. This usage is confirmed by the way Luguhu Naze refer to relatives when speaking the local Han dialect; they call them all *mama*, which leads to such usages as "In my house there are four mothers" (Wo jia you sige mama). Similarly, *evu* singles out the mother's brother, because mothers' brothers are the senior males of the household, in the same way that mothers and their sisters are the senior females. Once again, *emi* and *abu* are the residual terms, in this case referring to all relatives of the senior generation who are not household members, except the father, who, even in this strictly matrilineal system, is still a special case.

Language is also important as a marker of Naze identity in some areas, though not in others. In the concentrated community at Wodi, the language of everyday conversation for most people is Naze, though they are also fluent in the local Han dialect and some can also speak Nuosu, necessary for conversation with the hill-dwellers who come down to the valley to trade. In Wodi, people call themselves Naze in their own language, but when they speak Han, they call themselves Mengzu or Mengguzu—that is, Mongols. When their *ndaba* priests perform the ceremony to send the souls of the deceased back through a series of intermediate stops to the original homeland, everyone agrees that the original homeland must be someplace in Inner Mongolia, even though nobody can locate the exact spot anymore. This close association with Mongolia is another thing that distinguishes these Guabie Naze from their relatives around

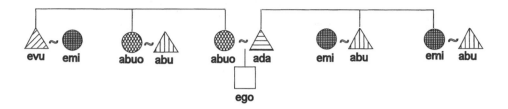

DIAGRAM 11.6. Kin terms used by matrilineal Naze at Lugu Lake

Lugu Lake, for many of whom the Mongolian *minzu* affiliation is not partic-ularly important. One local cadre told me that a Naze leader from Zuosuo near Lugu Lake had recently come to Guabie to advocate uniting to form a Mosuo autonomous county; he was first received cooly, but when he brought up the subject again at the following banquet, the locals objected to the point that a fist-fight erupted.

In other areas, the attachment to Mongolia is even stronger. Three hours' walk to the northeast of Wodi lies the headquarters of Dapo Mongolian Township, which was officially established in 1984 and whose tenth-anniver-sary celebration I attended in November 1994. Dapo is higher, more remote, and poorer than Wodi, lacking not only a road but also plans for a road, as well as electricity. Its population of 3,700 souls is about one-third Naze, so it, along with Yanhai at Lugu Lake, was qualified in the 1980s to become a Mongolian township.

Naze culture is weaker, and Mongolian ethnicity even stronger, in Dapo than in Wodi. I was there only briefly and did not get a chance to visit any Naze homes, but I found both dress and language, the other two ethnic markers, to be much more assimilated to Han ways than was the case down in the valley. For example, even for the celebration of ten years as a Mongolian township, only three or four of the several hundred women in attendance wore Naze-style clothing, though most middle-aged and older women in Wodi wore this style of clothing every day. When the visiting dignitaries were greeted by local Naze, they apologized that they did not know how to make *chiong*, or barley beer, so they gave us bottled beer instead. Naze in many parts of the township, where the ethnic groups are mixed, now speak Han at home, and even those who speak Naze are still bilingual.

It is thus rather startling that Mongolian ethnic identity is so strong, at least among Naze cadres in Dapo. When the Mongolian township was established, a representative from Yike Juu (Yikezhao in Chinese) League,[8] in western Inner Mongolia, came to the founding ceremony and left a plaque featuring a silver horse and a picture of Chinggis's tomb in the Ordos. Slogans commemorating the tenth anniversary were written in Mongolian as well as Chinese, even though there is nobody who can actually understand written Mongolian. Dapo people have even been offered adult-literacy classes in Mongolian, taught by a local Naze teacher who grew up speaking Han at home, learned Naze from playmates when he went to school, and recently spent three months in Muli learning to read and write the Mongolian script from a Muli Naze who had studied in Hohhot. He admitted to me that literacy classes in Mongolian were probably not appropriate for most Dapo Naze, who spoke Han anyway, but said they might work better in Wodi, where there were concentrations of monolingual Naze speakers. And the township head, also a local Naze, told me that their language and that of western Inner Mongolia, while different on the surface, were actually 70 percent the same.[9] Finally, the township party secretary wore a locally made rendition of a Mongolian riding robe, or *deel*, gray with an orange sash, when he presided over the anniversary ceremony; it was the only outfit of its kind I had ever seen, and he looked impressive in it with his six-foot frame, chiseled, dark-skinned features, and wavy white hair. When I asked him what it was called, he said *fuzhuang*, the Han word for "costume," something only minorities have (fig. 27).

At Guboshu in central Yanyuan, seat of another former *tusi* government, the situation combines aspects of Wodi and Dapo. Guboshu is extremely well-off economically for a Naze area, being situated less than an hour's drive from the county seat of Yanyuan, in a township that is mostly Han. It sports good roads, nearly 100 percent school attendance, and flourishing agriculture. The houses are identical to those found at Guabie, women wear skirts, there are no Buddhist temples or monks, people under forty speak almost entirely Han, and there is no thought of conducting schools in anything but the Han language. But my friend Wang Wenzhi, who told me not to go writing that they were anything but Mongols, hails from Guboshu.

There thus seem to be clear cultural differences between the Eastern and

---

8. A league (*meng* in Chinese, *aimag* in Mongolian) is an administrative unit that exists only in Inner Mongolia. It corresponds to a prefecture (*diqu* or *zizhi zhou*) in other areas of China.

9. In fact, there are no resemblances or connections whatsoever between Naze (a Tibeto-Burman language usually assigned, along with closely related Naxi, to the Yi branch) and Mongolian (an Altaic language), except insofar that both languages may have borrowed some of the same Buddhist terms from the Tibetan.

FIG. 27. The party secretary of Dapo Mongolian Township giving an
address at the celebration of the township's tenth anniversary

Western Naze, though they say they can understand each other's spoken languages; a couple of people from Guabie told me they could understand 90 percent of Lugu Lake people's speech, and another compared the degree of
difference to that between standard Chinese and the local Han dialect of
Liangshan, which is certainly a bridgeable gap. But in fact there is very little,
if any, interaction between Naze in northwestern and northeastern Yanyuan.
To be fair, it's hard to get from one place to the other; even if one has a private car at one's service, the trip would take two grueling days. By public transport and foot, it might take almost a week. But there is more to the separation
than that; even though both groups call themselves Naze and both are officially
classified as Mongols, they are importantly divided by cultural differences, especially in the kinship system; intermarriage is problematical when one group
has marriage and the other only visiting.

So when Zuosuo and Gaizu people say they feel a closer affinity with "Mosuo"
in Yunnan than with "Mongols" in Guabie, Dapo, or Guboshu, it is not surprising. It is interesting, however, that most intellectuals and leaders in Zuosuo
and Gaizu these days don't care much about being Mongols. The standard line
of most of them is that it is obvious the Naze have been in the area for two

thousand years or so, and even though Mongol armies were there in the thirteenth and fourteenth centuries, whatever Mongols remained were assimilated to Naze ways. What is most relevant is that the Naze in Ninglang and the Naze in Zuosuo, Qiansuo, Gaizu, and other parts of northwestern Yanyuan are one people. "Mosuo," the Yanhai and Gaizu people think, is not a particularly good name for them, since it is a Han invention and might have once been somewhat pejorative, so maybe "Mongol" is a good thing to be called, though they have little if anything to do with Mongolia. But as a Yanhai cadre said to me, if I write "Naze" I will not get any objections from anywhere. I have taken his advice to heart here, though that hardly resolves the problem.

Descendants of the last Zuosuo *tusi*, however, have a different take on the matter. They are patrilineal, and they are Mongolian. To understand why they feel such an affinity with Mongolia, we have to look at history.

HISTORY AND ETHNICITY

It is clear that the Naze link to Mongolia, and thus the claim of many Naze in Sichuan that they are Mongols (as well as their current *minzu* status as members of the Mengguzu), cannot rest on culture in any objective sense. The link, if it exists, is historical: many Naze claim to be descended from Qubilai Khan's Mongol armies that conquered this area in the process of reuniting China under their Yuan dynastic government. The Yuan forces established *tusi* in several places, and Naze think of themselves as the descendants of these local Mongol rulers.

Li Shaoming, a distinguished Sichuanese ethnologist, explored the validity of this claim in a 1986 article. He finds that, according to historical records, there were two periods when Mongol military forces occupied the current Naze area. The first of these was in 1253, when Qubilai (grandson of Chinggis and later immortalized by Coleridge, among others) led his Southern Expedition against the Dali kingdom, an independent power centered in what is now Yunnan. The second occupation was between 1393 and 1398, when an attempted uprising by a former Mongol garrison was suppressed by Ming troops, but only after prolonged fighting, and the defeated troops retreated to what are now Naze areas. So there is no doubt, according to Li, that there is "Mongol blood" among the present-day Naze. But, he says, all of the ruling families that claim descent from that time have Tibeto-Burman, not Mongolian, surnames, so that whatever Mongols mixed into the Naze population have long been Naze-ified (1986: 282). In other words, any cultural or linguistic influence from Mongolia has long been overwhelmed by the local culture, and in fact there appear to be no records indicating even a direct line of descent from the local rulers established by the Mongols to those rulers in the late Ming and Qing from whom descent can be traced in every generation.

Still, the families of local rulers seem to have identified with Mongolia since well before the ethnic identification project (Li Shaoming 1986: 279–80). And interestingly enough, the ruling families seem to have long traced their descent patrilineally, not only in the Eastern Naze area, where everyone is patrilineal, but also in the Lugu Lake area. La Pinzu, son of the last *tusi* of Zuosuo, is adamant about both his Mongolian ancestry and the nobility of his patriline. Shih Chuan-kang thinks that the family of the *tusi* of Yongning, in the heart of the matrilineal area, was originally Prmi (1994: 34–45), and this is certainly possible, though some Prmi in the Lugu Lake area have also adopted the duolocal household organization, which means that his Prmi origin would not necessarily explain his family's patrilineal descent, especially since there are patrilineal Naze in the Eastern area in townships where there are no Prmi at all.

The most we can say about history, then, is that there is a recent historical tradition of descent from Mongol armies. This historical tradition, paradoxically enough, acts as an aspect of culture; the technical language of ethnohistory has come to permeate arguments in the everyday discourse about ethnic identity, even though the ethnohistorical evidence, when looked at from outside, is rather equivocal.

THE QUESTION OF LANGUAGE

It is completely unclear at this writing when, how, or even whether the question of Naze identity will ever resolve itself. But before we leave it hanging to go on to the question of representation, we should deal once more with the issue of the relationship between the local field of ethnic-group interaction and identity, and the wider fields of *minzu* politics on a national and international scale. One of the reasons why the question of Naze identity is so vexing is that the Naze are dealing in the national and international arena not only with the hegemony of the Han-dominated state but also with the tyranny of the Han language. In that language, there is no way to say Naze, since Naze is not an official *minzu*. One can write a close approximation, *nari*, in Chinese characters, but many writers, such as Li Xingxing (1994), put it in quotation marks, giving it a less-than-legitimate status. When one is speaking Han, one says "Menggu" or "Mosuo"—there simply are no other Han words that are not obvious transliterations. So even if one discards the possibility that the Naze are a kind of Naxi, there are still only two possible designations for these people in the Han language, which is the language that counts in national discourse. We who speak and write in English, however, should be careful not to let the Han language take over our discourse. Rather than talk about Meng, Zang, and Yi in Sichuan, or Mosuo, Pumi, and Yi in Yunnan, we should do the local people a favor by referring, in English, to Naze, Prmi, and Nuosu, thus not prejudicing our own conclusions by speaking in Han categories.

At the same time, our Western anthropological pieties about how to refer to colonialized peoples hardly seem adequate to the Naze problem. Again, my friend Wang Wenzhi, though she would say "Naze" in her own language, would be disappointed in me if I don't just refer to the Naze as Mongolians when I write about them in a cosmopolitan discourse, and Charles McKhann changed his terminology from "Nari" to "Mosuo" on the recommendation of American-educated Shih Chuan-kang, who told him that was how the Naze in Yongning preferred to talk about themselves to the outside world. Of course, when they talk to the outside world, they speak Chinese. In rejecting the Han-language discourse, I am rejecting the imperial claims of the Chinese state to be able to categorize and control its ethnic subjects, but I am also denying members of the local ethnic groups the chance to have their own positions in arguments ratified by a cosmopolitan voice such as mine. They, like Jomo Kenyatta, are participants in the ethnological discourse as well. Kenyatta wrote in English (1938); they write in Han. Maybe I should just decide whether the Naze really are Mongols or not, and if they are, call them that, and if not, call them "Mosuo." But again, at least one person told me, "If you say 'Naze,' you won't get any objections from anywhere."

12 / Representing the Naze

T he struggles over identity, complex as they are, nevertheless constitute only one part of the Naze ways of being ethnic. Because of their
unusual kinship system, the Western Naze, at least, are far better known
to the world in general, and particularly the Chinese world, than their numbers (perhaps thirty thousand) and their location (scenic, but almost impossibly remote) would otherwise warrant. Because of their matrilineal social
system, and particularly because of the extreme, pure, uncompromising form
of matriliny that is represented by the duolocal system of residence, the Naze
have come to represent something other than just a small ethnic group living
near a pretty lake. They have come, at various times and in various contexts,
to represent a primitive stage of society, an ethnological archetype, a sexual
paradise, and an exotic tourist destination.

The Naze are, of course, not the only people to have entered arenas of
national or cosmopolitan discourse representing something other than themselves. Ever since Montaigne, small-scale societies have come to represent either
our own past or some kind of contrast to what we are, often combining these
two in a romantic image of what we have lost in the last few hundred or thousand years (S. Diamond 1974, Fabian 1991). This kind of representation has continued into recent decades, most strikingly in the case of the Tasaday, a small
group in a Philippine forest that was originally described as knowing nothing
of surrounding tribes, let alone of history or civilization, when some loggers
happened upon them in the early 1970s (Nance 1975). That they were later shown
to be a recent offshoot of other peoples living in the same region was a great
topic for anthropological self-examination, but in the popular discourse, once
they were no longer "really primitive," they were simply forgotten (Dumont
1988).

But representation as the primitive is not confined to those peoples totally
out of contact with civilization or those previously unknown. Miriam Kahn
has recently shown, for example, how Tahiti and the Tahitians have come to
represent a tropical paradise of sexual freedom and white beaches, even when

their own concerns have been more with subsistence, local politics, and softening the French colonial yoke (1995, 2000); this is but one instance of a tropical trope applied to peoples who may profit from it marginally through tourism but certainly do not understand it in their own categories. And the representation of minority *minzu* in contemporary China usually emphasizes their ancientness, primitivity, and display of characteristics of Han selves as they were in the distant past. Some of the earliest applications of ethnology, in the 1920s, were attempts to understand scientifically the cultures described in early classical books such as the eighth-sixth century B.C.E. *Classic of Poetry* (Shijing) (Chen Yongling 1998: 4). And there has been a continuing tradition, now reinforced by the Marxist model of cultural evolution, of viewing contemporary minorities as parallel to, or informative about, the past stages of the now-advanced Han civilization (Harrell 1995a: 15–17).

So the Naze are not alone in standing for something else in the minds of others. But in the context of today's China in particular, and to a lesser extent in the context of today's world in general, they are something special, and again it relates back to their matrilineal system. Outside awareness of this system has led the Naze to become objects with several diverse kinds of meanings in several separate but interlocking discourses.

REPRESENTATION AS PRIMITIVE: CHINESE ETHNOLOGISTS AND MORGAN'S PARADIGM

As mentioned in chapter 3, when the Communist Party took over China, their project of imposing Soviet-inspired Marxist ways of thinking and acting reached into the field of anthropology, which had previously been dominated by British-style structural-functionalism, American historicism, and Continental diffusionism (Chen Yongling 1998: 3–27; Guldin 1994: parts 3 and 4). In addition to delineating *minzu*, based ostensibly on Stalin's categories of nationality, and determining which of the five modes of production various communities employed before the land and democratic reforms, Soviet-style ethnology as it developed in China was concerned with probing further back into human social evolution by employing the ideas of the pioneer nineteenth-century American anthropologist Lewis Henry Morgan. In two massive works, *Systems of Consanguinity and Affinity of the Human Family* (1871) and *Ancient Society* (1877), Morgan set forth what he considered to be a comprehensive account of the progress of humankind through a series of stages from savagery to barbarism to civilization. In each of these stages, certain social, political, and technological institutions arose over and over in every society

Morgan examined. Karl Marx, toward the end of his life, became interested in ethnology for what it could tell him of the early stages of human material development, and he was particularly taken with Morgan's work, reading it carefully and taking extensive notes. After Marx's death in 1883, his sidekick Friedrich Engels took up the cause of Morgan and wrote *Die Ursprung der Familie, des Privateigentums und des Staats*,[1] which became a Marxist classic after the establishment of the Soviet Union. But while Engels's work found a place in every secondary school throughout the Communist Bloc until the end of the cold war, Morgan himself was reserved for specialists, and on the basis of Morgan's work Chinese ethnologists began constructing a picture of human social evolution as it happened to occur within the contemporary borders of the People's Republic.

One generalization that Morgan made in both of his books was that an important step in the progress of kinship systems was from matrilineal to patrilineal clans, occurring sometime during the lower or middle stages of barbarism. The Hodenosaunee, or Iroquois, the subject of Morgan's own ethnological researches, represented to him and to those who read his work the fullest development of matrilineal clan organization before property relationships developed to the point where males began to want their sons to inherit, and transmission of clan membership and property rights switched to the male line. In most parts of the world, however, the matrilineal stage was long past, recoverable only in myth and legend, and perhaps in those random customs and habits left over from the previous stage of evolution, because of the conservative nature of language (1870: 15). Actual matrilineal societies were quite rare, because humanity had mostly passed that stage.

When Chinese ethnologists were converted, forcibly or otherwise, to the Morganian paradigm, they used it quite rigorously to put order into what otherwise might have been the ethnological chaos of China's border regions, particularly the Southwest. When they came upon the matrilineal Western Naze, this was to them a real treasure. As Yan Ruxian and Song Zhaolin say in the introduction to their book on Yongning matrilineal organization,

> In 1877 the great ethnologist Morgan recognized that ethnological data preserved the human past. Thus, with an attitude of urgency, he called upon Americans to collect these facts that "will have no basis for their discovery after a few years." (1983: 1)

---

1. The Chinese title is *Jiating, siyou caichan yu guojia de qiyuan;* in English, it is usually known as *The Origin of the Family, Private Property, and the State* (Engels 1972 [1883]).

When Song Enchang and others first applied the Morganian/Marxist paradigm to the peoples of Lugu Lake in 1956, and when their researches were followed by more detailed investigations undertaken by Yan Ruxian and her colleagues beginning in 1962, they felt they were doing the same thing in China that Morgan had done in America a hundred years earlier: documenting for scholars of all nations the existence of institutions and peoples that would help them to understand their own past, and would help them to further develop their theoretical apparatus and deepen their comparative understanding (Yan and Song 1983: 2–6).

They and others who came after carried out extremely detailed investigations, many times over. Yan and Song had to walk over mountain trails for ten days from the Naxi center of Lijiang, entrusting their baggage to muleteers; they stayed in the Lugu Lake area for about three months. Yan returned several times with her husband, Yunnanese Yi scholar Liu Yaohan, and others, and logged a total of over a year of fieldwork, interrupted, of course, by the total stoppage of ethnological fieldwork and much persecution of ethnologists during the Great Proletarian Cultural Revolution (Yan and Liu 1986: 4). In addition, other teams of researchers carried out equally detailed investigations during the late 1950s and early 1960s, almost all of them in the various villages of Yongning Township, on the northern and eastern shores of Lugu Lake. These researchers included Wang Chengquan and Zhan Chengxu (1988a,b), and Zhou Yudong (1988).

The Naze, or at least the matrilineal segment of the Naze living reasonably close to Lugu Lake, were thus one of the most ethnographed peoples in the world, even though they were virtually unknown to the centers of anthropological research in Europe and North America. The several volumes of ethnography that came out of this early research generally treat the same series of topics: matrilineal clan organization, feudal systems of rule and exploitation, "walking marriage," and the historical reasons why the Mosuo, as they are generally called in the body of the texts (until the 1990s, "Naxi" still had to be used in the titles), retained their ancient matrilineal customs even though they were surrounded for hundreds if not thousands of years by people who were making the transition to patriliny. In addition, there is some attention given to collection of songs, stories, and other folkloric materials that support and clarify the nature of the social structure the ethnologists are analyzing. The reports contain mountains upon mountains of painstakingly collected and detailed data (the three volumes by Yan and Song, Yan and Liu, and Wang, Zhan, and Zhou between them are over a thousand pages, most of them large-format), including, for example, complete charts of the composition of eighty households (Wang and Zhan 1988a: 130–36) and meticulous drawings comparing the log-style courtyard houses of 1960s Yongning to various housing styles unearthed in archaeological researches on (presumably matrilineal) peoples who lived in north China from prehistoric times to the Han dynasty (Yan and Song 1983: chap. 7).

Chinese ethnologists' work in the 1950s, 1960s, and 1980s thus offers incomparable detail, presented primarily in service of the goal of reconstructing history through synchronic research. In Yan's most systematic work, she presents the various forms of family found in her researches in the Lugu Lake region— the clan family, matriarchal family, coexistent family, and patriarchal family— as representing successive stages in the development of the human family in general, with all of them existing at the same time in Yongning at the time of her researches (Yan and Song 1983: 292; Yan 1984). Her conclusions are neatly summarized in the English version of one of her articles:

> These families serve as a group of living fossils of the emergence and development of the monogamous family. Since they existed among the same nationality, they form the basis for a comparative study of the history of the family among other nationalities. (1984: 81)

To the Western anthropologist in the 1990s, the Chinese ethnological work on the Naze—classifying them, meticulously recording every household and then placing each family type into a predetermined evolutionary sequence, fitting everything together into a historically ordered mode of production, and then suggesting that they, like geologic fossils, can be used as exemplars of types that help to confirm nomothetic generalizations—all seems unbelievably objectifying and distancing. Some educated Naze who read some of these research reports are rumored to have felt the same way, and to have objected particularly strongly to being called "living fossils" (*huo huashi*) as if they were nothing but an object for study. But this is a reflection of the nature of Chinese anthropology in general; unlike its cosmopolitan counterpart, it has never questioned the possibility of an objective science of human society. And as long as it has not done this sort of questioning, it will continue to deal with the scientific facts of human societies in the same way any science deals with any kind of facts.

The ethnologists themselves seem to realize this. In the preface to their 1986 collection of fieldwork reports, Yan Ruxian and Liu Yaohan end on a wistful note that seems to indicate great self-awareness:

> Although we have been to the Lugu Lake region three times to conduct research and have accumulated more than a year of field time, in the end stretching out

over twenty-some years, we still depend almost entirely on translation and have been unable to acquire a grasp of the Mosuo language, so that crude approximations and ignorant mistakes have been unavoidable in our fieldwork. We await the criticism of Mosuo cadres and masses, and of readers in general. (1986: 4)

Chinese ethnologists have thus been, in important ways, prisoners of the science imposed upon them by the Communist Party in its literizing and nation-building projects. For the Mosuo themselves, one assumes all this investigation has been not much more than a colossal nuisance, but being called living fossils cannot have helped.

REPRESENTATION AS MATRILINEAL: COSMOPOLITAN ANTHROPOLOGY AND THE NAZE CASE

The Question of Mother-Right

Almost continuously since the publication of Johann Jakob Bachofen's *Das Mutterrecht* in 1861 (in Bachofen 1954), the question of matriliny has beguiled the Euro-centered world of anthropology, but matriliny has meant different things at different times. In the nineteenth century, Morgan was only one of many evolutionary anthropologists who assumed that matriliny, or "mother-right," was an earlier condition of humanity, one whose gentle communitarianism was doomed to fall before the onslaught of martial, competitive patriarchy. These ideas about matrilineal organization were also tied in with the various authors' evolutionary sequences of marriage-types; for Morgan, the family had evolved from communal forms of sexual union in the earliest days to a loose "pairing marriage" in the heyday of matrilineal clan organization, such as was represented by the Hodenosaunee, to the exclusivist monogamous institutions of the modern world. In the early to mid-twentieth century, matriliny became detached from matriarchy; for British social anthropology, it was simply another way of organizing male dominance, with power and property passing from uncle to nephew instead of from father to son (Radcliffe-Brown 1924, Richards 1950, R. Fox 1968). At the same time, marriage was declared to be cross-cultural, historically universal, varying in singularity and plurality but not in occurrence. Psychoanalysts saw matriliny as a feeble male end-run around the Oedipus complex (Jones 1925, Paul 1976), while a brief fad of sociobiology in the 1970s construed matrilineal institutions as a way of maximizing one's genetic legacy in the absence of "paternitycertainty," which they pronounced as a single word (van den Berghe 1979: 101–9).

In recent years, anthropology's attention has been diverted away from the study of kinship systems, but matriliny has not quite faded from view, because of the replacement of kinship by gender as a central area of study in the discipline. Since the late 1970s, anthropologists have again raised the issue of the universality of male dominance (a good review is Yanagisako and Collier 1987), and many scholars have either tried to redefine the issues of power, prestige, and dominance more precisely and analytically, or looked for social systems that might be construed as egalitarian, or both. These explorations have resulted in a more nuanced and sophisticated understanding of what is meant by dominance of one gender over the other; we now understand that equality does not and probably cannot mean the absence of differences (even putting aside, of course, physical differences between males and females) but will be found, if at all, in societies where gender roles are rather sharply divided but do not result in an overwhelming power or prestige differential between the genders (for a review, see Mukhopadhyay and Higgins 1988).

Onto this world stage, in the 1980s, come the Mosuo, that is, those Western Naze whose villages and towns are accessible enough to transportation to have facilitated anthropological research. At first, in the early 1980s, when books such as those of Yan and Song, Yan and Liu, and Wang and Zhan began to circulate in the community of Western China-specialists in anthropology, many of them assumed that there was a matrilineal group to be studied, known as the Naxi. And at least one Western anthropologist, Charles McKhann, did go to Lijiang in 1987 to conduct what was probably the first long-term research by a Western anthropologist in a village in China since the 1940s. But because of the confusion of names (McKhann knew better, but the rest of us did not), the people he studied were not the matrilineal folks at all—the Mosuo of Lugu Lake were then off limits to foreign researchers, since Ninglang County was a closed area (though there were at that time rumors of Lonely Planet people sneaking into the Lugu Lake area, and I was even invited for a brief visit in 1988, though the trip was later canceled), and the other Western Naze were even harder to reach, since no Westerner at that time had any hope of getting into Yanyuan or Muli.

Cosmopolitan anthropology thus came, in an ironic twist, to be represented in the Naze areas by three Chinese anthropologists working for doctoral degrees at North American universities: Shih Chuan-kang at Stanford, Weng Naiqun at the University of Rochester, and Guo Xiaolin at the University of British Columbia.[2] Aside from one piece by McKhann based on written

2. Actually, by the time Guo did her field research in 1992, it might have been possible for foreigners to do research at Lugu Lake; I spent several weeks in Yanyuan, including a visit to that

sources (1995), most of what anthropology outside of China knows about the Naze and the question of matriliny comes from these three authors' dissertations (Shih 2001, Weng 1995, Guo 1996). All three present detailed descriptions and analyses of Western Naze household structure, system of sexual unions, and matrilineal clan organization, and all use the Naze examples to address some of the ongoing issues that have brought to matrilineal institutions a disproportionate amount of attention in Western anthropology. In particular, Shih claims that the Naze social system disproves the principle of the universality of marriage, while Weng claims that the Naze present an example of true gender egalitarianism.[3]

The Question of the Universality of Marriage

In the 1960s there was a debate in anthropology over whether marriage was a universal human institution, as claimed by George Peter Murdock in his synthetic work *Social Structure* (1949). One case frequently brought up in light of this question was that of the Nayar of central Kerala, who until the late eighteenth century had a household and marriage system remarkably like that of the Western Naze, where people remained members of their mothers' households throughout their lifetimes, and men visited their sexual partners at night. Although this system seemed to lack many characteristics of marriage, most notably a male-female procreative/sexual pair living together, the consensus at the end of the debate was that the Nayar still had a form of marriage, since a woman did go through a kind of marriage ceremony with a man of an allied clan before she could begin other sexual relationships, and the pair thus joined had certain obligations to each other throughout life (Gough 1959, Leach 1961). In his dissertation, after a detailed description of the Naze "walking" system,

---

lake, in 1993, and already there were facilities being developed for foreign tourists. And by the mid-1990s, foreign researchers were able to go just about anywhere, as evidenced by my time in Guabie and McKhann's research in Eya, one of the most remote places in southwest China. But the Chinese researchers did have the jump, and it is thus their works on which we depend for most of our anthropological representations of the Western Naze.

3. It is not my purpose here to relate these authors' analyses in detail; all are based on intensive field investigation and present valuable data in a number of areas, not just those treated here. For the reader who wants to learn more about Naze society and culture than can be found in the brief account in chapter 11, and who does not read Chinese or who does not want to read through the filter of Morgan's model, I would recommend reading these three dissertations. My purpose here is to show how Naze come to represent something else, in this case how they have become data-points in some centuries-long scientific controversies.

which he calls by the native term *tisese*, or "going back and forth," Shih comes to the conclusion that the system was "entirely classless, noncontractual, nonobligatory, and nonexclusive," and forces us to rethink what he considers to be ethnocentric definitions (1994: 225) of marriage put forth by previous theorists:

> The Moso [*sic*] case decisively reveals to us that the traditional approach to the definition of marriage leads us to nowhere. We should no longer attempt to mend and refine the definition and hope in so doing someday we can make it really all-embracing. But rather, we should change the cultural connotation that we assigned to the term, which is beyond any wording and phrasing of the definition. . . . We have to admit the honorability and authenticity of alternative patterns of institutionalized sexual union other than marriage. (1994: 225–26)

The Western Naze thus become a data-point in a field of scientific inquiry, but they also become something else: a field for the affirmation of the honorable anthropological principle of cultural relativity, the refusal to judge the customs of other cultures by standards of our own. In this, it is safe to say that Shih is pointing the spearhead of his criticism as much at traditional Chinese ethnology, with its Morganian ideas of progress beyond where the Naze currently stand, and at Chinese official morality, which condemns the Naze system for being backward, immoral, and, in some cases, disease-provoking (Yan 1989: 85), as he is at the Westerners whose definitions of marriage are narrow and therefore ethnocentric.

It is interesting that this cultural relativity has not been completely shared by Naze intellectuals. For example, He Xuewen, writing in *Selected Compilation of Literary and Historical Materials from Ninglang* (Ninglang wenshi ziliao xuanji), takes issue with outside scholars' ideas that the Naze "walking marriage" was a promiscuous system, in which a woman could have multiple nonexclusive sexual relationships at one time. According to He, almost all walking relationships were serial, and people were severely criticized for not breaking off one relationship before starting another. Shih (1994: 58–61) disputes this, and his data seem irrefutable. But Naze intellectuals are now also caught up in ethnological discourses and are beginning to represent themselves (in this case, as moral people with a different system, rather than as examples of primitive immorality) at the same time as cosmopolitan scholars such as Shih are representing them as doing what Chinese official values would see as immoral, but pleading in the spirit of cultural relativity that this is as moral as any other system.

I once made a joke to a Naze friend and self-proclaimed supporter of male dominance (from Guboshu in the eastern, patrilineal area) about the matrilineal society at Luguhu, and she exploded, "Who says we had a matrilineal society? Who says we don't have marriage? Why do they write these things about us? Why don't they write that the Han have whorehouses?" To her, "matrilineal society" meant primitive and immoral; she seemed quite unconvinced by my subsequent feeble remarks about cultural relativity.

The Question of Gender Equality

As with the issue of the universality of marriage, anthropologists have been arguing for over a century about the question of whether male dominance is universal or not. Some of the early evolutionists thought not; they felt that the matriarchal systems that preceded modern patriarchy were built on a foundation of cooperation rather than hierarchy. In the early and mid-twentieth century, male dominance was assumed without being much argued, but since the rise of feminism in society and social science since the 1960s, these issues have come to the fore again, with various kinds of feminists taking different approaches to the question of how to measure equality and, once it is measured, whether there are egalitarian social systems or not.[4]

The place of matrilineal systems in the debate over gender (formerly sexual) equality has been complex. On the one hand, it has been clear for nearly a century that the mere existence of matrilineal descent and/or inheritance does not guarantee equal power or prestige between the genders—we need look no further for evidence than Malinowski's classic studies of the Trobriand Islanders (Malinowski 1929). On the other hand, it does seem that a disproportionate number (though by no means all) of the cases brought up by various scholars as candidates for sexual egalitarianism are societies with some kind of matrilineal kinship institutions. It is here that the Naze, once again, enter the stage of world anthropology.

Of the three ethnographers who have approached the Naze from cosmopolitan discourse, Weng Naiqun devotes the most attention to this particular issue. The body of his work consists of detailed analyses of both symbolic and material aspects of relationships between the genders in the context of the

---

4. I leave aside here feminist approaches to cultural critique, an area in which I am not competent. In the area of feminist comparative sociology, bearing on the questions of marriage and gender hierarchy to which the works of Shih and others are speaking, I have found work of the 1980s to be the most helpful, including Flax 1982, Collier 1988, Schlegel 1977, and Ortner 1981.

Naze household, paying particular attention to the factors of economic and ritual reciprocity, and to the voluntary nature of the system of sexual relations, which he calls the *a xia* system. He comes to the conclusion that Naze society has an "absence of male dominance" (1995: 229–33) because, unlike so many other societies where the relationship between the domestic and the public domains of action is antagonistic, with the result that the domestic is made subordinate to the public, in Western Naze society

> it is not hard to find a tendency to domesticate the public domain. . . . In other words, Naze society is domestic-oriented. The Naze always tend to maximize the domestic domain while minimizing the public domain. . . . Naze women are usually placed in the central position of a household. In other words, the domestic domain belongs to Naze women. Thus, the tendency to domesticate the public domain shows again the centrality of women in the Naze society. (1995: 220)

For Weng, the key to equality between women and men in Naze society is complementarity within the socially central household, which is held together by matrilineal bonds rather than by conjugal pairing (1995: 225–28). This distinguishes Naze society from the great majority of societies, where conjugal relationships are based on the exchange of women, and this results in the absence of male dominance among the Naze:

> Socially, the reproduction of their society is not based on any conjugal pairing form, but on the synthesis of mother-son and sister-brother relationships. Most Naze women are not exchanged by their men folk in marriage. They have the right to control their own sexual life and procreation. By having sexual partners who belong to different matrilineal kin groups and socially denying their genitor roles, Naze women are able to give birth to new members of their own households. In addition, by keeping their sons as well as brothers at home to practice various ancestral cults, they are able to ensure the perpetuation of their households on both spiritual and material levels. (1995: 231)

Weng thus uses the results of careful, sensitive fieldwork to draw conclusions using the Naze case to address current anthropological debates. His conclusions in this area, unlike those made by Shih about sexual morality and cultural relativism, are probably not threatening to anyone but the most diehard Confucian. Nevertheless, he does use the Naze to represent something else, again a data-point in a cross-cultural dialogue about male dominance.

REPRESENTATION AS INNOCENT:
WITHOUT MALE DOMINANCE OR SEXUAL REPRESSION

Both Shih and Weng use data about family, sex, and gender in Naze society to address larger issues, but these are primarily scholarly issues emerging from almost abstract, centuries-long conversations about human nature and human universals. For another group of witnesses, ranging from casual tourists to serious fiction and nonfiction writers, Naze represent something much more immediate: an example of a society whose egalitarianism and lack of sexual hypocrisy represent a model or example, a real occurrence of what is thus proven to be not a utopian, but a realizable ideal, in contrast to the writer's own society where sexual hypocrisy and male dominance go hand-in-hand to create what Engels portrayed as the reproductive side of the Marxian dystopia of capitalism (1972 [1883]: 100–105) and what certain critics since the May Fourth era have portrayed as the repressive male-dominance at the core of Chinese culture (see Barlow 1990).

A Feminist Past

One group of people who have recently noticed the Naze are the writers of speculative feminist histories, a genre that has been gaining popularity in recent decades (Reed 1974, E. Morgan 1972, Fisher 1979, Eisler 1987). These books, aimed at an English-speaking, intellectual audience, are retellings of history to refute what the authors consider to be the myth that male dominance is natural, universal, and inevitable. They accomplish this refutation by showing that, at some time in the distant past (this varies from one reconstruction to another, since data are very difficult to interpret in this way), humans lived a more peaceful, cooperative existence than they do now, that there was no organized warfare and no large-scale politics, and thus no way for men to gain the ascendancy of power and prestige that they now have. This reconstruction of society is supported in these works by a reconstruction of the symbolic or cultural systems of those former times, in which cosmology and ritual displayed complementarity, rather than antagonistic asymmetry, between male and female principles.[5]

---

5. In this brief discussion, I am glossing over very significant differences in the particular ways these authors reconstruct earlier, nonhierarchical phases of human society. Some, such as Reed, draw very closely on Morgan and Engels, while others, such as Fisher and Eisler, pay greater attention to the symbolic aspects. For our purposes here, what is important is that the Naze may be entering this discourse.

In 1995 I received an enthusiastic phone call from an author of one of the most widely read of these speculative feminist histories. She had just seen a videotape, made by a Chinese commercial producer, of the egalitarian, matrilineal society of the Mosuo of Lugu Lake, and I had been referred to her as a scholar who knew something about the area. She asked a series of interesting questions about the nature of the society, but was astonished that I had actually been there, since she assumed it was impossibly remote; she assumed that it would be impossibly remote because she had assumed that it was a remnant of a distant past when all of humanity was like this. The picture that she had gleaned of Naze society seemed accurate to me, but the idea she drew about its significance—that it was a Neolithic survival of a formerly larger pattern—seemed to me to be another instance of using the Naze, however accurately they were portrayed, to represent something else, in this case, an imagined past that held out hope for a better future.

A Chinese Present

Naze society and culture have served an even greater role for Chinese intellectuals dissatisfied with what they see as the sexual hypocrisy of both the Confucian and Communist versions of their own culture. In the tradition of such works as *Destiny of the Flowers in the Mirror* (Jing hua yuan), which depicts a looking-glass world where men have bound feet (Li Ruzhen 1986 [ca. 1800]), and particularly chapters 54 and 55 of the great vernacular novel *Record of a Westward Journey* (Xi you ji), in which Monkey and his traveling companions enter the Kingdom of Women and learn what it is like to be pregnant, among other things (Wu Cheng'en 1961 [16th cent.]: 620–42), recent writers have used Naze as their own Kingdom of Women that offers a contrast to Han Chinese society, where male dominance in both power and symbolic terms is taken for granted and where people perhaps need detailed and startling alternatives, whether fantastical or ethnographic, in order to be able to see the repression and hypocrisy of their own society more clearly.

The most prominent modern writer to adopt Naze society as a mirror for Han sexual hypocrisy is Bai Hua, whose 1988 novel *The Remote Country of Women* (Yuanfang you yige Nüer Guo) was translated by Qingyun Wu and Thomas O. Beebe into English in 1994. The novel is ingeniously constructed to tell two parallel stories that meet partway through the book. The first is the story of the cultural cadre Liang Rui, a typical Han Chinese male intellectual caught up in the destructive nonsense of the Cultural Revolution. He is sent to the countryside, witnesses all sorts of hypocrisy, including the sexual kind, takes up a secret affair with the daughter of a prominent cadre, is found out and sent to prison, and finally, when he is released, decides to go not back to the city, like most disillusioned Maoist youth, but rather to the most remote place possible, which turns out to be Lugu Lake. Meanwhile, Sunamei, a Mosuo girl, is growing up. There are rumblings of outside influence—Han cadres make Mosuo people get married against their will, for example—but her life is basically one of coming of age sexually, finding out about lovers, and becoming a Mosuo woman. But then she is chosen, because of her beauty and voice, for the county song-and-dance troupe, which is where Liang Rui is assigned after his release from prison. They fall in love, and, after he explains the concept of marriage over and over again, she finally agrees to marry him. But when they return to Sunamei's village by the lake, she has a couple of innocent trysts with former lovers (the Mosuo see nothing wrong in this), and finally, in a fit of anger and jealousy, Liang Rui burns her matrilineal house down and, though he still loves her, is ostracized by the community and has to leave her forever.

The contrasts that Bai Hua draws here are not only between egalitarianism and hierarchy, or between freedom and repression, but most importantly those old Lévi-Straussian ones between nature and culture; between the innocence of the Mosuo and the calculation of the Han, and between a sexuality based on natural feelings of attraction and one based on artificial and destructive feelings of possessiveness and jealousy.

The details of Naze society—the fine points of housing and dress, the ceremonies of puberty and death, the kinship terminology used in the Naze household—all are carefully inserted into Bai Hua's narrative to give it an air of authenticity. He depended, says a note in the English edition of his novel, greatly on the ethnographic works of Zhan Chengxu and Yan Ruxian, and made two visits to Lugu Lake. What he has done in the novel, however, is to attribute an ancientness and innocence to the Naze that do not seem to be directly extractable from the empirical facts of the case, and to impart to their thoughts a rich emotional content that would not be accessible to an outsider without an intimate knowledge of the language, which, as we have seen, even Zhan and Yan have never learned, let alone Bai Hua. For example (in Wu and Beebe's translation),

> From fragrant autumn to chilly winter, Sunamei's pinched face showed no smile. Quite unexpectedly, the silent anger made her look more mature and more beautiful. Like a patch of azaleas blooming on mountain peaks, beautiful Sunamei rose before the men from dozens of miles around, making them look up to her

and seek a path to reach her. When the swinging festival came in the first lunar month, Sunamei deliberately asked that her swing be five feet longer than the others. As soon as she got on, the swing flew high above the heads of the audience. The ruffles of her skirt danced like lotus leaves in a storm. Her self-confidence rose with her body. She giggled heartily, her calves beneath her feet, that the clapping and cheering for her were much louder than for any other woman. (1994: 124)

Without knowing it, Sunamei laid her face on Longbu's hairy chest. She did not know when and how he had unbuttoned his shirt, but she was not frightened by the strong heartbeat of a man. She thought to herself, "How did I pass the long narrow bridge I thought I could never cross?" (1994: 151–52)

Bai Hua himself has observed that in this book, he "intended to use the past as a mirror to see the present, . . . to use the values of [the] matrilineal model to challenge our conventional evaluations regarding the primitive versus the modern, and the barbarous versus the civilized" (1994: 373).

The Naze clearly come off in Bai Hua's book as nicer, more genuine people than the Han, and in their mirror one can perhaps see ugly truths about Chinese culture with unusual clarity. But again, despite ethnographic accuracy, it is not the Naze that Bai Hua is primarily concerned with. If it were, he would not assume that they somehow lived in the past. He is using them instead as a sign vehicle in a larger conversation, one about the self-criticisms of modernists and Chinese intellectuals. People at Lugu Lake have undoubtedly read this novel by now; it would be interesting to hear what they think of it.

REPRESENTATION AS EXOTIC:
PROMOTING TOURISM IN A VERY REMOTE PLACE

All the ways of representing the Naze described above occur mainly in intellectual discourses whose ends are primarily scientific or political. But there is another context where an idealized picture is emerging of the Naze, their lake, and their exotic matrilineal system. This is the arena of national and international tourism.

Tourism has become a big industry in China since the mid-1980s, and most of the tourists are domestic; there are both official tourists, organized into groups for work-junkets of various sorts, and an increasing number of private tourists, who spend some of their ever-increasing disposable income to join commercial tours or just travel on their own, alone or as families.

FIG. 28. Lugu Lake

Altogether, China reported over forty-six million foreign tourists, most of them from Hong Kong (Yearbook 1996: 281), and six hundred million domestic travelers (ibid.: 352) in 1995. Not all of these were what we would call tourists, but it is nevertheless clear that the travel industry has boomed in the 1990s.[6] Tourism seems, in general, to be directed at one or more of three things: history (ancient or revolutionary), scenery, and ethnicity. Lugu Lake (fig. 28) has the last two in abundance.

Ethnic tourism (van den Berghe and Keyes 1984) in contemporary China is usually promoted by tourist bureaus at various levels of government, who work with local cadres to develop facilities for feeding and lodging tourists, as well as routines for receiving and entertaining them. Developing routines often involves taking native practices, such as dress, song, dance, drink, and sometimes even ritual, and adapting and standardizing them into performances that fit tourist tastes and schedules (fig. 29). What is emphasized in the promotional literature as well as in the performances themselves is the ethnic character of the things being performed, although these deviate from what was

---

6. I am indebted to Tim Oakes for bringing these figures to my attention.

FIG. 29. Naze women serve *chiong* to tourists, in this case
a cadre delegation.

practiced in the local community before it entered into the collaboration with
the tourist agencies.[7] This results in a kind of perpetual cycle of authenticity:
first intrepid travelers and then tourist promoters search out the most remote
and "untouristy" places to market to tourists in search of the ethnically
authentic, but by the time the great mass of tourists reach these places, the
cultural practices have been modified for the tourist trade, prompting the pio-
neers to seek out even more remote places. The quest for authenticity is thus
only momentarily satisfied, if at all, and by the time something makes any
money, it is no longer authentic in the sense of being untouched by the money-
making activities.[8]

7. As I described briefly in chapter 9, and as Louisa Schein analyzes cogently in her recent
book (1999), this standardization of ethnic forms for tourist purposes is not something done to
the ethnic people by agents of the state or the Han center. In most parts of China, the most active
and successful ethnic tourism entrepreneurs are educated members of the local minority groups.

8. On the collaboration and negotiation between local cadres and tourism officials, and the
ethnic politics that permeate the process, see Cheung 1996. On the cycle of authenticity and the
futility of the quest for the untouched, see Oakes 1995, 1998.

But the quest for authenticity is not the only motivation behind the promotion of ethnic tourism. There is also the desire to portray, in the actions of the tourists as they interact with the local people, the unity of the various nationalities (*minzu tuanjie*) that make up the Chinese nation and to show them with some sort of ethnological precision, demonstrating not only the variety of the nation but also the progress from more primitive to more civilized or advanced forms. Ethnic tourism thus becomes a kind of history lesson on the evolution through the various modes of production, culminating in socialism.

In this context, the Naze at Lugu Lake have it all: they not only have exotic customs galore, culminating in the matrilineal household and "walking marriage," they also have plenty of local color in their clothes and housing, and some of the best scenery in China to boot. A 1991 article titled "The Kingdom of Women by the Shores of Lugu Lake" (Lugu Hu pan Nüer Guo) in the magazine *Touring Southwest China* (Xinan lüyou) described the delights waiting for the fortunate visitor to Lugu Lake:

> At Lugu Lake there is a Kingdom of Women; the Mosuo people who live together on the shores of the lake have mostly matrilineal consanguineal households where women hold power. To this day they still preserve their peculiar anachronism of "walking marriage."
>
> This March, after the travel propaganda work meeting held in Panzhihua by the Provincial Tourism Bureau, a group was organized to go to Lugu Lake to investigate tourism. This writer was chosen for the trip and was thrilled to have the opportunity to understand the peculiarities of marriage and human emotions in a Kingdom of Women. . . .
>
> When we got to Lugu Lake, it was immediately just like the Kingdom of Women. Coming forward to greet us was a group of Mosuo maidens with intricate hairdos, colorful blouses, and long skirts, holding out flowers. Some of them would be guides for us, some would sing for us, some would build fires to prepare for a picnic on the shore of the lake.

Naturally, the author wants to know about the marriage system. He has been instructed not to ask any women, so he seeks out a young man in a military jacket, who turns out to be a PLA veteran. The young man tells him that the Mosuo marriage system is based on love, and extracts a promise not to write nonsense: "Bu yao luan jiang." The writer is discouraged:

> This conversation made me sweat inside. The "walking marriage custom" of the matrilineal society of the Mosuo would certainly be of interest to the ordinary

reader, but it is a most sensitive question. If in the course of an interview one happened to say something wrong, it could easily lead to misunderstanding and discourtesy. Difficult! (Jin Yu 1991: 13)

These brief quotations sum up the representation of the Mosuo in Chinese tourist discourse. The selling point is the matrilineal system and the custom of "walking marriage." At first glance this might seem odd to the average North American or European, since we would not expect ordinary readers of tourist magazines to even know the word "matrilineal." But we must remember that history, as presented in Chinese secondary schools, is taught according to an evolutionary model, and the beginning stage of the evolutionary model is taken from Morgan's *Ancient Society* as reinterpreted by Engels, so that anyone who has been to junior high school (the vast majority of those with enough money to become ethnic tourists) will know that matrilineal organization belongs to the very early stages of human history and that the chance to actually see it in action is something quite special. In addition, the reference to the Kingdom of Women (Nüer Guo) resonates with images of sex-role reversal to everyone who has read or even seen the TV serialization of *Record of a Westward Journey*, which is to say nearly every literate Chinese.

But the Mosuo as represented in this tourist literature are not just ancient; because they are ancient, they are also mysterious and somewhat irrational. Walking marriage, which the Mosuo all defend as the best system, is nevertheless "a most sensitive question," and there is a fear, as there would be among visitors to any primitive people, of doing something wrong, violating an irrational but nonetheless sacred prohibition, and getting oneself in such trouble as to preclude the possibility of finding a good source of information.

In the end, the delegation finds out about walking marriage from a Mosuo man who is an official in the county tourist bureau and who has accompanied the delegation all along. He explains and defends the system, but he won't tell the questioners whether he himself has ever been in a walking marriage or not. Thus the state, in the person of the tourist bureau, finally controls the information and provides and controls the spokesman for the Mosuo. This, plus a few well-selected pictures of pretty women standing in front of dugout canoes and log houses, and dancing in a line, complete the article and give the prospective tourist an attractive picture—resolved, not totally impenetrable, but still mysterious enough to keep it attractive and entice people to want to go to Lugu Lake.

More recently the Mosuo have been introduced to foreign tourists, who, according to a recent Reuters report (O'Neill 1995b) now constitute 40 percent of visitors to Luoshui, the most accessible village on the Yunnan side of the lake. A series of reports by the reporter Mark O'Neill touch on many of the same themes as the account by Jin quoted above, but in a different way and with different emphases that indicate his was a European and North American audience:

> Mayor Tsizuoercheng has no doubt the lure of China's only matriarchal society and a crystal-clear lake ringed by soaring mountains will draw tourists to his remote constituency. Such attractions far outweigh the lack of electricity, running water, and flush toilets around Lugu Lake in southwestern Yunnan Province. . . .
>
> The majestic lake glistens over 22 square miles. Its clear waters are ringed by soaring mountains, and visitors can breathe in clean air and enjoy a sense of tranquility unimaginable in China's overcrowded cities. Perhaps the main draw card is the "walking marriage" system of the local Mosuo tribe, under which the men live in their mothers' homes and visit the homes of their partners in the evening and depart early next morning. (1995b)

> Every evening after dinner, Ruxiang Songlong Zeer leaves his mother's home and walks the short distance to the home of his lady companion, spending the night before returning home early next morning. His is a "walking marriage," a form of partnership unique in China to the 50,000 members of the Muosuo [sic] tribe who live round this lake deep in remote mountains in a corner of southwestern Yunnan province. . . .
>
> This matriarchal system means that, unlike most Han Chinese who prefer baby boys to baby girls, Muosuo welcome girls as much or more than boys. Female infanticide, which occurs in some parts of China, is unknown. (1995a)

Aside from the Euro-American obsession with flush toilets, there is other evidence that this material is promoting tourism to a world audience. They would not know the term "matrilineal," so the reporter substitutes the grossly inaccurate "matriarchal," which is bound to be even more confusing, since "patriarchal" no longer has any thing to do with patriarchs. And the Mosuo are referred to as a "tribe," a term familiar to Americans through cowboy and Indian movies, and to Britons through having colonized most of Africa. Also, he manages to mention that the rest of China is polluted, noisy, and crowded, and likes to kill baby girls. And of course he is writing about the promotion of tourism, rather than promoting tourism directly, though the picture he paints is quite attractive even without the flush toilets.

Jim Goodman, writing in Hong Kong's *South China Morning Post*'s travel section, is considerably more direct in his January 1997 piece, "Where women rule":

> We all have a favourite place, where we feel light-years away from our problems. Mine is the northern end of Lugu Lake in northwest Yunnan province, the most beautiful body of water in all of Southwest China.
>
> Augmenting the attraction, it is the homeland of one of Asia's rare matriarchal societies—the Mosuo people. Remote it certainly is, but not too difficult to reach. . . .
>
> Mosuo women are not the least bit shy with their guests. Archumaw, one of the livelier of the daughters of Jiaoma's house, reminded me that on my last visit I said I wanted to learn some Mosuo songs. . . .
>
> Now she was in the mood for another song and belted out one of those high-pitched, warbling tribal tunes that are so unique to the Mosuos.
>
> Foreign and Chinese guests at Luoshui usually contact the village youth there to perform a song and dance show around an evening bonfire. Luoshui's dance show-girls, in their braided turbans, bright jackets and long pleated skirts, line up beside young men in Tibetan cowboy hats, black jackets, boots and cummerbunds. Led by a flutist they dance around the fire. . . .
>
> Mosuos do not formally marry and their language has no words for husband or wife. The girl chooses the boy. He stays overnight with her but returns to his own mother's for meals and work assignments. Such affairs may last only temporarily, but they can also survive a lifetime. The system, practised by all Mosuos except the clans of the ex-ruling class, came under attack during the more radical decades of the recent past. But Mosuos by and large refused to register their "marriages" and are today even more inclined to retain their custom now that they have become famous for it. (Goodman 1997)

This is all fairly accurate, except the part about having no word for husband or wife. But like O'Neill's reports for Reuters, it is clearly geared toward a Western tourist audience. The emphasis is not on the ancient or historical, as in the Chinese tourist material, but on the exotic and unspoiled. There is no hint that the Mosuo represent our own past, but rather that they represent a friendly, hospitable people (here there is no hint of cultural sensitivity or trying to "unlock the mystery" of the walking marriage system) who live in a beautiful setting. We can get away from our troubles there. The question of whether the Mosuo have any troubles is left unanswered.

Representation and Counter-Representation

If the Naze (or their Western, matrilineal segment, anyway) have entered the stages of world scholarly, political, and tourist promotional discourses, if they have become the representations of the ancient, the exotic, the unencumbered, the egalitarian, they have had little choice in how these representations have been formulated, what their content was, or to whom they would be disseminated. Both the rumored dislike of being called "living fossils" and the young veteran's admonition not to write nonsense are evidence that Naze who have read or heard about the material written with them as subject have often had reason to object to its content or at least to its tone. But it would be a gross oversimplification to see the Naze as nothing but objects of other people's discourse, vehicles in other people's sign systems. Having learned about the world's fascination with them, they have begun to try to manipulate it for local ends.

There is, of course, some scholarly counterdiscourse, as represented by the article by He Xuewen on misconceptions about the marriage system. Those who choose to become educated, to become part of the Chinese national system, can represent themselves to a Chinese scholarly or even popular audience by judicious use of various kinds of print media. And at the same time, they are able to try to lure the tourist trade as a strategy for economic growth and raising the standard of living. The mayor of Luoshui, with his plans to convert the village economy from farming to tourism by 2005 (O'Neill 1995b), is nothing if not a cadre-entrepreneur of the ilk now running local industries and other money-making enterprises all over rural China. And perhaps the most striking example of the use of Naze representations for local goals was the Academic Conference on Sexology and Lugu Lake Culture, held in Xichang in the fall of 1996, followed by a four-day tour to Lugu Lake to see the matrilineal society in action. I was invited but did not attend. It occurred to me that people might resent a visit by an international delegation of sexologists, but it was a Naze doctor from Yanyuan who organized the conference. I don't know what local people think of him.

PART 4

RESIDUAL

AND

INSTRUMENTAL

ETHNICITY

13 / Ethnicity and Acculturation:
Some Little Groups

A ll of the groups we have examined so far have possessed ethnic identities that clearly differentiate them from the majority Han—the Nuosu
have an unassailable endogamy and, in most places, a distinct cultural
and linguistic heritage that renders their identity completely unproblematic,
even in cases where there has been some acculturation to Han ways. The identity of the Prmi and Naze is much more contingent; it is likely that the ethnic
identification program forced them to choose and crystallize an identity that
would otherwise have remained fluid. But there is little acculturation to Han
ways in most Naze and Prmi communities; their local identities are solidly
bounded (except where Prmi and Naze themselves overlap), and the contin-
gencies in their identities involve choices in the wider language of ethnic
identification between *minzu* or proto-*minzu* identities such as Meng, Zang,
Naxi, Mosuo, and Pumi.

To stop our discussion of ethnicity in Liangshan at this point, however,
would ignore one of the most important historical trends in southwest China:
the centuries-long process of acculturation to Chinese ways, which in the past
usually led after many generations to assimilation to Chinese identity, the identity that since ethnic identification has been uniformly referred to as Han.
Jonathan Unger has maintained, for example, in a recent article (1997), that
this millennia-old process has accelerated in recent years, as all over Yunnan
and Guizhou formerly culturally distinct communities have come to adopt the
ways of the majority, with only the increasingly artificial *minzu* designations
standing between many minority communities and complete assimilation.

Such processes of acculturation have certainly been significantly accelerated in the People's Republic, and particularly in the Reform Era, as transport,
communications, economic development, education, and popular culture have
spread to formerly inaccessible areas. But here as elsewhere, individual cases
are more complex than is conveyed by invoking a unidirectional process such
as acculturation, sinicization, or Hanification. In fact, in Liangshan the process
can be seen to have gone a number of directions, three of which are described

in this chapter. In many small ethnic enclaves, acculturation proceeds apace, and in some cases this leads to virtual or actual assimilation. In the first section of this chapter I describe what I conceive to be different stages in this process, as represented by several small enclave communities in Miyi County. In other, larger enclaves, acculturation is extremely evident but seems to have no effect on identity, rather in the manner of the Nuosu of Manshuiwan. In the second section I describe this process for a related but somewhat different case—the Lipuo of Pingdi Township in Panzhihua. Finally, there can sometimes be a resurgence of identity for instrumental purposes, even where acculturation is virtually complete. In the last section, I describe this process for the Shuitian people of Pingjiang and Futian Townships in Panzhihua, a place where an instrumental ethnic rationality has resulted in the maintenance of minority status as part of a strategy for economic development.

LITTLE GROUPS IN MIYI: ETHNICITY LOST?

Tucked in little ethnic pockets around the Lesser Liangshan area are tiny enclaves of people who claim an identity as a separate *minzu* but whose claims to *minzu* identity are not recognized by the Chinese state. In the metalanguage of ethnic classification, they are usually Yi, sometimes Han. Their own languages of ethnic identity are weak—they often do not speak any actual language of their own, or only the old people recognize a few words. They sometimes preserve what they proudly consider distinctive customs, but they do not practice very many of them, most of their practices having been assimilated to Han or occasionally Nuosu ways. Their ethnic languages are not so much dead languages—they are still spoken, sort of—but ghost languages, like ghost towns that might or might not still have a few people living in them, but where empty buildings testify to the former presence of something larger and more distinctive. Their ethnicity is in a sense residual; it was about to be forgotten and they were about to become ordinary Chinese farmers when ethnic identification came, and they were labeled as minorities. For some of them, whose acculturation has gone less far than others, this has meant that they will stay ethnic for a while, using their identity perhaps to gain minor perquisites such as a higher birth quota. Others will lose ethnic identity altogether, and although they may remain minority *minzu* in the official language of ethnic identification, they will be for all practical purposes no different at all from their Han neighbors and relatives. Still others will simply become Han, as did the ancestors of several hundred million central and southern Chinese. The townships of Hengshan, Puwei, and Malong in Miyi County are home to several such groups whose degrees of acculturation and assimilation can be arranged along a continuum from least to most merged.

These townships, which lie in rugged hills between the Anning and Yalong Rivers, were governed from the beginning of the Ming dynasty until the early twentieth century by a *tusi*, surnamed Ji, who was posted there from Guizhou by the first Ming emperor as part of his campaign to eliminate residual Mongol influence from the Southwest (Peng et al. 1992: 24). His own ethnicity was Nasu, or "Eastern Yi," a group that formed the ruling classes of much local society in western Guizhou and northeastern Yunnan (see Cheung 1995b). Currently, the population of this area is extraordinarily mixed, though the great majority of people are either Han or Nuosu. But in addition, I interviewed members of groups calling themselves Nasu, Abu, Hong Yi, Tazhi, Bai, Lisu, Yala,[1] and Shui. Some of these are alternative identifications for the same groups of people; each group and each identification applied to a group differs in the nature of the ethnic identity it expresses. They range from the Yala, who in the early 1990s still maintained a strong, if officially unrecognized, ethnic identity, through the Nasu/Abu/Hong Yi and the Tazhi/Bai, whose language seemed to be dying except for unintentional artificial life-support from the metalanguage of ethnic identification, to the Shui, who were simply becoming Han.

Yala

There are Yala or Lila or Niluo people in Hengshan and Malong Townships; they number a few hundred in each place. In Hengshan, they live in two villages, situated on opposite sides of the town; in Malong, where the town is hardly worth the name (though there is a paved street about one hundred meters long), they live in a little cluster of houses right above the market. Though most Yala dispute it, they are officially ethnically identified as Yi; the best they can do for separate recognition is to be mentioned in local sources as a branch of the Yi *minzu*. Knowledgeable local people in both places say that the Yala were the first people to get here, followed by the Han and, much later, the Nuosu. Though it is unclear exactly when the first Han came, it is certainly true that the Nuosu, despite their great numbers, are the most recent immigrants. The Yala, like the

---

1. *The Account of the Minzu of Miyi* (Peng et al. 1992) list four of these groups as subheadings under Yi: the Abu, Tazhi, Yala, and Niluo. It turns out, however, that Yala and Niluo are alternate words for the same group, which is represented in Hengshan and Malong Counties: Yala is a Han-language term, while Niluo (or Lila, as I heard it) is the name in the native language.

Nasu and Tazhi, trace their residence in the area to the Hongwu period (1368–98) at the beginning of the Ming dynasty.

Yala may have once been primarily endogamous. Their expressed ideal (no longer rigorously practiced in the current generation) was for bilateral cross-cousin marriage, and I recorded at least one present-day case of direct brother-sister exchange, along with a lot of marrying back and forth between pairs of clans, especially in Malong, where only two clans are represented. Some people told me that they did not marry Han before the Democratic Reforms but did marry Lisu, who have since left the area. Nowadays, marriage with Han is fairly common: of thirty-nine marriages in the last two generations of the families I interviewed, sixteen were reported to be with other Yala, twenty-one with Han, and two with Abu. There were several marriages between Yala in Hengshan and Yala from Malong, which, combined with the fact that almost half of all recent marriages are still within the small Yala community, indicates that ethnicity may still be a factor in marriage choice. Or perhaps it is just that people continue to marry their affines, who tend because of past history to be Yala. What the Yala do not do is marry the Nuosu, even though both are classified as parts of the Yi *minzu*. In neither community could any of the Yala recall a single case of intermarriage with Nuosu.

Yala spoken language (which is certainly a variety of Yi, though it has not been studied formally) is alive, and perhaps well. In Malong, even young adults seemed to speak Yala most of the time around the house, while of course being perfectly fluent in Han. In Hengshan, it appeared to me that Yala was losing ground, but middle-aged people could still converse in it. Some people said that there had been a written language; one knowledgeable Yala man, a doctor in Hengshan, told me that the written language was lost sometime during the Qing dynasty, and that this was a great shame, because without a written language there was no possibility that the Yala could gain official *minzu* status: they would have to remain Yi, though they had nothing to do with the local Yi.

In the languages of ritual and customs, Yala still communicate difference, but not particularly loudly. Several people told me that there had been an erosion of Yala customs in the last decade, particularly with the opening up of Hengshan to commercial agriculture. Still, people preserve a few distinctive wedding customs, such as the bride's not entering the groom's house until the stars come out, the groom's painting the faces of the bride's relatives, and the bride's being carried on the back of a relative into the groom's house. In addition, they time their celebration of the New Year differently from the Han; they scatter pine needles on the floor of the house and courtyard, and terminate their celebrations on the thirteenth day of the New Year rather than waiting for the Lantern Festival on the fifteenth, as the Han do. Finally, their burial customs are different. In Hengshan, we were told, they still cremate the dead (which immediately distinguishes them from the Han), but instead of just leaving the ashes with a little stone marker, as the Nuosu do, they put them in an urn and bury them. In Malong, they cremated the dead until the early twentieth century but then began to take up the practice of burial when urged by the Nasu *tusi* (see below). They had a lovely graveyard with big trees, but it was destroyed and the trees all cut down in the Cultural Revolution. One man said wistfully, however, that it didn't make much difference, since according to Yala belief the soul no longer lingers in the ashes after the cremation. It is ironic, perhaps, that all of these customs are also practiced by one or another group of Yi (Nuosu or Lipuo) who live fairly nearby and may have contributed, along with linguistic similarities, to ethnic identification of the Yala as a branch of the Yi.

The Yala thus seem to be a typical case (see Cheung 1995a, 1996) of a small group that formed an ethnic identity in a local context, distinguishing itself from its neighbors by a combination of descent and ethnic markers, but that was then classified according to cultural and linguistic criteria (as Stalin recommended) as a member of a larger category. They refuse to accept this category, on the surface claiming cultural differences such as their own written language and certain marriage customs, but the real reason is that in the local context they play a different role. In Malong in particular, the Yala settlement is adjacent to the small township center, and the Yala have been lowland farmers in the area for countless generations, as well as subjects of the *tusi* in Puwei for at least a few centuries. Their social position is different from that of the Nuosu, who arrived much later, live in the highlands, and were only loosely subject to the *tusi*. So, in the practical local language of ethnic identity, they claim differences of descent and culture to distinguish themselves from the Yi. The state, operating on broader criteria that do not take the local social context into account, classifies them as Yi without much hesitation. They are still some distance from being completely acculturated to Han language or customs, and refuse to identify with Nuosu, so their only recourse is to claim that they are a separate *minzu*.

Nasu

Nasu, Abu, and Hong Yi are different appellations for a single group, which is represented primarily in Puwei, the former seat of the Ji *tusi*. Members of the Ji clan (called Azhi in their native Nasu tongue) whom I interviewed agree with the official history that says this group came originally from Shuicheng in Guizhou in the Hongwu reign period of the early Ming (probably in the 1380s), where the Ji clan were local rulers. The first Ming emperor, Taizu, moved them here as part of his campaign to oust the last Yuan officials in the area and consolidate Ming rule; after an unsuccessful rebellion by other local leaders, the family was established as *tusi* in 1404 (Peng Deyuan et al. 1992: 24). With the Ji came Nasu people of eight other clans, eventually given Chinese surnames. Many of them were landlords in the area until the democratic reforms of 1956 abolished old forms of landholding.

According to older members of the Ji and some of its allied clans, the term Abu comes from a hasty mistake made by the ethnic identification teams in the mid-1950s. In the Nasu language, the term for "grandfather" is *apu*; tenants and retainers of the Nasu rulers and landlords were required to call the Nasu "Apu" as a term of respect. When the identification teams came and asked who those people were, they were told, "Apu," and this got written down as an ethnonym (Abu in Chinese), when properly it was an honorific designation for members of a ruling class. Actually, of course, insofar as Nasu were the rulers of the local native administration, they were a class as well as a ruling ethnic group. At any rate, they did not call themselves Abu (except when they were addressing their own grandfathers), but this became their designation in local ethnology (Peng Deyuan et al. 1992: 49–50), even though their *minzu* designation, because of their linguistic closeness to Nuosu and perhaps because of the classification of their more numerous relatives in Guizhou, was Yi. Nevertheless, at least one woman of the Bai surname insisted to me that her family were Abu*zu*, and that they had been misclassified as Yi.

Why were the Nasu called Hong Yi, or Red Yi? Probably because they were Yi (or, in the more common but pejorative Chinese-language designation used before 1956, Luoluo), but they were neither the Black Luoluo (Nuoho) aristocrats nor the White Luoluo (Quho) commoners of the Nuosu, but rather a third kind of Luoluo, which needed to be designated by a color, which turned out to be red.

The ideal marriage form for Nasu before the current generation was delayed exchange, or *patrilateral* cross-cousin marriage; although direct exchange of the Nuosu type was allowed, it was discouraged. Even today, with considerably more freedom of marriage, a young woman's mother's brother's household is supposed to be given rights of first refusal before she marries a nonrelative. In recent years, however, freedom of marriage has meant that a large number of Nasu young people are marrying Han. In one branch of the Ji family, for example, the eldest living generation had two marriages, both to

Nasu surnamed Bai; the next generation had seven marriages, six of them to Nasu surnamed Ma and one to a Han; the third generation so far has had nine marriages, three to Nasu named respectively Lu, Ma, and Bai, and the other six to Han. What is striking here is that Nasu have started marrying Han, to whose cultural ways they are largely assimilated, but they have not intermarried with Nuosu, who are their close linguistic and cultural relatives, and with whom they share the Yi *minzu* designation.

The ethnic languages of the Nasu in Puwei are fading. One old man of the Ji clan could give me a basic vocabulary list, and knew that his "native" language shared about 80 percent of its vocabulary with the Nuosu dialect spoken by his mountain neighbors (which he spoke fairly well himself), but his conversation had been in Han for the last five or six decades at least, and people under sixty seem to know not even a few words in the old language. I was told that the Ji clan once had a genealogy, which was destroyed in the Democratic Reforms; the first part was written in Yi and the second in Chinese, but nobody now knows how to write the Yi characters; once again this contrasts with the situation of the Nuosu.

There is no longer any form of distinctive dress for Nasu people, and what customs differ from those of the neighboring Han are just enough to serve as ethnic markers. For example, they celebrate the Chinese New Year (which Nuosu do not), but they celebrate it slightly differently from the local Han, leaving a carpet of pine needles on the floor from the thirtieth of the twelfth month of the old year until the sixth of the first month of the new. Their marriage rituals also differ slightly from the Han and considerably from the Nuosu. They also place their ancestral altars, in Yi fashion, on a high shelf in a back corner of the front room of their otherwise Han-style house, rather than having them on a central altar on the back wall, as Han everywhere do.

In short, while some Nasu people freely acknowledge that they are Yi, and related to the Nuosu, their languages of ethnicity in everyday life say otherwise. They resemble the Nuosu in none of their interactions with other groups in local society. While Nuosu preserve endogamy, Nasu intermarry frequently, with the result that Nuosu are about the only group that Nasu will not marry. While Nuosu preserve their spoken and written language, even when bilingual in Chinese, Nasu have lost their written language entirely and their spoken language almost. While Nasu customs are distinct in a few ways from those of the Han, they are more distinct from those of their purported ethnic relatives, the Nuosu. My guess is that if it had not been for the crystallization of *minzu* categories in the metalanguage of ethnic identification, the Nasu identity would be on its way to dying out; acculturation and contact would have led by now to assimilation. For now, only their classification as Yi (which some of them dispute) has kept them from becoming Han.

Tazhi

Not far from the clusters of Nasu that dot the otherwise Han villages on the Puwei plain live an even more problematical group of people, identified as Tazhi in the local ethnological sources (Peng Deyuan et al. 1992: 52). When I first visited Puwei, I made the acquaintance of a local elementary school teacher, who told me that she herself was Tazhi and that there were three surnames of Tazhi resident in the township—Lu, Luo, and Wang. They once had a language of their own, she said, but only a few old people still remembered it. Their most distinctive custom was patrilateral cross-cousin marriage, which still existed in the form of the right of first refusal for a young woman's mother's brother's family. She also outlined to me certain Tazhi customs for holidays and rites of passage, which sounded very similar to those of the Nasu and other Yi groups (but not the Nuosu) in the region. They had mistakenly been classified as Yi, but they were in fact a separate *minzu*.

When I jeeped up to one of the Tazhi villages the next morning, however, and talked to some members of the Lu and Luo families, they denied that there was such a thing as Tazhi. They told me that their ancestors had originally called themselves Tazhi but that ethnic identification investigators in the 1950s had told them that there was no such group, that Tazhi was simply a name given to these three families by the Ji *tusi* and that in fact these people are descendants of Bai from Yunnan whence they came, so that they should properly identify themselves as Bai. But then that evening, I asked the schoolteacher again, and she told me that they were Tazhi, and that despite the official ethnic identification as Yi, she still wrote "Tazhi" on forms when required to state her *minzu*. Finally, the next morning I returned again to the Tazhi village to speak to the man who reputedly remembered the language, and he said that Tazhi was the proper designation for his group, but that since the state authorities would not recognize such an identity, and since they were not Yi, some people advocated calling themselves Bai. He turned out to know only a few words of the Tazhi language.

If we return for a minute to the metalanguage of ethnohistory, we may be able to place this confusion into context, at least. It seems clear from the affinities of the Tazhi language and the bits of the history remembered by people in the communities that the Tazhi are culturally and linguistically closely related to, if not identical with, the Nasu. Since the Tazhi were clearly neither members nor affines of the ruling Ji clan (most marriages before the current generation were among the three surnames; I found one to a Ma surname, which is Nasu, and the rest were to Han or to a Lisu family that migrated to the area a few decades ago), they may have been given the designation White Yi or White Luoluo, in an analogy to the White, or *quho*, commoner-retainer clans of the nearby Nuosu. If so, it is but a small step from White Yi, or Bai Yi, to just plain Bai, which happens, coincidentally, to be the name of an official *minzu*, most of whom live near Dali in west-central Yunnan.

This interpretation is strengthened by another nearby example. In Malong Township, southwest of Puwei, there are a group of families who call themselves Bai, even though their official identification cards and household registration records designate them as Yi. These families say they came to Malong in the 1950s from a place called Zongfa, which is just south of Renhe District Town near Panzhihua City. Nowadays, the population of Zongfa is all Han, but Pingdi, one township to the south, is inhabited by people who call themselves Lipuo in their own language and Bai Yi in Chinese. It is quite likely that the self-designated Bai in Malong, like those of the Tazhi in Puwei who call themselves Bai, are descendants of people who were once known as Bai Yi and who have hit on the availability of the official *minzu* designation Bai to find themselves a name that is not Yi—that is to say, not the same as the Nuosu up in the mountains, whose customs and languages, as shown above, demonstrate very little Han influence. Similar cases have also been reported from other parts of Miyi by local ethnologists (Li Liukun 1992).

Again in the case of the Tazhi, we can see the impact of the metalanguage of ethnic identification upon the local languages of ethnic identity. The Tazhi, like the Nasu (with whom they probably share a common origin not more than seven hundred years ago), occupy an ecological and formerly a political niche that is not much different from that of the Han in surrounding areas or even in their own townships. Through intermarriage and through the acculturative processes of state education and propaganda, they are in the process of acculturating to Han ways. Their languages will probably be completely gone in another generation, and they can choose to keep certain of their distinctive customs or not. They are undergoing the process of "becoming Chinese" outlined by Brown (1996) for the lowland aborigines of Taiwan. But because ethnic identification has intervened, they have no prospect of becoming Han: they are, for the time being, classified as Yi. Wanting to reject any association with Nuosu, they have little choice but to cling to their identity as Nasu or Abu or Hong Yi or Tazhi or Bai.

Yet, when conducting field research in such places as Puwei or Malong, I sometimes began to wonder how important ethnicity really is in the daily lives of these families. They are certainly aware of opportunities to gain slight but significant preferential treatment through affirmative action, and certainly when anyone asks them, they know their own *minzu* (though they don't always agree on the name, even among themselves), and there are certain people who are recognized experts, always delegated to receive investigating visitors, whether foreign anthropologists or county-level officials. But their life, with the exception of a few ritual occasions, is identical to that of their Han neighbors and relatives. I was struck, for example, when conducting household censuses of the Lisu lineage in the Tazhi village mentioned above, that one of their senior members (the township Party secretary) did not know the *minzu* of one of his brothers' wives or one of his own sisters' husbands. Nobody knew what *zu* they were because nobody had ever asked them, he said.

Shui

In Puwei Township there are eleven families, all named Wang, who are known to be members of the Shui *minzu*. According to one of their members, they have been in Puwei for five generations, having fled troubles in Guizhou Province, from whence they originally came. They have little left of an identity except a name, and even that is perhaps not permanent.

Ever since they arrived in Puwei, a prohibition on marrying close relatives has meant that the Wangs have almost exclusively married Han spouses, so that descendants of Wang women are simply Han, while descendants of Wang men retain their identity as Shui, but all have Han mothers.

Perhaps because of this intermarriage and isolation from other Shui, Mr. Wang said there is nobody who remembers even a single word of the Shui language (possibly this has been true for more than one generation), and they neither practice any distinctively Shui customs nor even know what these might be. Unlike some other local, isolated groups in this area, they have made no attempt to contact their relatives back in "the old country."

In other words, the Shui in Puwei are completely acculturated to Han ways. And even the ethnic identification process may not in their case be enough to save them from complete assimilation. Mr. Wang stated, and I confirmed by looking, that the household registration records for the Wangs in fact listed them as Han. All that is left, then, is a true ghost identity, and Mr. Wang said the only reason they still clung to any idea of being Shui at all was that they "had a feeling in their hearts that they should not forget their roots." It is impossible to know how long such a feeling might last.

From the Yala to the Nasu and Tazhi to the Shui, then, there is a progression of greater and greater acculturation to Han (or perhaps better stated, southwestern Chinese rural) culture. Yala, unhappy to be classified as Yi, proceed as if they were, indeed, a separate *minzu*; theirs is a case in which the languages of ethnic identification and ethnic identity are clearly at odds. Nasu and Tazhi are more ambivalent. Some claim a separate identity (as Abu or Tazhi or even Bai), while others seem content enough to be Yi, especially since this designation does not really mean having to interact closely with Nuosu. It is a safe bet that in the absence of ethnic identification they would just be Chinese. Shui, having originally been identified as Shui, seem not to care much longer, and are in the process of complete assimilation to a Han identity.

THE LIPUO IN PINGDI: ETHNICITY RETAINED

In the part of Panzhihua that lies south of the Jinsha River, in what was formerly part of Yongren County, Yunnan, there are fifteen thousand or more Yi people whose origins and social ties lie not in Sichuan to the north, but in central Yunnan to the south. Speakers of the Central Dialect (Chen Shilin 1984: 4) of Yi, they call themselves Lipuo and their language, Libie. In 1987, 7,607 Yi, probably all of them Lipuo, lived in Pingdi, the southernmost township in Panzhihua City. In 1988 my colleagues I and spent two weeks in the primarily Lipuo village of Yishala, in the southeastern corner of Pingdi (fig. 30).[2] In terms of the scale of acculturation presented above, the Lipuo in Pingdi are perhaps slightly more acculturated in every way but language than the Yala, Nasu, and Tazhi, but they retain their Libie language as the ordinary medium of everyday speech and the first language of small children. Their identity, unlike those of any of the groups described above, appears not to have gone even the slightest distance toward assimilation, despite their acculturation to Han (or perhaps more accurately, Chinese) ways.

"Lipuo" is a self-designation; all Lipuo use the term when they are speaking the Libie language; its Han translation is "Yi." Lipuo are, for the most part, educated people and know that there are other kinds of Yi around; many make a

---

2. The description and analysis in this section are taken, with some modifications, from Harrell 1990. They apply only to Pingdi; it appears that cultural differences and the conscious use of cultural markers are much more prevalent in other Lipuo or Lolopo communities in Yongren to the south, described in the works of Erik Mueggler (1998a,b, 2000). As with any other group (such as the Nuosu, chaps. 7-9,), the content and structure of ethnic identity differs from community to community.

FIG. 30. The village of Yishala. Lipuo and Han homes are identical.

distinction between themselves as "White Yi" and the Nuosu as "Black Yi."[3] One retired schoolteacher told me he thought they might have a common origin. None of the Lipuo I talked to seemed to dispute the existence of a broader Yi category or their membership in it, but it was not terribly important to them; the relevant relationships were local, and locally "Yi" was a Han word for "Lipuo."

Similarly, Han peasants, who make up about 8 percent of the population of Yishala, readily divide their local world into Yi and Han. One's status as one or the other is purely a matter of ancestry in most cases.

Neither of these local definitions is in any way in conflict with the state classification of the Lipuo into the Yi *minzu*. Officially, most Yunnanese Yi, including the Lipuo, are considered to have been at a higher, feudal stage of social evolution than were the Nuosu; this is evidenced by the similarity of their social organization with that of the local Han. But that the Lipuo are Yi is indisputable, and can be seen from their language, festivals, and other customs, as

3. This Black-White Yi distinction has nothing to do with the *nuoho-quho* caste distinctions of the Nuosu of Liangshan. Both are simply different instances of the use of colors to designate ethnic groups, which is widespread all over southwest China.

well as their history. The state identification is thus entirely compatible with the local identity, and indeed frames the local identity in the wider discourse of ethnic identification.

Unlike most Nuosu, the Lipuo have a relationship with neighboring Han that can be characterized not by separation but by absorption. Like the Nuosu of Manshuiwan, Lipuo in Pingdi have absorbed Han culture for hundreds of years, while retaining their ethnic identity. But unlike either the Manshuiwan Nuosu or the highland Nuosu, the Pingdi Lipuo communities have also absorbed Han people, not by slave-raiding and incorporation as the lowest caste but by marriage of both Han women and men into Lipuo villages and families.

Lipuo and Han live intermingled—in the same townships, the same villages, the same households. In Pingdi in 1987 there were seven administrative villages (*cun*) containing 12,336 people, of whom 7,607 (62 percent) were Yi and 4,729 (38 percent) were Han. The villages themselves varied in ethnic composition from Yishala (91 percent Yi) to Matou, (only 37 percent Yi and 63 percent Han). Within the village of Yishala, Yi and Han live interspersed in no discernable pattern: strictly speaking, there are no Han households, since every household in the village has Yi members. But despite this interspersal and intermarriage, Lipuo retain a strong Yi identity.

This pattern of interspersal has a long history. The Lipuo people in Yishala recognize themselves as belonging primarily to four major lineages, three of which can trace their origin to soldiers who came with various armies during the Ming and Qing periods from more easterly parts of China: Nanjing, Huguang, and Jiangxi. I have as yet found no concrete evidence of Ming origins for these clans, but one villager has in his possession a boundary agreement with a neighboring village, dated 1654.

The dates of migration thus seem reasonable, but what about the places? Villagers were willing to consider the suggestion that their ancestors who came from eastern or central China were in fact Han soldiers, who were sent to military colonies and intermarried with local women. If this is true, Lipuo and Han have been living interspersed for several hundred years, a conjecture that is also supported by a quotation from a late-eighteenth-century gazetteer of Dayao County saying that Han and Yi lived all mixed together (Dayao 1904: 60–61).[4]

---

4. One should realize, however, that these mixed Lipuo-Han communities, though they display no geographical or ecological separation between the two *minzu* at the local level (that is, in the highland townships of Pingdi, Ala, and Dalongtan), are still highland communities from the

The economy of Lipuo and Han is similarly integrated and identical in the local context. Peasants in Pingdi are basically subsistence cultivators, but they are regularly tied into the market and the cash economy. There has been a market at Datian, down the valley, since at least the early part of this century (Dayao 1904:2, 2b); there is now a market at Pingdi, and villagers go regularly on the market days.[5] Many villagers in 1988 also had cash income from a variety of sources: wage work at the Pingdi Concrete Factory or the Pingdi Winery, manufacture of lime to sell to private parties building houses, hauling with small tractors, or work at a variety of other wage-paying jobs. On the average, probably a quarter to a half of a family's income was in cash, and people had considerable amounts of bought consumer goods in their houses. Bailagu, another village in Pingdi, farms vegetables commercially, and Yibuku, a valley satellite village of Yishala, grows sugarcane as a major cash crop. In short, the Lipuo and the Han in Pingdi are equally full participants in the market economy of Renhe and Yongren.

Politically, Lipuo and Han have long been integrated here. At least since the mid-Qing this area has come under direct civil administration of the Imperial, Republican, and then People's governments (Dukou 1985: 74). There has not for a long time been any *tusi* or other equivalent "ethnic official" to serve as intermediary with the governments. In this respect, Yi and Han have been treated equally.

In the People's Republic the essentially undifferentiated treatment of Yi and Han has continued. Pingdi underwent land reform, characteristic of Han areas, in 1950–51, instead of waiting for the milder Democratic Reforms, characteristic of minority areas such as those inhabited by the Nuosu, in 1956. In Pingdi, and indeed in the Lipuo areas in Yongren in general, land reform took place in essentially the same way as in exclusively Han areas. In Yishala five families were classified as landlords and several more as rich peasants; they were struggled against and their land taken away. All of them were Lipuo. After land reform, the agricultural system underwent the same steps of collectivization, communization, devolution to the production team, and finally individual contracting of land as was carried out in most of the country.

Intermarriage between Lipuo and Han has been common here, probably ever since the communities were founded by the union of Han military colonists

---

perspective of the larger-scale local system of Renhe District or Yongren County. Lowland villages are almost exclusively Han.

5. The date of establishment of the market at Pingdi is not mentioned in the 1904 Dayao gazetteer.

FIG. 31. A Lipuo mother-in-law ushering her Han daughter-in-law
into the bridal chamber

and local women. There are very few Han in the village who are married to other
Han, and our whole research team was witness to one wedding in which a Han
woman from outside married into a previously all-Lipuo household. Intermarriage between Lipuo and Han is facilitated by the similarity of the marriage
and family systems. Marriages are usually arranged by an introducer, who must
nowadays secure the permission of the couple to be married. Once this is accomplished, negotiations begin. Lipuo and Han give similar dowries at marriage,
so negotiations for marriage exchanges proceed on a common understanding
even if the families are of different ethnic groups. Also, the Lipuo marriage ritual is conducted in the Han language and takes Han forms (fig. 31).

Intermarriage is thus extremely common, and many children are born of
"mixed" marriages. A child of a mixed marriage must be designated as belonging to one *minzu* or the other, but there is a choice. In the Pingdi area, the child
of a Han mother and a Yi father would take the Yi *minzu*; the child of a Yi
mother and a Han father may take either *minzu*. This means that most children of mixed marriages end up Yi, since most intermarriages involve a Han
woman from outside the village marrying a Lipuo villager. So the absorption
of Han people into the Lipuo community continues.

This close and almost indiscriminant interaction has, I think, led to the remarkable identity of culture, politics, and social structure that one observes between Lipuo and Han in Pingdi. We can see this lack of distinction in the sociolinguistic pattern of diglossia. Lipuo at home and with other villagers customarily speak the Lipuo language, called Libie. Libie contains a lot of Han loan words, ranging from kinship terms (Harrell 1989) to words for modern things such as tractors and sociological investigations. Nevertheless, the ordinary conversation one hears in Yishala is in Libie, not Han.

Almost all the Lipuo, however, are bilingual; their Han speech is almost uniformly fluent and indistinguishable from that of the local Han. Children at first speak only Libie but learn Han quickly when they go to school, so there are virtually no monolingual Libie speakers in the community. Children in primarily Han households may grow up speaking only Han at home, or they may learn both languages simultaneously, but when they are of an age to be getting around the community, they learn the Libie language also, so that there are not very many monolingual Han speakers either.

The Han language is used with outsiders, of course, but it also has several uses internal to the community. Wedding and funeral rituals, both of which our team observed in Yishala, are conducted entirely in the Han language and almost entirely according to Han forms. In addition, villagers use writing frequently: from popular magazines to the inscriptions on tombstones, everything is written in Han characters. When Yishala people write letters to Lipuo relatives, they do so in the only script they know: Han. Since Lipuo belongs to the Central Branch of Yi (Bradley 2001), which has historically not had its own scripts, we can be fairly certain that as long as these people have been writing, they have been writing in Chinese. I have photocopies of several documents dating as far back as the tenth year of the Shunzhi reign period (1654) of the Qing dynasty, so it is safe to say that they have been employing Chinese writing for a very long time.

In this diglossic situation, there has not for a long time been any separation of or difference between Han and Yi educational systems. The Yishala village school has taught both Lipuo and Han children in the Han language since 1906. Yishala is now a highly literate community; almost all males and some females born before 1949 went to school, and seven men from Yishala completed junior middle school before 1949. Today over 90 percent of children attend at least some school, and a sizable number go on to junior and senior middle school, and occasionally college. There is essentially no difference, then, in education between Yi and Han.

As the Lipuo community has absorbed Han people, so has it absorbed Han

FIG. 32. The son of the deceased *(right)* leaning on a staff as guests arrive
at a Lipuo funeral, as prescribed in the classics

culture, to the point where there are no obvious ethnic markers that distinguish Lipuo from local Han. Both men and women dress in ordinary Chinese
shirt-and-trousers costume. Housing in this area, consisting of mud-walled
houses built around a courtyard, is identical among the two *minzu*. In the central room off the courtyard, houses have a shrine with four red papers pasted
on the wall: one to heaven and the nation, one to the stove god, one to the family's ancestors, and one on the floor to the earth god. These are the paraphernalia of Han folk religion in its southwestern variant.

Also shared with the Han are the rituals of marriage, mentioned above, and
burial (figs. 32–33). In short, there is little visible cultural difference between
Lipuo and Han. If natives are asked about cultural differences, however, they
can come up with them. For example, we were told that while both Lipuo and
Han celebrate the traditional Chinese lunar New Year, Han refrain from eating meat on the first day of the year, while Lipuo will eat meat, though they
will not slaughter the animal on that day. Similarly, in the typical wedding ritual, the bride's relatives paint the faces of the groom's parents (fig. 34) so that
they will not seem too imposing (a ritual shared with certain other Yi groups),
and on the evening of a wedding there is "ethnic dancing." Han of course par-

FIG. 33. Carving a headstone for a grave in Yishala

ticipate in this, but it is defined as a Yi custom. There are differences, then, that people can point to when they need a marker.

Finally, Lipuo social organization is essentially identical to, and thus compatible with, that of the local Han. The four lineages that dominate Yishala show the same structure and all the trappings of Han lineage organization (Freedman 1958, 1966; R. Watson 1985) and are different from Nuosu local lineages (Hill and Diehl 2001). In pre-land reform times, the lineages were corporate groups who held some land in common, used to finance ancestor worship. Certain branches continue collective worship at the ancestral graves today, though the land is gone. And, as mentioned, at least two of the lineages keep written genealogies, which contain no hint whatsoever that the lineages consist of non-Han people. Class was also, before land reform, the main principle of social inequality in the Lipuo communities. Land was privately owned and status was based primarily on landholding. Since land was marketable, this class standing was subject to mobility.

Because these central aspects of social organization—family, lineage, and class—were identical to those in Han communities, there were and are easy relationships between Lipuo and Han. Not only could families negotiate wed-

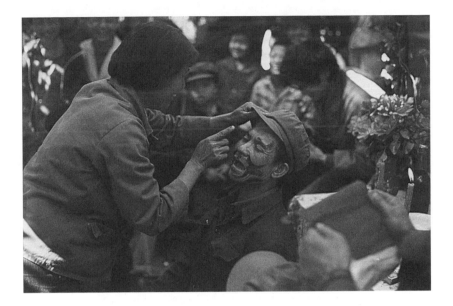

FIG. 34. The bride's relatives painting the faces of the groom's parents
at a Lipuo wedding

ding exchanges with no trouble, they could also evaluate one another's social
status in terms of the same criteria. Social organization, at least in the last century or so, does not seem to have formed a barrier to mobility or relationship
between the two groups. The question that of course presents itself is Which
came first—the integration or the similarity? In the long historical view, the
integration must have come first, unless we believe that the social organization and customs of the pre-Ming ancestors of the Lipuo were identical to those
of the Han, which seems highly unlikely. But once the process of demographic
and cultural absorption began, similarity and interconnectedness fed on each
other, leading to today's full integration.

In this situation of free relationship, cultural similarity, and social struc-
tural compatibility, the question that arises is What accounts for the continuing existence, indeed the continuing vigor, of Lipuo self-identity? What are
the barriers to assimilation and the assumption of Han identity? I think, in
fact, that there are three of these. First, there is the matter of habitus, an aspect
of ethnic identity treated by Bentley (1987). These people have thought of themselves as Lipuo for a long time, and they quite naturally, without thinking about
it, convey this identity to their children, for whom it remains part of their unex-

amined assumptions about their own place in the world. Since there are no pressures to assimilate, to take on a Han identity, and in fact no perceived advantage to doing so, the status quo remains unexamined and part of everyday experience.

Second, there is the current government policy of ethnic identification that applies to every individual. One has to be a member of some *minzu* or other if one is a citizen of China. And so people who are Yi marry other people who are Yi, and their children remain Yi. They cannot change their identity; they cannot simply become Han because they are culturally identical to, or culturally assimilated to, the Han *minzu*. In situations where there is even less "left of native culture" to serve as ethnic markers, people do not assimilate to Han identity once their minority identity has been established.

Third, there is in fact a perceived advantage in retaining Lipuo identity. Because Pingdi is a *minzu* township, it has gotten two medium-sized industrial plants (the cement factory and the winery) as well as several other government investment projects, and people can enter schools under special minority quotas, as well as legally bear two children within the state population-control program. The state has created a system in which minority status brings real advantages, which is a reason for claiming minority status. There are, however, two paradoxes in this situation. The first is that some of the benefits of minority status accrue to everybody in the minority district, not just to the members of the minority. Han people living in Pingdi are also allowed to have two children, and although they cannot use the minority quotas for school admission, they can of course share in the benefits of the factories built in the area, and of the cultural stations and other amenities the government has provided. So it is in the interest of the Han people as well that Pingdi be designated a minority township; for it to be so designated, a certain percentage of the population, no matter how Han culturally, has to be officially ethnically Yi.

The other paradox is that, in order for advantages of minority status to accrue to the Yi in this area, they need demonstrate only enough cultural difference from Han to be classified as a minority (language puts them over the top by itself) in order to receive the benefits of that status. They can become as Hanified as they please; they can equal or exceed their Han neighbors educationally or economically,[6] and once they are designated as minorities, they do not even

---

6. In fact, it looks good if they do so. The Han-controlled government likes to point out situations in which the "brother nationalities" are doing as well as or better than the Han: one frequently cited instance is the higher college admission rate among Koreans (who live mostly in the Yanbian [no relation] Korean Autonomous Prefecture) than among the Han.

need to retain the markers that got them the designation in the first place. So the nature of ethnic relations here, in which Yi absorb both Han people and Han culture, redounds to the benefit of everyone concerned, of all actors in the system: Lipuo, Han, and government. It is no wonder that, in this area, there is little of what we ordinarily think of as an ethnic problem. The stake of all actors in the system is the same. In this situation, acculturation can proceed even further than it has already, to the point where even language is lost, and ethnic identity will remain. The Lipuo in Pingdi are not that far yet, but we do have an example of such a situation: the Shuitian people.

THE SHUITIAN IN ZHUANGSHANG AND FUTIAN: ETHNICITY REGAINED

An Economic Success Story

When I first visited Panzhihua in 1987 to inquire of local authorities about the possibilities of conducting fieldwork there, I was told that there were three different kinds of Yi for me to study. There were the Liangshan Yi in various parts of Yanbian, who had preserved their ancient slave society system until 1956; there were the Yunnan Yi in Pingdi, who had long had a feudal mode of production; and there were some people in the western part of the municipality whom nobody knew too much about and who called themselves Shuitian,[7] but who ought to have more known about them.

As part of our 1988 field research, my colleagues and I went to a village called Zhuangshang in Pingjiang Township near the western extremity of Panzhihua, where we spent a week conducting household surveys and other interviews among the population, which was almost entirely Shuitian. In a 1990 publication, I had this to say about their ethnic identity:

> Although the Shuitian are officially classified as members of the Yi *minzu*, they reject this designation because they would prefer to be recognized as the Shuitian *zu*, so they are attempting to have their identity recognized as this separate *minzu*. They have been completely unsuccessful in this regard; the closest they have come is to have other people, unofficially at least, refer to them as the Shuitian Yi. Despite cultural, linguistic and social similarities to the surrounding Han population, the Shuitian people are firmly united in their assertion that they are not Han. . . .

7. There is no connection between the terms Shui (discussed earlier in this chapter) and Shuitian, though they both contain the character *shui,* or "water." The Shui are a recognized minzu, almost all of whom live in Guizhou, and whose language belongs to the Tai family.

The government has accepted [this claim], but it has used its own Stalinist criteria to classify them as Yi. The people of Zhuangshang presumably received this designation on the basis of their language (which would have been known to most of the older people alive at the time of classification in the mid-1950s), and perhaps such things as lighting torches on the twenty-fourth day of the sixth lunar month. But the Shuitian emphatically resist such classification; they use their own cultural criteria to point out that Yi, that is Nuosu, live in the mountains, eat *tuotuo rou* (big chunks of meat),[8] and wear funny costumes. The Shuitian, by contrast, live in the lowlands, eat rice, and wear ordinary clothes. They are not, in their own eyes, wild barbarians like the Nuosu. They are civilized people—how could they then be of the same minzu as the Yi? [Harrell 1990: 536–37]

By 1994, when I spent a week in the neighboring township of Futian, I heard nobody make any kind of strong claim for special status as a separate *minzu*. People still referred to themselves as Shuitian *zu* or Shuitian *ren*, but when asked readily agreed that Shuitian were a kind of Yi*zu*, and when they were either asked directly or being careful to speak correctly, readily identified their *minzu* as Yi. In addition, when I made brief visits back to Zhuangshang in both 1993 and 1994, the few people I talked to said that while some villagers don't like it, everyone now accepts, for pragmatic reasons, the designation of Shuitian as a kind of Yi. What happened in the interim?

For one thing, between 1988 and 1994 the Shuitian in both Futian and Zhuangshang did extremely well economically. I wrote of my first visit to Zhuangshang,

The southwestern corner of the township, where Jingtang, Kuqiao, Laluo, and Zhuangshang lie, is dry, undeveloped, and poorly served by transport. Zhuangshang itself is the poorest village in this corner of the township, with a *per capita* income in our survey of only around 424 *yuan*, not low enough to qualify it for state aid as an officially impoverished (*pinkun*) area, but low enough that it has no electricity, no bicycles (some families could afford them, but they couldn't get anywhere on them, so people use donkeys as their main means of carrying things), many people dress in patches, and all houses are built of unplastered mud walls. [Harrell 1993: 89]

---

8. The text in the original printed article is corrupt at this point. I have substituted a coherent, if perhaps less elegant version from an earlier draft.

According to people there, the situation in Futian was about the same in the late 1980s, with a per capita income of around ¥400 and a primarily subsistence economy. But since then, there has been rapid economic development, most dramatically in Futian, but also in Zhuangshang. In Futian the official per capita income in 1993 was ¥1,343; even with the considerable inflation that took place in China during that six-year interval, this is a startling improvement. Annual per capita income of individual production cooperatives ranged from ¥833 to ¥2,299. The three that are almost completely Shuitian Yi had average incomes of ¥1,724, ¥1,539, and ¥1,767, somewhat above the average for the township as a whole.

These income figures are also reflected in the changed standard of living in Futian in general, and in the Shuitian communities in particular. In the three production cooperatives that are all Shuitian, most people have recently built new houses with concrete floors, tile roofs, and piped-in running water from a local spring. Over half the families have televisions, and increasing numbers are purchasing washing machines and refrigerators. There are even a few households that have small trucks used for agricultural hauling. Zhuangshang has experienced similar development; from a place with no electricity and a shortage of irrigation water (caused by the water having been diverted by a local coal mine), in 1993 it boasted a per capita income of around ¥1,100 *yuan*— enough electricity for about half the families to have televisions, piped-in water in almost every household, and a new reservoir that was expected to solve their springtime irrigation problems beginning in 1995.

Futian has followed a model that would probably be familiar to those concerned with recent economic development in rural China. The township government has invested resources heavily in township and village enterprises, or *xiangcun qiye*; in 1994 they owned seventeen of these, including three coal-washing plants, a gas station, a papain plant, a coking factory, a mining company with six mines, a construction materials company, a wholesaling corporation, a construction company with four hundred workers, a gas station, some brick and tile kilns, and a driving school on the streets of Panzhihua City. The companies together had a total income of ¥21 million, of which something like ¥1 million was available from remitted taxes and another ¥200,000 from outright profits, both available for investment in education and rural infrastructure such as roads.

With the input from township investment in infrastructure, and with recently increased availability of agricultural extension programs, farmers of Futian have been able to increase their cash income greatly from three sources. Many areas have a grain surplus, which people can use to feed livestock or to sell on the open market. Scientific pig-breeding has also been introduced, and many households find this a source of increased income. In one village, because all breeding is done by artificial insemination, male pigs are castrated and sold as soon as they reach the most advantageous weight. And most dramatically, silkworm production was begun in 1991 and took off very quickly. The township government brought in an extension agent to teach silkworm-raising methods, and three households raised them that year. By 1994 about sixty families of the 109 in Tangba Village, which has the highest Shuitian population, raised silkworms, and their income according to official figures totaled ¥127,000, or slightly over ¥1,000 per household.

Development has led to increases in personal consumption, but some profits have also been plowed back into infrastructure and education, with the result that all production cooperatives (most of which are small natural villages) are now accessible by jeep roads of varying quality, and most also have running water. Local schools have improved their rates of pupil retention and graduation, and school officials are proud of the fact that Futian's children are taught every subject mentioned in the national "Outlines for Elementary Education," including natural science starting from the first grade and laboratory sciences in the upper grades.

Futian has thus become a success story, like so many other communities in rural China where there has been rapid development of cash crops and local enterprises in the past ten years. But Futian is special, because it is a minority township, or *minzu xiang*, by virtue of the fact that 1,320 of its 3,711 people, or 35.6 percent, are minorities, all but about 250 of them Shuitian Yi. This means that they are not just a run-of-the-mill success story (after all, they still lag far behind rural areas near China's coastal cities, and are not among the richest villages even in Panzhihua or Liangshan); rather, they are a demonstration that minorities can make it, living proof that even in one of the poorest parts of the country members of minority *minzu* can achieve economic development. The "Futian Model," with its agriculture- rather than migration-based development, its judicious use of local resources, and its reinvestment of profits from township and village enterprises, has begun to be advanced as a paragon for other minorities to follow in their own efforts at development (Li Xingxing 1995).

In my own opinion, Futian does not seem like much of a breakthrough for minorities. It is a lowland village near a medium-sized city, with good, relatively flat land and good soil; relatively good transport access, especially for a mountainous region; a tradition of schooling that goes back well before the establishment of the People's Republic; and a population 100 percent fluent in the Han language. Futian can certainly be a model for how to develop a com-

286

munity without destroying it, at least in the short run, but there is nothing about this model that makes it particularly suited to minorities, and it would be outrageous to think that a place like Mishi, with none of these advantages, or even one of the much better off natural economies around Lugu Lake or Baiwu, has any of the conditions necessary to emulate Futian in its pattern of economic takeoff. But probably because economic development in minority regions has been such a vexing problem for Chinese authorities generally, some people have seized on Futian, despite its special situation, as at least a real example of a minority community that has experienced development. And since Futian is, willy-nilly, a minority model, in a sense its presentation of self to the outside world must be of a minority community. As long as Futian's cadres, teachers, and ordinary people present themselves as successful minorities, they will continue to garner the outside attention that has contributed to their success. It is in this context that the current ethnic consciousness of many of Futian's Shuitian people has evolved in the last few years.

The Shuitian and Acculturation

The Shuitian, according to researches into their language, belong to the Western Branch of the Yi, one of the two who are more closely related linguistically to Lahu and Lisu than to the other Yi branches, and who are not known historically to have ever had a script for writing their language (Bradley 2001). In their own language, which is fading in Futian and gone in Zhuangshang, they call themselves Laluo (Björverud 1998). There has been little historical research into the origins of these particular Laluo, but people in Tangba Village related a legend:

> The ancestors of the three surnames—Li, Ni, and Hu—who constitute the entire population of the three hamlets that make up the ethnic core of Tangba, originally came from Yangshu Tang, Yangliu Wa, near Zhaotong in northeastern Yunnan. They originally all lived together, 360 households, in a stone-walled village [shi zhaizi]; this may have been located at the site of the current No. 1 Production Cooperative, where there are still some ruins of such a structure [I went to see these—a gate and some steps—myself]. They had a tenant, however, who got into some sort of dispute with them and burned all the wooden buildings inside the wall. With the buildings were burned any historical records that might have existed, so nobody knows how long ago this might have been. Any records they might have had would have been written in Chinese, since nobody knows of any evidence that there was ever a Shuitian writing system. When the walled

village was burnt, the surnames dispersed, and now they are found in Futian, Zhuangshang, and Taiping in what is now Panzhihua, and in many parts of Huaping County in Yunnan.[9]

According to older residents of Tangba, during the early part of the twentieth century this was a generally poor area, and *minzu* (which is the word Shuitian people often use to refer to themselves) were uniformly poor, and many of them worked as tenants for either the He or the Lu, two Han landlord families. But there were also poor Han peasants. The tenants usually lived in rudimentary houses provided by the landlords, and in addition to the rents paid to the landlords they also paid duties to the Gao *tusi*, who is remembered as having been Han himself, even though he collected duties only from the *minzu*. There were two traditional-style private schools in the township, and some of the *minzu* boys went there to study *The Three Character Classic*, *The Thousand-Character Text*, and some of the Confucian classics known as the Four Books. The only girl students, however, were Han. At that time, older people told us, people still mostly spoke the *minzu* language at home, though they were of course bilingual. Older people did not remember women ever wearing skirts, but they remember hearing their elders say that Shuitian women used to wear them, and in the early part of the twentieth century people still wove hempen cloth.

The picture one gets from talking to older people is that immediately before the founding of the People's Republic, there were still cultural and linguistic differences between Shuitian and Han. They were, however, integrated into the same economy of mixed tenants and small freeholders, as indicated by the fact that unlike Nuosu areas in Liangshan, for example, they underwent the ordinary process of the violent, class-struggle land reform, just like Han communities everywhere in China. Some of the local landlords in Futian were struggled against; in Zhuangshang, there were no landlords or rich peasants, though some people remember going to the neighboring Han Catholic village of Jingtang to participate in struggle sessions.

In the last forty or fifty years, however, any significant cultural differences that might serve as ethnic markers seem to have disappeared among the Shuitian in Zhuangshang and Futian. In Zhuangshang in 1988, there was already nobody who could speak the Shuitian language, and although it was lasting a bit longer in Futian, by 1994 even middle-aged people, though they could speak some,

9. All of this seems plausible with the exception of the number of households. The area is far too small to have held 360 families.

still felt much more at home in Chinese. All people could tell us in 1988 in Zhuangshang was that people were probably a bit darker-skinned on the average than the Han, and that they pronounced a very few words differently, such as *yinba* for "salt" in contrast to local *yanba*, as pronounced by Han in neighboring communities. In Futian in 1994, people could not name any customs that distinguished them from local Han—their marriage, funeral, and burial practices were all the same, and what ancestral altars I saw in both Futian and Zhuangshang were entirely in the local Han style.

A Resurgent Identity

Where people do make a lot of comments about ethnic differences, however, is in terms of character. For example, the Party secretary of the Shuitian-majority Tangba Village, herself a Han, along with two of her fellow cadres, both Shuitian, were eager to extol the virtues of the *minzu* to us. They are, of course, hospitable, or *hao ke*, something that is almost invariably said of minority *minzu* everywhere in China. This is a problem, of course, in one sense, since it means they "don't have a commodity-economy mind-set" (*meiyou shangpin jingji guannian*), another thing that is often said about minorities. On the other hand, their lack of economic killer-instinct makes them better able to undertake cooperative projects. A young woman who was among the leaders in the production of silk in Futian told us that if one producer does not have enough mulberry leaves at the crucial time between the last molting and the spinning of the cocoon, when it is difficult to keep up with the voracious appetites of the squirming larvae, another producer who had extra leaves she was not expecting to need would just allow her neighbor to go pick some and not charge her or expect anything in return. Han, however, would of course ask for money. Similarly, the village head told us that he borrows a room, free of charge, to raise silkworms in the township head's nearby large compound. Minorities, he told us, would never charge rent.

Speaking about character differences is only one way in which cadres and others in Futian emphasize their minority identity. They also like to stress how far they have come as a minority success story, but do not neglect to mention how far they still have to go. For example, my research companion in Futian in 1994, Yan Dezong, was telling some local cadres and farmers how much better the economic situation seemed in Futian than in his home village near Chongqing, to which he had recently returned for a family funeral. Immediately, local cadres responded that this must not be the case, since he after all comes from a Han area.

I think that all this presentation of self as minorities who have made it is probably carefully calculated to ensure that Futian retains its status both as a minority township (which can receive certain development aid from higher authorities, and whose residents can be eligible for certain perquisites) and as a model township, which receives solicitous attention from government agencies and from ethnological researchers alike. One discussion with a group of cadres of mixed ethnicity elicited the opinion that while there may be character differences between Han and *minzu* (the Han work harder when young, and the *minzu* when middle-aged, for example), really everybody is pretty much the same. But they all agreed that they worked hard to get Futian recognized in the early 1980s as a Yi township precisely so that they could get favorable treatment: everybody there, including the Han, has a flat two-child quota regardless of the sex of the children, and middle school students who are classified as minorities (though not, in contrast to the birth quota, the Han from minority areas) get an extra ten points added to their scores on the examinations for entry into vocational high schools, or *zhongzhuan*. For similar reasons, when Han marry minorities, the children always take the minority nationality.

Another way of pushing their case as a model minority community is to court visiting anthropologists. Futian was not in my original plans for field research when I went to Chengdu in October 1994; I changed my plans to accommodate it because I learned that the indefatigable Li Xingxing (who also wrote about the ethnicity of the Naze) was writing about Futian as an example of successful development in a minority area (Li Xingxing 1995) and that the township had become a long-term project of the provincial Nationalities Research Institute. When we visited the township head's house for lunch, he told me that I was not the first anthropologist to have been there; both Li Xingxing and his patron Li Shaoming (himself a member of the Tujia *minzu*) had eaten lunch at the same table. Mikhail Kriukov, an eminent Russian ethnologist who now teaches in Taiwan, had come only to the township and had not actually visited the villages.

This frank and unashamed instrumentalism goes a long way, I think, toward explaining both why the minority people of Zhuangshang and Futian try so hard to retain their minority status, in spite of their own admission of having no cultural barriers to intermarriage or to other interaction between them and their Han neighbors, and why by 1994 they had given up, for the time being at least, their earlier resentment over being identified as Yi. Most people in Futian in 1994 still did not come out with the term Yi entirely spontaneously; in the course of normal conversation they called themselves either Shuitian or, more commonly, just plain *minzu*. But when asked specifically which *minzu* they belonged to, none had any hesitation volunteering the name Yi.

It appears to me that the newfound prosperity of the Shuitian people would not be seriously threatened if they were to lose their minority status; they have come too far already. But it is still prudent not to take any chances. And fighting one minority designation just to get another that would not bring any added advantages seems chancy and therefore imprudent. When I was in Zhuang-shang in 1988, people were angry. They had experienced a decline in agricultural income because of the diversion of their water by the coal mine; they had experienced a cutoff of their electricity in response to their attempts to get the mine to give them back their water; they had unsuccessfully filed suit against the mine to try to get the water returned and the electricity turned back on. Being called Yi, getting lumped in with those barbarian Nuosu, was just another insult, and Yi status was visibly not doing them any good anyway. As a young man said to me in 1993, "When you were here before was the most difficult time." By 1993–94 things had changed for the better, and only the most diehard local loyalist would have failed to see the advantages of instrumental ethnicity.

It was thus entirely on instrumental grounds that the ethnic identity of the Laluo people of Zhuangshang and Futian was based in the mid-1990s. The process of acculturation had already gone so far that relatives did not always know the ethnicity of their own in-laws, and nobody could think of any cultural markers that distinguished one group from another. But unlike the Shui of Puwei or even the nearby Nasu and Tazhi, whose acculturation seemed to be leading them in the direction of assimilation, the Shuitian were standing firm, ideally as Shuitian but anyway as Yi. The *minzu* designation was so valuable that it brought along with it a real ethnic identity, even in the absence of ethnic conflicts or sharp local ethnic boundaries.

PART 5

DEFAULT

ETHNICITY:

THE

HAN

14 / The Majority as Minority

On the 30th of the old year, New Year's Eve of the year of the
Chicken, 1993, fifty-nine-year-old Han peasant Xu Guojun lay on his
side on the pine-needle-strewn dirt floor after dinner, head propped
on his elbow next to the fire, which burned day and night in a little
hearth next to the mud wall in the front room of his family's house.
Things are better now, he said, since the reforms, but really only
since Li Wusha became township head three years before. Yi, he
said, are better than Han at that sort of thing, since they think of
the collective welfare, while Han people think only of themselves.

For all the local ethnic communities described so far in this book, the
Han Chinese have constituted some kind of "other," whether it be a
haunting Hxiemga presence for the Nuosu of Mishi, an acculturating
force and developmental rival or partner of the Shuitian in Futian, or a neighbor and possible affine for the Lipuo of Pingdi. But Liangshan as a whole is
not a relatively pure minority enclave like Tibet or southern Xinjiang. Over
half the population of Liangshan Prefecture, and over 80 percent of Panzhihua,
are Han Chinese. To complete the puzzle of ethnic identity and ethnic dialogue in our study area, we still need to insert one more piece: identity and
ethnic relations as seen from the perspective of the local Han Chinese.[1]

Studying the Han is in some ways difficult, because there is a "thusness"
about Hanness that resists analysis or even data-gathering. Hanness is like
Whiteness in the United States; it is an unmarked characteristic that can be
delineated only in contrast to an ethnic other (Blum 1994). And much has been
made of the fact that "Han" itself is a constructed category, and a relatively

---

1. Actually, we should also examine at least two more pieces beyond the Han: the Hui Muslims
who have built a network of trading communities from Chengdu to Kunming, and the little enclaves
of Tai, Lisu, and Miao who were moved to Liangshan for historical and military reasons in the
Ming and Qing dynasties. But this book is too long already.

recent one at that (Gladney 1991: 81–87; Zhuang Wanshou 1996b: 48–51). This is true when one looks for the unifying characteristic, the cultural, historical, or genealogical unity that holds together Hakka from Jiangxi and boat people from Guangdong with Northwesterners who speak dialects with Altaic suffixes on their sentence-final verbs. It takes work, the work of conscious ethnic-group building, to come up with cultural markers (Watson 1993), historical common experience, or genealogical fictions such as the Han's being children of the Yan and Huang emperors.

However constructed the notion of an internally unified Han group may be, however, there is little doubt that when we examine local Han communities in mixed areas such as Liangshan, we find a clear sense of ethnic boundary between people who now call themselves Hāchu (the local dialect pronunciation of Hanzu), whatever they may have called themselves before the ethnic identification, and the ethnic other, whom they now mostly call *minchu* (the local version of *minzu*) in public, and sometimes more pejorative names in private. Hāchu is certainly a category constructed in opposition to *minchu*, but it is no less real in local Han farmers' lives for that. And, my earlier protestations notwithstanding (Harrell 1990), no ethnicity is purely local, but is rather a result of a global-local interface in which local people operate. Ethnic identity and ethnic relations for the Han communities around Liangshan are compounded of local, everyday relations between themselves and their *minzu* neighbors, mixed with their ideological connection to that billion-strong constructed entity known as the Han people. Examining the Han in Liangshan should thus enable us not only to complete the picture of ethnic relations in this region, but to shed further light on the processes of ethnic change examined in chapter 13, and also to offer a case study that will contribute to the understanding of the power of an idea: the idea of the Han.

FOUR KINDS OF HAN RESIDENTS

There are, roughly speaking, four kinds of Han in our study area. First, there are short-term migrants from poor areas, there to work on construction projects such the one underway while Yan Dezong and I were doing our village interviews in Futian. Unless they establish residence, however, they do not much enter into interethnic relations. Second, of the slightly more than half of the resident population of Liangshan and Panzhihua that are Han, many, of course, have migrated from other parts of China as a result of the industrialization and other development policies that the Party has followed since the 1950s. These are mostly urbanites: there are administrative and technical cadres (though administrative cadres in Liangshan tend to be Yi), managers and engineers in the great state extractive enterprises, workers in those same factories, researchers, and schoolteachers. The city (that is, the urban area, not the municipal administrative region, or *shi*) of Panzhihua is almost entirely Han, and even in urban Xichang the Han are about 95 percent of the population. These urban Han are not very involved in ethnic relations unless they are administrative cadres or in some cases teachers, and they will not be considered in detail here.

Third, aside from the urban population, large proportions of the village dwellers are Han.[2] All along the Anning River Valley, from Mianning through Xichang, Dechang, and Miyi, and in the Jinsha Valley at Huili and Huidong, the agricultural population is overwhelmingly Han. Even in smaller valleys and plains, Han farmers predominate. In the large plain around Yanyuan, for example, there are whole townships with almost no Yi population, and traveling south from the city of Panzhihua into the mountains, one has to climb out of the fertile bottomlands into the foothills before one encounters even the culturally sinicized Lipuo. In Ganluo and Jinyang, at the opposite ends of Liangshan, there are rural patchworks of Han and Nuosu that produced the important bicultural Republican-era leaders Leng Guangdian and Long Yun, respectively.

In all of these areas, Han Chinese village life has gone on for decades or centuries more or less as it has anywhere else in China, and without much apparent influence from the surrounding Nuosu and other minority peoples. People speak local dialects that are influenced by the regional standards of Chengdu and Kunming but have their own local flavors, more Yunnanese than Sichuanese in their use of the retroflex initials not found in Chengdu or Chongqing, and in their lack of palatization in words such as *ke*, meaning "to go." Some dialectologists suspect that there might be Tibeto-Burman influences in southwestern Chinese, but the almost completely monolingual speakers in these areas are unaware of any resemblances between their own languages and those of the *minchu*, as they ordinarily refer to minorities. For these Han villagers, the minority presence is similar to, or perhaps even less important than, the haunting presence of the Hxiemga for the Nuosu of Mishi. In Liangshan, of course,

2. I know of no source that cross-tabulates population by urban/rural and *minzu*. However, it is possible to estimate the size of the rural Han population in Liangshan Prefecture by taking the total Han population in the 1990 census, 1.98 million, subtracting the urban total for Xichang (about 180,000, almost all Han) and the other county towns (probably another 200,000, roughly half of them Han), and getting a total rural population of about 1.6 million Han, which is just over half of the total rural population of approximately 3.1 million (Dangdai 1992: 1, 16-17). For Panzhihua, applying a similar reasoning process yields a rural population that is about 75 to 80 percent Han (Du Weixuan et al. 1994: 74, 130-33).

Han live in a minority autonomous area, and if they know who the top local leaders are, they know that most of them are Yi and some are even Zang. They see the "Yi Bao," the "Yi bros," on the streets and in the markets but don't pay much attention to them. They are simply living in Chinese peasant communities that happen to be situated in regions of the country where there are also minority communities. Their life is not very different for it.

Fourth, there is still another sort of Han people in Liangshan and the remoter parts of Panzhihua: those whose villages are tucked away in little valleys and hillsides in semiremote corners of the mountains, sometimes separate from and sometimes combined with villages populated by other ethnic groups. In their own townships and villages, they form distinct minorities, and despite their emotional and cultural connection to the billion-plus Han Chinese in the country as a whole, on the extreme periphery they are outnumbered, and despite the political and economic dominance of Han people in the Chinese polity and economy, in their local communities they exercise no kind of dominance at all. They are likely to meet and interact with members of other ethnic groups every day; in many places they have had a tradition of intermarriage with ethnic minorities for at least the last two generations, and sometimes much further back than that. Many of them are partially or fully bilingual. It is through the study of these peripheral Han, who come into daily contact with minorities, that we can shed new light on ethnic relations as seen from the Han side, as well as on the power of the idea of Han.

THE HAN OF BAIWU

Xu Guojun, who opined that Yi were better cadres than Han, and his family, together with their relatives and neighbors in Lianhe Village, contiguous with the lower end of Baiwu Town (see chap. 8), are one such remote Han community. In 1993, when Ma Erzi and I conducted a complete census, there were 160 of them, in twenty-one households. One immediately striking fact is that they are no wealthier or better-educated than their Prmi covillagers or the Nuosu in the village attached to the other end of town. In this subsistence farming area, standards of living do not vary much from one household to another, regardless of ethnicity, unless they have some outside source of income. All of the homes of the local Han have dirt floors and mud walls, and almost all of the thatched roofs have been replaced with tile during the last decade or so. Electricity was connected to the town in 1993, and by 1998 Han and minorities alike had lightbulbs in their houses, and televisions were becoming increasingly common (Ma Erzi, personal communication).

Grain-growing is not going to make anybody rich in a cold, high place like Baiwu, and in 1994 there was not a single rural industry in the entire township. To have a chance to break out of a bare subsistence economy, people in Baiwu and other highland areas in Yanyuan must rely on commercial agriculture, and in the last few years they have started planting apple trees. The stereotype, of course, is that Han have business sense, while minorities, just emerging from a primitive or slave economy based in more generalized reciprocity, are unlikely to be able to succeed as entrepreneurs. But in fact, Han and minorities are just about equally likely to become orchard entrepreneurs or to be left behind. Twenty-one of forty-six Nuosu families in Hongxing, and ten of twenty-one Han families in Lianhe—that is, between 40 and 50 percent of each ethnic group—have invested in orchards (see table 7.2). Similarly, there are Han shopkeepers in the little private stores in Baiwu Town, but there are also Nuosu; the vaunted entrepreneurial activity of the Han Chinese seems not to have been able to dominate the "tribal" Yi in a place like Baiwu.

The situation in education, another area where minorities stereotypically lag behind Han, is less balanced than the economic scene—in the schools of Baiwu, Nuosu and Prmi on the whole do better. In 1993 we conducted a survey of the educational levels of all families in the two villages connected to Baiwu Town, as well as some of the surrounding communities. Table 14.1 shows the results. The Han of Lianhe ranked below all Nuosu categories except former slaves and villagers of Changma (an hour-and-a-half walk from the school) and below their Prmi neighbors in male education; they also ranked below the Prmi but slightly above most of the Nuosu in female education. Ma Erzi told me that when he went to school in Baiwu Town in the 1960s, the Nuosu students were poorer but more diligent than the Han. At first, the Nuosu were at a disadvantage, since classes were taught in a language they didn't understand. But by the third or fourth grade, they were trading diligence for consumption privileges. Some of the Han students at that time could afford to rent comic books, a luxury beyond the reach of their Nuosu schoolmates. So the more academically inclined of the Nuosu boys made a deal: they would do the Han boys' homework in return for the loan of comics. In fact, all twelve natives of Baiwu Township who have gone to college or technical school have been Nuosu, without a Prmi, Naxi, or Han among them.

Part of the lack of motivation for education among Han in places such as Baiwu may stem from the perceived lack of opportunities for social mobility. Getting into college is just about out of the question, coming from such poor schools as are available in these remote districts, and a high school education does not lead anywhere in a Yi autonomous prefecture where local and middle-

TABLE 14.1.

Differential Educational Attainment of Ethnic Groups in Baiwu Zhen

	Mgebbu (Yi) Yangjuan				Former Slaves (Yi) Yangjuan				Yi Clans Hongxing				Prmi and Naxi Lianhe				Han Lianhe				Yi and Zang Changma			
	Single		Married		Single		Married		Single		Married		Single		Married		Single		Married		Single		Married	
Sex	M	F	M	F	M	F	M	F	M	F	M	F	M	F	M	F	M	F	M	F	M	F	M	F
Illiterate	2	16	23	50	2	11	6	12	10	13	22	33	2	0	6	12	4	2	9	12	7	9	5	12
Self-ed old-style few years	7	9	15	4	1	0	7	3	6	3	9	0	2	1	11	4	7	3	14	3	10	0	5	0
Elem. grad	0	0	12	1	0	0	1	1	1	0	4	0	1	0	5	3	1	0	0	0	0	0	5	0
Jr. high	6	0	12	1	0	0	1	0	4	0	10	1	2	0	6	4	7	2	5	1	1	0	1	0
Sr. high	3	0	4	3	0	0	0	0	0	0	1	0	0	1	1	0	0	0	0	0	0	0	0	0
College	5	0	2	1	0	0	0	0	0	0	0	0	0	0	0	0	0	0	0	0	0	0	0	0
In school	34	13	—	—	8	2	—	—	23	5	—	—	12	8	—	—	13	7	—	—	5	0	—	—
TOTAL	57	38	68	60	11	13	15	16	44	21	46	34	19	10	29	23	32	14	28	16	23	9	16	12
In school (%)	70	34	—	—	73	15	—	—	52	24	—	—	63	80	—	—	41	50	—	—	22	0	—	—
Jr. high (+%)	60	0	26	8	0	0	7	0	19	0	24	3	28	50	23	17	37	28	18	6	6	0	6	0
Sr. high (+%)	36	0	9	7	0	0	0	0	0	0	2	0	0	50	3	0	0	0	0	0	0	0	0	0

SOURCE: Harrell and Ma 1999: 229.

level official posts go preferentially to minorities. Also, it is difficult for remote Han to go on past junior middle school even if they want to. Most of the places in the relatively good schools—the No. 1 Middle School in Yanyuan City for the Baiwu people, or equivalent schools in other counties—go either to Han from the core Han districts, where the elementary and lower-middle-school education is much better, or to minorities, who are given affirmative action points on the entrance exams. In Yanyuan, as in many counties, the minority middle school, where only a few Han students are typically allowed to study, has the reputation of being the second-best school in the county. This pattern is repeated at the prefectural level, where again the minority middle school is regarded as a relatively good school (Schoenhals 2001, n.d.). Remote Han are thus in a position similar to that of poor Whites in the United States in the era of affirmative action, whose perception is often that the few places not claimed by the middle and upper class go to disadvantaged minorities.

In both economic and educational terms, then, life for the remote Han is not much better or worse than it is for their minority neighbors, and this is in great contrast to the Han in Han areas. Shuanghe Township, about a thirty-minute drive from Yanyuan City on the Han-dominated Yanyuan Plain, can serve as a contrasting example. There every village has a five- or six-year school, and the town elementary school graduates about sixty students per year, over 80 percent of whom go on to middle school in the township. Televisions and other minor appliances are commonplace in new houses that are increasingly built of brick, and there are even a few local industries (such as a not-too-distant cement plant) to offer a potential way out of the poverty of subsistence farming. And even these areas are on the Yanyuan high plain, a poor region in general, impoverished and fully agricultural in comparison to the Han townships in the Anning Valley and even to ethnically mixed areas such as Futian and Manshuiwan.

OUTNUMBERING, HYBRIDIZATION, AND THE IMPORTANCE OF BEING HAN

In addition to relative poverty and lack of economic or educational opportunity, there is an even more important contrast between Han in Han areas and Han as minorities in minority areas. The Han-area Han can live their lives in almost total ignorance of minority society and culture—it is almost unheard of, for example, for Han people from the areas in and around Yanyuan City to know anything at all of the Nuosu language. It was not at all atypical when, speaking my rudimentary *Nuosu ddoma* with a couple of friends on the street in Yanyuan City, I was approached by an elderly Han lady who said to me, "You know *their language*!? I have lived here all my life and never managed to learn a word of it." By contrast, Nuosu in core areas who know a little Han are usually proud of the fact, even if they are disdainful of the culture that sustains that tongue. In Puwei, even the Tazhi and Nasu are forgetting their Tibeto-Burman tongues, and there are Han-dominated mixed areas where minority languages are fast disappearing if they are not already gone, as in the Shuitian community of Zhuangshang (see chap. 13). But for the remote Han, life is lived in the context of minority language, culture, and society, and it is impossible for them to avoid contact with and knowledge of minority culture.

Our friend Mr. Xu of Baiwu may serve as an example. His wife is a Prmi, so all of his seven children are minorities, taking advantage of the minor but significant affirmative action benefits available to them and their descendants in schooling and birth quotas. Because of the ethnic intermarriage, Xu's house has a hybrid floor plan. Entering their front room, one finds two altars. At the rear of the room is the Han-style altar, surrounded by red papers marking this as a place to worship heaven, earth, and the nation in the middle, the stove god on the stage left, the ancestors on the stage right, and the earth god underneath. Along the right side of the room as one enters, there is the whitewashed earth altar of the Prmi, topped at the New Year season by pine and other branches, and dedicated to the worship of the household deity Zambala.

When Xu's son was married to a local woman who was Naxi (who in Baiwu are almost completely acculturated to local Prmi ways, which in turn have absorbed considerable Han influence), the wedding ceremony was as hybrid as the house it was conducted in. There were pine needles scattered on the floor, and plenty of Tibetan-style foods such as butter tea and barley beer, though in Baiwu the Nuosu also like to drink butter tea. Other than that, however, Han customs prevailed, since the groom's father is a Han: the bride and groom made obeisances to heaven, earth, and ancestors, and at the ensuing meal young women dressed up in brightly colored sweaters or blazers lurked with aluminum scoops of rice, ready to fill the half-empty bowls of the unsuspecting diners, who were then semiobligated to try to finish eating them. In the evening the bride and groom served drinks to the guests, receiving in return money that would become part of the bride's personal fund (fig. 35). So actually this wedding joined a Prmi (or Zang, anyway) boy with a Han father to a Naxi girl with a Prmi mother, using mainly Han rites, with a few Prmi touches thrown in. A large number of guests were Nuosu.

All over the remote regions of Lesser Liangshan, this kind of cultural

FIG. 35. The bridal couple exchanging drinks for money
at an interethnic wedding in Baiwu

hybridization occurs through intermarriage. And the Han are the most intermarrying of groups in these situations. I have visited a large number of villages and townships where remote Han live intermixed with other ethnic groups,
and never do the Han express any cultural or normative barriers against marrying anyone of any other *minzu*. Particularly since the establishment of the
People's Republic, such intermarriage has become common, and smaller ethnic groups with fewer available brides are particularly likely to marry Han. For
example, a hamlet in Liziping Township in Muli County, deep in the mountains, has twenty-two households—eighteen Miao and four Han. Local people
estimated that about a third of the marriages in recent years had been between
Miao and Han. One of the homes I visited, which had a Han daughter-in-law,
continued to follow Miao customs of ancestral worship, though the daughter-
in-law, married only six months before, had not yet learned much of the Miao
language. Similarly, in the Yala community at Malong in Miyi County (see chap.
13), there was little intermarriage with Han before the founding of the People's
Republic, but since then twenty-one of thirty-nine marriages have been with
Han. Although the architecture and lifestyle of the Yala now conform in most

respects to the local Han norm, they still preserve certain distinctive ritual and calendrical customs (along with their Tibeto-Burman language) that serve to distinguish them unequivocally as a minority group, despite the large number of Han brides marrying into the community.

Han peasants like Mr. Xu, whom we met in chapter 7, can usually speak Nuosu, though they do so only when facing monolingual Nuosu speakers. Here, I think, Mr. Xu exemplifies a Han attitude that persists even in the most remote periphery and which serves to remind us that ethnicity is not exclusively a relation of difference but is also a relation of inclusion. For these remote Han, however poor and disadvantaged they may feel, still think of themselves as superior to minorities in at least some respects. Mr. Xu is not the only Han in Baiwu who speaks Nuosu, and I have met Han who are so fluent in that language as to almost pass for natives. But even in these remote regions, the linguistic structure is set up in such a way that the Han language penetrates almost everywhere, and it is much more likely that minority people will find Han language useful than the other way around. After all, higher education and most governmental functions are carried out either exclusively in Han or in Han plus some other language; rarely is a minority tongue without translation used. Therefore, even remote, bi- or tri-lingual Han can be proud that their own language is the most important one and often look with disdain upon other languages.

One example of this sort of disdain comes in school situations. In most of the non-Han regions of Liangshan, particularly in the Western areas, which are not as exclusively Nuosu as the core area, schools teach primarily in Han, but also require Nuosu language classes of all students, regardless of their ethnicity. Teachers report that when Han students end up in these classes, it is often difficult to motivate them to study hard. One Nuosu-language teacher in Guabie, where the Nuosu are a majority of the township population, but there are enclaves of Naze and Han who do not ordinarily use the Nuosu language, told me that Han students who did not learn Nuosu at home were particularly difficult to teach. They could not pronounce Nuosu words at all well (indeed, in one of his classes that I observed, he gave several pronunciation tips for the *Hāchu tongxio*, or "Han classmates"), and since grades in Nuosu classes no longer count on the middle school entrance exams, Han students simply didn't care, and goofed off annoyingly in class.

Other Han, who might be expected to know minority languages, somehow get by without them. For example, Mr. Zhang, an old man from Muli, was originally from a Han family who were tenants of a *nuoho* landowner. One year his family owed the landlord three silver ingots but could produce only two, so the landlord captured him and he worked for nine years in the lord's house

FIG. 36. A Han family in Baiwu sweeping the tombs and presenting
offerings a few days after the New Year holiday

as a slave. But now, forty years later, living in Baiwu, a community with a majority Nuosu population, he remembers only a few words of the language.

Pride in one's language, of course, connects even remote Han to a national
culture and to an idea of a Han *minzu*, as well as to the possibility of wider
outside connections than are possible for most minorities. For example, it is
quite common when conducting censuses of Han families to find daughters
who have married men from distant cities or even other provinces and have
gone to live with their husbands' families there. One daughter of the Duan family in Baiwu, who was visiting at the New Year in 1993, had such an urban aspect
about her dress and deportment that I was not surprised to learn that she had
married a man from Nanchong and had lived for awhile in Chengdu before
moving back to his rural home. I have met people whose children have married as far away as Hebei and Shandong.

There is, then, among most remote Han people, a kind of cultural or ethnic pride, expressed in China-wide connections and in condescension toward
minority languages, which for some is about the only advantage or superiority they can claim over their numerically and politically dominant, and sometimes wealthier, "minority" neighbors. Once, when I went tomb-sweeping with

some Baiwu Han families (fig. 36), a teenage girl got irritated at her little brother, who was doing one of those irritating things that little brothers do, and called him a Luoluo, a pejorative term for a Nuosu (my colleague Ma Erzi, who had come along, gently pointed out that *he* was a Luoluo, but the point was lost, for the time being anyway, on the exasperated teenager). The little boy's reply unconsciously reflected the predicament of the remote Han: I don't remember exactly what he said, but it began with the exclamation *abbe*, which is what people say in the local Han dialect when they are startled or frustrated, as a boy would be when called a dirty name by his sister. *Abbe*, of course, is borrowed directly from the Nuosu language.

REMOTE HAN AND THE PROCESSES OF ETHNIC CHANGE

There seems to be no doubt that, over the *longue durée* of Chinese history, the trend has been for the central culture, represented in the governmental and scholarly institutions of the Confucian elite, to acculturate those on the periphery and eventually to assimilate them to the point that they identify with the local Chinese, the people who in recent centuries have come to call themselves Han. As we saw in chapter 13, this process, known conventionally as "sinicization" (Shepherd 1993: chap. 11), can take a variety of forms, as seen from the perspective of the "non-Chinese" or "minorities" who are undergoing the process. But of course the process is two-sided: it is not just a local minority undergoing a change that is instigated and controlled by a government or even an ideology (the idea of the Han); at the same time it is a process of interaction between the local minority people and the local Han. To understand the process fully, we must reexamine it from the Han perspective.

It seems quite probable that in the past, the kinds of close everyday interaction and intermarriage that went on between Han (or its pre-essentialist equivalent) and minorities usually resulted in what Melissa Brown (1996) has described as the "long-route" process toward sinicization. As more and more Han (usually men) moved into a community, there would be a gradual acculturation to Han ways, and when the acculturation had been complete for a few generations, people would no longer stigmatize the locals as *fanzi* or *manzi* (foreigners or barbarians), and they would be Chinese peasants, pure and simple. Several variations of this process (most of them incomplete) have been described in chapter 13. But the reverse process is also possible, and it is also documented that in the short run and in more remote areas at least, acculturation often went the other way. Particularly in Nuosu communities, where Han peasants were sometimes captured and made into slaves, they lost their Han culture and identity within two generations. The two hamlets in Mishi that together were once known as Jiefang Cun, or Liberation Village (see chap. 6), are good examples of this. Nowadays, when villagers tell their stories, they mention having been slaves but never mention having ancestors from the Hxiemga. And back in Baiwu at least one former slave family, completely Nuosu in culture and identification, still remembered that they had a grandmother who had been a Han.

In recent decades, with affirmative action an important component of minority policy, there seems to have arisen a third kind of process, where sinicization proceeds apace on the cultural front, as people trade their original language, economy, and customs for those of the generic "Chinese peasant," known locally as Han customs and culture (Unger 1997), but never even consider the possibility of changing their identity to become Han in identification as well as in culture. In this process, which was described for the Shuitian in chapter 13, Han people who enter minority communities do not become either agents of sinicization or objects of the inverse process, since the *minzu* identities are fixed by the ethnic identification process. Rather, the local Han are minor agents of cultural sinicization (the major agents are the schools and the propaganda system in general), while at the same time they become the parents and ancestors of people whose identity will be other than Han. In the past, this was a transitional stage in a process that eventually led toward cultural acceptance as Han, but now, because the descendants of mixed marriages almost always choose the non-Han identity, it is possible to become more and more Chinese culturally while still remaining firmly members of an ethnic minority category in an ethnically mixed community. Paradoxically, when these communities evolve, the role of the Han in them is not necessarily a predominant or leading one. In places such as Baiwu or Liziping or even Manshuiwan, the Yi or Miao or Prmi join the cultural community of Chinese through their direct contact with state institutions, particularly the schools and increasingly the market economy. If, as happened in Baiwu for example, a young Naxi becomes a traveling merchant and goes all over the Southwest selling stuff, he becomes competent in the ways of China's new market culture, fluent in standard Chinese and not just the local Han dialect, and able to operate as an urban migrant in a Chinese city without reference to his ethnicity. But he retains that ethnic identity nevertheless. And the culture to which he has assimilated is not that of the local, backward, poor, and peripheral Hāchu in his village but rather that of urbanizing, modernizing China.

In light of this experience, we need to reexamine our notions of China as a Han-dominated society. The status of being an official member of the Han minority confers no privilege or ability to dominate in its own right. As the Shuitian and Tai peasants of Futian are economically better off than people around Chongqing, where Yan Dezong came from (see chap. 13), so the Nuosu dominate the political, cultural, and educational landscape of Baiwu, and to a lesser extent of Yanyuan County as a whole. The route to mobility is not facilitated by Han status; in fact, in the era of affirmative action, Han identity can be a handicap.

Does this mean that minorities are equal in Chinese society? Of course not. Insofar as they are recognized as minorities, they are constantly stigmatized as backward, dirty, lazy, and a host of other negative stereotypes. And insofar as they do not necessarily grow up familiar with or sympathetic to Han culture, they have little chance to succeed in business, education, or politics. The poverty and isolation of a place like Mishi is testimony to this kind of disadvantage. But when members of minority *minzu* can get a college education (which is much more difficult for the Nuosu of Baiwu than it would be for an ordinary worker's daughter in Shanghai, but it does happen), when they can make money selling things, when they become indistinguishable in their behavior from the Chinese norm, then they have equal respect and opportunity. What is dominant, then, or perhaps better said, hegemonic, is a cultural and behavioral norm, not the Han as a group; in fact it is clear that such an internally diverse category as Han is not a group at all. China is best seen as dominated not by an ethnic group, but by a social elite of cadres, intellectuals, and, increasingly, businesspeople, who espouse a particular model of culture—socialist, modern, educated, Chinese—whose content is that of the standardized national culture called, in a shorthand way, Han culture, or *Hanzu wenhua*.

In a place like Baiwu, the local Han have only marginally better access to this cultural model than do the Nuosu or Prmi, and the opportunity structure created by affirmative action has probably equalized the local playing field, as it certainly has in Manshuiwan, another place where the Nuosu are wealthier and more successful than the Han. The place is bilingual and bicultural, after all. A place like Mishi is entirely different—only one person from there has ever made any money, and only one has ever been to college.

IMPLICATIONS

The remote Han thus tell us about a series of issues. They tell us, and they sometimes complain a bit about it, that affirmative action works. Though there is still overwhelming Han dominance in education and entrepreneurship at the prefectural and even county levels, those from certain ethnically mixed local communities such as Manshuiwan and Baiwu who have been successful have almost all been minorities. And the pattern repeats itself politically at the higher levels of county and prefecture. There are many Han cadres at these levels, particularly in the technical and financial areas that require better specialized education than is available in many minority communities. But almost all of the Han cadres are from outside; natives who make it to high places in government are almost invariably minorities.

In addition, the remote Han shed light on the process of sinicization, which has been going on, a few steps forward and a few back, for at least two thousand years in this area. The most important lesson is that this process is not a one-way thing. Depending on the demographic, military, and political conditions in a specific locality at a particular time, minorities may become Han, Han may become the parents of minorities, and these days, minorities may acculturate to Han ways at the same time that the children of Han are developing strong and unequivocal minority identities.

Finally, the remote Han also tell us that even though they are at a marked political and educational disadvantage with respect to their minority neighbors (and no particular economic advantage one way or the other), they also retain a kind of cultural pride in their Han heritage, expressed sometimes through negative stereotypes and ethnic slurs but more often through pride in their own language, disdain for the languages of others, and the memory and possibility of long-distance connections with Han in other parts of the country. This is the power of an idea, which is perhaps more appropriately called "Chinese culturalism" (Townsend 1992, Levenson 1968). The premodern empires up to and including the Qing were founded on an idea of universal cultural superiority, in which dynasties of varied ethnic origin—even the "alien" or "non-Chinese" rulers in the case of the Yuan, Qing, and other "conquest dynasties"—sometimes managed to control the means of cultural reproduction through the performance of acts that came under the direction of the Board of Rites, including, most importantly, the examination rites that guarded the gates to official privilege, wealth, and status. All of this is supposedly changed with the equality of *minzu* and the criticism of "Han chauvinism" in the People's Republic. But in fact it is still the universal cultural norm, now justified in terms of its supposed modernity and advanced economy, that is important in setting the standard for the country. The remote Han both gain and suffer from this modern version of culturalism. They gain in that they can feel culturally superior to their neighbors, and feel part of a group that extends all the way to Hebei and Gansu. They lose in that the cultural standard is only a little bit more accessible to them in their mountain hollows than it is to the ethnic Other next door.

In conclusion, I want to come back to Mr. Xu, and his comment that Yi think of collective good, while Han think only of their own families. The poorest family I interviewed the whole time I was in Baiwu was a Han family, and when we went to their house, we found an old lady home alone in a ramshackle, unkempt courtyard. It was right after the New Year, but there were no red couplets on her doorway, and she explained that they were too poor to celebrate. Her eldest son had never married, and her second daughter-in-law was dead, leaving her and her second son to raise five grandchildren, two of whom had quit school out of poverty that year at ages twelve and thirteen, and two others of whom never went beyond the second grade. Her third son, a truck driver, had lost his truck to a raging river, and then drowned trying to save the vehicle. There was no Lei Feng campaign in his memory. My Nuosu colleague was quick to point out that this would never happen among the Nuosu. Someone, a clan-mate perhaps, would give a poor family *something*—a couple of chickens maybe—so they could celebrate the New Year.

CONCLUSION

Comparing Ways of Being Ethnic

Thus do the peoples of Liangshan live their lives as ethnics: as members of local communities, almost all of whom come into regular or occasional contact with members of different communities and with the representatives of the Chinese state; and also as members of state-designated categories, or *minzu*, who come into contact with members of other *minzu* and with the state that so designates them. In some senses, then, the people of Liangshan are participants in a common system of ethnic and *minzu* relations. But this is not a simple system in the conventional sense, in which individual components relate to each other in terms of a series of rules or expectations. The *minzu* system, imposed by the Communist Party in the 1950s, was an attempt to create such a uniform system, using a series of uniform criteria (common territory, language, economy, and culture) to define a list of fifty-some equivalent categories whom the state and Party apparatus could treat in equivalent ways. But as chapters 5 through 14 illustrate, this *minzu* system was superimposed upon a complex local reality in which members of local and regional communities related to each other in a variety of ways according to a variety of identities based on different combinations of the four factors specified in the *minzu* definition and other factors that are not there, such as religion, class, and political control or allegiance. Rather than simplifying the reality of ethnic relations, the imposition of the *minzu* system further complicated it in the sense that the preexisting categories did not cease to exist upon the classification of everyone into *minzu* categories, but rather added another level of complexity that consists of the relationship of the local groups and their preexisting identities to the larger identities of the *minzu* system. Thus if there were many ways of being ethnic in Liangshan in 1850 or 1950, there are even more ways of being ethnic now. Having described, in chapters 5 through 14, a fairly representative sample of these ways (there are many others, of course), four tasks remain for the conclusion to this study: a systematic comparison of the ways of being ethnic in the communities described, an attempt to explain the diversity of ways of being ethnic, a reflection on what this local material means for the study of ethnic relations at the turn of the twenty-first century, and a reflection on what this might mean for the future of China as a nation.

CHARTING THE WAYS OF BEING ETHNIC

If we return to our conceptualization of an ethnic group's identity as composed of both in-group solidarity and out-group boundaries—both of them built on the triple bases of culture, kinship, and history—we can formulate a chart of the differential importance of these different bases of identity in the communities described in this book. Table 15.1 attempts to indicate the importance of each basis for each group.

This table divides the bases of ethnic identity into mechanisms of internal solidarity and of external relations, both those that maintain and those that blur intergroup boundaries. In each section, cultural, kinship, and historical bases of solidarity and bounding are explored. Cultural bases of solidarity are divided into the "habitual" (in Bourdieu's sense [1990: 52–65]), which are so ingrained as to be second nature to those who practice them, and the "invented" (Hobsbawm and Ranger 1983), which are conscious attempts to create and maintain a sense of a common culture. Cultural mechanisms of boundary maintenance are divided into "incomprehension" of the culture of the ethnic other and schismogenesis (Bateson 1958: 171–97), the conscious building of cultural traits that are different from those of the other. The one cultural mechanism of boundary blurring is acculturation, which of course can go in either direction across the boundary, but is usually adoption by non-Han peoples of Han ways.

Kinship mechanisms of solidarity consist of genealogical consciousness and group-endogamy, which together make the members of a group related by descent and affinity. Kinship mechanisms of boundary maintenance include the reinforcement of genealogical separateness that is a characteristic of caste systems (Mandelbaum 1970: chap. 8), as well as prohibitions on exogamous marriages. Boundary blurring through kinship occurs as intermarriage between members of the group and members of other groups.

History builds solidarity through creating narratives of a common past, and also tells members of an ethnic group how to think of the ethnic other—as a historic enemy or as a historic ally.

Table 15.1 indicates the strength or weakness of these mechanisms of ethnicity for each of the communities discussed in chapters 5 through 14. These include the local Nuosu communities of Mishi, Baiwu, and Manshuiwan, along with the Nuosu and other Yi elites who participate in the creation of a larger

Yi identity. All the Prmi communities described in chapter 10 are treated together, though further research in other areas might well turn up differences. Three columns treat the Naze: the eastern, patrilineal groups; the western, matrilineal groups around Lugu Lake as I saw them in my own research; and the representation of the Lugu Lake people in ethnographic, fictional, and tourist discourses. Four of the Yi groups experiencing acculturation, as described in chapter 13, occupy the next columns, followed by the Han of Han areas and the Han of minority areas described in chapter 14. Finally, the last column characterizes the official model of *minzu* relations, which, although it exists nowhere in its ideal form, influences the reality of ethnic relations in every local and regional community.

KINDS OF ETHNICITY

The first things that are apparent, at a gross level, in table 15.1 are the differences between the four types of ethnicity portrayed by the Nuosu, by the Prmi and Naze (with the exception of the Naze as portrayed), by the other Yi described in chapter 13, and by the Han. An obvious and important pattern is that the groups described in chapter 13, as might be expected, show more mechanisms of boundary crossing—cultural and kin-based—than do either the Nuosu (with the exception of Manshuiwan) or the Prmi and Naze. In other words, these groups are becoming part of a Chinese nation both syntagmatically and paradigmatically—they are becoming *more like* other Chinese, and they are also becoming *more integrated* with them. They are undergoing the process sometimes known as sinicization. But the process is not yet anywhere near complete, because they all still show some mechanisms of in-group solidarity, including historical and genealogical consciousness in all the groups, and very strong knowledge of history among the Shuitian. It is likely, as mentioned above, that assigning a *minzu* identity to these groups promoted their historical and perhaps their genealogical consciousness, and thus prolonged the existence of in-group solidarity, even as the projects of state- and nation-building promoted mechanisms of boundary crossing and discouraged mechanisms of boundary maintenance.

The Prmi and Naze (with the exception of the portrayed Naze) do not differ greatly from the smaller Yi groups in the degree to which they maintain or blur and cross boundaries. Where they differ, for the most part, is in the greater strength of their in-group solidarity mechanisms. There are still a lot of habitual cultural traits, particularly language, maintained in these communities, where all the chapter 13 groups except the Yala have basically converted to

TABLE 15.1

Ways of Being Ethnic in Liangshan

	Nuosu				Prmi	
	Mishi	Baiwu	Man-shuiwan	Yi leaders		Patri-lineal
In-group solidarity						
Cultural commonality						
Habitual	++	+	w	w	+	+
Invented	+	+	+	++	+	+
Kin relatedness						
Genealogical	++	++	++	+	+	+
Endogamous	++	++	+	+	w	o
Historical continuity	+	+	++	++	+	+
Out-group boundary maintenance						
Cultural distinctiveness						
Incomprehension	++	o	o	o	o	o
Schismogenesis	+	++	o	+	+	+
Kin unrelatedness						
Caste barriers	++	++	o	+	o	+
Exogamy prohibition	++	++	w	+	o	o
History of conflict	++	+ +	+	w	+	w
Out-group boundary blurring						
Culture—Acculturation	w	+	++	+	o	+
Kinship—Intermarriage	o	o	+	+	o	+
History of cooperation	o	+	++	++	?	+

Legend

+ Clearly present
++ Extremely strong, important in maintaining group identity
w Weak; not important in creating and maintaining group identity
o Absent
? Insufficient data; probably not important

Naze		Other Yi				Han		Minzu model
Matri-lineal	Por-trayed	Yala	Tazhi-Nasu	Lipuo Yishala	Shuitian	Han areas	Minority areas	
++	++	+	w	+	w	++	+	++
++	o	w	w	w	w	+	+	o
+	+	+	+	+	+	+	+	+
+	+	o	o	o	w	+	o	o
+	+	+	+	+	++	+	++	++
o	+	o	o	o	o	++	o	+
++	+	+	o	o	w	o	o	o
?	o	o	w	o	o	o	o	o
o	+	o	o	o	o	o	o	o
++	+	+	+	+	+	+	+	+
w	o	+	++	+	++	w	+	++
w	w	+	+	+	+	w	+	++
?	o	?	?	+	w	w	+	+

Chinese in their everyday speech. In addition, Prmi and patrilineal Naze cadres and intellectuals, at least, have invented a whole series of connections to their respective *minzu*—Tibetan and Mongolian—which are strong sources of in-group solidarity. By contrast, the Yala, Tazhi/Nasu, and Shuitian all have problems with their *minzu* status as Yi and thus do not take advantage of this potential mechanism of solidarity.

There is an immediate difference within this larger group, however, between the patrilineal Naze and the Prmi on the one hand, and the matrilineal Naze on the other. The matrilineal Naze have, in addition to their own language, their social system, a strong cultural basis for in-group solidarity. It seems to me that the nature of this cultural solidarity lies somewhere between the habitual and the invented: it is certainly habitual in the sense that it is ingrained and, in the core areas around Lugu Lake, anyway, relatively unquestioned. But this is not because of any ignorance of the alternatives—*because* the Naze have been portrayed in so many ways by outsiders, and because they are aware of these portrayals, and the portrayals have moved their social system at least part way from the realm of the habitual to the realm of the invented, or at least consciously promoted.

The Naze in the ethnological, feminist, and touristic portrayals are something else altogether. All the portrayals depend on Naze ethnicity being a much more culturally based and habitual thing than it actually is. For any of the portraits to be effective, they must show the Mosuo as innocently living apart from the surrounding society and from the programs of the Chinese state—at most, Mosuo can be victims of Han ethnocentrism or communist repression, but they cannot be shown as understanding why the repression is taking place or what to do about it. They must thus show habitual, not invented, cultural practices, incomprehension of the Han, complete kinship separation from all of their neighbors, and a history of little contact with the outside— and that, of course, conflictual.

If the portrayals of the Naze in various outside media are fantasies with little basis in the reality of this small group that has always had to live in close proximity with a variety of neighbors, the picture painted of them is not unlike the reality of some of the Nuosu, particularly in remote, purely Nuosu areas such as Mishi. There, almost all the mechanisms of in-group solidarity and boundary maintenance are operative, and there are few modes of boundary crossing. Cultural differences are primarily habitual, and understanding of Han ways is minimal. There is, of course, in the era of ethnic revival, some conscious reinvention of Nuosu traditions in schismogenetic opposition to those of the Hxiemga, but these are not important in the lives of most people there.

And all the workings of the kinship system serve to strengthen internal ties and weaken external ones. Particularly important here are genealogy and caste, which work hand in hand. Caste membership is, of course, a function of the relative ranking of clans, and clan membership is the most basic of identities for any Nuosu, along with gender. Everyone is immediately classified at birth, and no classification, except a slave one that someone would want to hide, permits any overlap between Nuosu and Han.

In Baiwu, caste membership and endogamy are still important forces, uniting Nuosu and excluding outsiders (in this case, Prmi and Naze as well as Han). But there they work in a context where cultural barriers are not as strong altogether, and what cultural barriers do exist are much more conscious and to an extent invented for the purposes of schismogenesis—Nuosu women in Baiwu, for example, wear skirts almost all the time; in Mishi they usually wear pants. The weaker nature of cultural barriers in a mixed area such as Baiwu means that some acculturation has in fact gone on, as indicated in the bottom rows of table 15.1.

Manshuiwan, paradoxically, looks in many ways much more like most Prmi, Naze, and even other Yi communities than it does like the Nuosu communities of Mishi and Baiwu. Cultural differentiation is almost absent, with the exception of language and the continuing use of religious ceremonies, and in contrast to Baiwu there is little or no attempt to re-create or reinvent Nuosu cultural tradition there. In fact, Manshuiwan people often comment on how different they are from the Nuosu up in the mountains. Kinship solidarity is somewhat stronger, with an important genealogical consciousness, but exogamy is weak, and many more people marry Han than marry mountain Nuosu. And importantly, the oral histories of Manshuiwan mix tales of conflict against Han with tales of cooperation and Nuosu participation in such cosmopolitan institutions as the imperial examination system.

The Yi cadres and intellectuals described in chapter 9 have a view of ethnicity that does not coincide exactly with those of any of the three Nuosu communities or four other Yi communities profiled in table 15.1. This is because they are at least partly constrained by the *minzu* model, both having to make their arguments in terms of the Yi category rather than some more local identity and seeing the size of the Yi category as an opportunity to build a larger ethnic coalition. But there are other ways in which their identity departs from the *minzu* model. For one thing, they cannot entirely shake endogamy, given their own constituency in a caste- and clan-conscious ethnic group. For the same reason, they cannot be rid of caste altogether, though it was officially abolished forty years earlier. And they must consciously invent all sorts of "ethnic culture," from beauty contests to lacquered chopsticks, while the official model pretends that these things are part of an ancient tradition. Finally, while most of these ethnic leaders accept the idea of social evolution, they do not agree with the companion idea that to advance is to become more like Han. They thus combine aspects of the official *minzu* model with long-present Yi pride in their genealogy and culture, and distrust of almost all things Han.

Finally, we come to the Han themselves. As the acculturators in most cultural interactions, both the Han of Han areas and the Han of minority areas display almost no mechanisms of boundary maintenance. Even though the Han-area Han approach minority cultures with almost total and usually deliberate incomprehension, they do not feel that their own, "superior" culture belongs entirely to them. Both kinds of Han, but those from minority areas in particular, employ mechanisms of boundary crossing through intermarriage, historical inclusiveness ("We all are children of the Yellow Emperor"), and acculturation of minorities to the Han's own ways. And whereas most Han people have a strong genealogical consciousness (back to the Yellow Emperor again), Han genealogy has long allowed intermarriage and adoption as ways of gaining membership in kin groups. In short, Han ethnicity is like the most primordial and habitual Nuosu ethnicity of places like Mishi in that it rests on cultural pride and incomprehension of the other, but it differs radically from Nuosu ethnicity in that it is ultimately inclusive on the cultural, kinship, and historical levels. It is quite difficult to become Nuosu; it is easy to become Han.

EXPLAINING WAYS OF BEING ETHNIC

If we group these ways of being ethnic into four broad types—the primordial, exclusive, cultural ethnicity of the Nuosu (chaps. 5–9); the historical, contingent ethnicity of the Prmi and Naze (chaps. 10–12); the residual, instrumental ethnicity of the smaller groups (chap. 13); and the primordial, inclusive ethnicity of the Han (chap. 14), we immediately wonder why, when all these groups are interacting locally and regionally with each other, the bases of their various ethnic identities are so different. Why does Nuosu language hold up in an enclave of three hundred people, while Prmi and Naze often die out in enclaves of similar or even somewhat larger size? Why are Prmi perfectly pleased with being either Zang or Pumi, while Yala and Shuitian are quite reluctant to be Yi? Why is the culturally and historically based ethnicity of the Han an inclusive one, while the culturally and genealogically based ethnicity of the Nuosu is so exclusive? To use a familiar extended metaphor, if all these groups are playing in the same social arena, why are they playing by such different rules? How can soccer and rugby exist on the same playing field at the same time?

These questions are of more than just theoretical interest. The kinds of ethnic identity displayed, for example, by the smaller groups feed right into the current version of the "literizing project" or "civilizing project" of the Chinese state. They retain a separate identity, but it is not an oppositional one. Clearly, if they had not been identified as members of minorities in the 1950s, they would be well on their way to complete assimilation by now, and some of them would be almost there. Their identity as separate ethnic groups is in a sense a creation of the Chinese state; it poses no threat to the state's projects. The Prmi and Naze are slightly more problematical, since there is a definite cultural basis to their ethnicity, and since many of them identify with the Mongolian or Tibetan minorities, whose larger manifestations in Mongolia and Tibet do create potential problems for state control. But their identities tend strongly toward multivalence—Prmi before the ethnic identification process were Tibetan religiously, often Chinese politically, and just plain Prmi culturally. Many Naze were also Tibetan religiously, Mongolian nostalgically, and locally very distinct culturally. Theirs is another identity that is unlikely to be oppositional, though the potential is there as long as the linguistic and cultural differences persist as potential ethnic markers. Nuosu identity, on the other hand, is strongly oppositional—for many Nuosu, including not a few leaders and intellectuals, the world is composed of two important categories of people—Nuosu and Hxiemga—and the former are genealogically and morally superior to the latter, making the Hxiemga the usurpers of the Chinese nation. For now, Nuosu oppositionalism is not to China but to the Han, and this distinguishes it from much of the true ethnic nationalism in Tibet, Xinjiang, and to a lesser extent Inner Mongolia. But it is still oppositional, and thus remains a potential flashpoint for ethnic conflict. If we can explain the conditions under which these different types of ethnic identity developed, we might be better able to predict and prevent ethnic conflict in similar situations.

Philosophers of social science such as Jon Elster (1983: 13–88) and Daniel Little (1991) distinguish intentional from functional explanations. Intentional explanations rely on the intentionality of actors making rational choices in pursuit of certain utilities, or benefits. The most commonly used intentionalist model is that of neoclassical economics, in which actors pursue profits in a market system. But profits in a market are only one way to define goals to be pursued, and the intentionality of individual actors can be invoked in support of a wide variety of utilities. Functional explanations eliminate the necessity of intentionality in explanation—outcomes survive because they are beneficial for those who bring them about, whether the benefits are intended or not. In other words, beneficial actions are selected out from other actions, because they are beneficial to the actors. The most widely used functional explanation is Darwinian natural selection, but again the logic of selection is not confined to speciation or to biology. It is also clear to most philosophers that social phenomena are very complex and that the presence of intentionality as an explanatory factor does not preclude the simultaneous presence of selection. Both intention and selection can help us understand the differences in ethnicity among Nuosu, Han, and Prmi-Naze and the little groups described in chapter 13.

Selection will produce different results only with different starting conditions. If there are four basic types of ethnicity in Liangshan, all of them must have been selected for in the contexts of the particular groups that hold them, which means that in order to understand the differences among the four modes of ethnic identity, we must investigate the different conditions that caused different modes to be selected for the different groups. We can begin with the difference between Han inclusivity and Nuosu exclusivity. At least since the late Song dynasty (see chap. 4), the encounter between Han and Nuosu has been unequal in the broad arena of southwest China as a whole. This was not always so in the preceding millennium, and the exact factors that enabled the Han to get the upper hand are not completely clear, but we may suggest the military and bureaucratic backing of larger empires for local Han military and civil outposts, along with the comparative advantage of a marketized, locally specialized economy over a subsistence economy. With the ability to expand, at least in certain very broad niches (river valleys and plains with high agricultural potential and good transport, such as the Anning Valley), the best strategy for the Han was to be inclusive, enabling them to occupy all those ecological zones in which the advantages of their economy and bureaucracy were sure to prevail. Drawing boundaries around themselves would stop the expansion, both demographically and geographically, so that if there were any Han communities that acted this way, they would have rapidly been replaced by communities that were more aggressively and inclusively assimilationist, allowing intermarriage and pursuing a strategy of cultural imperialism. This selective advantage, it seems to me, explains both the cultural basis and the inclusive nature of Han ethnicity.

Despite Han regional advantage, however, the Nuosu political and social system, formed by a process of tribalization (see chap. 2) on the edges of Han civilization, was advantageous in its own environment. In the sparsely populated and sparsely populable hills, agricultural surpluses were difficult to produce, negating the advantages of the Han market economy, and administration and military control were extremely expensive, negating the advantages of the Han bureaucratic system. As long as the Nuosu remained in their mountain fastnesses, they could keep the Han at bay, as clearly evidenced by the lack of bureaucratic administration in the heart of Liangshan clear until 1950. But they could not hope to expand geographically into Han areas or to expand demographically at the expense of the Han, because of their demonstrated disadvantages in highly productive areas. They could expand only into other areas ecologically similar to their original homeland, such as the areas in the mountains west of the Anning River, where most of the mixed communities described in this book are located.

Probably the most adaptive political response to Han expansion was the one the Nuosu ended up with—the tribalization represented in the caste and clan system that prevailed in the core areas and indeed drove the *tusi*—the representatives of the bureaucracy—out of most of the core area as late as the eighteenth and nineteenth centuries. This tribalization, of course, involved the formation of a clan-based political order, in which each person's social position was to a large extent genealogically determined. Birth said the most important things about a person—Loho or Shama, *nuoho* or *quho*, Nuosu or Hxiemga. Preserving the genealogical basis of group membership, and tying genealogical membership to cultural language, thought, and behavior shored up the boundaries against Han incursion in those areas where the Nuosu system was equal to or more adaptive than the commercial-bureaucratic system of the Han. Rigid barriers to membership would not allow the Nuosu to expand into the fertile valleys and plains, but they could not do that anyhow, at least not without the kind of acculturation represented in Manshuiwan. This way, they preserved their own political and social integrity in the mountains. They did, of course, allow Han to join the system, but only involuntarily as captured slaves, who came in on the lowest level of influence and prestige. This exclusive system based on culture and genealogy allowed the Nuosu to preserve their polity in Liangshan, and led to the nature of Nuosu ethnic identity that has carried over even several decades into the People's Republic.

Turning to the more contingent ethnicity of the Prmi and Naze, we have to begin by admitting that if their social systems had any advantage at all over either Nuosu or Han systems, that advantage was not ecologically based. In the high mountain basins and narrow river valleys where the Prmi and Naze now live, Han-style agriculture could do just as well, as evidenced by the expansion of rice cultivation near Lugu Lake in recent years (Shih 2001). These groups also appear to have been too small demographically and too widely dispersed to form any kind of polity that would be strong beyond an individual local-ity, except in alliance with a stronger neighbor. For most of the Yuan, Ming, and Qing periods, this stronger ally was the imperial bureaucratic state, which found it administratively efficient to rule indirectly through local ethnic rulers, or *tusi*; the Tibetan state could also be useful as a supporter in areas where the imperial state found it advantageous to concentrate even fewer resources. Boundary crossing was thus necessary for such small groups if they were to survive at all, and it is not surprising that they have a history of marrying Han and absorbing Han culture. They could never hold their own against a Chinese military-bureaucratic machine determined to subdue them, or for that mat-ter against militant and demographically superior Nuosu clans. But the Nuosu were unwilling to cross boundaries, for reasons outlined above, so that the only boundaries that the Prmi and Naze could cross were those with the Han (who of course practiced inclusion as a primary strategy of domination) or with each other. We can thus see that contingent ethnicity was the most adaptive strat-egy for these groups.

Contingent ethnicity of this sort, with its multivalent ties and its adaptive boundary-crossing, can play into the hands of the Han strategy of inclusion and absorption, and this is what seems to have happened with the smaller groups described in chapter 13. The boundary crossing and alliance making that they did in previous centuries eventually resulted in such a degree of cultural mix-ing that it became adaptive for individuals to acculturate even more rapidly. We can see this in situations such as that of the Nasu in Puwei or the Shuitian in Zhuangshang, whose language is no longer of any use. If we keep in mind that selection works at the individual level, we can see how it would no longer be to the advantage of individuals to maintain group cultural distinctiveness beyond a certain point. Only the designation as members of minorities, and the preferential policies extended to minorities in the 1980s and 1990s, have kept these people from complete acculturation and eventual assimilation.

It is thus clear that the ways of being ethnic adopted by the Han, the Nuosu, and the other groups conferred selective advantage on the members of those groups as long as the demography and ecology of the various groups remained as they did. One can also explain the different modes of ethnic identity in terms of individual intention, an explanatory strategy particularly useful when applied to the maintenance of ethnic groups in the present. Intentionality, for example, best explains the strong feelings of ethnic identity among such people as the Shuitian and Yala, or even the somewhat acculturated Prmi of Baiwu. Cadres who argue in the bureaucracy and the legislative organs for bet-ter treatment of their ethnic groups, as well as individuals of doubtful ances-

try who continue to try to be recognized as minorities despite their almost complete acculturation to Han ways, are pursuing a strategy of individual advantage through preferential policies, but the result is that a group maintains an
ethnic consciousness even though there are few cultural or kin-based mechanisms of solidarity. Naze cadres who insist that they are Mongolians, or their
Prmi counterparts who call themselves Zang, do so in order to gain an ally, as
their ancestors did. In this case the allies are the cadres and intellectuals of the
Mongolian and Tibetan *minzu*; the result is that these ethnic groups continue
a strategy of multivalence. And cadres of the Nuosu, the only group in this
region other than the Han large enough to make it feasible to have schooling
and bureaucracy conducted in their own language, argue for a larger and more
inclusive Yi *minzu*, one that would include the Lisu, Lahu, and Hani, and which
might be the basis of a provincial-level Yi autonomous region like those granted
to the Mongolians, Tibetans, Uygur, Hui, and Zhuang. In order to mobilize
local support for such a project, they must continue to draw clear genealogical lines between Yi and others, even if they include in the Yi category peoples
such as the Shuitian, Yala, and Lipuo.

THINKING ABOUT ETHNICITY THROUGH LIANGSHAN

The 1990s saw a lot of talk about the Cold War bringing the end of the nation-
state.[1] Despite its origins in the newest version of Eurocentric narcissism, this
discourse has pointed out some interesting phenomena, including some very
important changes in Europe itself. One now drives from Germany to France
with nothing but a rest stop and a sign announcing the border; with the Euro's
introduction as a common currency, money changers are going the way of border guards and passport stamps. A visa for a Chinese visitor is good for nine
countries. And of course many important decisions affecting people's economic
life are made by the proverbial "faceless bureaucrats in Brussels." At the same
time, regional autonomy in administration, culture, and education is a reality
in regions from Flanders to Catalonia, which as early as 1992 proclaimed itself
in its Olympic advertising to be "a country in Spain."

In addition, immigration has created new, transnational communities,
people who no longer give up the old country for the new, but maintain transnational connections including dual citizenship and often, as in the case of Hong
Kong-Vancouver businesspeople, transnational households. International

---

1. For a critical review, see Bornträger 1999.

capital, of both the investment and the cultural sorts (the latter coming with the advent of cheap communications by telephone, fax, and e-mail) is often said to herald the demise of nationality and national sovereignty, and to presage a world in which cultural communities will be less and less localized, and cross-cutting ties of language, religion, and, decreasingly, nationhood will turn us from a worldwide patchwork of ethnic groups and nations into a worldwide network of cultures and interest groups.[2]

This transformation from cultural nationalism to cross-national pluralism might well be the next stage in the development of ethnic relations, comparable to the shift from the multiethnic empire to the culturally uniform nation-state described in chapter 2. If cross-national pluralism is the next model of ethnic relations, however, there is evidence that it will not completely displace the nation-state model any time soon. At the same time as the Euro comes into being, new nationalisms and new histories are being created not so far away from Brussels—in the Balkans and the Caucasus, for example—and existing nation-states such as Romania, Iraq, Japan, Korea, and many others show little sign of relinquishing either administrative and military sovereignty or their cultural and educational projects of promoting nationalism and national history, even if some of the citizens of some of these states participate in transnational migration and communication. If the nation-state is dying, its death will stretch out over decades, if not centuries, and in the meantime the peoples of Liangshan will have to deal with the state nationalism of the People's Republic of China.

The relevance of the Chinese case, and of southwest China in particular, for understanding ethnicity in the current historical moment lies not only in the size and ethnic diversity of China, but also in the fact that China has never succeeded in becoming a nation-state in the classical sense, but has promoted, especially since 1980, a program of rabid nationalism combined with a commitment to limited ethnic and cultural diversity. In other words, China, having never become a nation-state in the unified sense of France or Japan, is now faced with the prospect that it may never become one, if the forces of transnationalism and globalism proceed as rapidly in Asia as they have in Europe. If China is moving toward participation in the transnational network model, as advocates of the death of the nation-state would predict, then there is a chance

2. I am indebted to Jonathan Lipman for the patchwork-network contrast, which he originally used to analyze the different forms of social organization of Chinese Muslims (Lipman 1984). For varied and interesting discussions of Chinese transnationalism and its implications for the world order of the near future, see the essays in Ong and Nonini 1997.

of a kind of federal solution to China's festering ethnic conflicts, a solution in which Tibet, Xinjiang, and Inner Mongolia would become federal states with a true measure of cultural, educational, economic, and administrative autonomy, remaining within China in the same way that Flanders remains part of Belgium or Catalonia is a country that is still in Spain. But the price of such autonomy is unquestioned loyalty to the center, and this does not seem to be in the offing for any of these large peripheral regions.

We can think about federalism in Inner Mongolia, Xinjiang, or Tibet partially because those regions fit the national model of ethnicity, subscribed to by nation-state builders and Stalinist nationality theorists alike, where a people, a territory, a language, an economy, and a culture coincide with each other and make up an entity that is destined either to become a nation in its own right (the wish of certain local nationalist factions) or to become absorbed and assimilated into the governing nation-state, as Turkey has been trying to do with the Kurds. Federalism represents a third solution to ethnic or national diversity of this sort.

Southwest China, however, forces us to think differently. Groups such as the Prmi or the Yala can never become states in a federal system—they are not only too few and too local, but are also too dependent on relationships with the center. There are many more Nuosu, and they are much more concentrated, especially in Greater Liangshan, but still they hardly fit the model of a possible federal state—their settlement is still too ecologically determined, with too few of them in the agriculturally productive and accessible lowlands, and they in turn are ultimately dependent on their economic and administrative connections to the Chinese center. So if China does become less centralized and more federal, it will not be able to take care of the ethnic groups of the Southwest as it does those around its northern and western peripheries: the units that make up the federation cannot be ethnically determined except in the kind of artificial way that has produced the current "autonomous" prefectures and counties. As we have seen throughout this book, the peoples of Liangshan are ethnic in a way that is different from that of the Catalans or Uygur or Kurds. Ethnic identity coincides only loosely with region, and in some places it does not even coincide with culture or language. If economic development opens up the wider world to significant numbers of minority people from Liangshan, they may well participate in transnational communication and migration (after all, there have been two international Yi studies conferences—in Seattle and Trier), but they will have only limited opportunities to develop ethnically inspired regional autonomy of the kind we see in the subnational regions within the European community.

If anyone in Liangshan has a case for a federal territory, it is of course the Nuosu, but at present there is no such recognized unit as Nuosu in the Chinese lexicon of ethnic or national groups. Nuosu are Yi, and Nuosu leaders know that if they have any chance at a larger regional autonomous polity based on ethnicity, it will be a Yi polity, incorporating parts of Yunnan and Guizhou as well as Liangshan. This is indeed one of the reasons why Nuosu and other Yi leaders have engaged in the kinds of cultural national construction described in chapter 9—they must build a wider ethnic identity if it is to mean anything in a future federal political system. This is another reason, I think, why many Prmi and Naze leaders are so ready to identify themselves as Tibetans or Mongolians—they need to position themselves this way in order to take advantage of any kind of ethnic federalism, which will certainly carve out only the larger chunks for federal status.

We thus see that the different ways of being ethnic will continue to be important even if the overall mode of ethnic relations, not having changed completely from the empire model of ethnic division of labor to the nation-state model of ethnic assimilation, now goes in a new direction of pluralist networking. The opportunities to participate in any networks that may emerge in this area in the future are different for people who practice different ways of being ethnic in the present. This is as likely to be true for hill peoples in India or Southeast Asia, for mixed and shifting linguistic collectivities in the Caucasus, or for native populations in the Andes as it is for the peoples of Liangshan. Ethnicity is rarely a unified phenomenon, and the close study of a place like Liangshan thus serves as an illustration of this fact and as an admonition to take both scholarly and political account of it.

IMPLICATIONS FOR CHINA

Most of the types of ethnic identity described in this book are not particularly oppositional by world standards, and as such are little threat to the unity of the Chinese polity. Aside from the fact that none of the local groups except the Nuosu and perhaps the Lipuo are big enough to pose more than a very local problem anyway, the sorts of ethnic consciousness that involve boundary crossing and only a minimum of boundary maintenance are not only no threat to the state's proposed multiethnic order; they in fact support it, and in return for this support the local communities receive modest sorts of preference and assistance, and limited freedom to develop certain areas of culture and language. Throughout China's Southwest, there are many regions where minorities and Han live in this kind of intermixed way, and there is likely to be little trouble if the government continues to pursue the present policies—it is to the advantage of members of minority groups to go along.

The Nuosu in Liangshan, of course, are different, and are the only group in the region that poses even a conceivable threat to Chinese state hegemony. As mentioned above, their identity is both habitually and calculatedly oppositional, and there are enough of them to make such an oppositional strategy advantageous. There was a large-scale rebellion against the Democratic Reforms in 1956–58, and although there has been no such military opposition since, many people—even cadres and especially some intellectuals—still glorify the memory of those rebels. A similar rebellion under today's conditions seems unlikely, and even less likely of success than the Quixotic effort of the 1950s, since there are now more roads that could be used by the Chinese army. But other forms of opposition are still possible, and the resentment of such current phenomena as extractive industry and Han immigration fits only too well with the exclusivist, us-and-them view of Nuosu-Hxiemga relations that persists so strongly in the villages.

There are, however, reasons to think that Nuosu-Han relations will remain peaceful, even though ridden by constant tension, distrust, and resentment, and will not lead to a war of independence. Most important, this is because Nuosu opposition is expressed against the Han and against current policies, not against China as a nation or against the concept that they are Chinese citizens. Nuosu belong to no nation at all unless they belong to China, and in fact the main oppositional historical narrative of various Yi scholars has been one that sees the Yi as the founders of a Chinese nation whose pride of place has been usurped by the Han, rather than as a separate nation of their own. Nuosu will oppose what they consider slights and abuses, but not contest the fact that they are citizens of China.

Another reason that ethnic relations are likely to remain peaceful is the ultimate smallness of the Nuosu as a people and of Liangshan as a region. There are only two million Nuosu, and although there are seven million total Yi, the Yi in other regions such as Guizhou and Yunnan are much more acculturated and much more economically integrated with the surrounding Han and other ethnic groups than are the Nuosu in Liangshan. And Liangshan is surrounded on at least three sides by predominantly Han areas. Any effort at violent confrontation, in other words, would be doomed from the start, and unlike the tragic heroes of 1959, everybody in Liangshan now knows that China is huge and the Han population is over a billion, so that any kind of uprising would be fruitless.

Finally, there is the degree to which Nuosu cadres and intellectuals have thrown in their lot with the Chinese state. Unlike many intellectuals in Xinjiang, for example, who think of China as a Han state that occupies their territory, Nuosu leaders think of China as a state that ought to be less Han, especially in its local manifestations. They chafe not against China but against the fact that China, even locally, is Han dominated. In a paradoxical sense, in order to advance local autonomy, they need to participate more fully in Chinese state-building, to co-opt economic development, education, and cultural projects for local and ethnic advantage. This strategy involves resentment and competition but not outright separatism.

In this way, the situation in the whole Southwest contrasts with that in places such as Tibet, Xinjiang, and Inner Mongolia, where many people question whether China is the nation of which they ought to be citizens. Mongols, Uygurs, and Tibetans can all point to a time in the past when they were independent state polities in their own right, and Mongols can of course point to a Mongolian state that exists in the present. Uygurs can look at the newly independent -stans of Central Asia and dream of a Uyguristan or East Turkistan among them. Not only does it seem just barely feasible that one of these areas might pull off a war of independence, it also seems historically plausible that they be independent nations, because they once were. Nuosu have no such claim on the past or present. They, as much as their smaller, more compromising neighbors, must make their way in China, their own way of being ethnic.

Glossary

Chinese terms are followed by Chinese characters.
Nuosu terms appear in boldface type, and words from other languages are
indicated as such.

abo father's sister; mother's
brother's wife

Abu 阿布 a mistaken ethnonym
for Nasu in Puwei

ada father

amo mother

assa female cross-cousin of a man

Ba (Tib.) self-designation of
Khams-pa Tibetans in Muli

baga village or hamlet

Bai 白 the name of a *minzu*

Bailang geshi 白狼歌诗 "Song
of Bailang"

Baima 白马 an ethnic group in
northwestern Sichuan that claims
to be separate from the Zang

baipi shu 白皮书 "white-cover
books," first editions of the ethnological reports of the 1950s

baixing 百姓 the commoner
retainers of a *nuoho* lord

ban 班 class of students that
studies all subjects together

bazi 坝子 flat alluvial plain

bazong 把总 local official subordinate to the Muli king

bimo Nuosu priest

bingtuan 兵团 soldier corps,
the Xingjiang military construction corps

bla-ma (Tib.) incarnate lama

buhao shua 不好耍 doesn't
play happily

buluo 部落 tribe

buzu 部族 tribal ethnic group

can dou 餐豆 string beans

Can tu si; feng niang mi 蚕吐丝;
蜂酿蜜 "Silkworms extrude
silk; bees ferment honey"

chengbao 承包 to lease or
contract out an economic
asset

chiong (Prmi) Tibetan-style barley beer

ci fangyan 次方言 subdialect

cobi a Nuosu funerary ritual

cun 村 village or administrative village

cunxiao 村校 village elementary school

cyvi Nuosu clan

dachun 大春 late or summer agricultural season

da Han minzu zhuyi 大汉民族主义 "great Han chauvinism"

Dai 傣 a *minzu*, most of whose members call themselves Tai

dazi 鞑子 a pejorative term for Mongols

Dedai 德傣 Dai of Dehong

ddobaq (Naxi) priest of the local tradition, same as *dongba*

deel (Mong) Mongolian-style riding robe

dianshi ji 电视机 television set

diaozhu 吊柱 "hanging" vertical posts

difang zhi 地方志 local histories or local gazetteers

diqu 地区 ordinary prefecture

divaddu small paddle for applying lacquer

djaba (Naze and Prmi) monk; Buddhist priest

dongba 东巴 Naxi priest of the local tradition (same as *dobbaq*)

dongba wen 东巴文 script used by *dobbaq* or *dongba*

duilian 对联 parallel couplet posted on a doorway or altar

fangyan 方言 dialect

fang zhi 方志 local histories; local gazetteers

fanzi 番子 foreigners; barbarians

fu 副 vice- or associate- office

funzoddu pivot-point on a lathe-frame

fuzhuang 服装 "costume," referring to ethnic dress

Gami (Prmi) Khams-pa Tibetans

gaitu guiliu 改土归流 "replacing the local and restoring the posted," a reform movement to replace *tusi* with centrally appointed bureaucrats

gaoshan Yizu 高山彝族 mountain Yi

gaxy household slave

Gelug-pa (Tib.) the "orthodox" sect of Tibetan Buddhism

gemo master artisan

gongzuo 工作 to work for wages

grwa-pa (Tib.) monk

guahao jianshe　挂好建设　"grasp construction"

guifan Yiwen　规范彝文　"regularized Yi writing," the new standard Nuosu script based on the traditional script

Hāchu tongxio　汉族同学　(Liangshan dialect)　Han classmates

hangue (Prmi)　priest of the local tradition

Hanzu wenhua　汉族文化　Han culture

hao ke　好客　hospitable

hexin diqu　核心地区　the "nuclear area" of Liangshan

Hou Han shu　后汉书　*History of the Later Han Dynasty*

huagao　花槁　wild cherry wood

huajiao　花椒　Sichuan peppercorns

huang jiu　黄酒　Tibetan-style barley beer

Huayang guo zhi　华阳国志　*Records of Foreign Countries*

hui shuohua de gongju　会说话的工具　"tools that could talk" (slaves)

Huizu　回族　the Hui, or Chinese Muslim, *minzu*

huofo　活佛　"living Buddha," a Chinese term for a Tibetan incarnate lama

huo huashi　活化石　living fossil

Hxiemga　Han

Hxiemgamo　Han woman

ichy　long-handled wooden spoon

Ji　吉　a *tusi* surname from Puwei, Miyi

jin　斤　unit of weight equal to .5 kg.

jieshy vala　pleated felt cape and woven fringed cape; distinctive Nuosu clothing

juren　举人　holder of the second, or provincial examination degree under the Qing

Kurshy　Nuosu New Year celebration

kuzzur　soup tureen

lama　啦嘛　Chinese term for a Tibetan monk, or *grwa-pa* (not necessarily an incarnate lama)

lao baixing　老百姓　common people

laoshi hao　老师好　"We wish you well, teacher"

Laoshih zaijian　老师再见　"Goodbye, teacher"

li　李　plums; also the surname Li

333

Lisu 傈僳 the name of a *minzu*

liti shehui 立体社会 "vertical society" where altitude correlates with ethnicity and social organization

liuzu fenzhi 六祖分枝 "the breakup of the six ancestors," the origin of the different Yi peoples

long de chuan ren 龙的传人 descendants of the dragon

lu 路 road; trail

luohou 落后 backward

Luoluo or Lolo 倮猡 an old, somewhat pejorative term for Yi and related peoples

mama 妈妈 mama (surprise!)

Man shu 蛮书 *Book of Barbarians*

manzi 蛮子 barbarians

Manzu the Manchu *minzu*

maoniu 牦牛 yak

meiyou shangpin jingji guannian 没有商品经济观念 lacking in a commodity-economy mind-set

meng 盟 "league," a Mongolian administrative district equivalent to a prefecture

Menggu ren 蒙古人 Mongols

Mengzu 蒙族 or Mengguzu 蒙古族 the Mongolian *minzu*

mgajie a lower, dependent stratum of Nuosu society

mgava buckwheat pancakes

mgehni wild cherry wood

Miao 苗 the name of a *minzu* that includes Hmong and their relatives

Miao Man tu ce 苗蛮图册 "Miao albums"; picture albums of southwestern peripheral peoples

minban 民办 community supported (of a teacher)

Mingai 民改 short form of Minzhu Gaige

minwei 民委 nationalities commission

Minzhu Gaige 民主改革 "Democratic Reform," revolutionary social transformations in minority areas in the 1950s

minzu 民族 ethnic group or "nationality"

minzu ban 民族班 special class for minority students

Minzu Daxue 民族大学 Nationalities University in Beijing

minzu gongzuo 民族工作 "nationalities work," bureaucratic activities concerned with minorities

minzu jianshi 民族简史 concise histories of *minzu*

minzu shi 民族史 ethnohistory

minzu shibie 民族识别 ethnic

("nationalities") identification or classification

minzu tuanjie 民族团结 unity among *minzu*

minzuxue 民族学 ethnology; the study of *minzu*

minzu xueyuan 民族学院 "nationalities institute," a college for members of minority *minzu*

minzu zhongxue 民族中学 minorities middle school

mishuzhang 秘书长 chief-of-staff of a bureaucratic office

monyi mother's sister; father's brother's wife

Mosuo 摩梭 a Han-language name for the western Naze

mu 亩 a unit of land comprising about 1/6 acre or 1/15 hectare

muluo 木螺 log-cabin building style

Nari 纳日 one way to write "Naze" in Chinese

Naxi 纳西 the name of a *minzu*

ndaba (Naze) priest of the local tradition

ndeggu mediator

Ni a classical name for Yi peoples, found in several Yi languages

nüer guo 女儿国 "kingdom of women"

nuli 奴隶 slave

nuo *see* **nuoho**

nuoho the aristocratic caste among the Nuosu, called *hei Yi* 黑彝 in Chinese

Nuosu bburma Nuosu writing

Nuosu ddoma Nuosu spoken language

Nuosumo Nuosu woman

Nuosu muddi Nuosu area; Liangshan

nzymo the highest stratum of the Nuosu caste system; the stratum that produced *tusi*

onyi mother's brother; father's sister's husband

onyisse a woman's mother's brother's son

pavu father's brother; mother's sister's husband

pian qu 片区 "slice district," an area including several townships within a county

pingba Yizu 平坝彝族 lowland Yi

pinkun 贫困 poor, impoverished

pinyin 拼音 romanization system

pochan dizhu 破产地主 bankrupt landlord

Pumi 普米 a *minzu* including the Prmi of Yunnan

puzi 堡子 (Liangshan dialect) village; hamlet

qiangjiu luohou 抢救落后 rescue the backward

Qiang yuzhi 羌语支 Qiang branch of the Tibeto-Burman language family

qiaobuqi 瞧不起 be arrogant toward or have contempt for

qiema tiny lacquer brush

qu 区 former administrative unit comprising several townships

quho the commoner caste of Nuosu, called *bai Yi* 白彝 in Chinese

qunuo the top stratum of the **quho**

ren 人 "people," a designation for an ethnic group within an officially recognized *minzu*

Renda 人大 short for Renmin Daibiao Dahui

Renmin Daibiao Dahui 人民 代表大会 People's Congress, the legislature

Renmin Zhengfu 人民政府 People's Government, the administrative bureaucracy

Renmin Zhengzhi Xietiao Weiyuanhui 人民政治协调 委员会 People's Consultative Conference, a kind of forum for approving policies, which also compiles local history materials

shaoshu minzu 少数民族 minorities or minority *minzu*

sheng 生 "raw," referring to relatively unacculturated peoples

Shehui lishi diaocha baogao 社会 历史调查报告 *Reports of Social and Historical Investigations*

shi 市 city or municipality as an administrative unit

Shi ji 史记 *Records of the Historian* by Sima Qian, written in the 2nd and 1st centuries B.C.E.

shi zhaizi 石寨子 stone-walled village

shu 熟 "cooked," referring to semi-acculturated peoples

shuangwen ban 双文班 bilingual class

shuangyu jiaoyu 双语教育 bilingual education

shui 水 water; name of a *minzu* in Guizhou

Shuiniu shuiniu guo; huangniu huangniu guo 水牛水牛过 黄牛黄牛过 "Water buffaloes get it on with water buffaloes; oxen get it on with oxen"

Shuitian　水田　a self-appellation of certain lowland peoples whose language belongs to the Yi family

shuohma　rhododendron

shushu　叔叔　father's younger brother

siheyuan　四合院　four-sided courtyard house

sishu　私塾　private school teaching the traditional Confucian curriculum

ssakuo　brave person; war leader

ssema　lacquer brush

suga　wealthy person in Nuosu society

sunyi　shaman

tai Han hua　太汉化　too Hanified

tongban tongxue　同班同学 schoolmates of the same class

tongyi duominzu guojia　统一多民族国家　unified country of diverse nationalities (or ethnic groups)

tubaihu　土百户　very low-ranking local ruler

Tudi Ye　土地爷　the local "earth god" deity

tumu　土目　low-ranking local ruler

tuotuo rou　坨坨肉　"chunk-chunk meat," a Han name for the Nuosu style of eating meat

tuqianhu　土千户　low-ranking local ruler

tusi　土司　local native ruler

tuyu　土语　local language variety

vala　woven, fringed woolen cape

voshe　pork

wen　文　writing; literary; literized

wen shi ziliao　文史资料　"literary and historical materials," compiled by each county's *zhengxie*

xiang　乡　rural township

xiangcun qiye　乡村企业　township and village enterprises

xiang shijie xuanchuan Yizu wenhua　向世界宣传彝族文化　propagandizing Yi culture to the world

xiaochun　小春　early or spring agricultural season

Xichu　(西族)　a local term for Prmi, used east of Lugu Lake

Xidai　西傣　Dai of Xishuangbanna (Sipsong Panna)

Xifan　西番　"Western Bar-

barians," an old name for
Qiangic speakers

"Xinan yi liezhuan" 西南夷列传
"Record of the Southwestern
Barbarians," from *Records of
the Historian* (*Shi li*) by Sima
Qian

xiongdi minzu 兄弟民族
brother nationalities or
fraternal ethnic groups

xiucai 秀才 holder of the lowest
examination degree under the
Qing dynasty, also called
shengyuan

yamen 衙门 office of the imperial government, applied also to
the office of a *tusi*

Yan Huang zisun 炎黄子孙
children and grandchildren
of the emperors Yan (Shen
Nong) and Huang (the
Yellow Emperor)

yatou 丫头 female household
slave in Han society

Yi 彝 the name of a *minzu*

"Yi bao" 彝胞 "Yi bros.," a
folksy, somewhat condescending
Han-language name for Nuosu

yifu 衣服 clothes

Yiwen ban 彝文班 class taught
in the Nuosu language

Yiwen xuexiao 彝文学校 Yi-
language school

Yizu chuantong zhishifenzi 彝族
传统知识分子 traditional Yi
intellectuals

Yizu Hanzu shi liang jia 彝族汉族
是两家 "Yi and Han are two
separate families"

Yizu xiang 彝族乡 designated Yi
township

yuangen 圆根 mild, flat turnip

yuoshe mutton

yuwei 语委 language committee
of a local government

yuwen 语文 (Chinese) language,
referring to a class in school

Zangyu 藏语 "Tibetan"
language; also refers to other
languages spoken by Zangzu

Zangzu 藏族 the Tibetan
minzu

Zangzu zizhi xian 藏族自治县
Zang autonomous county

zhen 镇 township

Zhengxie 政协 short for
Renmin Zhengzhi Xietiao Weiyuanhui

zhixi 枝系 "branch" of a
minzu

Zhoguoco people of China
(translation of *Zhongguo ren*)

Zhongguo ren 中国人 Chinese
people; people of China

Zhonghua minzu 中华民族 the
Chinese nation

zhongzhuan 中专 vocational high school

zizhi qu 自治区 autonomous region, equivalent to a province

zizhi xian 自治县 autonomous county

zizhi zhou 自治州 autonomous prefecture

-zu 族 *minzu* (suffix form)

zzo adze

zzowo lathe rotor

Bibliography

AAA (American Anthropological Association)

1976 (1971)   Principles of Professional Responsibility, Adopted by the Council of
               the American Anthropological Association May 1971. Reprinted as an
               appendix to Michael A. Rynkiewich and James P. Spradley, eds., *Ethics
               and Anthropology: Dilemmas in Fieldwork*. New York: Wiley.

Ahern, Emily M.

1972   *The Cult of the Dead in a Chinese Village*. Stanford: Stanford University
               Press.

Anderson, Benedict R. O'G.

1991   *Imagined Communities*. 2nd ed. London and New York: Verso.

Atwood, Christopher

1995   "The Japanese Roots of the Communist Autonomy Project in Inner
               Mongolia." Paper presented at the Annual Meeting of the Association
               for Asian Studies, Washington, D.C.

Azha Muga

1994   "Leng Guangdian xingban jiaoyu he qiangzheng wo dushu de qing-
               kuang" (Leng Guangdian's promotion of education and the circum-
               stances under which he got me to go to school). *Liangshan minzu yanjiu*
               4: 183–89.

Bachofen, Johann Jakob

1954 (1861)   *Mutterrecht und Urreligion*. Ed. Rudolf Marx. Stuttgart: Rudolf Kröner
               Verlag.

Bai Hua

1994 (1988)   *The Remote Country of Women* (Yuanfang you yige Nüer Guo). Trans.
               Qingyun Wu and Thomas O. Beebe. Honolulu: University of Hawaii
               Press.

Bamo Ayi

1994   *Yizu zuling xinyang yanjiu* (Research on ancestral spirit beliefs of the
               Yi). Chengdu: Sichuan Minzu Chubanshe.

2001   "On the Education of the Bimo." In Stevan Harrell, ed., *Perspectives on the Yi of Southwest China,* 118–34. Berkeley and Los Angeles: University of California Press.

Barlow, Tani

1990   "Theorizing Women: *Funü, Guojia, Jiating.*" *Genders* 10: 132–60.

Batatu, Hanna

1978   *The Old Social Classes and the Revolutionary Movements of Iraq.* Princeton: Princeton University Press.

Bateson, Gregory

1958 (1936)   *Naven: A Survey of the Problems Suggested by a Composite Picture of the Culture of a New Guinea Tribe drawn from Three Points of View.* Stanford: Stanford University Press.

Bentley, G. Carter

1987   "Ethnicity and Practice." *Comparative Studies in Society and History* 29, no. 1: 24–55.

Bhabha, Homi

1990   *Nation and Narration.* London: Routledge.

Björverud, Susanna

1998   *A Grammar of Lalo.* Lund: Department of East Asian Languages, Lund University.

Blum, Susan D.

1994   "Han and the Chinese Other: The Language of Identity and Difference in Southwest China." Ph.D. diss., University of Michigan.

Borchigud, Wurlig

n.d.   "Mongols and the Inner Mongolian Autonomous Region." In Stevan Harrell and Dru C. Gladney, eds., *Minority Profiles for the PRC.* Washington, D. C.: World Bank, forthcoming.

Bourdieu, Pierre

1990 (1980)   *The Logic of Practice.* Stanford: Stanford University Press.

Bradley, David

1990   "Language Planning for China's Minorities: The Yi Branch." In D. Laycock and W. Winter, eds., *A World of Language: Presented to Professor S. A. Wurm on his 65th Birthday,* 81–89. Canberra: Department of Linguistics, Australian National University.

2001   "Language Policy for the Yi." In Stevan Harrell, ed., *Perspectives on the Yi of Southwest China,* 195–213. Berkeley and Los Angeles: University of California Press.

Brown, Melissa J.

1996   "On Becoming Chinese." In Melissa J. Brown, ed., *Negotiating Eth-*

nicities in China and Taiwan, 37–74. Berkeley: University of California Institute of East Asian Studies.

CCP Xide (Zhongguo Gongchandang Xide Xian Weiyuanhui Zuzhi Bu [Organization Department of the Xide County Communist Party])

1991   *Zhongguo Gongchandang Sichuan Sheng Xide Xian zuzhi shi ziliao* (Materials on the organizational history of the Chinese Communist Party in Xide County, Sichuan). Xide: Zhongguo Gongchandang Xide Xian Weihuanhui Zuzhi Bu.

Chang, Kuang-chih

1977   *The Archaeology of Ancient China*. 3rd ed. New Haven: Yale University Press.

1980   *Shang Civilization*. New Haven: Yale University Press.

Chen Changyou

1992   *Qian xibei Yizu meishu* (Fine arts of the Yi of northwestern Guizhou). Guiyang: Guizhou Minzu Chubanshe.

Chen Shilin

1985   *Yiyu jian zhi* (Concise account of the Yi language). Beijing: Zhongguo Minzu Chubanshe.

Chen Tianjun

1987   "Lun Yizu gushi fenqi" (Discussion of the periodization of ancient Yi history). In Zhongguo Xinan Minzu Yanjiu Hui, ed., *Xinan minzu yanjiu, Yizu zhuanji* (Research on southwestern *minzu*, Yi special collection), 107–19. Kunming: Yunnan Renmin Chubanshe.

Chen Yongling

1998   "The History of Ethnology in China." In idem, *A Collection of Chinese Ethnological Studies*, 1–72. Taipei: Hong-Yih Publishing Co.

Chen Zongxiang and Deng Wenfeng

1979   "'Bailang ge' yanjiu shuping" (A summary and critique of research on the "Song of Bailang"). *Xinan Shifan Xueyuan xuebao* (Southwest Teachers College bulletin), no. 4: 48–55.

1991   *"Bailang ge" yanjiu* (Research on "The Song of Bailang"). Vol. 1. Chengdu: Sichuan Renmin Chubanshe.

Cheung, Siu-woo

1995a   "Subject and Representation: Identity Politics in Southeast Guizhou." Ph.D. diss., University of Washington.

1995b   "Millenarianism, Christian Movements, and Ethnic Change among the Miao in Southwest China." In Stevan Harrell, ed., *Cultural Encounters on China's Ethnic Frontiers*, 217–47. Seattle: University of Washington Press.

1996   "Representation and Negotiation of Ge Identities in Southwest Guizhou." In Melissa J. Brown, ed., *Negotiating Ethnicities in China and Taiwan*, 240–73. Berkeley: University of California Institute of East Asian Studies.

Chiang Kai-shek (Jiang Jieshi)

1947   *China's Destiny*. New York: Macmillan.

Collier, Jane F.

1988   *Marriage and Inequality in Classless Societies*. Stanford: Stanford University Press.

Connor, Walker

1984   *The National Question in Marxist-Leninist Theory and Strategy*. Princeton: Princeton University Press.

Dangdai Liangshan Bianxie Zu

1992   *Dangdai Liangshan* (Contemporary Liangshan). Chengdu: Bashu Chubanshe.

Dayao

1904   *Dayao Xian zhi* (Gazetteer of Dayao County). Dayao.

Diamant, Neil J.

1999   *Revolutionizing the Family: Politics, Love, and Divorce in Urban and Rural China, 1949–1968*. Berkeley: University of California Press.

Diamond, Norma

1995   "Defining the Miao: Ming, Qing, and Contemporary Views." In Stevan Harrell, ed., *Cultural Encounters on China's Ethnic Frontiers*, 92–116. Seattle: University of Washington Press.

Diamond, Stanley

1974   *In Search of the Primitive: A Critique of Civilization*. New Brunswick, N.J.: Transaction Books; distributed by E. P. Dutton.

Ditu Ji

1983   *Zhonghua Renmin Gongheguo fen sheng dituji (Hanyu pinyin ban)* (Provincial atlas of the People's Republic of China [pinyin edition]). Shanghai: Ditu Chubanshe.

Dreyer, June Teufel

1976   *China's Forty Millions: Minority Nationalities and National Integration in the People's Republic of China*. Cambridge, Mass.: Harvard University Press.

Du Weixuan et al., eds.

1994   *Panzhihua Shi zhi* (Gazetteer of Panzhihua Municipality). Chengdu: Sichuan Kexue Jishu Chubanshe.

Du Yuting

1985   *Jinuozu jianshi* (Brief history of the Jinuo *minzu*). Kunming: Yunnan Minzu Chubanshe.

Dukou Shi Wenwu Guanli Chu, comp.

1985   *Dukou Shi wenwu, kaogu, lishi, minzu yanjiu ziliao xuanji* (Selected materials on the artifacts, archaeology, history, and ethnic groups of Dukou). Panzhihua: Panzhihua Shi Wenwu Guanli Chu.

Dumont, Jean-Paul

1988   "The Tasaday, Which and Whose? Toward the Political Economy of an Ethnographic Sign." *Cultural Anthropology* 3, no. 3: 261–75.

Dwyer, Arienne M.

1998   "The Texture of Tongues: Languages and Power in China." In William Safran, ed., *Nationalism and Ethnoregional Identities in China*, 68–85. London and Portland: Frank Cass.

Eickstedt, Egon Freiherr von

1944   *Rassendynamik von Ostasien*. Berlin: Walter de Gruyter.

Eisler, Riane

1987   *The Chalice and the Blade: Our History, Our Future*. San Francisco: Harper and Row.

Elster, Jon

1983   *Explaining Technical Change*. Cambridge: Cambridge University Press.

Endicott-West, Elizabeth

1989   *Mongolian Rule in China: Local Administration in the Yuan Dynasty*. Cambridge, Mass.: Harvard Council on East Asian Studies.

Engels, Friedrich

1972 (1883)   *The Origin of the Family, Private Property, and the State*. Trans. Alick West. New York: International Publishers.

Evans-Pritchard, E. E.

1940   *The Nuer*. Oxford: Oxford University Press.

Fabian, Johannes

1983   *Time and the Other: How Anthropology Makes Its Object*. New York: Columbia University Press.

Fan Ke

n.d.   "The Ethnic Politics of being Islamic in South Fujian." Ph.D. diss., University of Washington.

Fei, Xiaotong

1981   *Toward a People's Anthropology*. Beijing: Renmin Chubanshe.

Fisher, Elizabeth

1979   *Woman's Creation*. New York: McGraw Hill.

Flax, Jane

    1982   "The Family in Contemporary Feminist Thought: A Critical Review." In Jean Bethke Elshtain, ed., *The Family in Political Thought*. Amherst: University of Massachusetts Press.

Foucault, Michel

    1977   *Discipline and Punish: The Birth of the Prison*. Trans. Alan Sheridan. London: Allen Lane.

Fox, Robin

    1968   *Kinship and Marriage: An Anthropological Perspective*. Harmondsworth: Penguin.

Freedman, Maurice

    1958   *Lineage Organization in Southwestern China*. London: Athlone Press.

    1966   *Chinese Lineage and Society: Fukien and Kwangtung*. London: Athlone Press.

Fried, Morton H.

    1967   *The Evolution of Political Society*. New York: Random House.

    1983   "Tribe to State or State to Tribe in Ancient China?" In David N. Keightley, ed., *The Origins of Chinese Civilization*, 467–94. Berkeley and Los Angeles: University of California Press.

Friedman, Edward, Mark Selden, and Paul Pickowicz

    1991   *Chinese Village, Socialist State*. New Haven: Yale University Press.

Fu Yuyao

    1983   "Yanyuan, Muli er xian minzu lishi wenhua kaocha jilue" (Report of investigations into the ethnic history and culture of the two counties of Yanyuan and Muli). In Li Shaoming and Tong Enzheng, eds., *Yalong Jiang xialiu kaocha baogao* (Report of investigations along the lower course of the Yalong River). Chengdu: Zhongguo Xinan Minzu Yanjiu Xuehui.

Gellner, Ernest

    1987 (1983)   "Nationalism and the Two Forms of Cohesion in Complex Societies." In *Culture, Identity, and Politics*, 6–28. Cambridge: Cambridge University Press.

Gladney, Dru C.

    1991   *Muslim Chinese: Ethnic Nationalism in the People's Republic*. Cambridge, Mass.: Harvard University Press.

Goldstein, Melvyn C.

    1989   *A History of Modern Tibet, 1913–1951: The Demise of the Lamaist State*. Berkeley and Los Angeles: University of California Press.

1997   *The Snow Lion and the Dragon: China, Tibet, and the Dalai Lama.* Berkeley and Los Angeles: University of California Press.

Goldstein, Melvyn C., and Cynthia M. Beall

1990   *Nomads of Western Tibet.* Berkeley and Los Angeles: University of California Press.

Goodman, Tom

1997   "Where women rule." *South China Morning Post,* "The Review," 4 January 1997, p. 6.

Gough, Kathleen

1959   "The Nayars and the Definition of Marriage." *Journal of the Royal Anthropological Institute* 89: 23–34.

1961   "Nayar: Central Kerala." In David M. Schneider and Kathleen Gough, eds., *Matrilineal Kinship,* 298–384. Berkeley and Los Angeles: University of California Press.

Guldin, Gregory Eliyu

1994   *The Saga of Anthropology in China: From Malinowski to Moscow to Mao.* Armonk, N.Y.: M. E. Sharpe.

Gunter, Michael M.

1994   *The Changing Kurdish Problem in Turkey.* Conflict Studies 270. London: Research Institute for the Study of Conflict and Terrorism.

Guo Xiaolin

1996   "Rice Ears and Cattle Tails." Ph.D. diss., University of British Columbia.

Guojia Minwei

1981   *Zhongguo shaoshu minzu* (China's minorities). Beijing: Renmin Chubanshe.

Guo Moruo

1972   "Gudai wenzi zhi bianzheng de fazhan" (The dialectics of the development of ancient writing). *Kaogu xuebao* 29, no. 1: 1–3.

Haley, Brian D., and Larry R. Wilcoxon

1997   "Anthropology and the Making of Chumash Tradition." *Current Anthropology* 38, no. 5: 761–94.

Han, Almaz

1999   "Split Identities: Making Ethnic/Minzu Subjects in Inner Mongolia, People's Republic of China." Ph.D. diss., University of Washington.

Hansen, Mette Halskov

1999   *Lessons in Being Chinese: Minority Education and Ethnic Identity in Southwest China.* Seattle: University of Washington Press.

Hanson, Allan

1989   "The Making of the Maori: Culture Invention and Its Logic." *American Anthropologist* 91, no. 4: 890–902.

Harrell, Stevan

1989   "Ethnicity and Kin Terms Among Two Kinds of Yi." In Chien Chiao and Nicholas Tapp, eds., *Ethnicity and Ethnic Groups in China*, 179–98. Hong Kong: New Asia Academic Bulletin.

1990   "Ethnicity, Local Interests, and the State: Yi Communities in Southwest China." *Comparative Studies in Society and History* 32, no. 3: 515–48.

1992   "Aspects of Marriage in Three Southwestern Villages." *China Quarterly* 130: 323–37.

1993   "Geography, Demography, and Family Structure in Three Southwestern Villages." In Deborah Davis and Stevan Harrell, eds., *Chinese Families in the Post-Mao Era*, 77–102. Berkeley and Los Angeles: University of California Press.

1995a   "Introduction: Civilizing Projects and the Reactions to Them." In Stevan Harrell, ed., *Cultural Encounters on China's Ethnic Frontiers*, 1–36. Seattle: University of Washington Press.

1995b   "The History of the History of the Yi." In Stevan Harrell, ed., *Cultural Encounters on China's Ethnic Frontiers*, 63–91. Seattle: University of Washington Press.

1995c   "Jeeping against Maoism." *positions* 3, no. 3: 728–58.

1996a   "Introduction." In Melissa J. Brown, ed., *Negotiating Ethnicities in China and Taiwan*, 1–18. Berkeley: University of California Institute of East Asian Studies.

1999   "Nuosu Lacquerware: A Traditional Craft and Its Recent Transformations." Paper presented at the Conference on Chinese Vernacular Cultures, Berkeley, March 1999.

2000a   "The Changing Meanings of Work in China." In Barbara Entwisle and Gail E. Henderson, eds., *Re-Drawing Boundaries: Work, Household, and Gender in China*, 67–76. Berkeley and Los Angeles: University of California Press.

2000b   *Tianye zhong de zuqun guanxi yu minzu rentong: Zhongguo xinan Yizu yanjiu* (Field studies of ethnic relations and identity: Research on the Yi of southwest China). Trans. Bamo Ayi and Qumo Tiexi. Nanning: Guangxi Minzu Chubanshe.

2001   (ed.) *Perspectives on the Yi of Southwest China.* Berkeley and Los Angeles: University of California Press.

Harrell, Stevan, and Bamo Ayi

    1998   "Combining Ethnic Heritage and National Unity: A Paradox of Nuosu (Yi) Language Textbooks in China. *Bulletin of Concerned Asian Scholars* 30, no. 2: 62–71.

Harrell, Stevan, Bamo Qubumo, and Ma Erzi

    2000   *Mountain Patterns: The Survival of Nuosu Culture in China.* Seattle: University of Washington Press.

Harrell, Stevan, and Ma Erzi

    1999   "Folk Theories of Success Where Han Aren't Always the Best." In Gerard Postiglione, ed., *China's National Minority Education*, 213–41. New York: Garland Press.

Haug, Sarah W.

    1995   "From Many Cultures, One Nation: Ethnic and Nationalist Identity in Belizean Children." Ph.D. diss., University of Washington.

He Xuewen

    1991   "Yongning Mosuo ren de hunyin ji qi xisu" (Marriage and its customs among the Mosuo people of Yongning). In *Ninglang wenshi ziliao xuanji* (Selected compilation of literary and historical materials from Ninglang), 255–64. Ninglang: Ninglang Zhengxie

Heberer, Thomas

    1989   *China and Its National Minorities: Autonomy or Assimilation.* Armonk: M. E. Sharpe.

    2001   "Nationalities Conflict and Ethnicity in the People's Republic of China, with Special Reference to the Yi in Liangshan Autonomous Prefecture." In Stevan Harrell, ed., *Perspectives on the Yi of Southwest China*, 214–37. Berkeley and Los Angeles: University of California Press.

Heller, Maria

    1988   "Introduction." In Maria Heller, ed., *Codeswitching: Anthropological and Sociolinguistic Perspectives.* Berlin, New York, and Amsterdam: Mouton de Gruyter.

Henderson, Gail E., Barbara Entwistle, Li Ying, Yang Mingliang, Xu Siyuan, and Zhai Fengying

    2000   "Re-Drawing the Boundaries of Work: Views on the Meaning of Work (Gongzuo)." In Barbara Entwisle and Gail E. Henderson, eds., *Re-Drawing Boundaries: Work, Household, and Gender in China*, 33–50. Berkeley and Los Angeles: University of California Press.

Hill, Ann Maxwell, and Eric Diehl

    2001   "A Comparative Approach to Lineages among Xiao Liangshan Nuosu

(Yi) and Han." In Stevan Harrell, ed., *Perspectives on the Yi of Southwest China*, 51–67. Berkeley and Los Angeles: University of California Press.

Hinton, William

1966   *Fanshen: A Documentary of Revolution in a Chinese Village*. New York: Vintage.

Ho, Ping-ti

1976   *The Cradle of the East*. Chicago: University of Chicago Press.

Horowitz, Donald

1985   *Ethnic Groups in Conflict*. Berkeley and Los Angeles: University of California Press.

Hostetler, Laura

2001   *Qing Colonial Enterprise: Ethnography and Cartography in Early Modern China*. Chicago: University of Chicago Press.

Hsieh, Shih-chung

1987   "Minzuzhi daode yu renleixuejia de kunjing" (Ethnographic Ethics and the predicament of the anthropologist). *Dangdai* (Contemporary) 1987, no. 2: 20–30.

1995   "On the Dynamics of Tai/Dai Lue Ethnicity." In Stevan Harrell, ed. *Cultural Encounters on China's Ethnic Frontiers*, 301–28. Seattle: University of Washington Press.

Hu Qingjun

1981   *Ming-Qing Yizu shehuishi lunzong* (Essay on the social history of the Yi in the Ming and Qing). Shanghai: Shanghai Renmin Chubanshe.

Huoni Ddossijie Bburpur Woyuohxo

1989   *Huoni Ddossijie* (Han-Yi dictionary). Chengdu: Sichuan Minzu Chubanshe.

Jackson, Jean E.

1983   *The Fish People: Linguistic Exogamy and Tukanoan Identity in Northwest Amazonia*. Cambridge and New York: Cambridge University Press.

Jennings, Francis

1984   *The Ambiguous Iroquois Empire*. New York: W. W. Norton.

Jiang Yingliang

1948   "Liangshan Yizu de nuli zhidu" (The slave system of the Liangshan Yi). *Zhuhai xuebao* (Zhuhai journal) 1: 17–53.

Jiang Yongxing

1985   "Cong Guizhou minzu shibie gongzuo tanqi" (Discussion on the basis of Guizhou's ethnic identification work), *Minzu yanjiu jikan* (Ethnic research quarterly) (Guangxi) 2: 303–16.

Jike Zehuo

1990   *Wo zai shengui zhi jian* (My life among the ghosts and spirits). Kunming: Yunnan Minzu Chubanshe.

Jin Yu

1991   "Lugu Hu pan Nüer Guo" (Kingdom of Women on the shores of Lugu Lake). *Xinan lüyou* (Southwest travel) 28: 13–15.

Jiwu Muliu (Jjivo Munyu)

n.d.   "Liangshan Yizu Jiwu gongyi shijia" (The artisan clan Jjivo of the Liangshan Yi). Unpublished paper.

Jones, Ernest

1925   "Mother-right and the Sexual Ignorance of Savages," *International Journal of Psycho-Analysis* 6: 109–30.

Kahn, Miriam

1995   "Heterotrophic Dissonance in the Museum Representation of Pacific Cultures." *American Anthropologist* 97, no. 2: 324–38.

2000   "Tahiti Intertwined: Ancestral Land, Tourist Postcard, and Nuclear Test Site." *American Anthropologist* 102, no. 1: 7–26.

Kenyatta, Jomo

1938   *Facing Mount Kenya: The Tribal Life of the Gikuyu.* With an introduction by B. Malinowski. London: Secker and Warburg.

Keyes, Charles F.

1976   "Toward a New Formulation of the Concept of Ethnic Group." *Ethnicity* 3: 203–13.

1996   "Ethnicity." In Thomas J. Barfield, ed., *The Blackwell Dictionary of Anthropology*, 152–54. Oxford: Basil Blackwell.

Khan, Almaz

1995   "Chinggis Khan: From Imperial Ancestor to Ethnic Hero." In Stevan Harrell, ed., *Cultural Encounters on China's Ethnic Frontiers*, 248–277. Seattle and London: University of Washington Press.

Leach, Edmund

1954   *Political Systems of Highland Burma.* London: Athlone Press.

1961   "Polyandry, Inheritance, and the Definition of Marriage, with Particular Reference to Sinhalese Customary Law" (with prefatory note). In idem, *Rethinking Anthropology*, 105–13. London: Athlone Press.

Legendre, A.-F.

1913   *Au Yunnan et dans le massif du Kin-ho (Fleuve D'or).* Paris: Plon Nourrit et. Cie.

Levenson, Joseph R.

1968 *Confucian China and Its Modern Fate*. Vol. 1. Berkeley: University of California Press.

Lévi-Strauss, Claude

1966 *The Savage Mind*. Chicago: University of Chicago Press.

Li Fanggui

1985 "Zhuge Liang nanzheng daoguo Dukou meiyou" (Did Zhuge Liang's southern expedition reach Dukou [Panzhihua]?). In Dukou Shi Wenwu Guanli Chu, comp., *Dukou Shi wenwu, kaogu, lishi, minzu yanjiu ziliao xuanji* (Selected materials on the artifacts, archaeology, history, and ethnic groups of Dukou), vol. 1: 146–47. Dukou: Dukou Shi Wenwu Guanli Chu.

Li Haiying et al.

1985 "Yanbian Xian Hongbao Gongshe Miaozu diaocha" (Investigation of the Miao of Hongbao Commune, Yanbian County). In Dukou Shi Wenwu Guanli Chu, comp., *Dukou Shi wenwu, kaogu, lishi, minzu yanjiu ziliao xuanji* (Selected materials on the artifacts, archaeology, history, and ethnic groups of Dukou), vol. 1: 44–60. Dukou: Dukou Shi Wenwu Guanli Chu.

Li Liukun

1992 "Miyi Baizu shi wei Yizu zhong de Baiyi kaozheng" (A proof that the Bai of Miyi are really the Baiyi, a kind of Yi). In *Miyi wenshi ziliao* (Literary and historical materials on Miyi), vol. 5: 116–18. Miyi: Miyi Zhengxie.

Li Ruzhen

1986 *Jing hua yuan* (Destiny of flowers in the mirror). Beijing: Renmin
(c. 1800) Wenxue Chubanshe.

Li Shaoming

1986 "Lun Chuan-Dian bianjing Nari ren de zushu" (Discussion of the ethnic categorization of the Nari people of the Sichuan-Yunnan border area). *New Asia Academic Bulletin* 6: 279–90.

Li Xiaoting

1969 "Cong ji zhong shiqian he youshi zaoqi taowen de guancha lice Zhongguo wenzi de qiyuan" (Extrapolating the origin of China's writing from observations of several kinds of prehistoric and early historic pottery inscriptions). *Nanyang xuebao* (Nanyang University journal), no 3, 1–28.

Li Xingxing

1994 "Chuan-Dian bian 'Nari' ren zucheng wenti de youlai yu xianzhuang" (The history and current status of the question of the ethnonym of the 'Nari' people of the Sichuan-Yunnan border). *Minzu yanjiu dong-tai*, no. 1: 7–11.

1995　"Futian Yangshi" (The Futian model). In Li Xingxing and Luo Yongzhi, eds., *Panzhihua Liegu Shang de changdian* (The advantages of the Panzhihua Rift Valley), chap. 1. Chengdu: Sichuan Minzu Chubanshe.

Li Yifu

1986　"Tantan jianli zhongguo minzu gainian tixi de wenti" (Chatting about the question of the establishment of China's system of concepts about *minzu*). *Minzu yanjiu* 1986, no. 4: 12–17.

Liangshan Yizu Zizhi Zhou Gaikuang Bianxie Zu

1985　*Liangshan Yizu Zizhi Zhou gaikuang* (General account of Liangshan Yi Autonomous Prefecture). Chengdu: Sichuan Minzu Chubanshe.

Lietard, Alfred

1913　*Au Yun-nan: Les Lo-lo p'o*. Münster: Aschendorffsche Verlagsbuch-handlung.

Lilley, Ian

1992　"Papua New Guinea's Human Past: The Evidence of Archaeology." In R. D. Attenborough and M. P. Alpers, eds., *Human Biology in Papua New Guinea: The Small Cosmos*. Oxford: Clarendon Press.

Lin Yaohua

1961　*Lolo of Liangshan* (Translation of *Liangshan Yijia*, 1947). New Haven: Human Relations Area Files Press.

1987　"Zhongguo xinan diqu de minzu shibie" (Ethnic identification in the southwest Chinese area"). In *Yunnan shaoshu minzu shehui lishi diaocha ziliao huibian* (Collection of materials from historical and socio-logical investigations of minority nationalities in Yunnan), 1–6. Kunming: Yunnan Renmin Chubanshe.

1993　"Shilun dangdai Liangshan qu dengji guannian de cancun xingtai" (Preliminary discussion of the survival of caste thinking in contem-porary Liangshan). In Zhongyang Minzu Xueyuan, Minzu Xue Xi, Minzu Yanjiu Suo, eds., *Minzu, zongjiao, lishi, wenhua* (Ethnicity, religion, history, culture), 1–16. Beijing: Zhongyang Minzu Daxue Chubanshe.

1994　*Liangshan Yijia de ju bian* (The great transformation of the Liangshan Yi). New edition of *Liangshan Yijia* (1947), with additions. Beijing: Shangwu Yinshuguan.

Lipman, Jonathan N.

1984　"Patchwork Society, Network Society: A Study of Sino-Muslim

Communities." In Raphael Israeli and Anthony Johns, eds., *Islam in Asia*, vol. 2: 246–74. Jerusalem: Magnes.

Little, Daniel

1991   *Varieties of Social Explanation: An Introduction to the Philosophy of Social Science.* Boulder: Westview Press.

Litzinger, Ralph A.

1995   "Making Histories: Contending Conceptions of the Yao Past." In Stevan Harrell, ed., *Cultural Encounters on China's Ethnic Frontiers*, 117–39. Seattle: University of Washington Press.

Liu Yaohan

1985   *Zhongguo wenming yuantou xintan* (A new approach to the origin of Chinese civilization). Kunming: Yunnan Renmin Chubanshe.

Liu Yu

2001   "The Heroic Age of the Liangshan Yi." In Stevan Harrell, ed., *Perspectives on the Yi of Southwest China*, 104–17. Berkeley and Los Angeles: University of California Press.

Lu Hui

1994   *Des Montagnes Fraîches au gouvernement du Yunnan, genèse et destin historique d'un clan yi en Chine.* Ph.D. diss., École des Hautes Etudes en Sciences Sociales, Paris.

2001   "Preferential Bilateral Cross-Cousin Marriage among the Yi in Liangshan." In Stevan Harrell, ed., *Perspectives on the Yi of Southwest China*, 68–80. Berkeley and Los Angeles: University of California Press.

Ma Changshou

1985   *Yizu gudai shi* (Ancient history of the Yi). Edited by Li Shaoming. Shanghai: Shanghai Renmin Chubanshe.

Ma Erzi

1992   "Qiantan Liangshan Yizu Degu" (A superficial discussion of the Ndeggu of the Liangshan Yi). *Liangshan minzu yanjiu* 1: 99–107.

1993   "Dui jiu Liangshan Yizu shehui jiegoude zai renshi ji 'Heiyi' 'Baiyi' de bianxi" (On a reexamination of the social structure of old Liangshan, and of the distinction between "Black Yi" and "White Yi"). *Liangshan minzu yanjiu* (Liangshan ethnic studies), 1993: 38–48.

2001   "Names and Genealogies Among the Nuosu of Liangshan." In Stevan Harrell, ed., *Perspectives on the Yi of Southwest China*, 81–93. Berkeley and Los Angeles: University of California Press.

Ma Xueliang, ed.

1987   *Cuanwen congke* (Collected inscriptions in Old Yi writing). Chengdu: Sichuan Minzu Chubanshe.

Mackerras, Colin

1994 *China's Minorities: Integration and Modernization in the Twentieth Century*. Hong Kong: Oxford University Press.

Malinowski, Bronislaw

1929 *The Sexual Life of Savages*. New York: Harcourt, Brace, and World.

Mandelbaum, David

1970 *Society in India*. Vol. 1: *Continuity and Change*. Berkeley and Los Angeles: University of California Press.

Matisoff, James A.

1991 "Sino-Tibetan Linguistics: Present State and Future Prospects." *Annual Review of Anthropology* 20: 469–504.

McKhann, Charles F.

1989 "Fleshing Out the Bones: The Cosmic and Social Dimensions of Space in Naxi Architecture." In Chien Chiao and Nicholas Tapp, eds., *Ethnicity and Ethnic Groups in China*, 157–77. Hong Kong: New Asia College, the Chinese University of Hong Kong.

1995 "The Naxi and the Nationalities Question." In Stevan Harrell, ed., *Cultural Encounters on China's Ethnic Frontiers*, 39–62. Seattle and London: University of Washington Press.

Mead, Margaret

1975 *Blackberry Winter: My Earlier Years*. New York: Washington Square Press.

Morgan, Elaine

1972 *The Descent of Woman*. New York: Stein and Day.

Morgan, Lewis Henry

1870 *Systems of Consanguinity and Affinity of the Human Family*. Smithsonian Contributions to Knowledge, 218. Washington: Smithsonian Institution.

1877 *Ancient Society*. New York: Henry Holt.

Morris-Suzuki, Tessa

1996 "A Descent into the Past: The Frontier in the Construction of Japanese Identity." In Donald Denoon, Mark Hudson, Gavan McCormack, and Tessa Morris-Suzuki, eds., *Multicultural Japan: Palaeolithic to Postmodern*, 81–94. Melbourne: Cambridge University Press.

Mueggler, Erik

1998a "A Carceral Regime: Violence and Social Memory in Southwest China." *Cultural Anthropology* 13, no. 2: 167–92.

1998b "The Poetics of Grief and the Price of Hemp in Southwest China." *Journal of Asian Studies* 57, no. 4: 979–1008.

2001   "A Valley/House: Remembering a Yi Headmanship." In Stevan Harrell, ed., *Perspectives on the Yi of Southwest China*, 144–69. Berkeley and Los Angeles: University of California Press.

Mueller, Herbert

1913   "Beiträge zur Ethnographie der Lolo." *Baessler Archiv für Ethnographie* 3: 39–69.

Mukhopadhyay, Carol C., and Patricia J. Higgins

1988   "Anthropological Studies of Women's Status Revisited: 1977–1987." *Annual Review of Anthropology* 17: 461–95.

Muli Zangzu Zizhi Xian

1985   *Muli Zangzu Zizhixian gaikuang* (General description of Muli Zang Autonomous County). Chengdu: Sichuan Minzu Chubanshe.

Murdock, George Peter

1949   *Social Structure.* New York: Macmillan.

Nance, John

1975   *The Gentle Tasaday: A Stone Age People in the Philippine Rain Forest.* New York: Harcourt Brace Jovanovich.

Naughton, Barry

1988   "The Third Front: Defense Industrialization in the Chinese Interior." *China Quarterly* 115 (Autumn): 351–86.

Oakes, Timothy

1995   "Tourism in Guizhou: Place and the Paradox of Modernity." Ph.D. diss., University of Washington.

1998   *Tourism and Modernity in China.* London and New York: Routledge.

O'Neill, Mark

1995a   "Matriarchy rules in corner of man-dominated China." Reuters@clarinet.com.

1995b   "Tourism changes remote Chinese village." Reuters@clarinet.com.

Ong, Aihwa, and Donald Nonini, eds.

1997   *Ungrounded Empires: The Cultural Politics of Modern Chinese Transnationalism.* New York and London: Routledge.

Ortner, Sherry

1981   "Gender and Sexuality in Hierarchical Societies: The Case of Polynesia and Some Comparative Implications." In Sherry B. Ortner and Harriet Whitehead, eds., *Sexual Meanings: The Cultural Construction of Gender and Sexuality*, 359–409. Cambridge and New York: Cambridge University Press.

Pan Jiao

n.d.   "Theories of Ethnic Identity and the Making of Yi Identity." Paper presented at the Second International Yi Studies Conference, Trier, June 1998.

Pan Wenchao

1987   "Shilun Liangshan Yizu nuli shehui de dengji huafen" (Preliminary discussion of the allocation of caste statuses in Liangshan Yi slave society). In Zhongguo Xinan Minzu Yanjiu Hui, ed., *Xinan minzu yanjiu, Yizu zhuanji* (Research on southwestern *minzu*, Yi special collection), 321–34. Kunming: Yunnan Renmin Chubanshe.

Paul, Robert A.

1976   "Did the Primal Crime Really Take Place?" *Ethos* 4, no. 3: 311–52.

Peng Deyuan et al.

1992   *Miyi minzu zhi* (Account of the *minzu* of Miyi). Miyi, Sichuan: Miyi Minzu Zhi Bianji Xiaozu.

Peng Wenbin

n.d.   "Ersuzu/Fanzu, and Zangzu: Identities Claimed and Imposed." Unpublished paper.

Peng Yingming

1985   "Guanyu wo guo minzu gainian lishi de chubu kaocha" (A preliminary investigation concerning the idea of *minzu* in our country). *Minzu yanjiu* 1985, no. 2: 5–11.

Potter, Jack, and Sulamith Heins Potter

1990   *China's Peasants: Ethnography of a Revolution.* Cambridge: Cambridge University Press.

Qi Qingfu

1987   "Nanzhao wangshi zushu kaobian" (Considering the debates about the ethnicity of the ruling families of Nanzhao). In Zhongguo Xinan Minzu Yanjiu Hui, ed., *Xinan minzu yanjiu, Yizu zhuanji* (Research on southwestern *minzu*, Yi special collection), 136–51. Kunming: Yunnan Renmin Chubanshe.

Qubi Shimei and Ma Erzi

2001   "Homicide Cases in Old Liangshan." In Stevan Harrell, ed., *Perspectives on the Yi of Southwest China*, 94–103. Berkeley and Los Angeles: University of California Press.

Radcliffe-Brown, A. R.

1924   "Mother's Brother in Southern Africa." *South Africa Journal of Science* 21: 542–55.

Reed, Evelyn

1974   *Woman's Evolution.* New York: Pathfinder Press.

Richards, Audrey J.

1950   "Some Types of Family Structure Amongst the Central Bantu." In A. R. Radcliffe-Brown and Daryll Forde, eds., *African Systems of Kinship and Marriage*, 207–51. London and New York: Oxford University Press.

Rock, Joseph F.

1930   "The Glories of the Minya Konka," *National Geographic Magazine* 63, no. 4: 389–437.

1948   *The Ancient Na-khi Kingdom of Southwest China*. Cambridge: Harvard University Press.

Rudelson, Justin Jon

1997   *Oasis Identities: Uyghur Nationalism Along China's Silk Road*. New York: Columbia University Press.

Schein, Louisa

1989   "The Dynamics of Cultural Revival among the Miao in Guizhou." In Chien Chiao and Nicholas Tapp, eds., *Ethnicity and Ethnic Groups in China*, 199–212. Hong Kong: New Asia Academic Bulletin.

1997   "Gender and Internal Orientalism in China." *Modern China* 23, no. 1: 69–98.

1999   *Minority Rules: The Miao and the Feminine in China's Cultural Politics*. Durham: Duke University Press.

Schlegel, Alice

1977   *Sexual Stratification: A Cross-Cultural View*. New York: Columbia University Press.

Schoenhals, Martin

1993   *The Paradox of Power in a People's Republic of China Middle School*. Armonk, N.Y.: M. E. Sharpe.

2001   "Education and Ethnicity among the Liangshan Yi." In Stevan Harrell, ed., *Perspectives on the Yi of Southwest China*, 238–55. Berkeley and Los Angeles: University of California Press.

n.d.   *Caste and Class Turned Inside-Out*, unpublished book ms.

Schwartz, Ronald D.

1994   *Circle of Protest: Political Ritual in the Tibetan Uprising*. New York: Columbia University Press.

Shepherd, John Robert

1993   *Statecraft and Political Economy on the Taiwan Frontier, 1600–1800*. Stanford: Stanford University Press.

Shih, Chuan-kang

2001   *The Yongning Mosuo*. Stanford: Stanford University Press.

Sichuan Minzu Yuyan Xuehui

1990   *Guifan Yiwen yingyong yanjiu* (Research into the use of standard Yi script). Chengdu: Sichuan Minzu Chubanshe.

Sichuan Renmin Guangbo Diantai

1990   *Gulao wenzi chongfang guangmang* (Old script restored to the lime-light). Chengdu: Sichuan Minzu Chubanshe.

Sichuan Sheng Bianji Zu

1985   *Sichuan sheng Liangshan Yizu shehui lishi diaocha zonghe baogao* (Summary volume of historical and social investigations on the Yi of Liangshan in Sichuan Province). Chengdu: Sichuan Sheng Shehui Kexue Yuan Chubanshe.

1987   *Sichuan Yizu lishi diaocha ziliao, dangan ziliao xuanbian* (Collected and edited materials from oral history and archival sources on Yi history in Sichuan). Chengdu: Sichuan Sheng Shehui Kexue Yuan Chubanshe.

Sichuan Sheng Minzu Yanjiu Suo

1980   *Baima Zangren zushu wenti taolunji* (A collection of discussions on the ethnic categorization of the Baima Tibetans).

1982   *Sichuan shaoshu minzu* (The minorities of Sichuan). Chengdu: Sichuan Minzu Chubanshe.

Siu, Helen F.

1989   *Agents and Victims in South China.* New Haven: Yale University Press.

Snow, Edgar

1938   *Red Star over China.* New York: Grove Press.

Sonyel, Salahi R.

1993   *Minorities and the Destruction of the Ottoman Empire.* Ankara: Turkish Historical Society Printing House.

Sun Yat-sen (Sun Zhongshan)

1928   *San Min Chu I: The Three Principles of the People.* Trans. Frank W. Price, ed. L. T. Chen (Chen Liting). Shanghai: The Commercial Press.

Swain, Margaret Byrne

1989   "Developing Ethnic Tourism in Yunnan, China: Shilin Sani." *Tourism Recreation Research* 14 (1): 33–39.

1990   "Commoditizing Ethnicity in Southwest China." *Cultural Survival Quarterly* 14, no. 1: 26–29.

Tash, Abdul Qader

1997   "The Position of Muslims in France." *Arab View*, March 9. http://www.arab.net/arabview/articles/tash16.html

Townsend, James

    1992   "Chinese Nationalism." *The Australian Journal of Chinese Affairs* 27: 97–130.

Trawick, Margaret

    1990   *Notes on Love in a Tamil Family.* Berkeley and Los Angeles: University of California Press.

Turner, Victor

    1968   "Muchona the Hornet: Interpreter of Religion." In *The Forest of Symbols*, 131–50. Ithaca, N.Y.: Cornell University Press.

Unger, Jonathan

    1997   "Not Quite Han: The Ethnic Minorities of China's Southwest." *Bulletin of Concerned Asian Scholars* 29, no. 3: 67–78.

Upton, Janet L.

    1999   "Schooling Shar-khog: Time, Space and the Place of Pedagogy in the Making of the Tibetan Modern." Ph.D. diss., University of Washington.

    2000   "Notes Toward a Native Tibetan Ethnology." *Tibet Journal* 25, no. 3: 3–26.

van den Berghe, Pierre L.

    1979   *Human Family Systems: an Evolutionary View.* New York: Elsevier North Holland.

van den Berghe, Pierre L., and Charles F. Keyes

    1984   "Tourism and the Ethnic Division of Labor." *Annals of Tourism Research* 11: 343–52.

Wallerstein, Immanuel

    1984   *The Politics of the World-Economy: The States, the Movements, and the Civilizations.* Cambridge and New York: Cambridge University Press.

Wang Chengquan and Zhan Chengxu

    1988a   "Ninglang Xian Yongning Qu Zhongshi Xiang Naxizu fengjian lingzhu zhi, azhu hunyin he muxi jiating diaocha" (Investigation into the feudal lord system, *azhu* marriage, and matrilineal households of the Naxi of Zhongshi Township, Yongning District, Ninglang County). In Wang Chengquan and Zhang Chengxu, *Ninglang Yizu Zizhi Xian Yongning Naxizu shehui ji muxi zhi diaocha* (Investigations into the society and matrilineal system of the Naxi of Yongning in Ninglang Yi Autonomous County).

    1988b   "Ninglang Xian Yongning Qu Kaiping Xiang Naxizu fengjian lingzhu zhi, azhu hunyin he muxi jiating diaocha" (Investigation into the feudal lord system, *azhu* marriage, and matrilineal households of the Naxi of Kaiping Township, Yongning District, Ninglang County). In Wang

Chengquan and Zhang Chengxu, *Ninglang Yizu Zizhi Xian Yongning Naxizu shehui ji muxi zhi diaocha* (Investigations into the society and matrilineal system of the Naxi of Yongning in Ninglang Yi Autonomous County).

Watson, James L.

1980   "Transactions in People: The Chinese Market in Slaves, Servants and Heirs." In James L. Watson, ed., *Asian and African Systems of Slavery*, 223–50. Berkeley and Los Angeles: University of California Press.

1993   "Rites or Beliefs? The Construction of a Unified Culture in Late Imperial China." In Lowell Dittmer and Samuel S. Kim, eds., *China's Quest for National Unity*, 80–103. Ithaca: Cornell University Press.

Watson, Rubie S.

1985   *Inequality among Brothers: Class and Kinship in South China*. Cambridge and New York: Cambridge University Press.

Wellens, Koen

1998   "What's in a Name? The Premi in Southwest China and the Consequences of Defining Ethnic Identity." *Nations and Nationalism* 4, no. 1: 17–28.

Weng Naiqun

1995   "The Mother House." Ph.D. diss., University of Rochester.

Wolf, Margery

1985   *Revolution Postponed: Women in Contemporary China*. Stanford: Stanford University Press.

Wu Cheng'en

1961   *Xi you ji* (Record of a westward journey). Hong Kong: Shangwu
(16th c.)   Yinshuaguan.

Wu Guoqing

1994   "Jieshao kaiming jinbu renshi Leng Guangdian Xiansheng." (An introduction to Mr. Leng Guangdian, an enlightened and progressive personage). *Liangshan minzu yanjiu* 4: 189–95.

Wu Jingzhong

1993   *Liangshan Yizu Fengsu*. (Customs of the Liangshan Yi). Chengdu: Sichuan Minzu Chubanshe.

2001   "On the Nature and Origins of the Nzymo." In Stevan Harrell, ed., *Perspectives on the Yi of Southwest China*, 35–48. Berkeley and Los Angeles: University of California Press.

Xide Xianzhi

1992   *Xide xianzhi* (Gazetteer of Xide County). Chengdu: Chengdu Dianzi Keji Daxue Chubanshe.

Xie Benshu

1988   *Long Yun Zhuan* (Biography of Long Yun). Chengdu: Sichuan Minzu Chubanshe.

Xie Shouchang

1931   *Zhongguo gujin diming da zidian* (Great dictionary of ancient and modern place-names of China). Shanghai: Commercial Press.

Xinan Minzu Yanjiu Xuehui

1987a   *Xinan minzu yanjiu, Yizu zhuanji* (Researches into southwestern *Minzu*, Yi special collection). Kunming: Yunnan Minzu Chuban She.

1987b   *Xinan minzu yanjiu, Yizu yanjiu zhuanji* (Researches into southwestern *minzu*, Yi research special edition). Chengdu: Sichuan Minzu Chubanshe.

Yan Ruxian

1984   "A Living Fossil of the Family—A Study of the Family Structure of the Naxi Nationality in the Lugu Lake Region." Trans. Xing Wenjun. *Social Sciences in China* 3, no. 4: 60–83.

1989   "Marriage, Family, and Social Progress of China's Minority Nationalities." In Chiao Chien and Nicholas Tapp, eds., *Ethnicity and Ethnic Groups in China*, 79–87. Hong Kong: New Asia Academic Bulletin.

Yan Ruxian and Chen Jiujin

1986   *Pumi zu* (The Pumi nationality). Beijing: Renmin Chubanshe.

Yan Ruxian and Liu Yaohan

1986   *Yongning Naxizu shehui ji muxi zhi diaocha* (Investigation of the society and matrilineal system of the Yongning Naxi). Kunming: Yunnan Renmin Chubanshe.

Yan Ruxian and Song Zhaolin

1991   *Yongning Naxizu de muxi zhi* (The matrilineal system of the Naxi of Yongning). Kunming: Yunnan Renmin Chubanshe.

Yanagisako, Sylvia Junko, and Jane Fishburne Collier

1987   "Toward a Unified Analysis of Gender and Kinship." In Jane Fishburne Collier and Sylvia Junko Yanagisako, eds., *Gender and Kinship: Essays Toward a Unified Analysis*, 15–50. Stanford: Stanford University Press.

Yang, Martin C.

1945   *A Chinese Village*. New York: Columbia University Press.

Ye Dahuai and Mao Erha

1984   *Yanbian minzu zhi* (Record of the ethnic groups of Yanbian). Yanbian: Yanbian Xian Minzu Shiwu Weiyuanhui.

Yearbook of China Tourism

1996   *Zhongguo lüyou nianjian* (Yearbook of China Tourism). Beijing: Zhongguo Lüyou Chubanshe.

Yi Mouyuan
1987   "Shilun lishishang Liangshan diqu zhengquan de minzu xingzhi" (Preliminary discussion of the ethnic character of historical governments in the Liangshan area). In Zhongguo Xinan Minzu Yanjiu Hui, ed., *Xinan minzu yanjiu, Yizu zhuanji* (Research on southwestern *minzu*, Yi special collection), 302–20. Kunming: Yunnan Renmin Chubanshe.

Yuan Yayu, ed.
1992   *Dangdai Liangshan Yizu shehui yu jiating* (Society and family in contemporary Liangshan). Chengdu: Sichuan Daxue Chubanshe.

Zeng Zhaolun
1945   *Liangshan Yiqu gaikuang* (The general situation in the Yi areas of Liangshan). In *Liangshan Yiqu diaocha ji* (Record of investigations in the Yi areas of Liangshan). Chongqing: N.p. (Trans. Josette M. Yen as *The Lolo District in Liangshan*. New Haven: HRAF Press.)

Zhong Dakun, ed.
1992   *Liangshan Yizu, The Yi Nationality of Liangshan Mountain*. Beijing: Renmin Meishu Chubanshe.

Zhou Xiyin
1987   "Shilun Yizu jindaishi shang de liang ci geming douzheng" (Preliminary discussion of two revolutionary struggles in modern Yi history). In Zhongguo Xinan Minzu Yanjiu Hui, ed., *Xinan minzu yanjiu, Yizu yanjiu zhuanji* (Southwest nationalities research, Yi research special collection), 453–70. Chengdu: Sichuan Minzu Chubanshe.

Zhou Yudong
1988   "Labo Xiang Naxizu lingzhu jingji he jiating hunyin diaocha" (Investigation of the feudal lord economy and the family and marriage of the Naxi of Labo Township). In Wang Chengquan and Zhang Chengxu, *Ninglang Yizu Zizhi Xian Yongning Naxizu shehui ji muxi zhi diaocha* (Investigations into the society and matrilineal system of the Naxi of Yongning in Ninglang Yi Autonomous County).

Zhuang Wanshou
1996a   *Taiwan lun* (About Taiwan). Taipei: Yushan.
1996b   *Zhongguo lun* (About China). Taipei: Yushan.

Zimei Yixue Yanjiu Xiaoxu (Bamo Ayi, Bamo Qubumo, and Bamo Vusamo)
1992   *Yizu fengsu zhi* (Record of the customs of the Yi). Beijing: Zhongyang Minzu Daxue Chubanshe.

Index